W Juliet

Volume 11

Story & Art by Emura

W Juliet
Volume 11

Story and Art by Emura

Translation & English Adaptation/Naomi Kokubo & Jeff Carlson
Touch-up Art & Lettering/Krysta Lau, Imaginary Friends Studios
Graphic Design/Hidemi Sahara
Editor/Carrie Shepherd

Managing Editor/Annette Roman
Director of Production/Noboru Watanabe
Vice President of Publishing/Alvin Lu
Sr. Director of Acquisitions/Rika Inouye
Vice President of Sales & Marketing/Liza Coppola
Publisher/Hyoe Narita

Printed in the U.S.A.

Published by VIZ Media, LLC
P.O. Box 77010
San Francisco, CA 94107

10 9 8 7 6 5 4 3 2 1
First printing, July 2006

T 251551

www.viz.com
store.viz.com

PARENTAL ADVISORY
W JULIET is rated T for Teen and is recommended for ages 13 and up. This book contains mild sexual situations/humor and alcohol and tobacco usage.

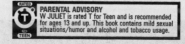

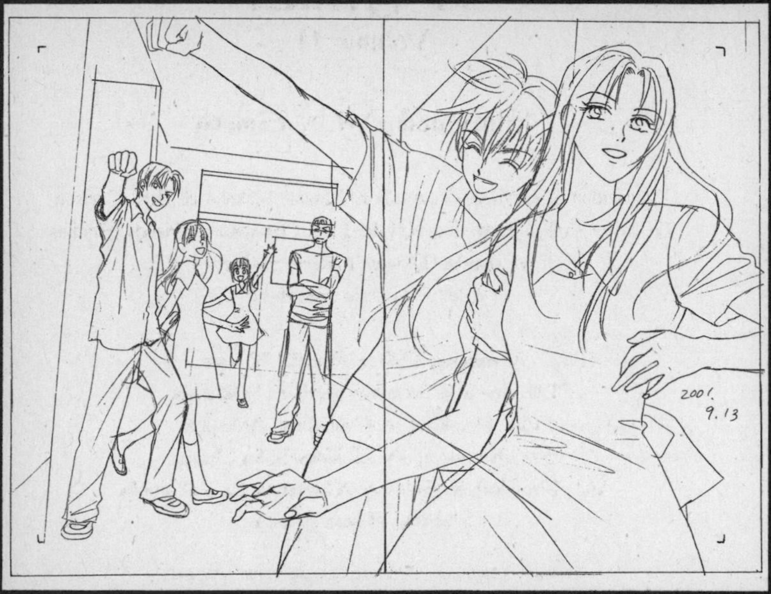
2001.
9.13
2001 Hana to Yume No. 22 draft cover art (B4 size)

2002 Zensa Phone Card, draft

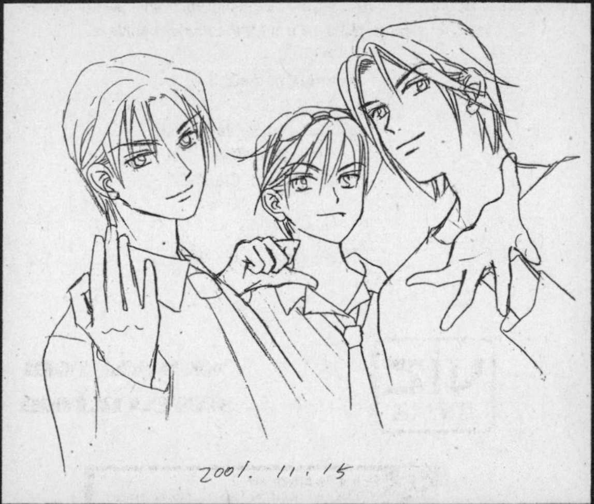
2001. 11. 15

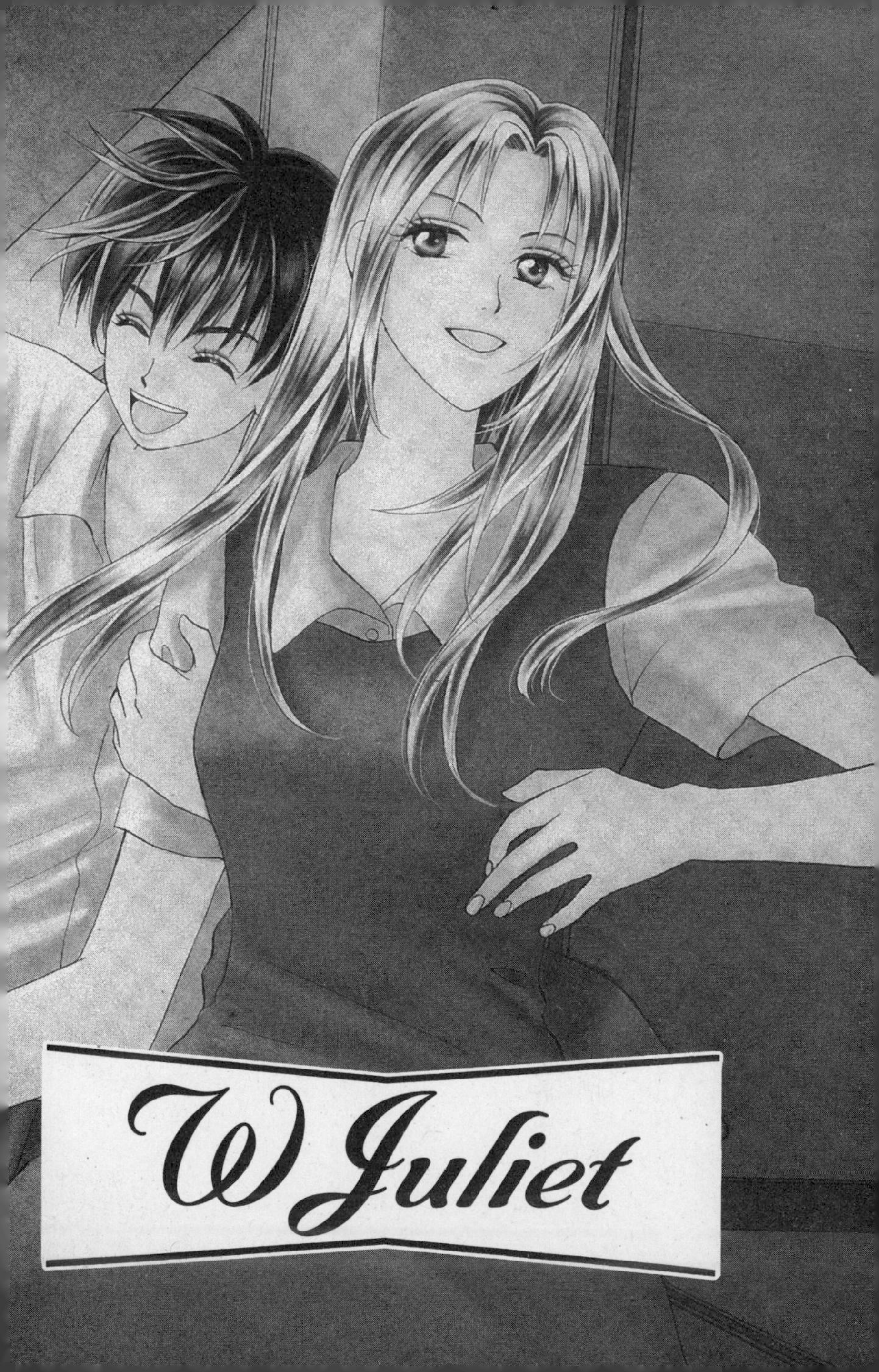
W Juliet

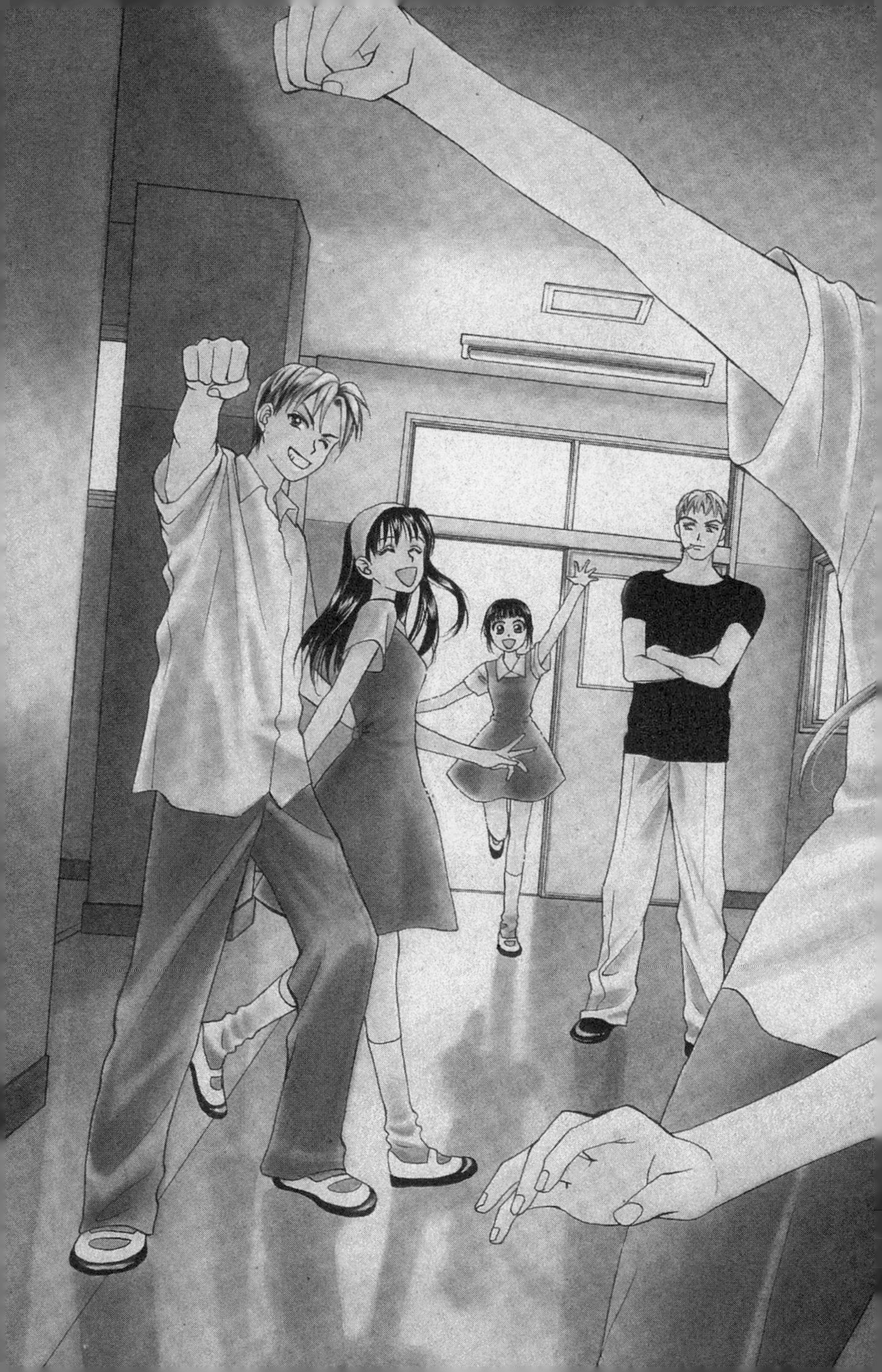

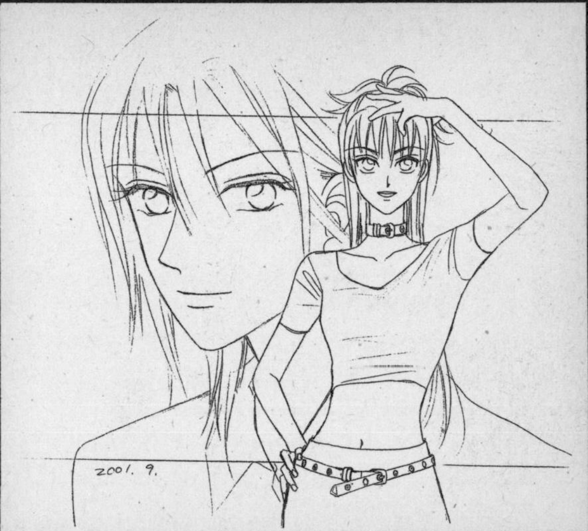
2001. 9.

2001 HCD W Juliet

Jacket Front ↑ Back ↓

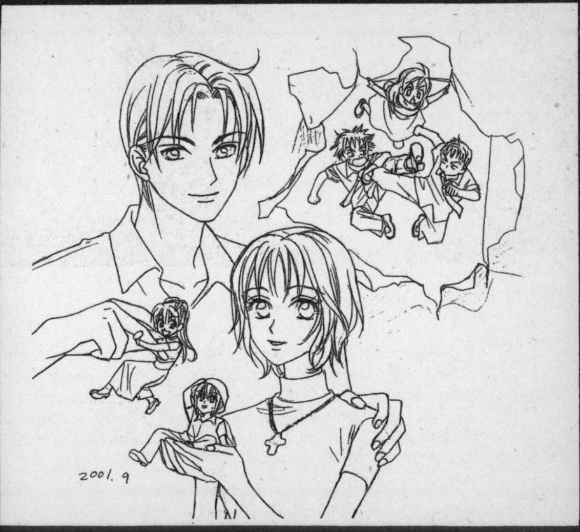
2001. 9

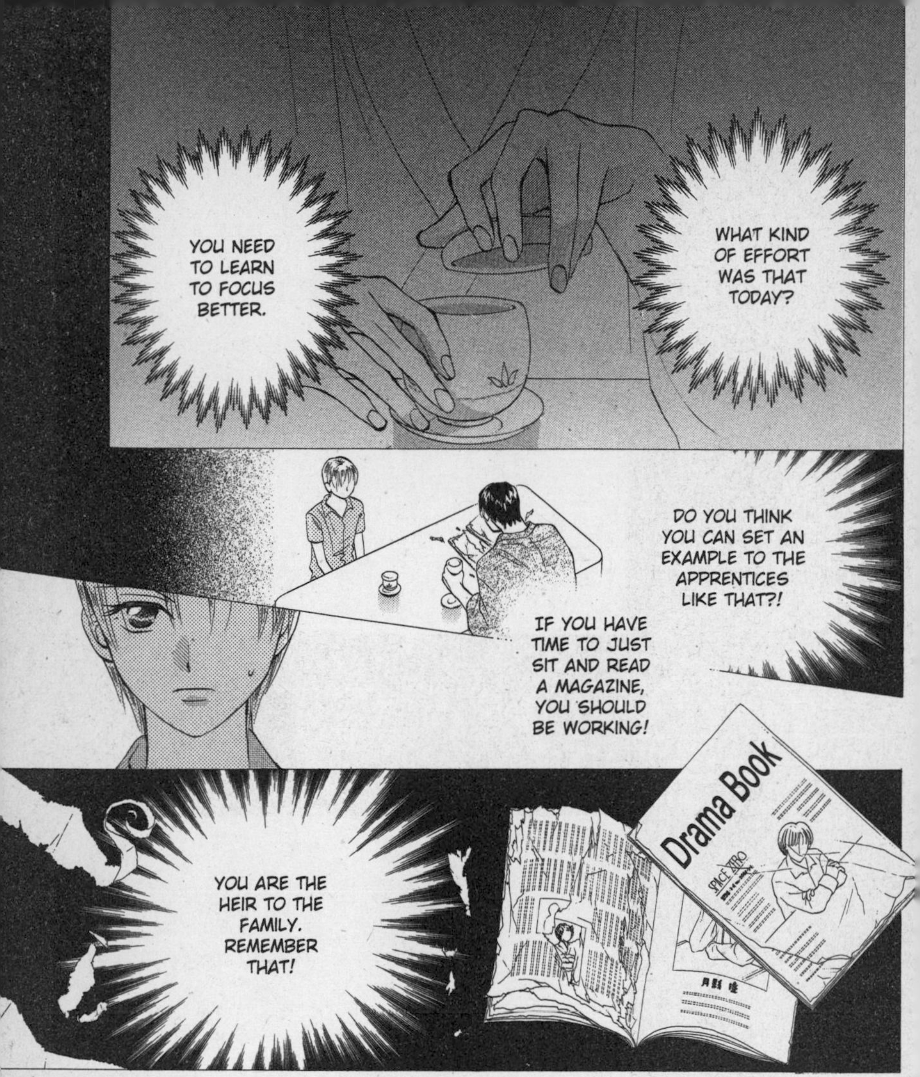
WHAT KIND OF EFFORT WAS THAT TODAY?
YOU NEED TO LEARN TO FOCUS BETTER.
DO YOU THINK YOU CAN SET AN EXAMPLE TO THE APPRENTICES LIKE THAT?!
IF YOU HAVE TIME TO JUST SIT AND READ A MAGAZINE, YOU SHOULD BE WORKING!
Drama Book
YOU ARE THE HEIR TO THE FAMILY. REMEMBER THAT!

—Behind the Scenes Story ①—

I wanted to come up with something unexpected...and this is the result. (Laugh) A sweet tooth just doesn't suit Masumi, the father. But some say "he's cute." I'm not a fussy eater, but I shy away from strong flavors or oily foods. I can eat them, but whenever I do, I end up dead with heartburn several minutes later. I like simple and light food! So (?) I support yogurt rather than flan caramel.

I'm totally hooked on yogurt with aloe in it at the moment! It's supposed to be good for the stomach.

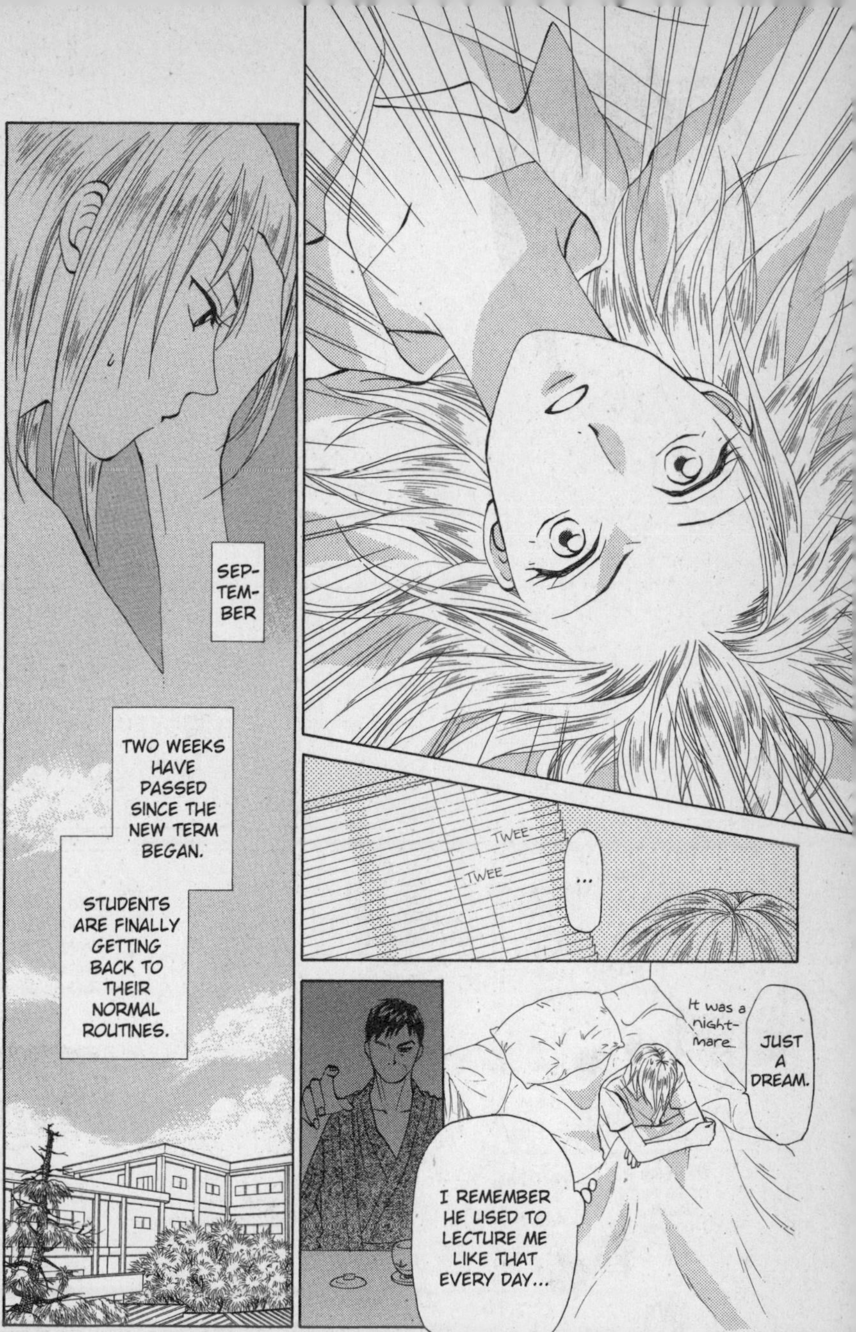
...
TWEE
TWEE
JUST A DREAM.
It was a nightmare...
I REMEMBER HE USED TO LECTURE ME LIKE THAT EVERY DAY...
SEPTEMBER
TWO WEEKS HAVE PASSED SINCE THE NEW TERM BEGAN.
STUDENTS ARE FINALLY GETTING BACK TO THEIR NORMAL ROUTINES.

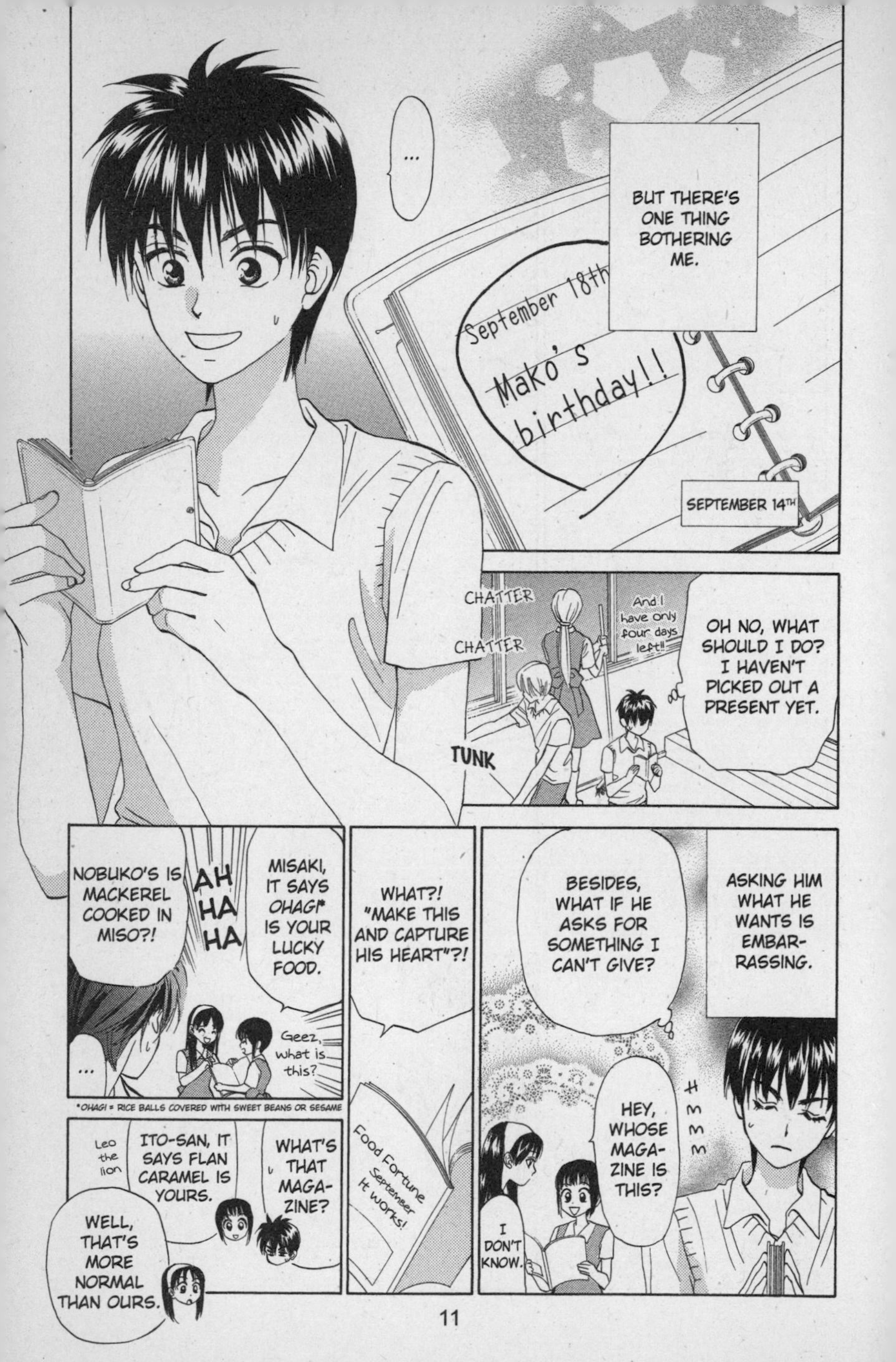
BUT THERE'S ONE THING BOTHERING ME.
September 18th
Mako's birthday!!
SEPTEMBER 14TH
...
OH NO, WHAT SHOULD I DO? I HAVEN'T PICKED OUT A PRESENT YET.
And I have only four days left!!
CHATTER
CHATTER
TUNK
ASKING HIM WHAT HE WANTS IS EMBAR-RASSING.
BESIDES, WHAT IF HE ASKS FOR SOMETHING I CAN'T GIVE?
HMMM
HEY, WHOSE MAGA-ZINE IS THIS?
I DON'T KNOW.
WHAT?! "MAKE THIS AND CAPTURE HIS HEART"?!
Food Fortune September It works!
MISAKI, IT SAYS OHAGI* IS YOUR LUCKY FOOD.
AH HA HA
NOBUKO'S IS MACKEREL COOKED IN MISO?!
Geez, what is this?
...
*OHAGI = RICE BALLS COVERED WITH SWEET BEANS OR SESAME
WHAT'S THAT MAGA-ZINE?
ITO-SAN, IT SAYS FLAN CARAMEL IS YOURS.
Leo the lion
WELL, THAT'S MORE NORMAL THAN OURS.

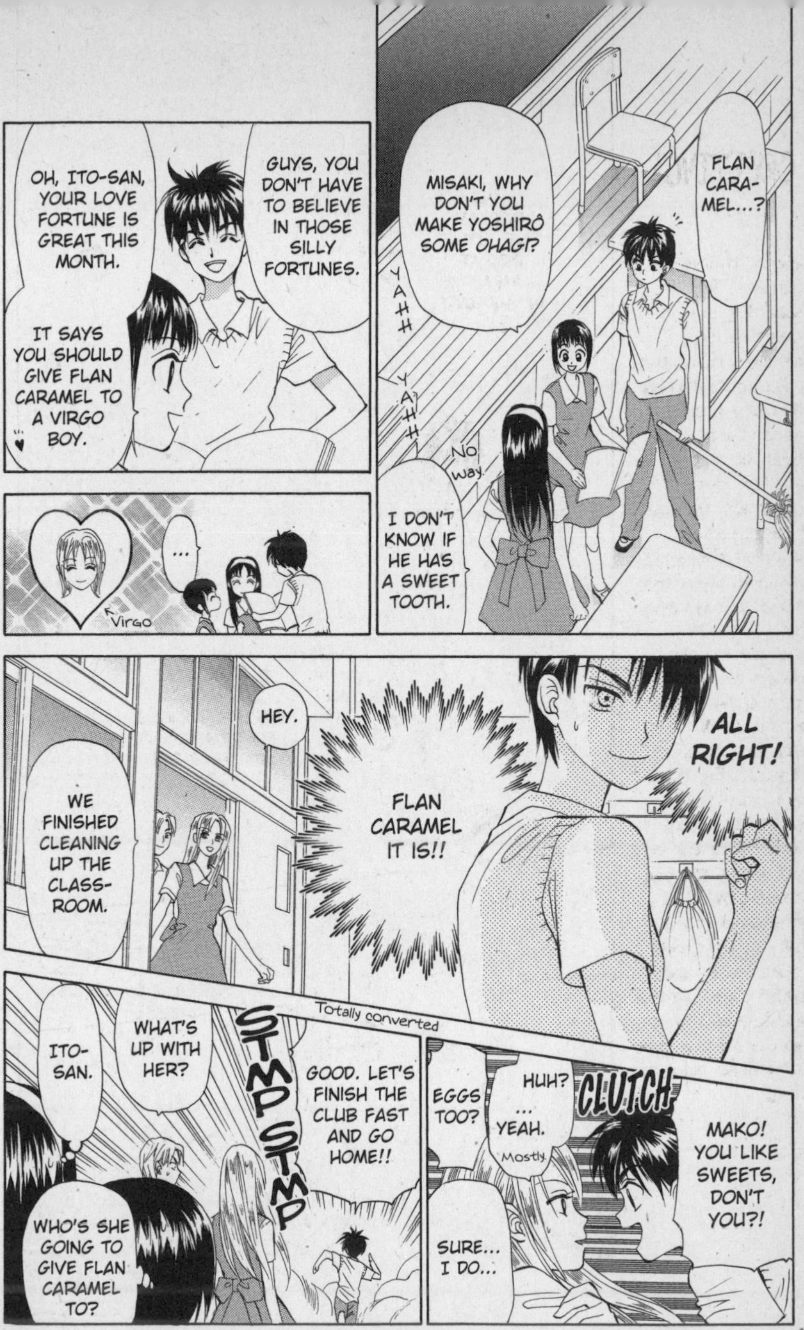
FLAN CARAMEL...?
MISAKI, WHY DON'T YOU MAKE YOSHIRÔ SOME OHAGI?
YAHH
YAHH
No way.
I DON'T KNOW IF HE HAS A SWEET TOOTH.
GUYS, YOU DON'T HAVE TO BELIEVE IN THOSE SILLY FORTUNES.
OH, ITO-SAN, YOUR LOVE FORTUNE IS GREAT THIS MONTH.
IT SAYS YOU SHOULD GIVE FLAN CARAMEL TO A VIRGO BOY.
...
Virgo
ALL RIGHT!
FLAN CARAMEL IT IS!!
Totally converted
HEY.
WE FINISHED CLEANING UP THE CLASSROOM.
MAKO! YOU LIKE SWEETS, DON'T YOU?!
CLUTCH
HUH? ... YEAH.
Mostly.
EGGS TOO?
SURE... I DO...
GOOD. LET'S FINISH THE CLUB FAST AND GO HOME!!
STMP STMP
WHAT'S UP WITH HER?
ITO-SAN.
WHO'S SHE GOING TO GIVE FLAN CARAMEL TO?

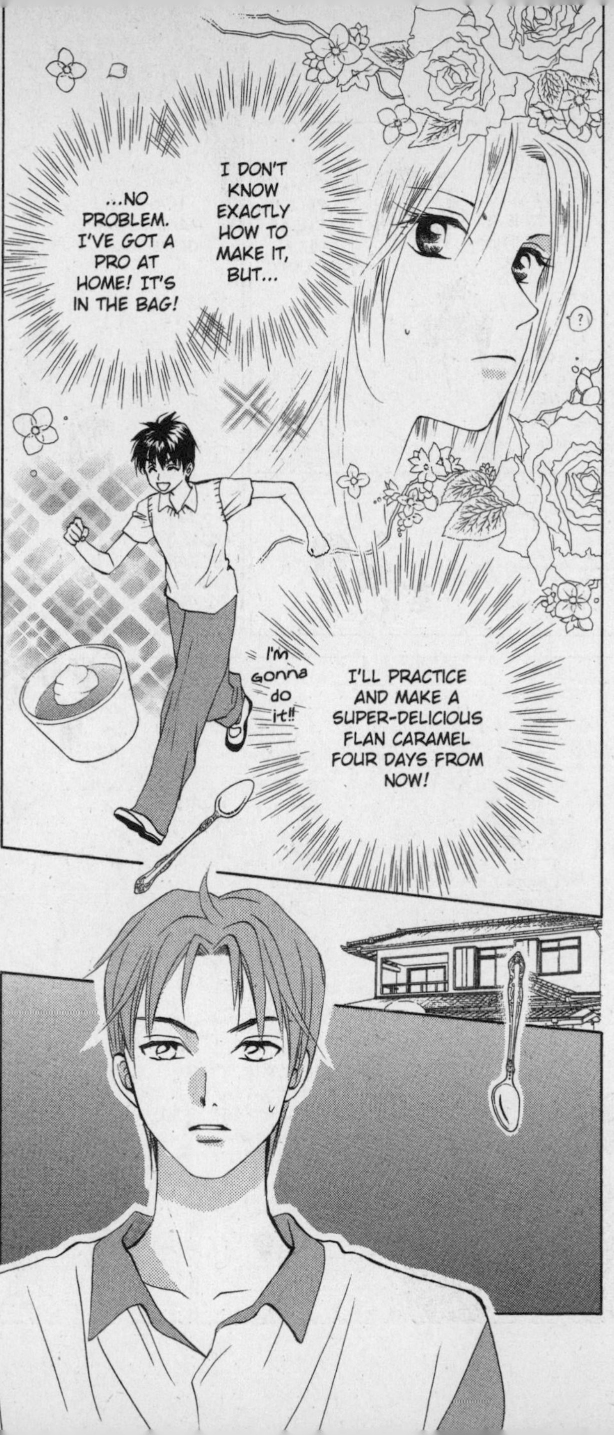
I DON'T KNOW EXACTLY HOW TO MAKE IT, BUT...
...NO PROBLEM. I'VE GOT A PRO AT HOME! IT'S IN THE BAG!
I'LL PRACTICE AND MAKE A SUPER-DELICIOUS FLAN CARAMEL FOUR DAYS FROM NOW!
I'm gonna do it!!

GREETINGS.

Hello, this is Emura. The summer sun is getting so strong now that I feel dizzy lately. (Laugh) Compared with the cold winter, I prefer the summer, though. I can't handle winter. Because I'm oversensitive to cold, my hands and fingers refuse to move when it gets too chilly. My brain gets frozen too. (Laugh) By the way, right before volume 11 was released, the **W Juliet Character Book** was published. It's full of illustrations that have never been seen by the public before. If you are interested, please pick it up. ♪

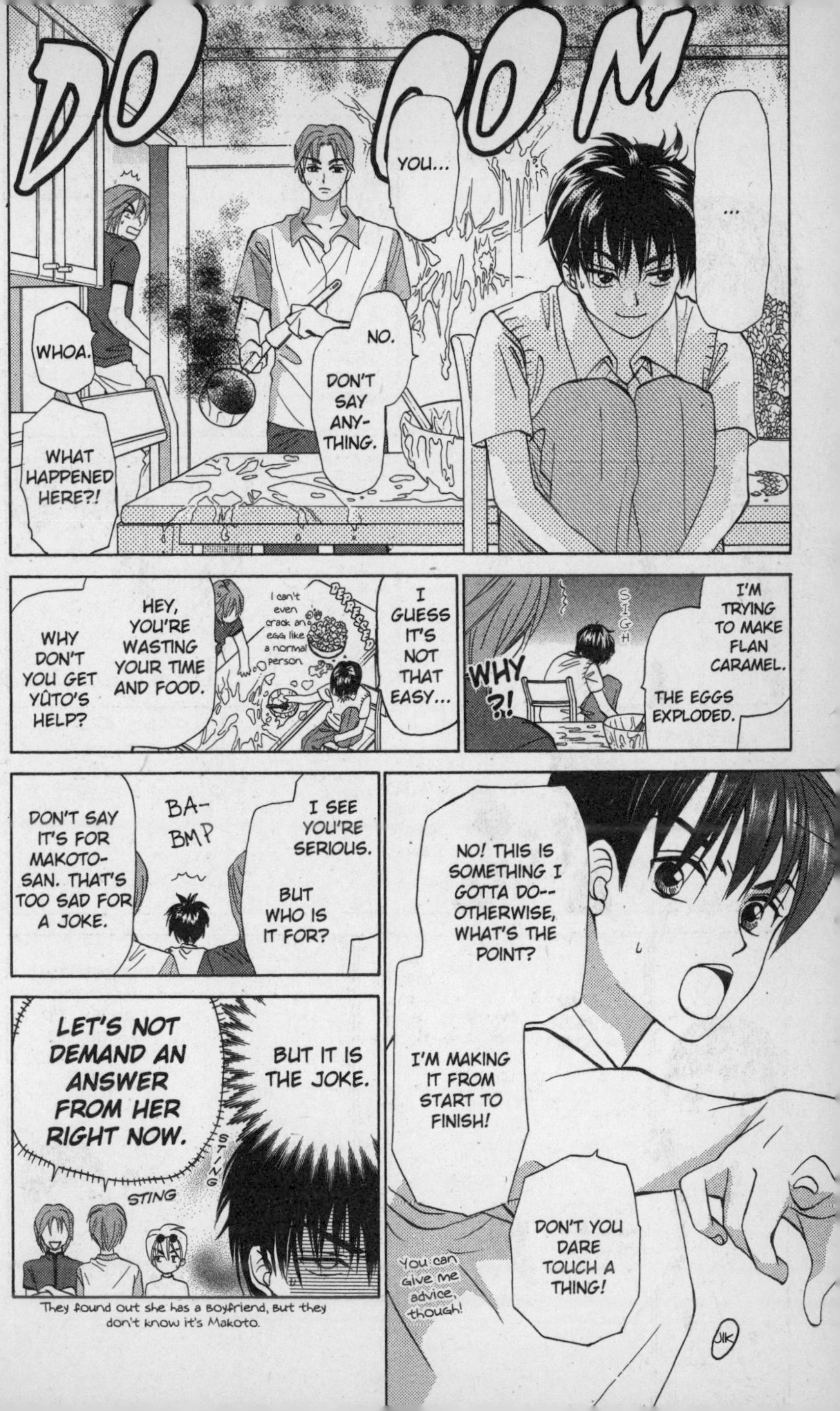
DO COM
...
YOU...
NO.
DON'T SAY ANYTHING.
WHOA.
WHAT HAPPENED HERE?!
I'M TRYING TO MAKE FLAN CARAMEL.
THE EGGS EXPLODED.
SIGH
WHY ?!
I GUESS IT'S NOT THAT EASY...
DEPRESSED
I can't even crack an egg like a normal person.
HEY, YOU'RE WASTING YOUR TIME AND FOOD.
WHY DON'T YOU GET YÛTO'S HELP?
NO! THIS IS SOMETHING I GOTTA DO--OTHERWISE, WHAT'S THE POINT?
I'M MAKING IT FROM START TO FINISH!
DON'T YOU DARE TOUCH A THING!
You can give me advice, though!
JIK
I SEE YOU'RE SERIOUS.
BUT WHO IS IT FOR?
BA-BMP
DON'T SAY IT'S FOR MAKOTO-SAN. THAT'S TOO SAD FOR A JOKE.
BUT IT IS THE JOKE.
LET'S NOT DEMAND AN ANSWER FROM HER RIGHT NOW.
STING
STING
They found out she has a boyfriend, but they don't know it's Makoto.

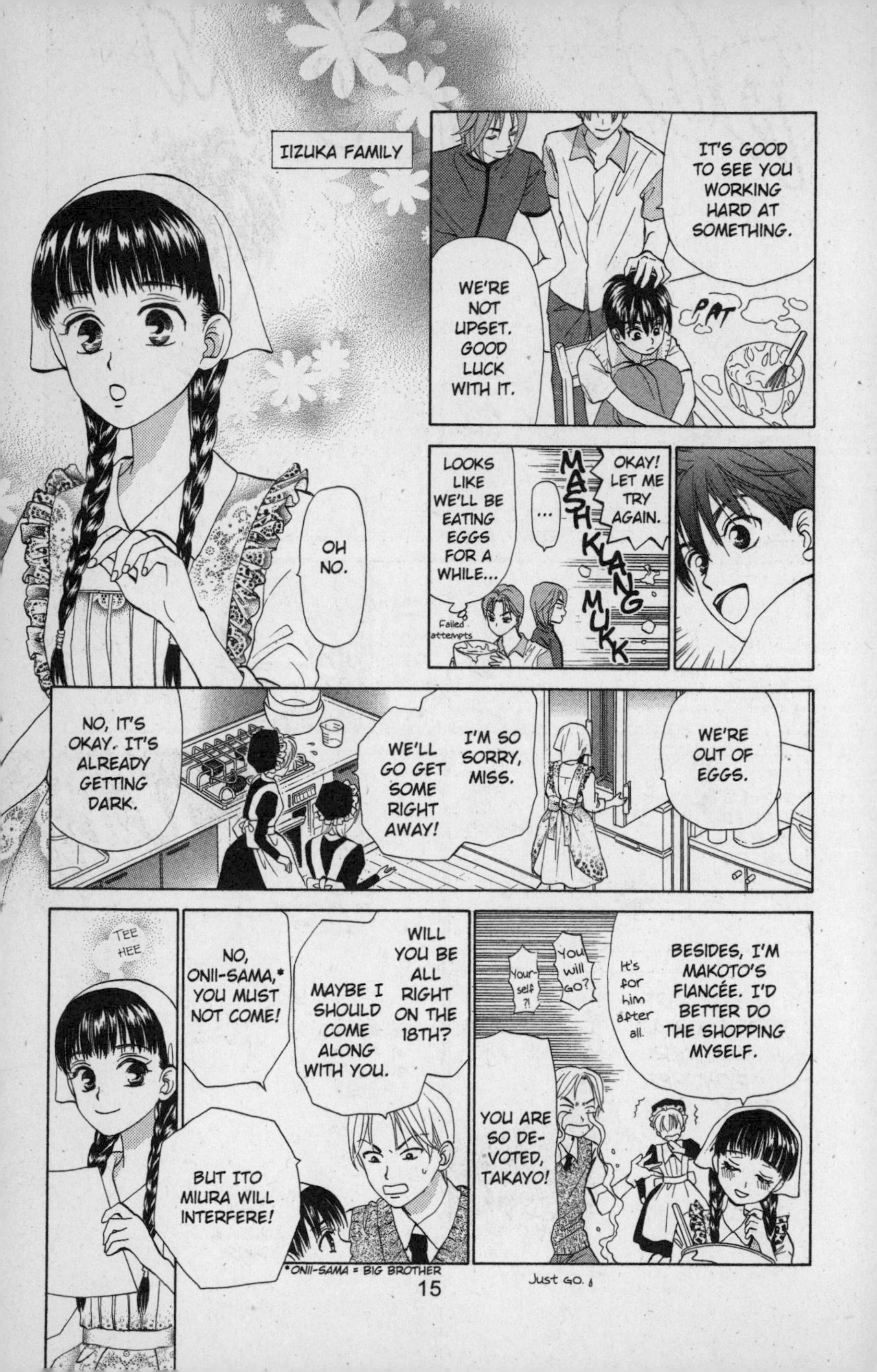
IIZUKA FAMILY
IT'S GOOD TO SEE YOU WORKING HARD AT SOMETHING.
PAT
WE'RE NOT UPSET. GOOD LUCK WITH IT.
OKAY! LET ME TRY AGAIN.
MASH
KLANG
MUKK
...
LOOKS LIKE WE'LL BE EATING EGGS FOR A WHILE...
Failed attempts
OH NO.
WE'RE OUT OF EGGS.
I'M SO SORRY, MISS.
WE'LL GO GET SOME RIGHT AWAY!
NO, IT'S OKAY. IT'S ALREADY GETTING DARK.
BESIDES, I'M MAKOTO'S FIANCÉE. I'D BETTER DO THE SHOPPING MYSELF.
It's for him after all.
You will GO?
Your-self ?!
YOU ARE SO DE-VOTED, TAKAYO!
Just GO.
WILL YOU BE ALL RIGHT ON THE 18TH?
MAYBE I SHOULD COME ALONG WITH YOU.
NO, ONII-SAMA,* YOU MUST NOT COME!
TEE HEE
BUT ITO MIURA WILL INTERFERE!
*ONII-SAMA = BIG BROTHER

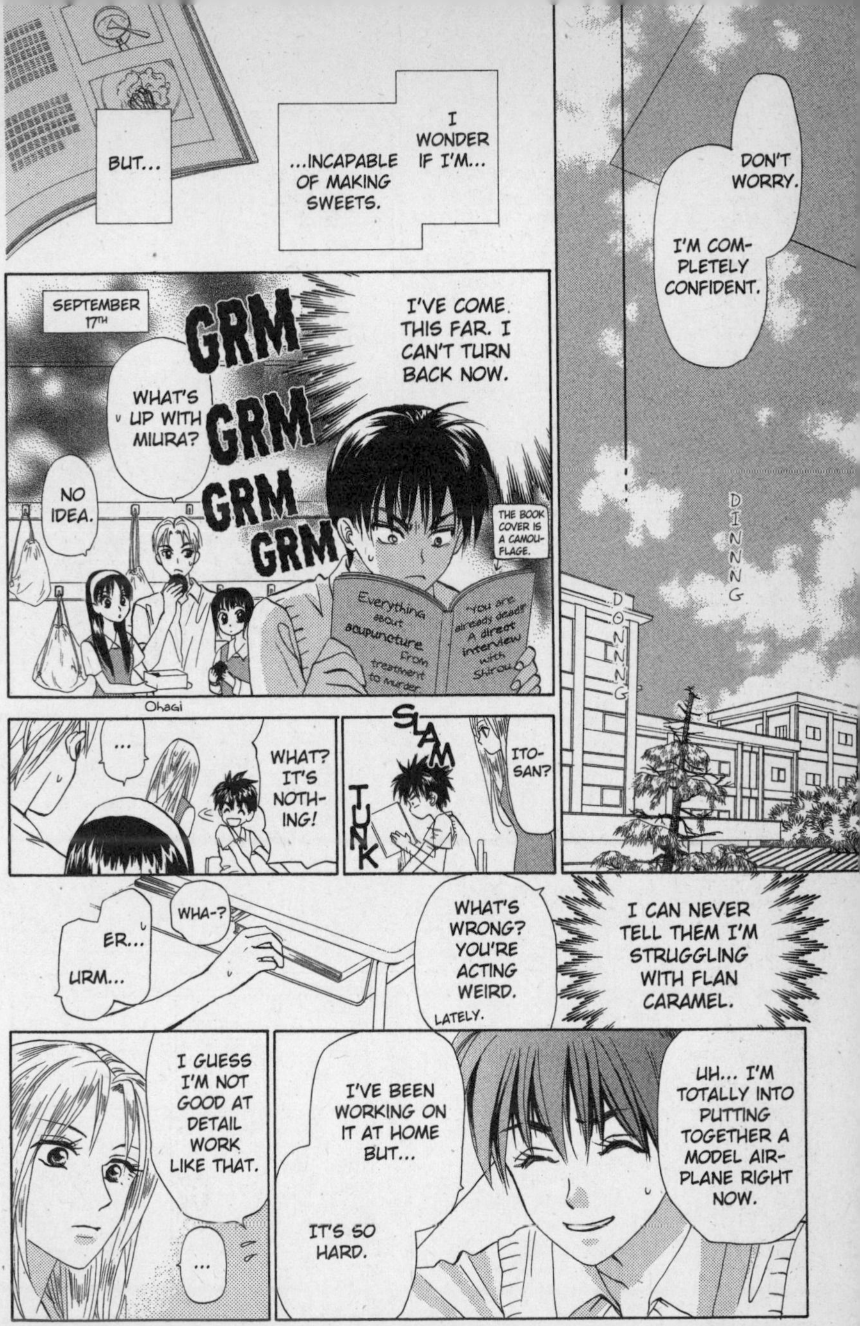
DON'T WORRY.
I'M COMPLETELY CONFIDENT.
DINNNG
DONNNG
I WONDER IF I'M...
...INCAPABLE OF MAKING SWEETS.
BUT...
I'VE COME THIS FAR. I CAN'T TURN BACK NOW.
GRM GRM GRM GRM
THE BOOK COVER IS A CAMOUFLAGE.
"You are already dead!" A direct interview with Shirou
Everything about acupuncture From treatment to murder
SEPTEMBER 17TH
WHAT'S UP WITH MIURA?
NO IDEA.
Ohagi
ITO-SAN?
SLAM
TUNK
WHAT? IT'S NOTHING!
...
I CAN NEVER TELL THEM I'M STRUGGLING WITH FLAN CARAMEL.
WHAT'S WRONG? YOU'RE ACTING WEIRD.
LATELY.
WHA-?
ER...
URM...
UH... I'M TOTALLY INTO PUTTING TOGETHER A MODEL AIRPLANE RIGHT NOW.
I'VE BEEN WORKING ON IT AT HOME BUT...
IT'S SO HARD.
I GUESS I'M NOT GOOD AT DETAIL WORK LIKE THAT.
...

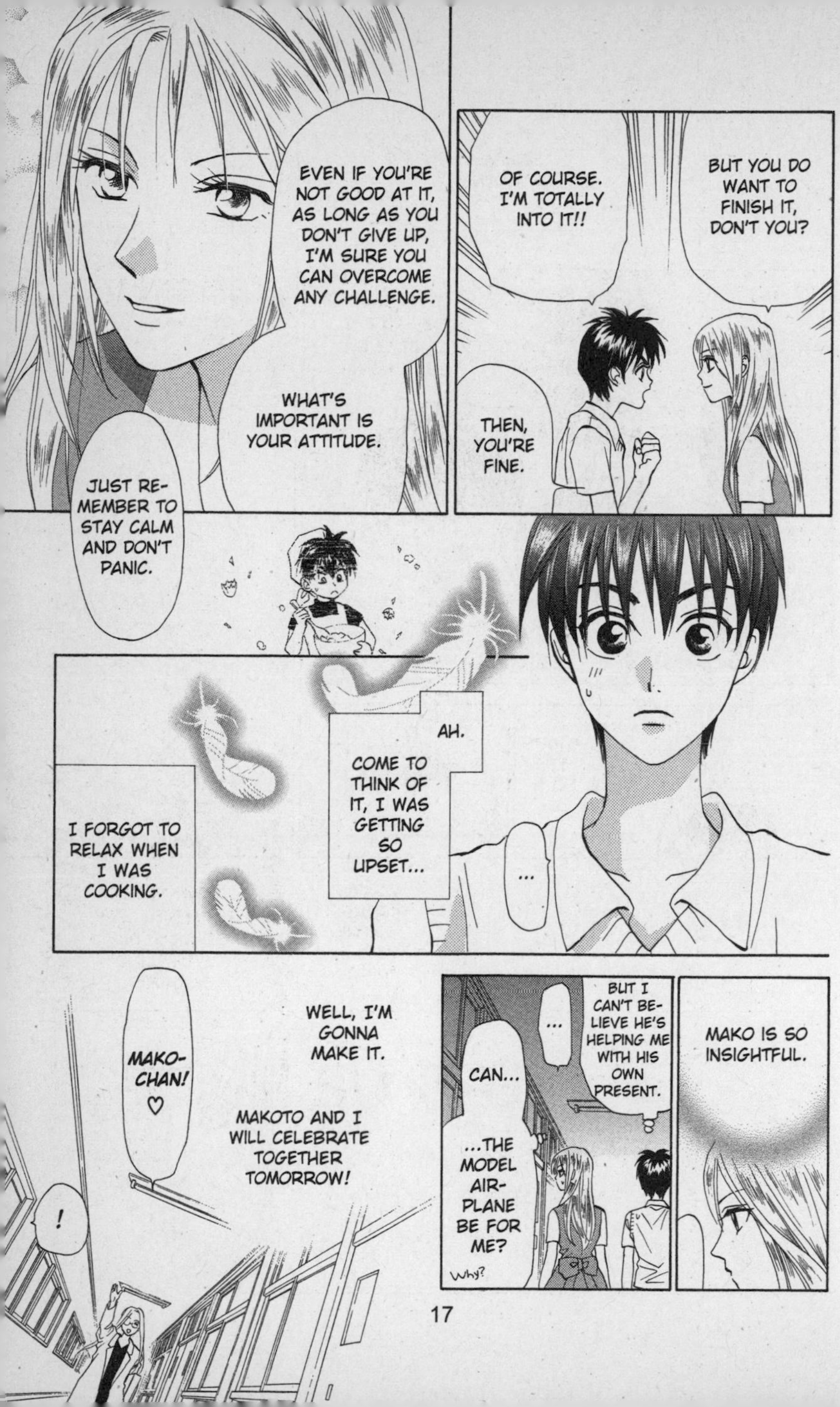
BUT YOU DO WANT TO FINISH IT, DON'T YOU?
OF COURSE. I'M TOTALLY INTO IT!!
THEN, YOU'RE FINE.
EVEN IF YOU'RE NOT GOOD AT IT, AS LONG AS YOU DON'T GIVE UP, I'M SURE YOU CAN OVERCOME ANY CHALLENGE.
WHAT'S IMPORTANT IS YOUR ATTITUDE.
JUST RE-MEMBER TO STAY CALM AND DON'T PANIC.
...
AH.
COME TO THINK OF IT, I WAS GETTING SO UPSET...
I FORGOT TO RELAX WHEN I WAS COOKING.
MAKO IS SO INSIGHTFUL.
BUT I CAN'T BE-LIEVE HE'S HELPING ME WITH HIS OWN PRESENT.
...
CAN...
...THE MODEL AIR-PLANE BE FOR ME?
Why?
WELL, I'M GONNA MAKE IT.
MAKOTO AND I WILL CELEBRATE TOGETHER TOMORROW!
MAKO-CHAN! ♡
!

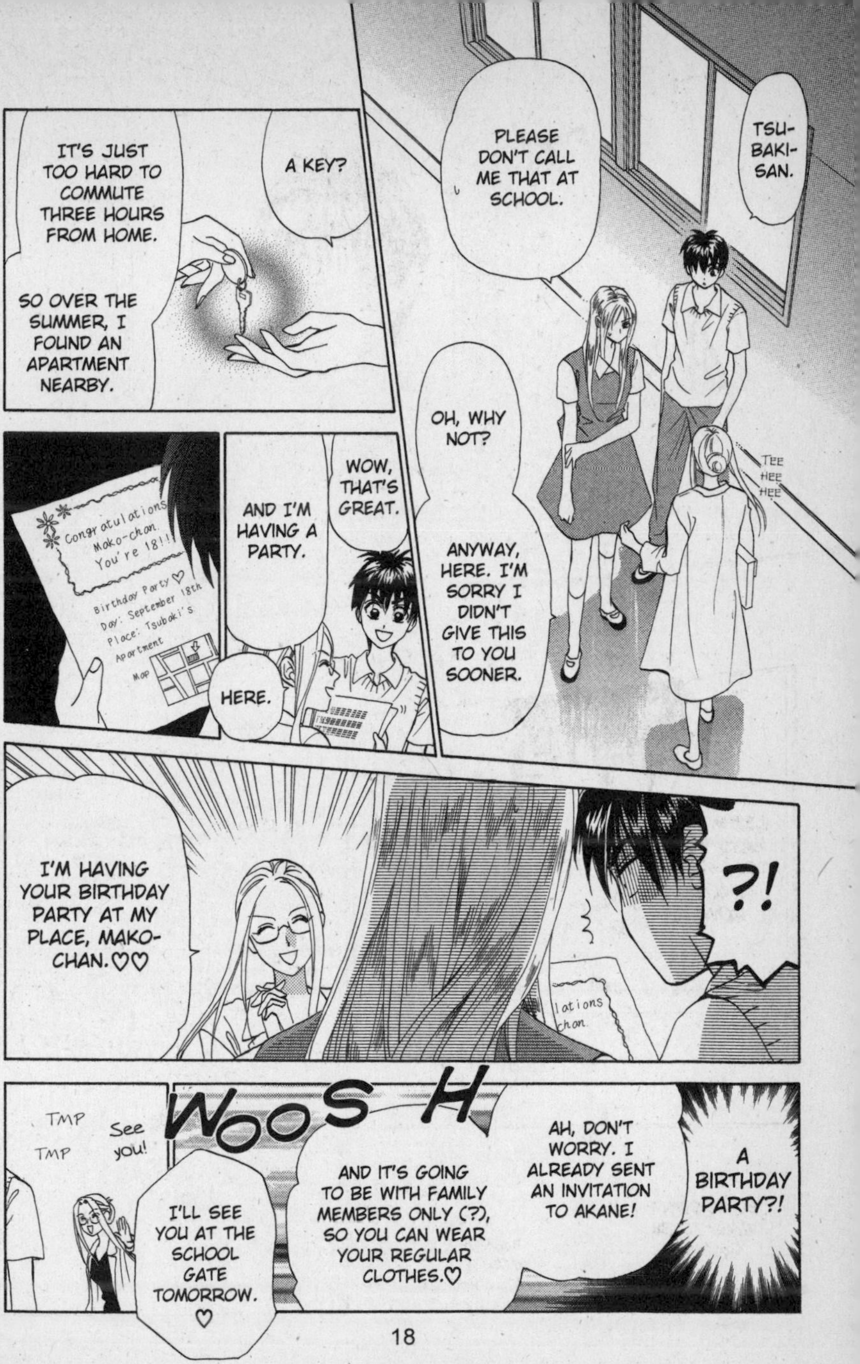
TSU-BAKI-SAN.
PLEASE DON'T CALL ME THAT AT SCHOOL.
OH, WHY NOT?
TEE HEE HEE
ANYWAY, HERE. I'M SORRY I DIDN'T GIVE THIS TO YOU SOONER.
A KEY?
IT'S JUST TOO HARD TO COMMUTE THREE HOURS FROM HOME.
SO OVER THE SUMMER, I FOUND AN APARTMENT NEARBY.
WOW, THAT'S GREAT.
AND I'M HAVING A PARTY.
HERE.
Congratulations Mako-chan. You're 18!!
Birthday Party ♡
Day: September 18th
Place: Tsubaki's Apartment
Map
?!
I'M HAVING YOUR BIRTHDAY PARTY AT MY PLACE, MAKO-CHAN.♡♡
lations
chan.
A BIRTHDAY PARTY?!
AH, DON'T WORRY. I ALREADY SENT AN INVITATION TO AKANE!
AND IT'S GOING TO BE WITH FAMILY MEMBERS ONLY (?), SO YOU CAN WEAR YOUR REGULAR CLOTHES.♡
WOOSH
I'LL SEE YOU AT THE SCHOOL GATE TOMORROW. ♡
See you!
TMP
TMP

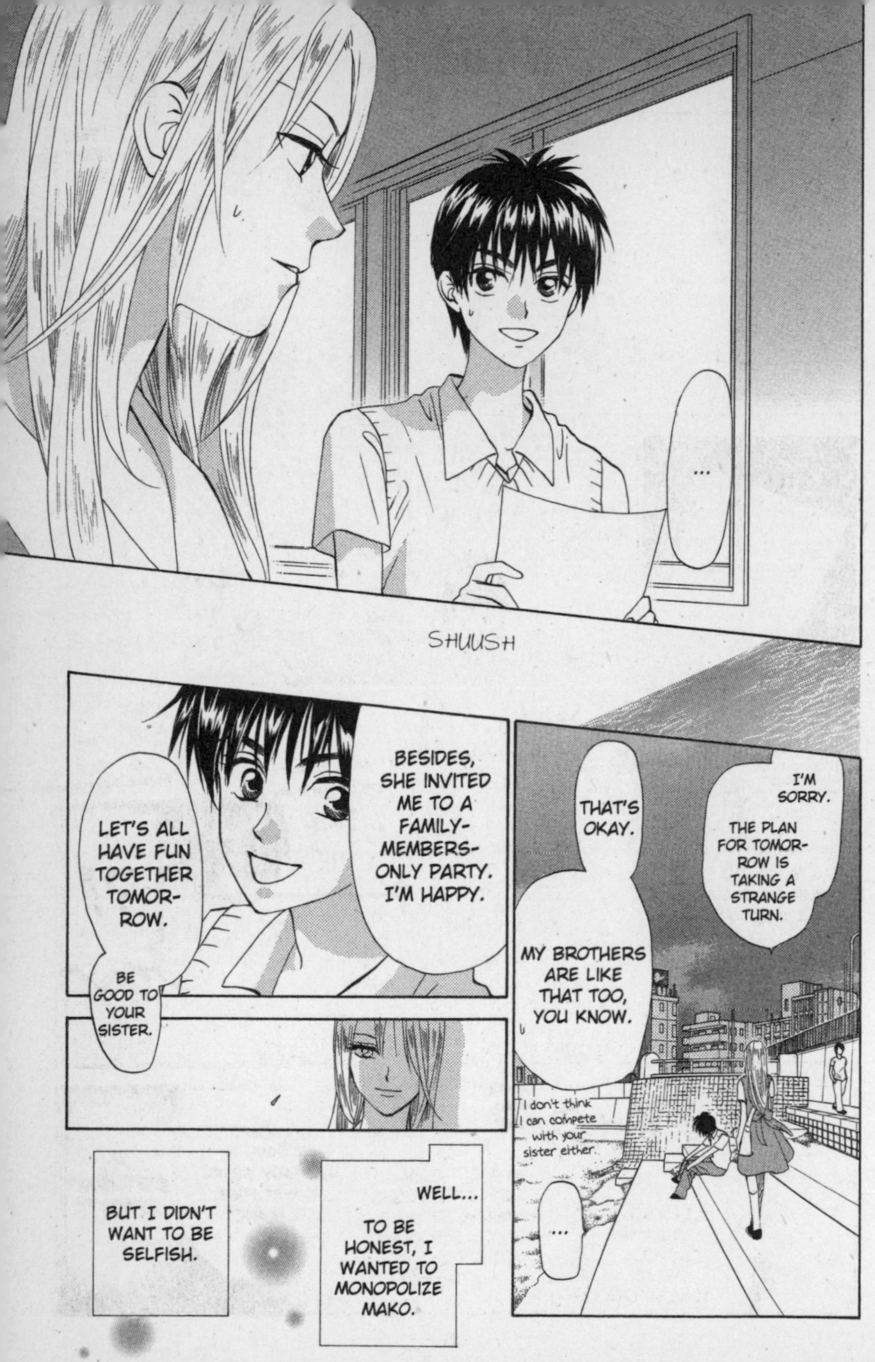
...
SHUUSH
I'M SORRY.
THE PLAN FOR TOMORROW IS TAKING A STRANGE TURN.
THAT'S OKAY.
MY BROTHERS ARE LIKE THAT TOO, YOU KNOW.
I don't think I can compete with your sister either.
...
BESIDES, SHE INVITED ME TO A FAMILY-MEMBERS-ONLY PARTY. I'M HAPPY.
LET'S ALL HAVE FUN TOGETHER TOMORROW.
BE GOOD TO YOUR SISTER.
WELL...
TO BE HONEST, I WANTED TO MONOPOLIZE MAKO.
BUT I DIDN'T WANT TO BE SELFISH.

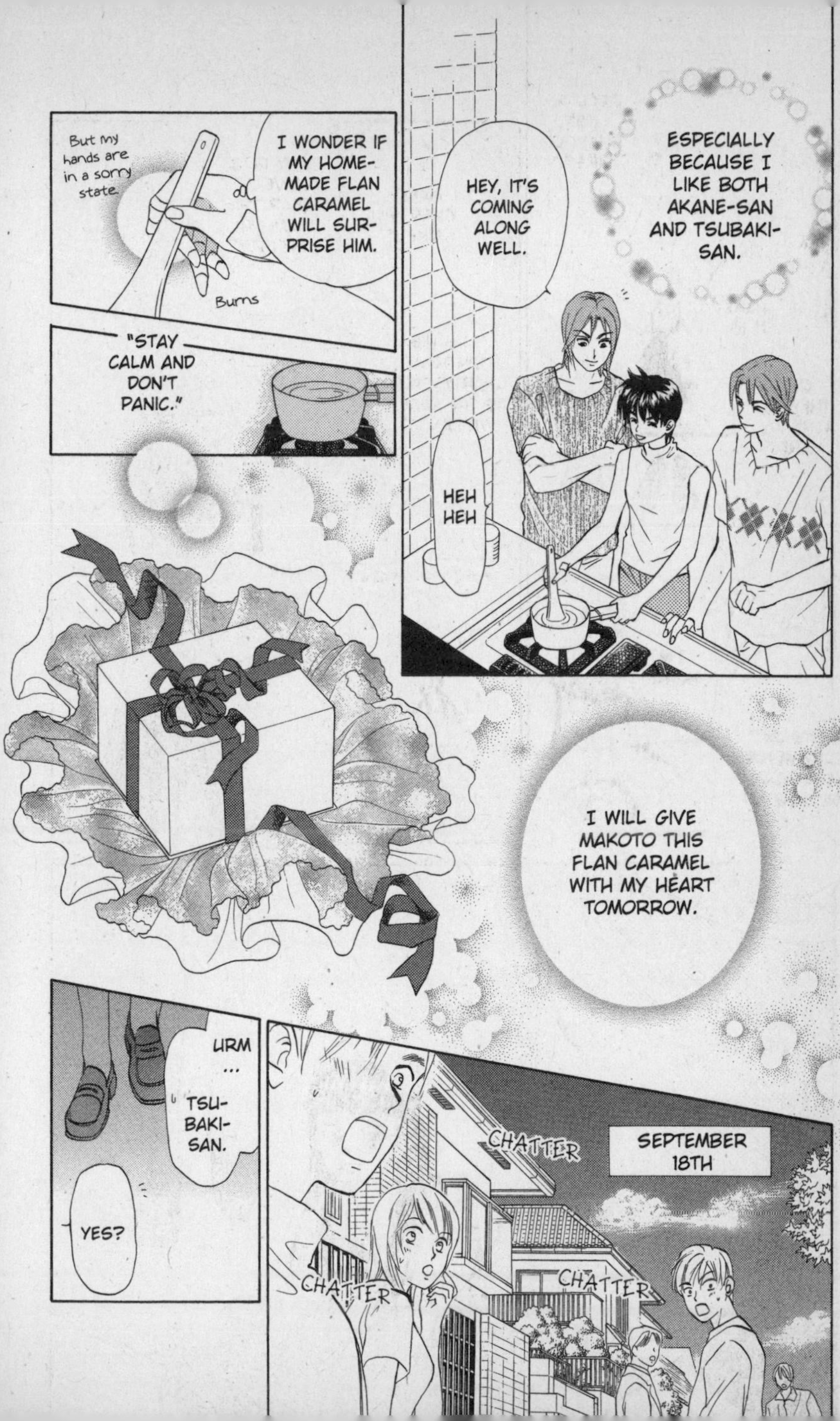
ESPECIALLY BECAUSE I LIKE BOTH AKANE-SAN AND TSUBAKI-SAN.
HEY, IT'S COMING ALONG WELL.
HEH HEH
I WONDER IF MY HOME-MADE FLAN CARAMEL WILL SUR-PRISE HIM.
But my hands are in a sorry state
Burns
"STAY CALM AND DON'T PANIC."
I WILL GIVE MAKOTO THIS FLAN CARAMEL WITH MY HEART TOMORROW.
SEPTEMBER 18TH
CHATTER
CHATTER
CHATTER
URM ... TSU-BAKI-SAN.
YES?

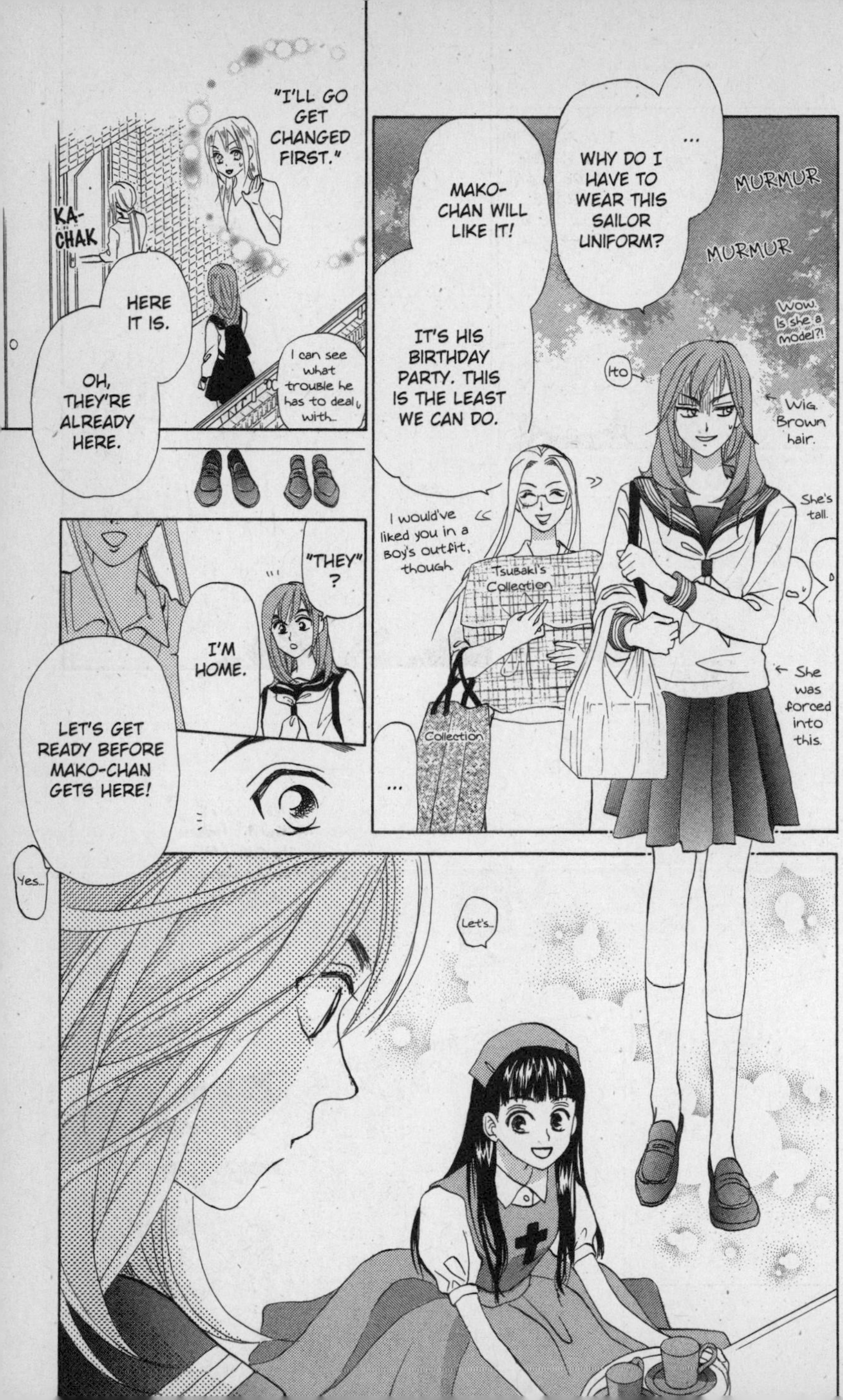
...
WHY DO I HAVE TO WEAR THIS SAILOR UNIFORM?
MURMUR
MURMUR
MAKO-CHAN WILL LIKE IT!
IT'S HIS BIRTHDAY PARTY. THIS IS THE LEAST WE CAN DO.
Wow. Is she a model?!
Ito
Wig. Brown hair.
She's tall.
She was forced into this.
I would've liked you in a boy's outfit, though.
Tsubaki's Collection
Collection
...
"I'LL GO GET CHANGED FIRST."
KA-CHAK
I can see what trouble he has to deal with...
HERE IT IS.
OH, THEY'RE ALREADY HERE.
"THEY"?
I'M HOME.
LET'S GET READY BEFORE MAKO-CHAN GETS HERE!
Yes...
Let's...

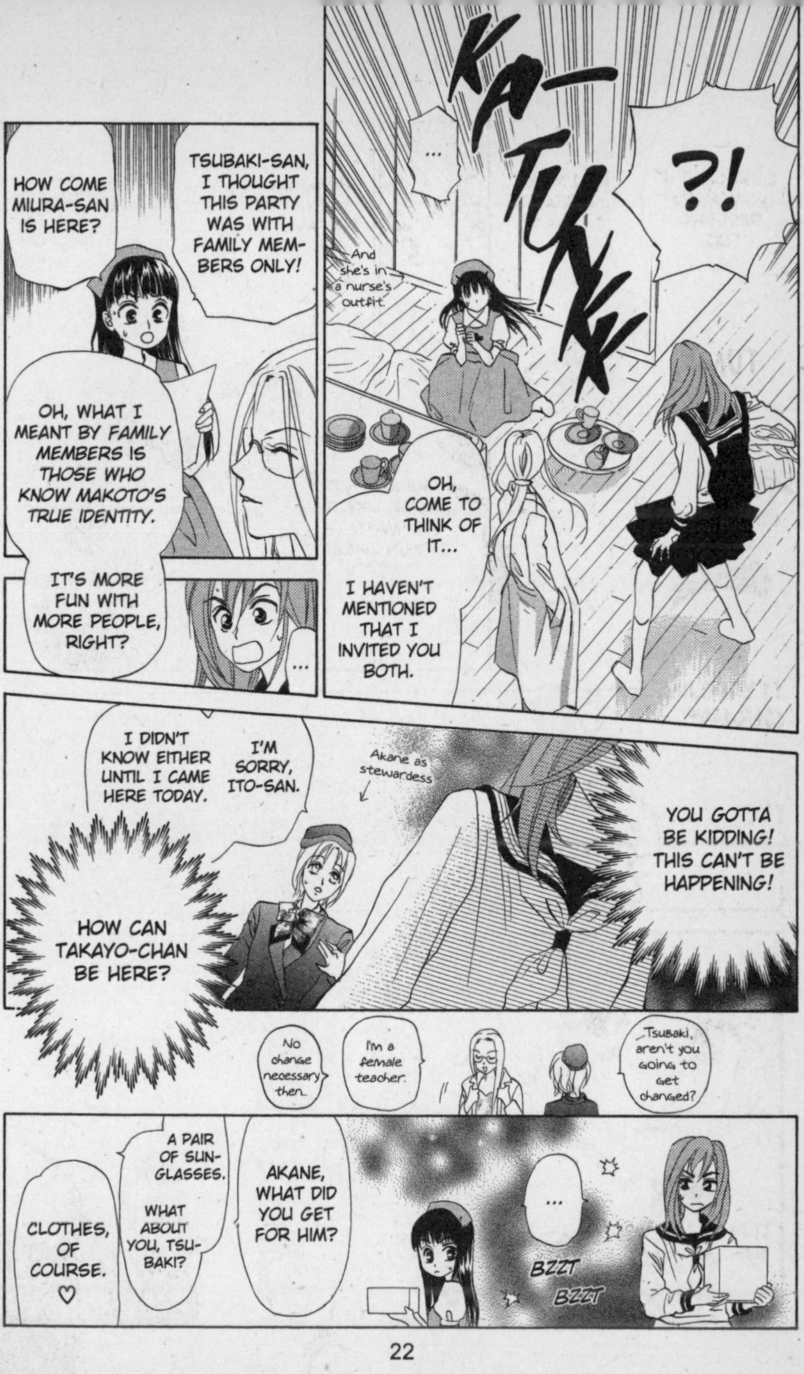
KA-TUNKK
?!
...
And she's in a nurse's outfit.
OH, COME TO THINK OF IT...
I HAVEN'T MENTIONED THAT I INVITED YOU BOTH.
TSUBAKI-SAN, I THOUGHT THIS PARTY WAS WITH FAMILY MEMBERS ONLY!
HOW COME MIURA-SAN IS HERE?
OH, WHAT I MEANT BY FAMILY MEMBERS IS THOSE WHO KNOW MAKOTO'S TRUE IDENTITY.
IT'S MORE FUN WITH MORE PEOPLE, RIGHT?
...
YOU GOTTA BE KIDDING! THIS CAN'T BE HAPPENING!
Akane as stewardess
I'M SORRY, ITO-SAN.
I DIDN'T KNOW EITHER UNTIL I CAME HERE TODAY.
HOW CAN TAKAYO-CHAN BE HERE?
Tsubaki, aren't you going to get changed?
I'm a female teacher.
No change necessary then.
...
BZZT
BZZT
AKANE, WHAT DID YOU GET FOR HIM?
A PAIR OF SUNGLASSES.
WHAT ABOUT YOU, TSUBAKI?
CLOTHES, OF COURSE. ♡

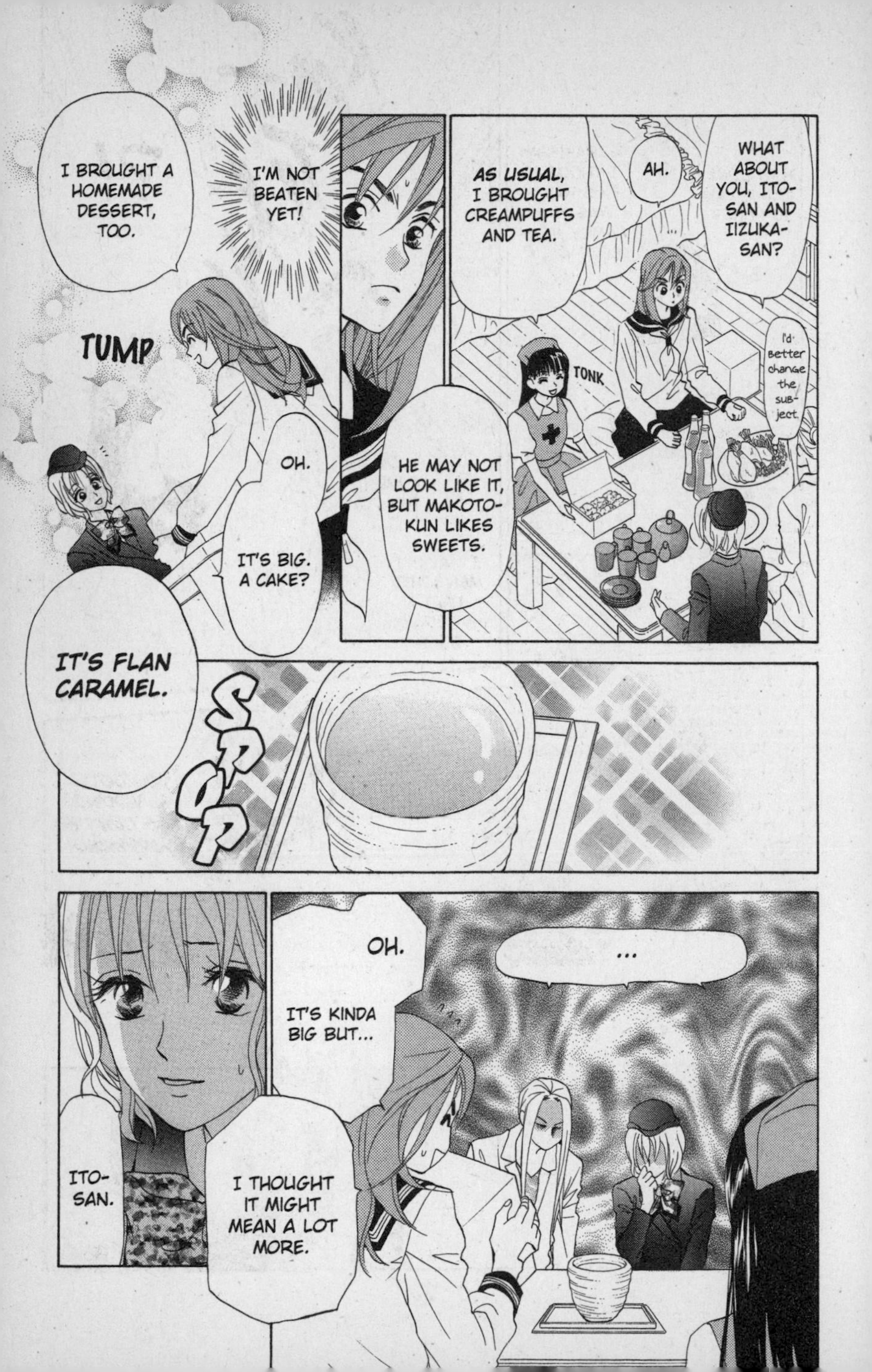

WHAT ABOUT YOU, ITO-SAN AND IIZUKA-SAN?
AH.
AS USUAL, I BROUGHT CREAMPUFFS AND TEA.
I'd better change the subject.
TONK
HE MAY NOT LOOK LIKE IT, BUT MAKOTO-KUN LIKES SWEETS.
I'M NOT BEATEN YET!
I BROUGHT A HOMEMADE DESSERT, TOO.
TUMP
OH.
IT'S BIG. A CAKE?
IT'S FLAN CARAMEL.
SPOP
...
OH.
IT'S KINDA BIG BUT...
I THOUGHT IT MIGHT MEAN A LOT MORE.
ITO-SAN.

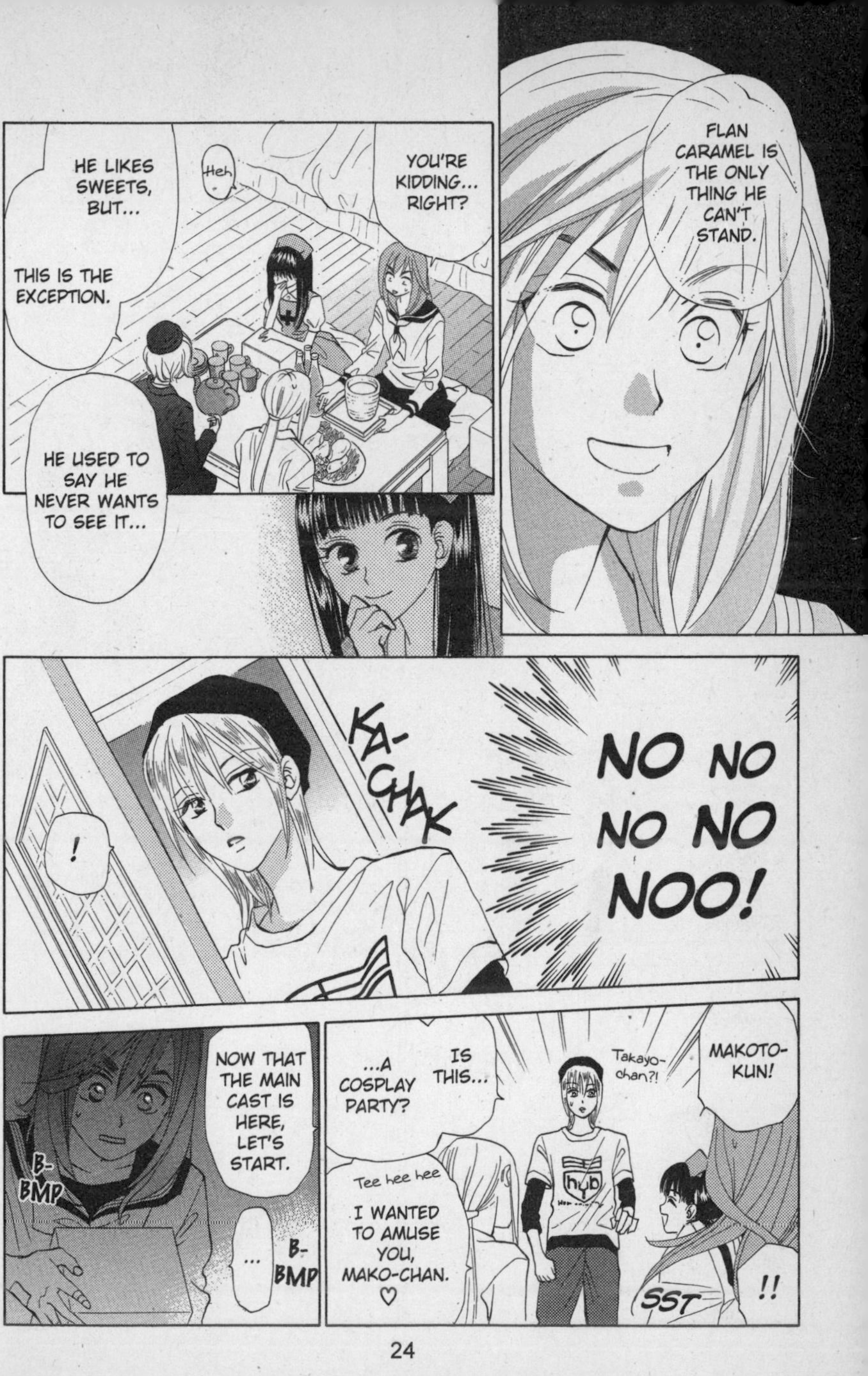
FLAN CARAMEL IS THE ONLY THING HE CAN'T STAND.
YOU'RE KIDDING... RIGHT?
Heh
HE LIKES SWEETS, BUT...
THIS IS THE EXCEPTION.
HE USED TO SAY HE NEVER WANTS TO SEE IT...
NO NO NO NO NOO!
KA-CHAK
!
MAKOTO-KUN!
Takayo-chan?!
IS THIS...
...A COSPLAY PARTY?
Tee hee hee
I WANTED TO AMUSE YOU, MAKO-CHAN. ♡
!!
SST
NOW THAT THE MAIN CAST IS HERE, LET'S START.
B-BMP
...
B-BMP

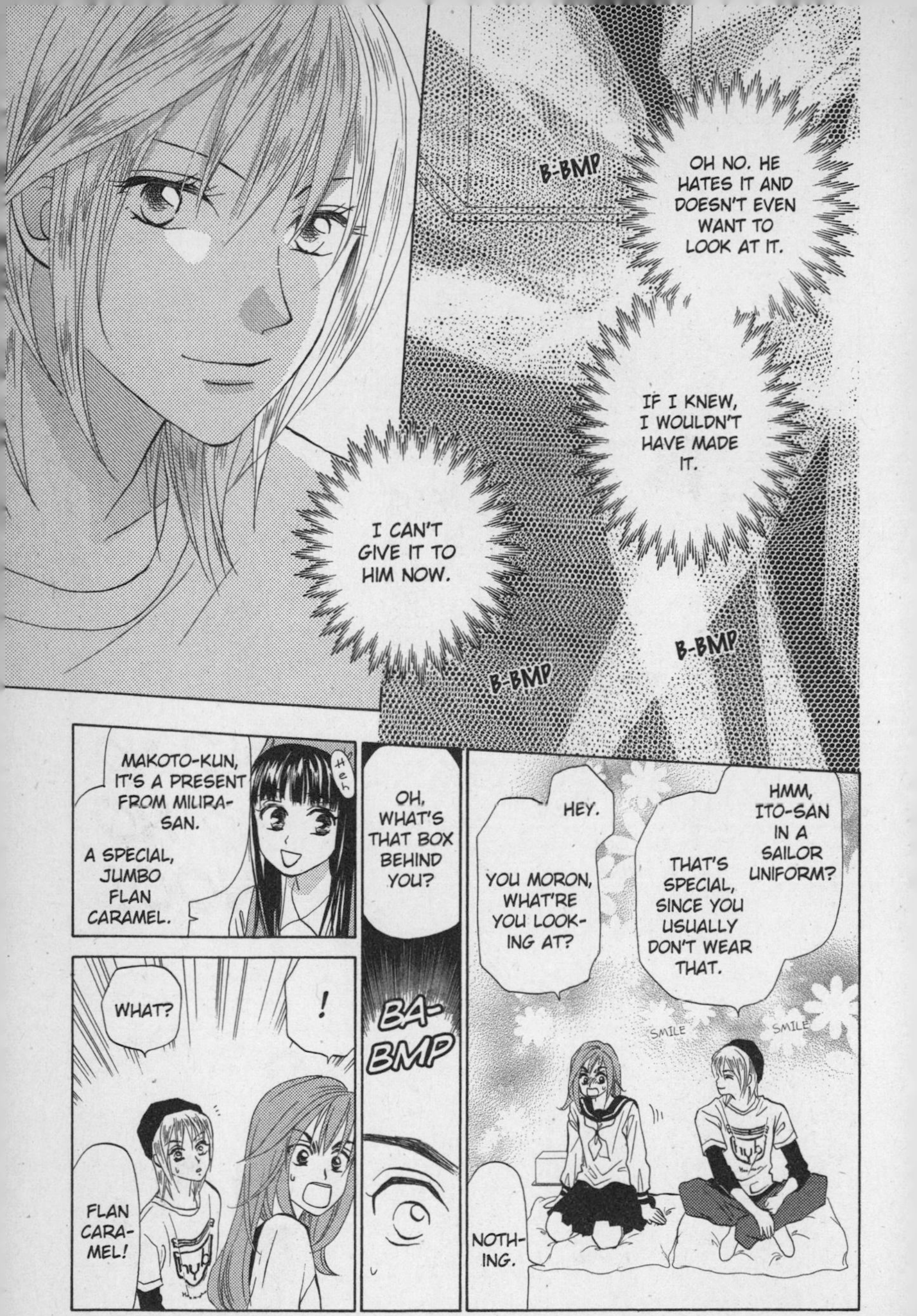
B-BMP
OH NO. HE HATES IT AND DOESN'T EVEN WANT TO LOOK AT IT.
IF I KNEW, I WOULDN'T HAVE MADE IT.
I CAN'T GIVE IT TO HIM NOW.
B-BMP
B-BMP
HMM, ITO-SAN IN A SAILOR UNIFORM?
THAT'S SPECIAL, SINCE YOU USUALLY DON'T WEAR THAT.
HEY.
YOU MORON, WHAT'RE YOU LOOKING AT?
SMILE
SMILE
NOTHING.
OH, WHAT'S THAT BOX BEHIND YOU?
BA-BMP
MAKOTO-KUN, IT'S A PRESENT FROM MILIRA-SAN.
Heh
A SPECIAL, JUMBO FLAN CARAMEL.
!
WHAT?
FLAN CARAMEL!

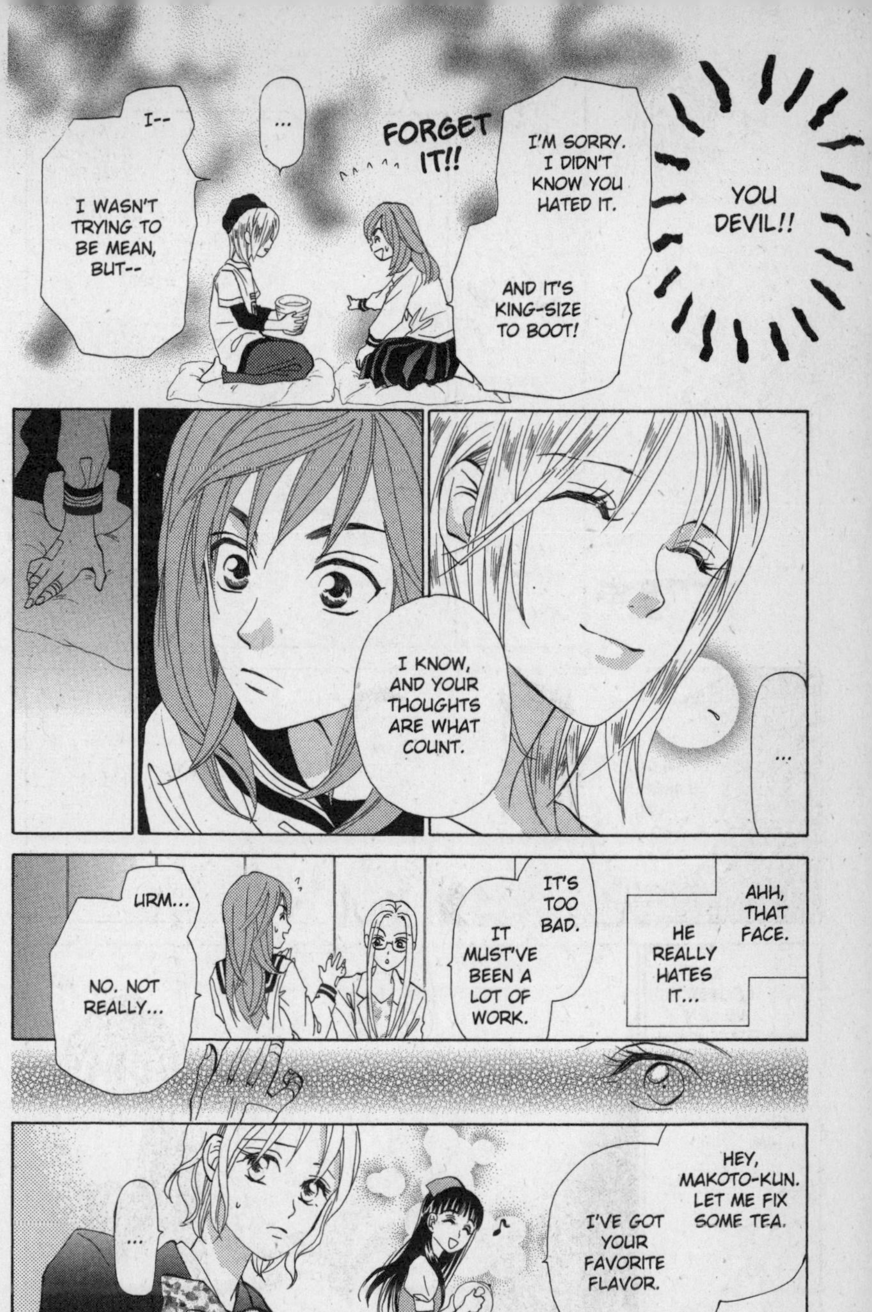
YOU DEVIL!!
I'M SORRY. I DIDN'T KNOW YOU HATED IT.
AND IT'S KING-SIZE TO BOOT!
FORGET IT!!
...
I--
I WASN'T TRYING TO BE MEAN, BUT--
...
I KNOW, AND YOUR THOUGHTS ARE WHAT COUNT.
AHH, THAT FACE.
HE REALLY HATES IT...
IT'S TOO BAD.
IT MUST'VE BEEN A LOT OF WORK.
URM...
NO. NOT REALLY...
HEY, MAKOTO-KUN. LET ME FIX SOME TEA.
I'VE GOT YOUR FAVORITE FLAVOR.
...

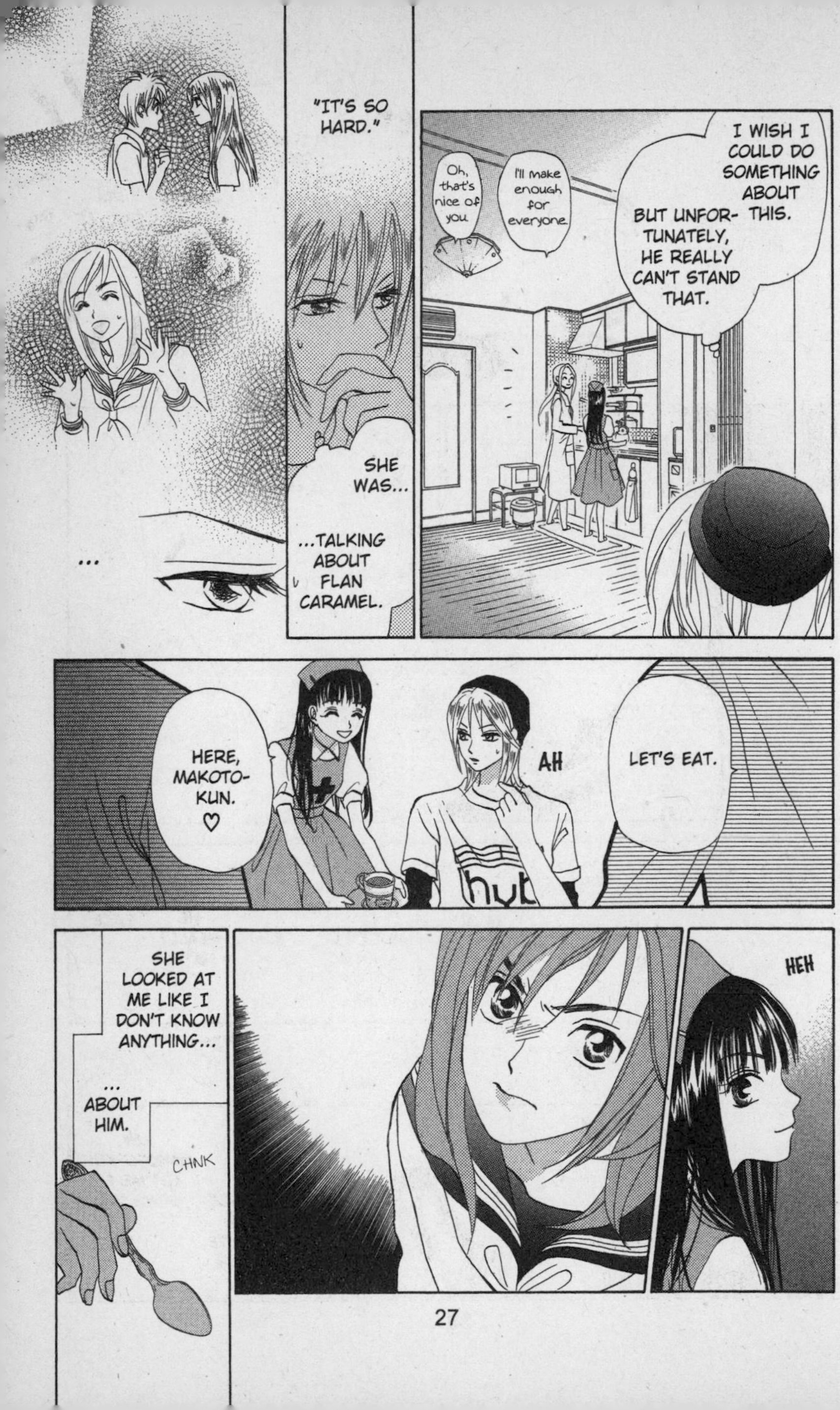
I WISH I COULD DO SOMETHING ABOUT THIS.
BUT UNFORTUNATELY, HE REALLY CAN'T STAND THAT.
I'll make enough for everyone.
Oh, that's nice of you.
"IT'S SO HARD."
SHE WAS...
...TALKING ABOUT FLAN CARAMEL.
...
LET'S EAT.
AH
HERE, MAKOTO-KUN. ♡
HEH
SHE LOOKED AT ME LIKE I DON'T KNOW ANYTHING...
...ABOUT HIM.
CHNK

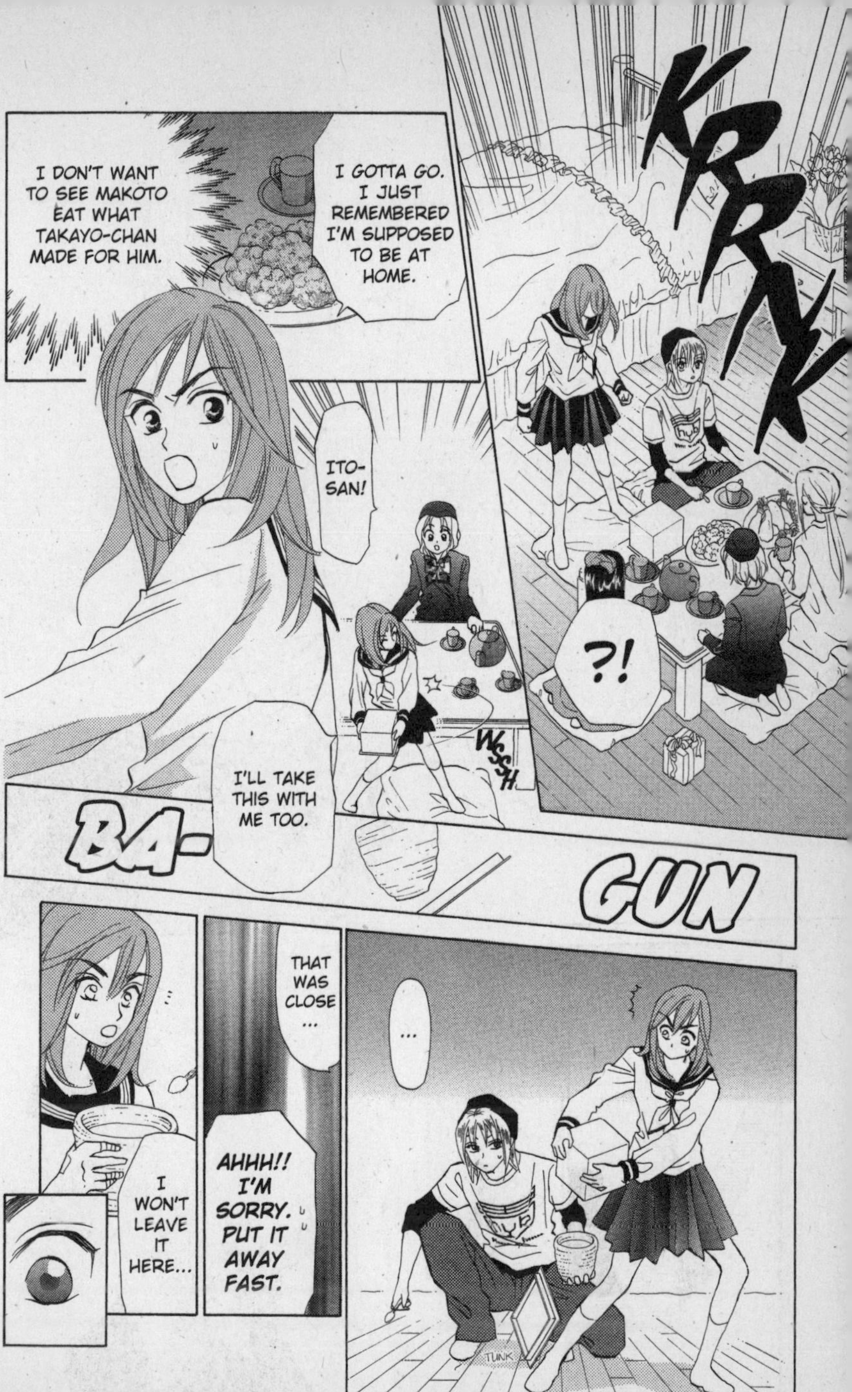
KRRNK
?!
I GOTTA GO. I JUST REMEMBERED I'M SUPPOSED TO BE AT HOME.
I DON'T WANT TO SEE MAKOTO EAT WHAT TAKAYO-CHAN MADE FOR HIM.
ITO-SAN!
I'LL TAKE THIS WITH ME TOO.
WSSH
BA-
GUN
...
TUNK
THAT WAS CLOSE ...
AHHH!! I'M SORRY. PUT IT AWAY FAST.
I WON'T LEAVE IT HERE...

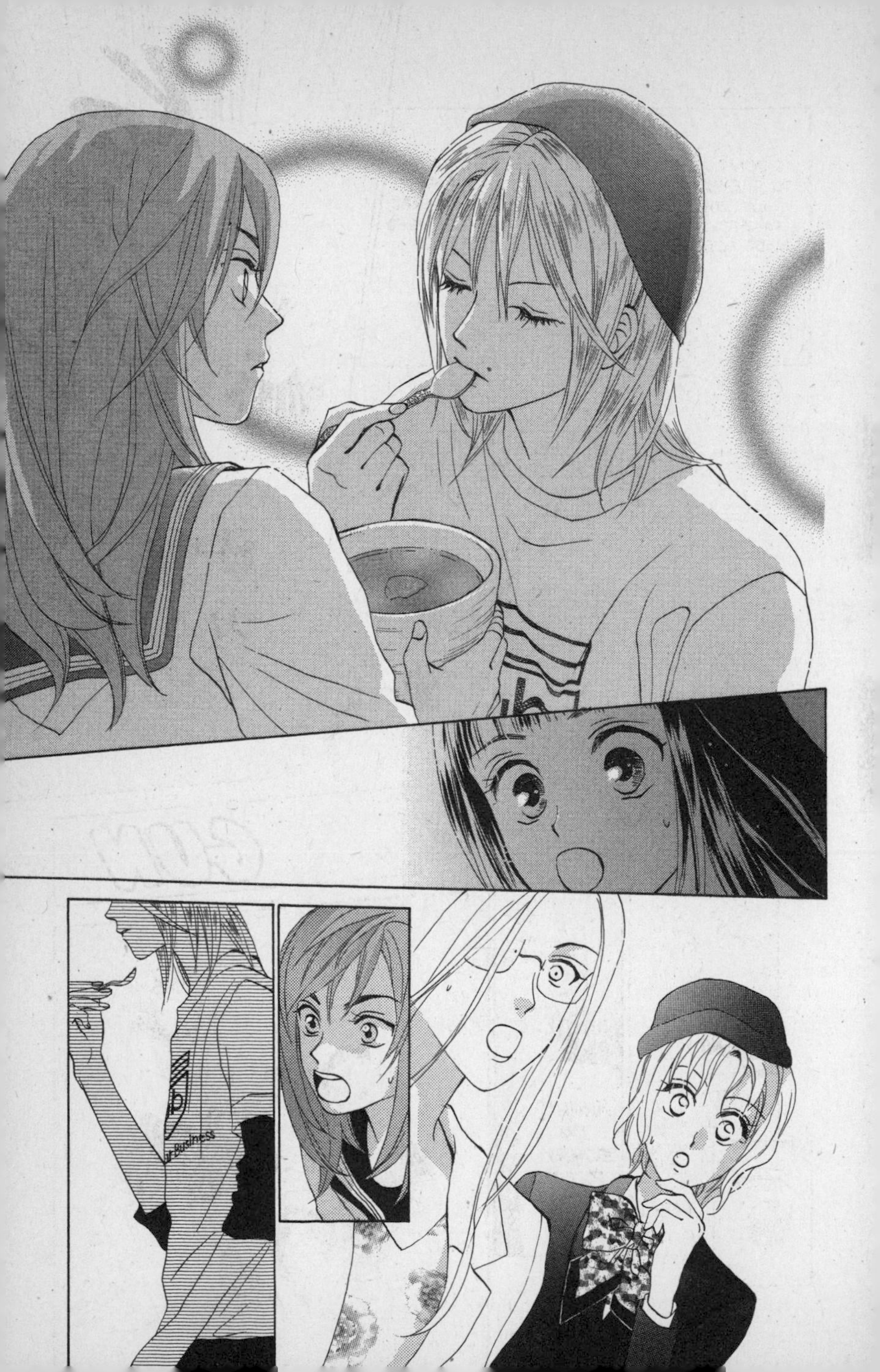
Business

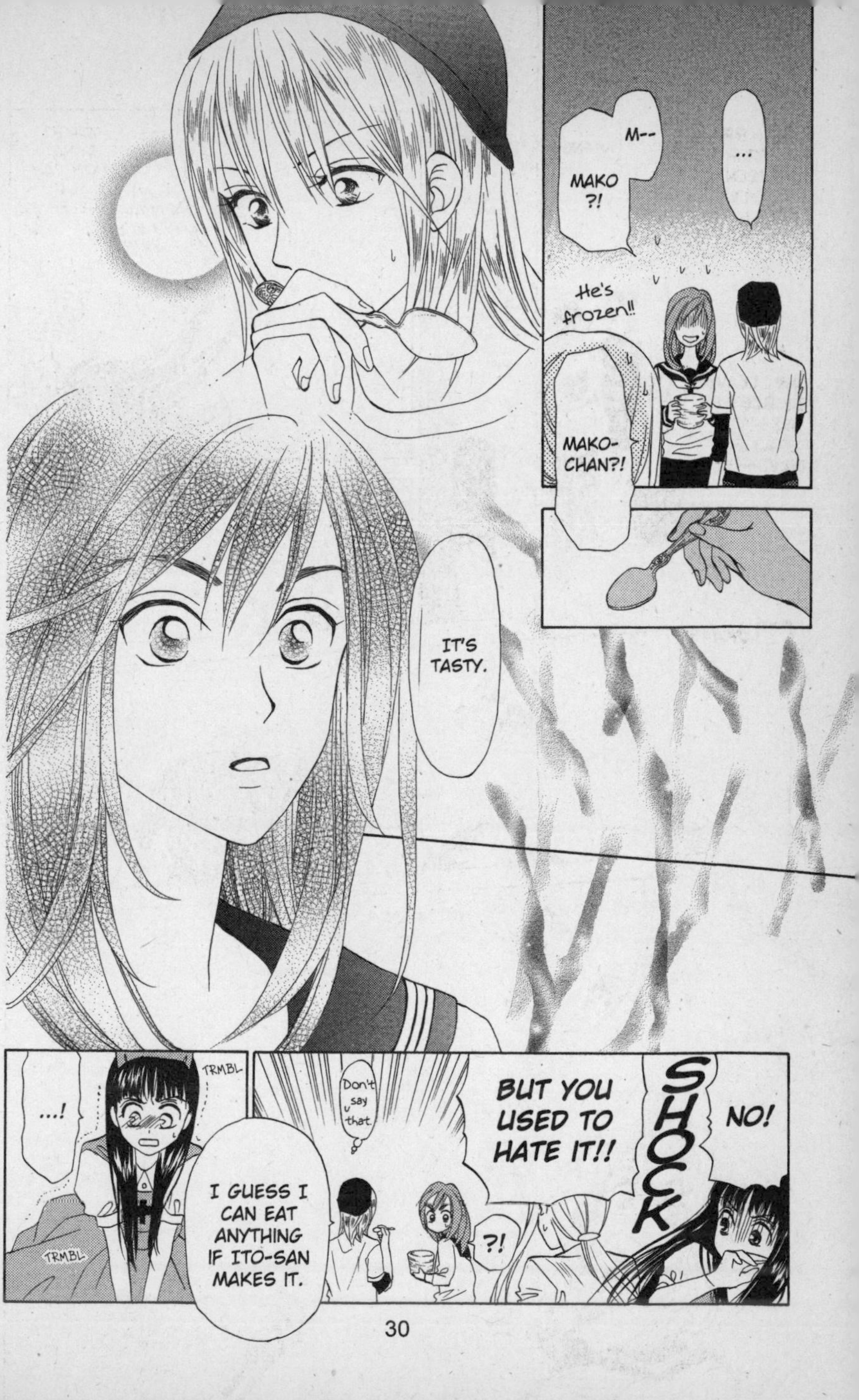
...
M--
MAKO ?!
He's frozen!!
MAKO-CHAN?!
IT'S TASTY.
NO!
SHOCK
BUT YOU USED TO HATE IT!!
Don't say that.
?!
I GUESS I CAN EAT ANYTHING IF ITO-SAN MAKES IT.
TRMBL
...!
TRMBL

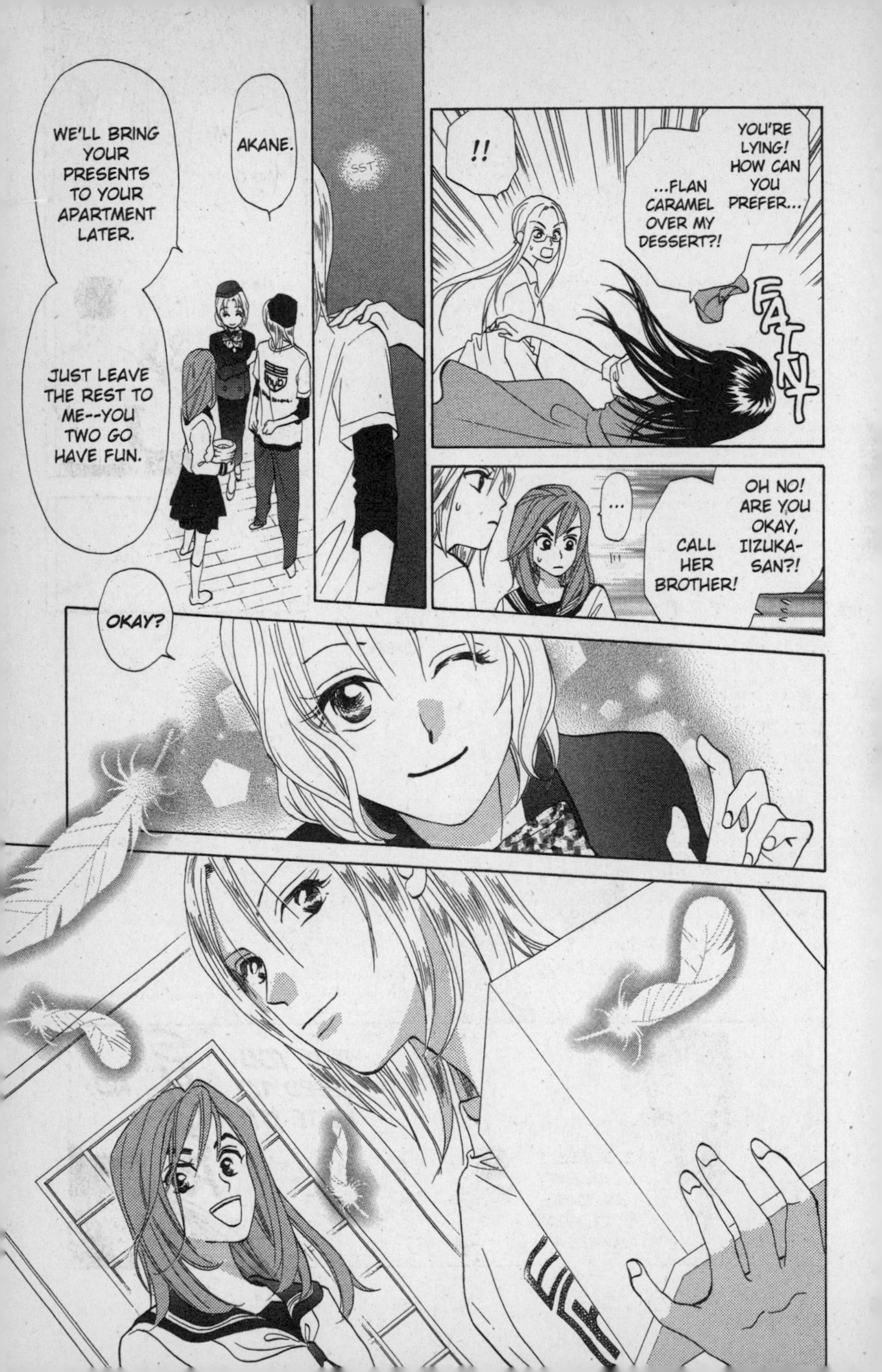
YOU'RE LYING! HOW CAN YOU PREFER...
...FLAN CARAMEL OVER MY DESSERT?!
!!
FAINT
OH NO! ARE YOU OKAY, IIZUKA-SAN?!
CALL HER BROTHER!
...
AKANE.
SST
WE'LL BRING YOUR PRESENTS TO YOUR APARTMENT LATER.
JUST LEAVE THE REST TO ME--YOU TWO GO HAVE FUN.
OKAY?

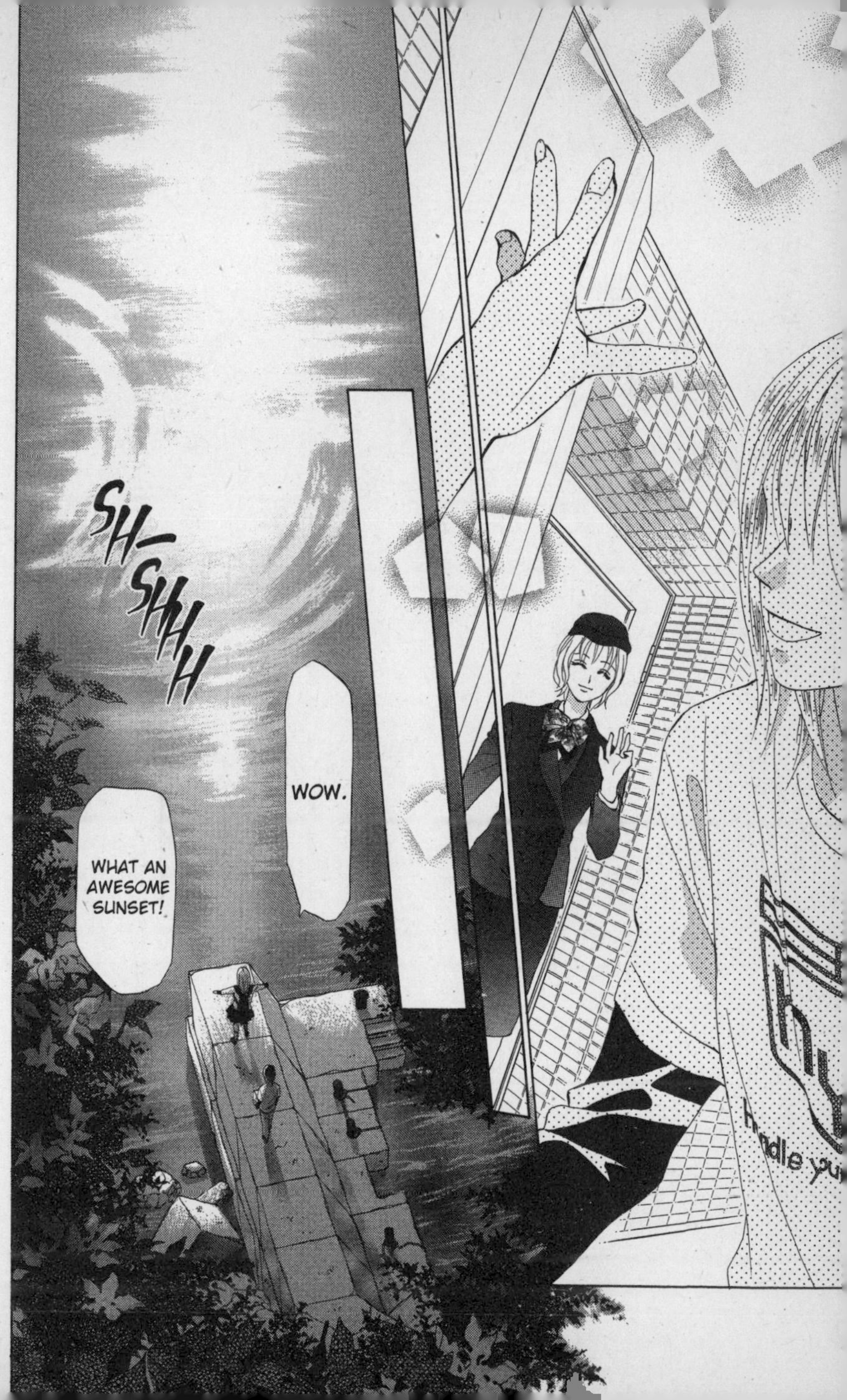
SH-SHHHH
WOW.
WHAT AN AWESOME SUNSET!

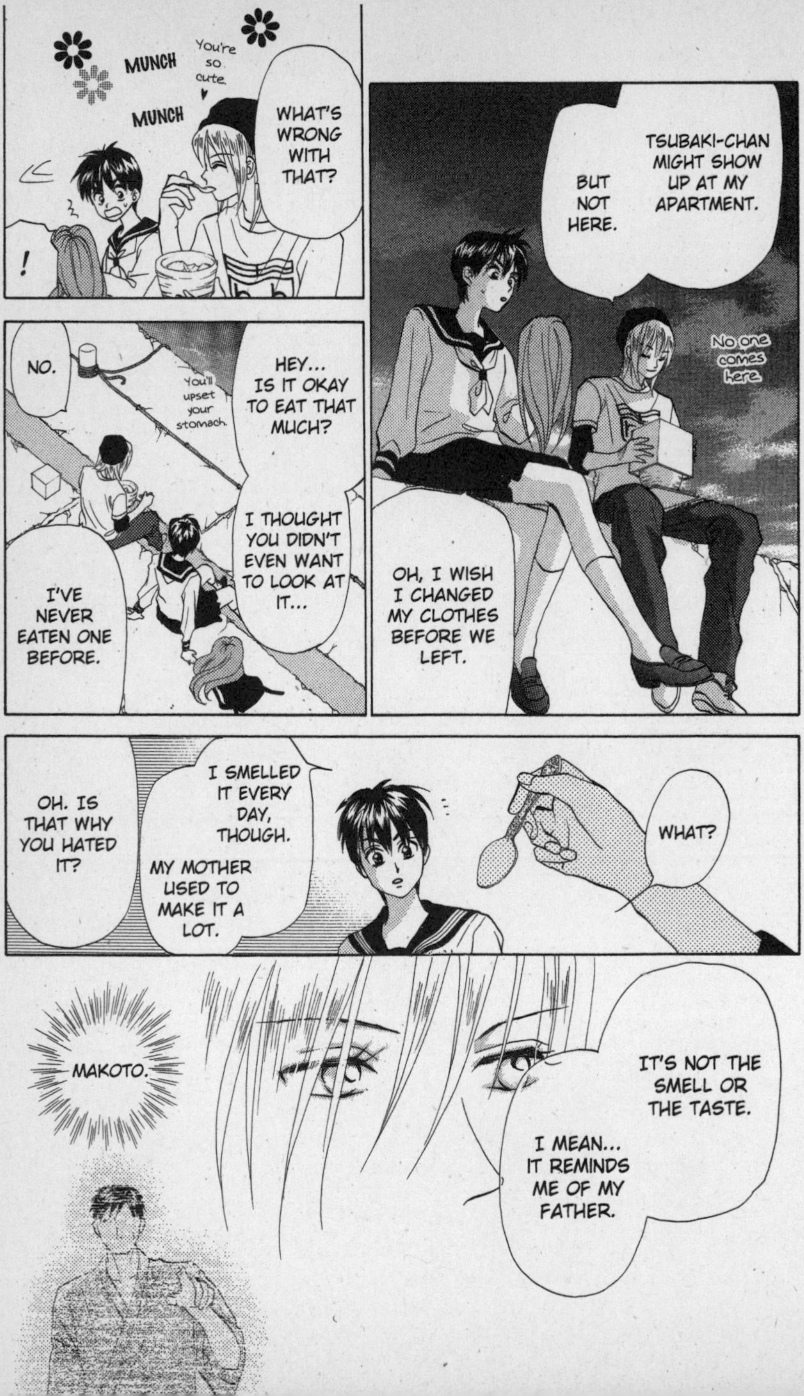
TSUBAKI-CHAN MIGHT SHOW UP AT MY APARTMENT.
BUT NOT HERE.
No one comes here.
OH, I WISH I CHANGED MY CLOTHES BEFORE WE LEFT.
WHAT'S WRONG WITH THAT?
You're so cute.
MUNCH
MUNCH
!
HEY... IS IT OKAY TO EAT THAT MUCH?
NO.
You'll upset your stomach.
I THOUGHT YOU DIDN'T EVEN WANT TO LOOK AT IT...
I'VE NEVER EATEN ONE BEFORE.
WHAT?
I SMELLED IT EVERY DAY, THOUGH.
MY MOTHER USED TO MAKE IT A LOT.
OH. IS THAT WHY YOU HATED IT?
IT'S NOT THE SMELL OR THE TASTE.
I MEAN... IT REMINDS ME OF MY FATHER.
MAKOTO.

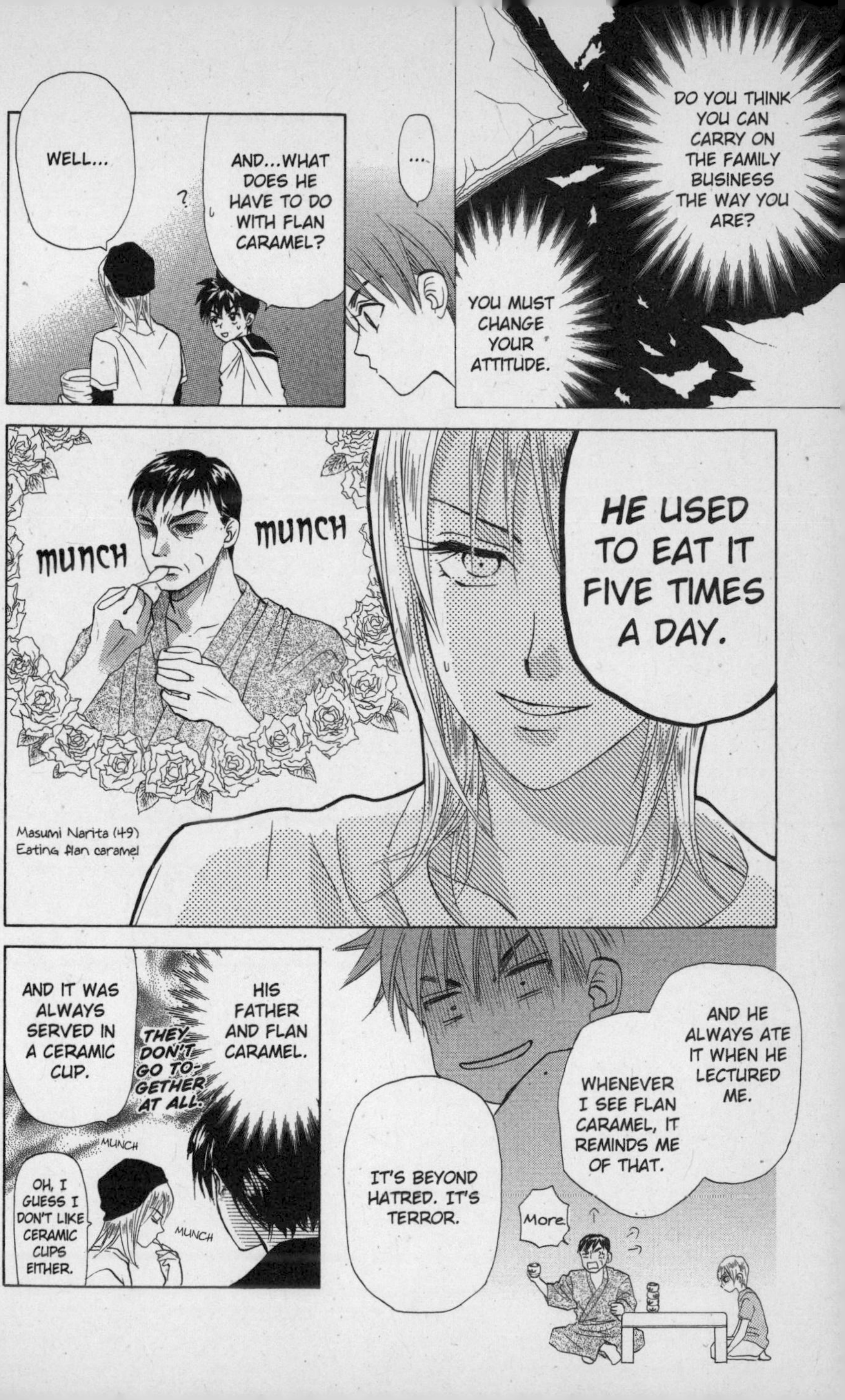
DO YOU THINK YOU CAN CARRY ON THE FAMILY BUSINESS THE WAY YOU ARE?
YOU MUST CHANGE YOUR ATTITUDE.
...
AND...WHAT DOES HE HAVE TO DO WITH FLAN CARAMEL?
?
WELL...
HE USED TO EAT IT FIVE TIMES A DAY.
MUNCH
MUNCH
Masumi Narita (49) Eating flan caramel
AND HE ALWAYS ATE IT WHEN HE LECTURED ME.
WHENEVER I SEE FLAN CARAMEL, IT REMINDS ME OF THAT.
IT'S BEYOND HATRED. IT'S TERROR.
More.
HIS FATHER AND FLAN CARAMEL.
THEY DON'T GO TO-GETHER AT ALL.
AND IT WAS ALWAYS SERVED IN A CERAMIC CUP.
MUNCH
MUNCH
OH, I GUESS I DON'T LIKE CERAMIC CUPS EITHER.

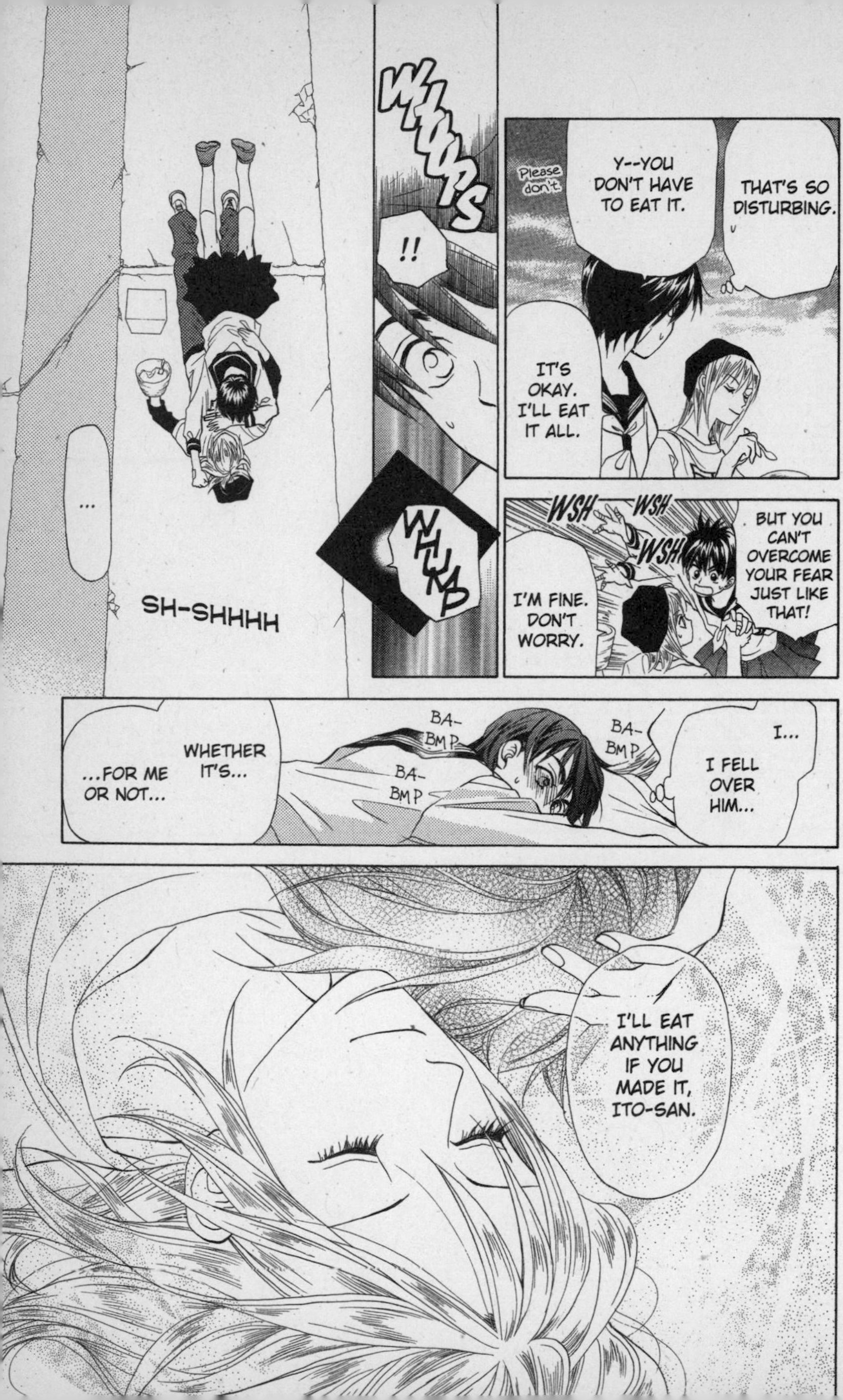
THAT'S SO DISTURBING.
Y--YOU DON'T HAVE TO EAT IT.
Please don't.
IT'S OKAY. I'LL EAT IT ALL.
WSH WSH WSH
BUT YOU CAN'T OVERCOME YOUR FEAR JUST LIKE THAT!
I'M FINE. DON'T WORRY.
WHUMPS
!!
WHUMP
SH-SHHHH
...
I...
I FELL OVER HIM...
BA-BMP
BA-BMP
BA-BMP
WHETHER IT'S...
...FOR ME OR NOT...
I'LL EAT ANYTHING IF YOU MADE IT, ITO-SAN.

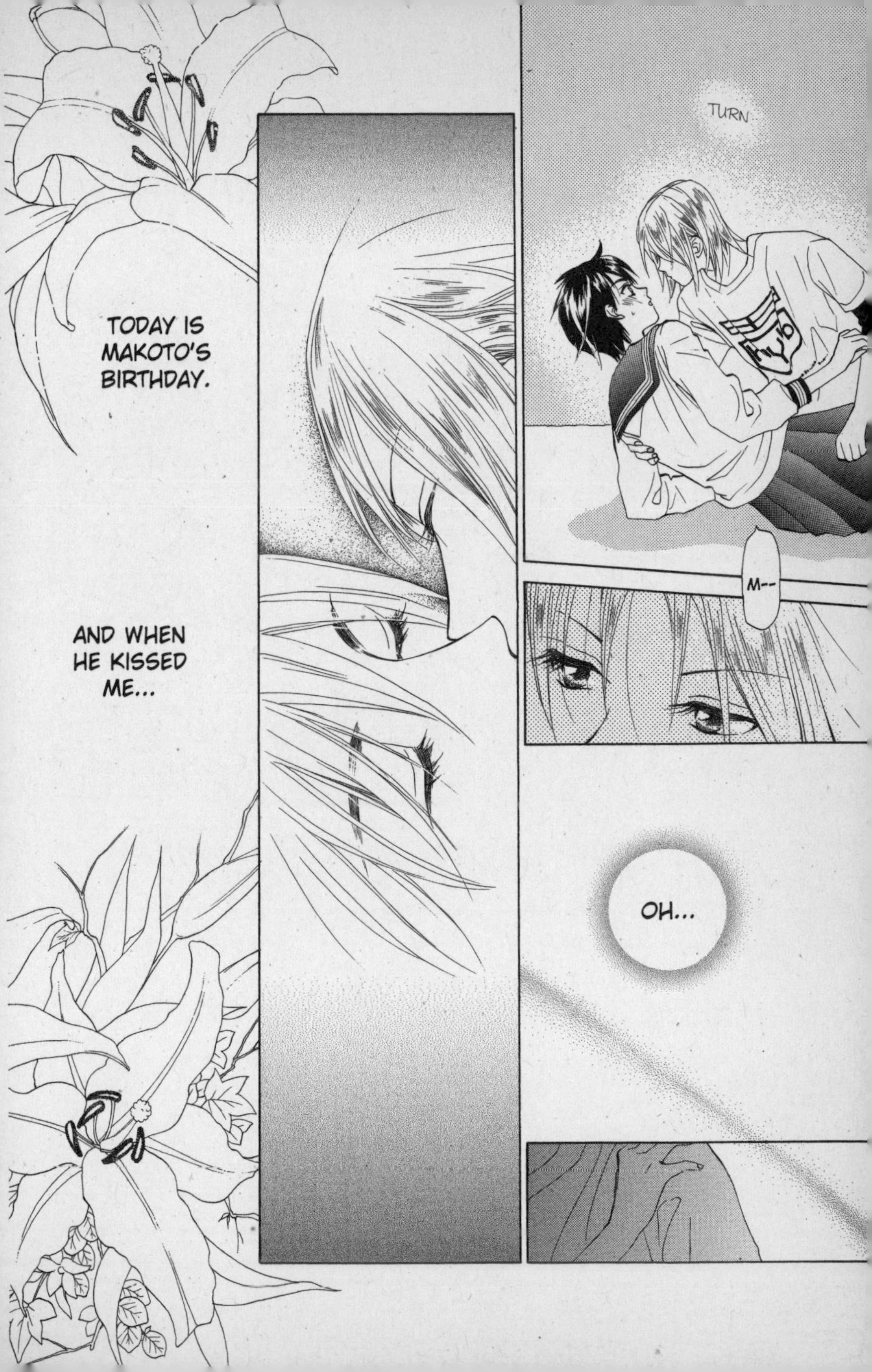
TURN
M--
OH...
TODAY IS MAKOTO'S BIRTHDAY.
AND WHEN HE KISSED ME...

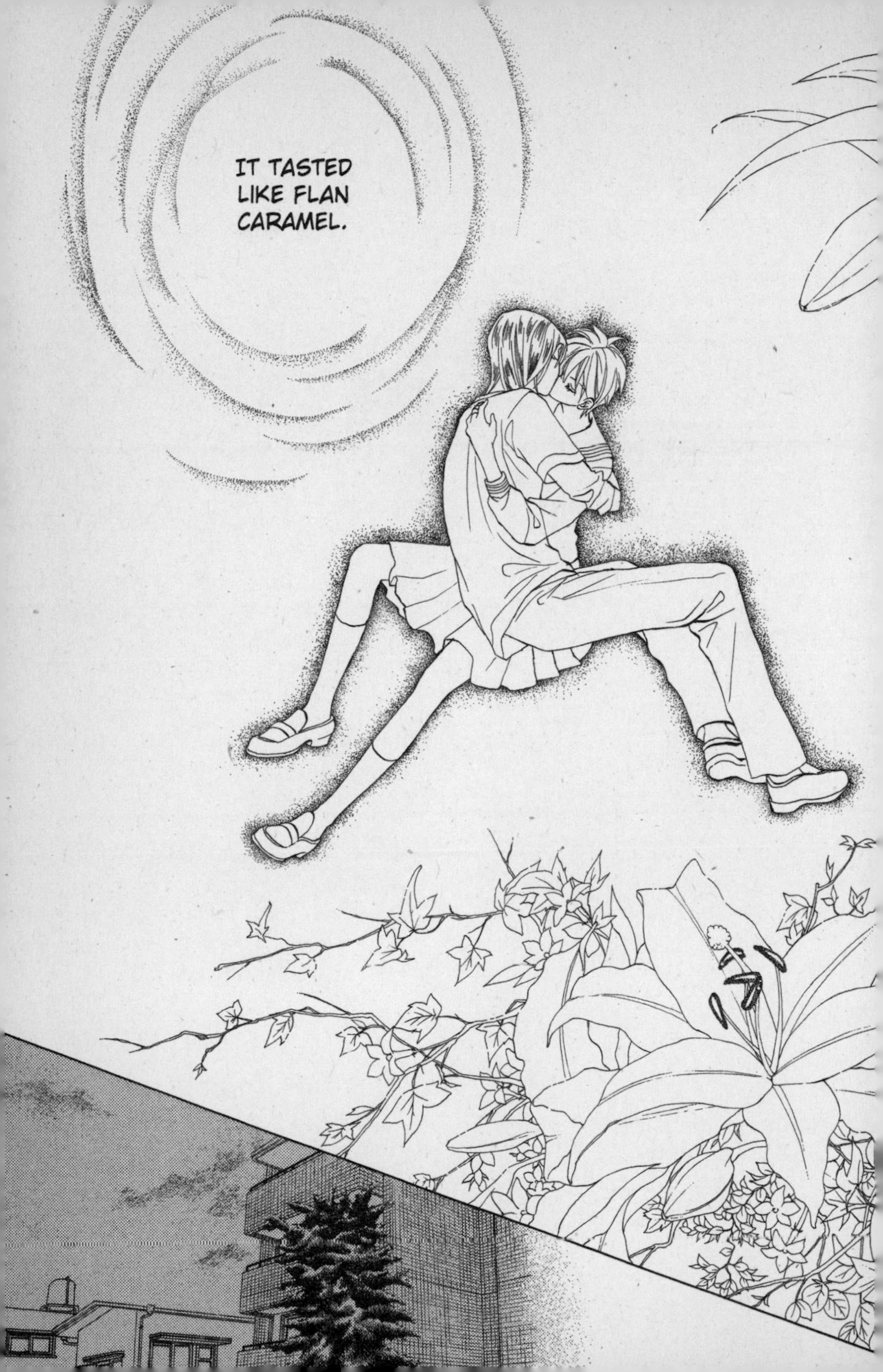
IT TASTED LIKE FLAN CARAMEL.

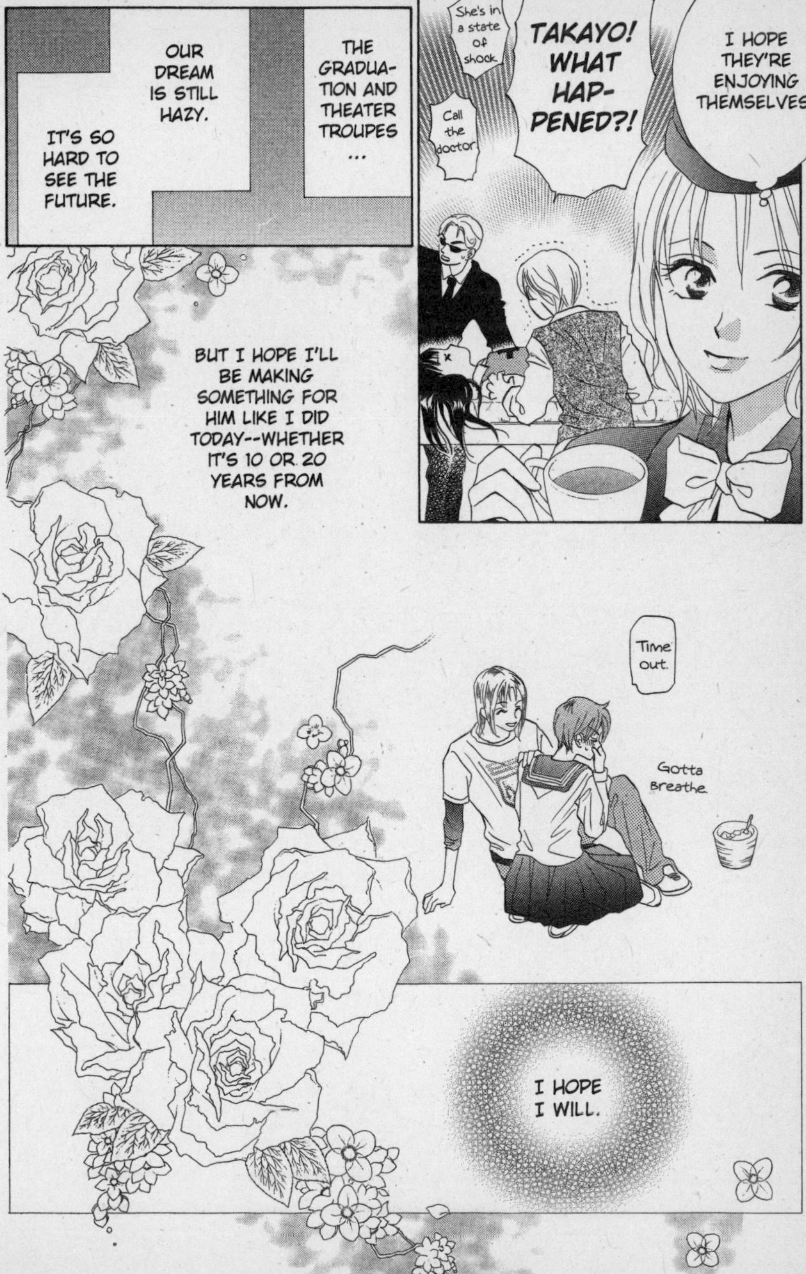
I HOPE THEY'RE ENJOYING THEMSELVES.
TAKAYO! WHAT HAP-PENED?!
She's in a state of shock.
Call the doctor
THE GRADUA-TION AND THEATER TROUPES ...
OUR DREAM IS STILL HAZY.
IT'S SO HARD TO SEE THE FUTURE.
BUT I HOPE I'LL BE MAKING SOMETHING FOR HIM LIKE I DID TODAY--WHETHER IT'S 10 OR 20 YEARS FROM NOW.
Time out.
Gotta Breathe
I HOPE I WILL.

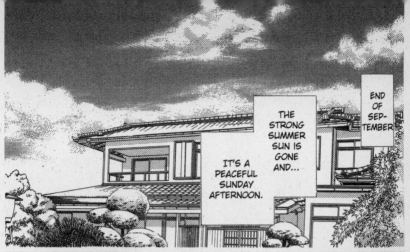

END OF SEP-TEMBER
THE STRONG SUMMER SUN IS GONE AND...
IT'S A PEACEFUL SUNDAY AFTERNOON.
I GUESS I'LL POLISH THE DOJO FLOOR TODAY.
FIRST SON • RYÛYA (22)
OH NO. THE SPECIALS AT THE SUPER-MARKET END AT 3 P.M.
Ads
SECOND SON • YÛTO (22)
SHAKE SHAKE
HUH? WE'RE OUT OF MILK.
FIRST DAUGH-TER • ITO (18)

—Behind the Scenes Story ②—

Tatsuyoshi's popularity is increasing rapidly! I received many letters saying "I really understand him" from those who have siblings. Thank you. ♪

They might fight, but Tatsuyoshi does care about Ito. And the girl who appears at the end is Rie-chan. She appears in *Nana-iro no Shinwa* (Rainbow Myth). If you're interested, please take a look.

It's about seven mysteries, and it has nothing to do with love. But I hope you'll enjoy it too.

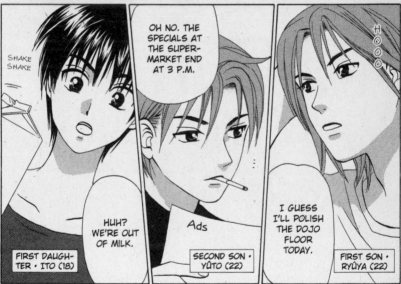

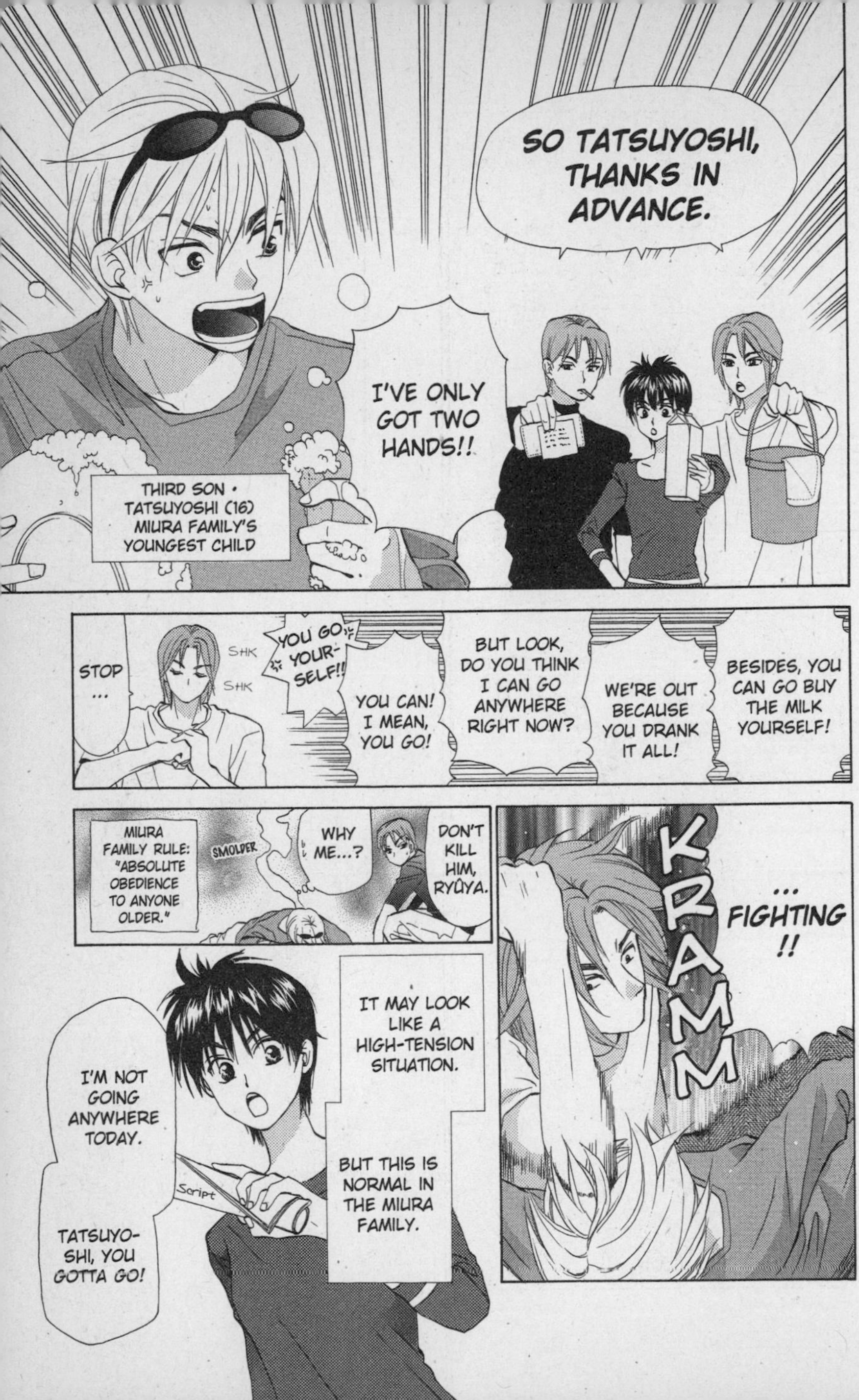
SO TATSUYOSHI, THANKS IN ADVANCE.
I'VE ONLY GOT TWO HANDS!!
THIRD SON • TATSUYOSHI (16) MIURA FAMILY'S YOUNGEST CHILD
BESIDES, YOU CAN GO BUY THE MILK YOURSELF!
WE'RE OUT BECAUSE YOU DRANK IT ALL!
BUT LOOK, DO YOU THINK I CAN GO ANYWHERE RIGHT NOW?
YOU CAN! I MEAN, YOU GO!
YOU GO YOURSELF!!
SHK
SHK
STOP ...
KRAMM
... FIGHTING !!
DON'T KILL HIM, RYÛYA.
WHY ME...?
SMOLDER
MIURA FAMILY RULE: "ABSOLUTE OBEDIENCE TO ANYONE OLDER."
IT MAY LOOK LIKE A HIGH-TENSION SITUATION.
BUT THIS IS NORMAL IN THE MIURA FAMILY.
I'M NOT GOING ANYWHERE TODAY.
TATSUYOSHI, YOU GOTTA GO!
Script

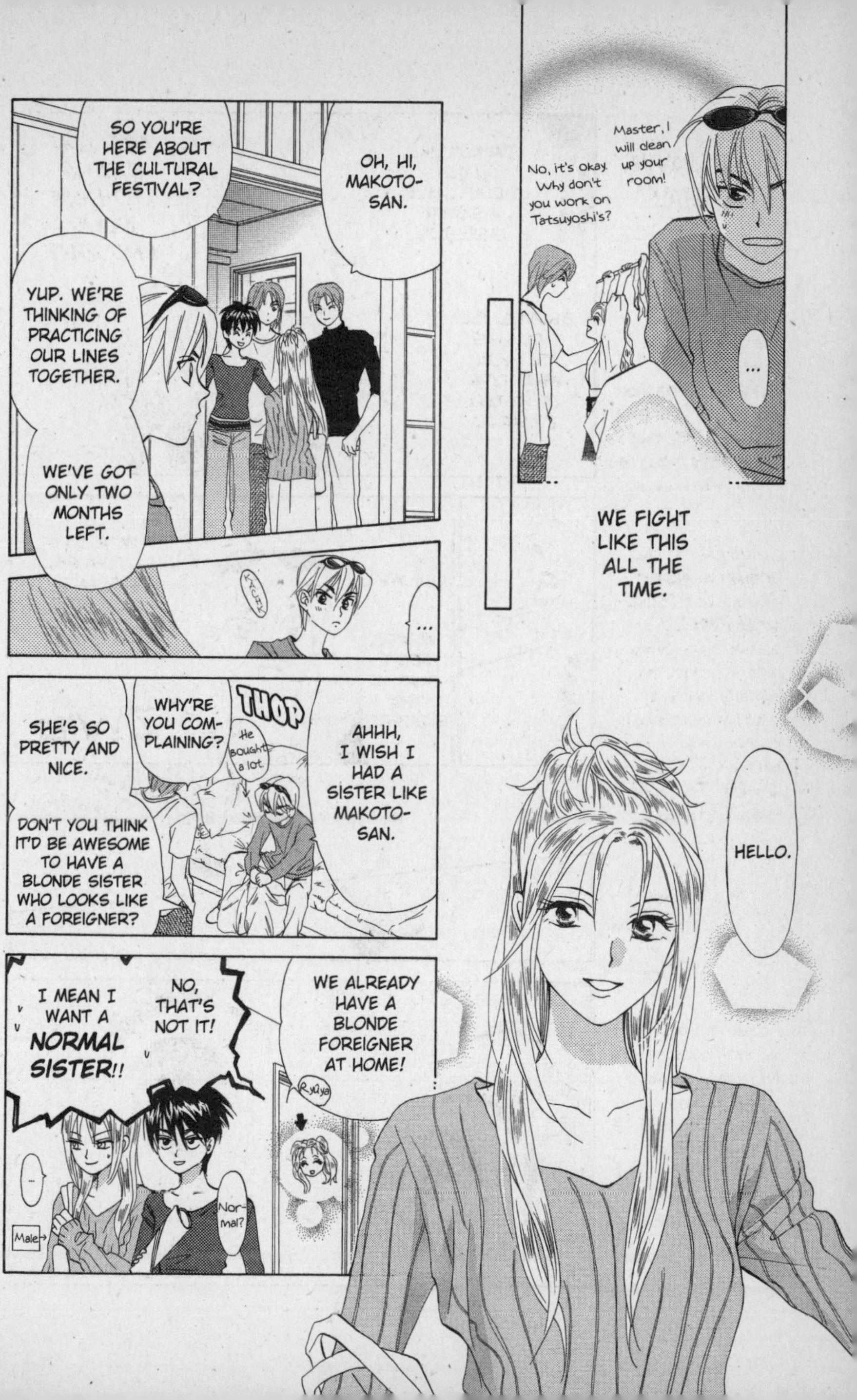
Master, I will clean up your room!
No, it's okay. Why don't you work on Tatsuyoshi's?
...
WE FIGHT LIKE THIS ALL THE TIME.
HELLO.
OH, HI, MAKOTO-SAN.
SO YOU'RE HERE ABOUT THE CULTURAL FESTIVAL?
YUP. WE'RE THINKING OF PRACTICING OUR LINES TOGETHER.
WE'VE GOT ONLY TWO MONTHS LEFT.
...
KACHK
AHHH, I WISH I HAD A SISTER LIKE MAKOTO-SAN.
THOP
He bought a lot.
WHY'RE YOU COMPLAINING?
SHE'S SO PRETTY AND NICE.
DON'T YOU THINK IT'D BE AWESOME TO HAVE A BLONDE SISTER WHO LOOKS LIKE A FOREIGNER?
WE ALREADY HAVE A BLONDE FOREIGNER AT HOME!
Ryuya
NO, THAT'S NOT IT!
I MEAN I WANT A NORMAL SISTER!!
Normal?
...
Male

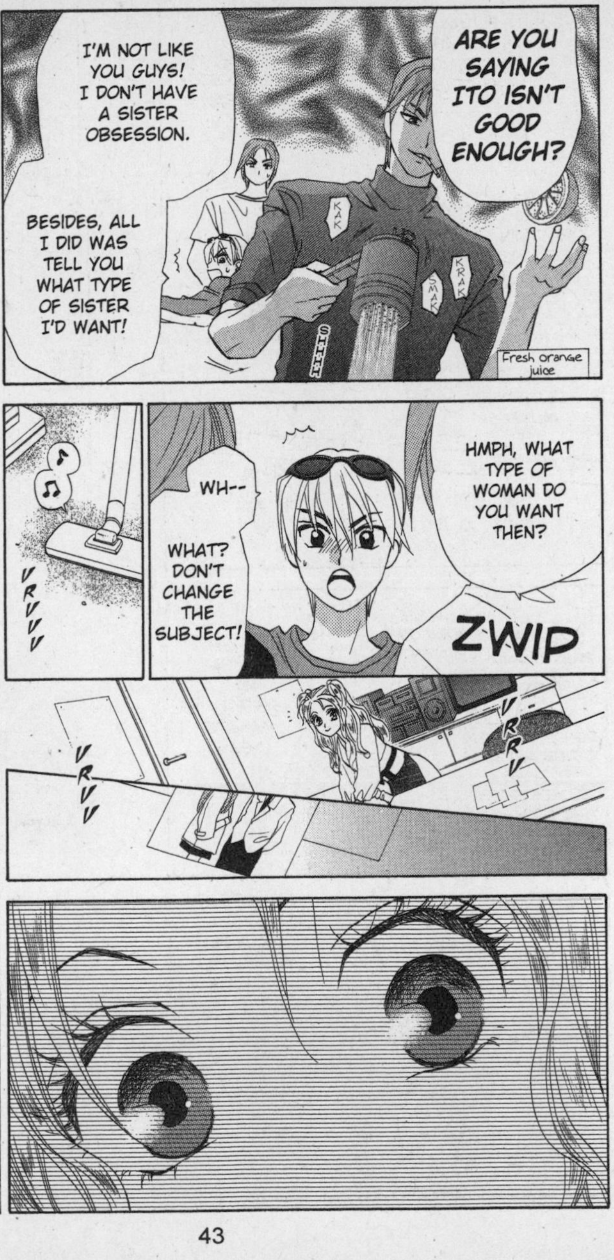
ARE YOU SAYING ITO ISN'T GOOD ENOUGH?
KAK
KRAK
SMAK
I'M NOT LIKE YOU GUYS! I DON'T HAVE A SISTER OBSESSION.
BESIDES, ALL I DID WAS TELL YOU WHAT TYPE OF SISTER I'D WANT!
SHHHH
Fresh orange juice
HMPH, WHAT TYPE OF WOMAN DO YOU WANT THEN?
ZWIP
WH--
WHAT? DON'T CHANGE THE SUBJECT!
VRVVV
VRRV
VRVV

ABOUT DRAWING MATERIALS

I receive a lot of letters asking about what materials I use when I draw. Maybe it's easier to understand if you look at the **Character Book**.

Am I nagging or what?

First of all, the **drawing paper**. I always use **135g from I●C**. Because 110g ones are so thin I'm afraid I might end up cutting them when I work on the tones. So I use thicker ones.

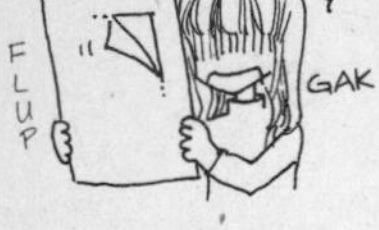
FLUP
GAK

I used to do that when I was submitting work before my debut... I applied pressure too hard! If you end up cutting it, tape it from behind.

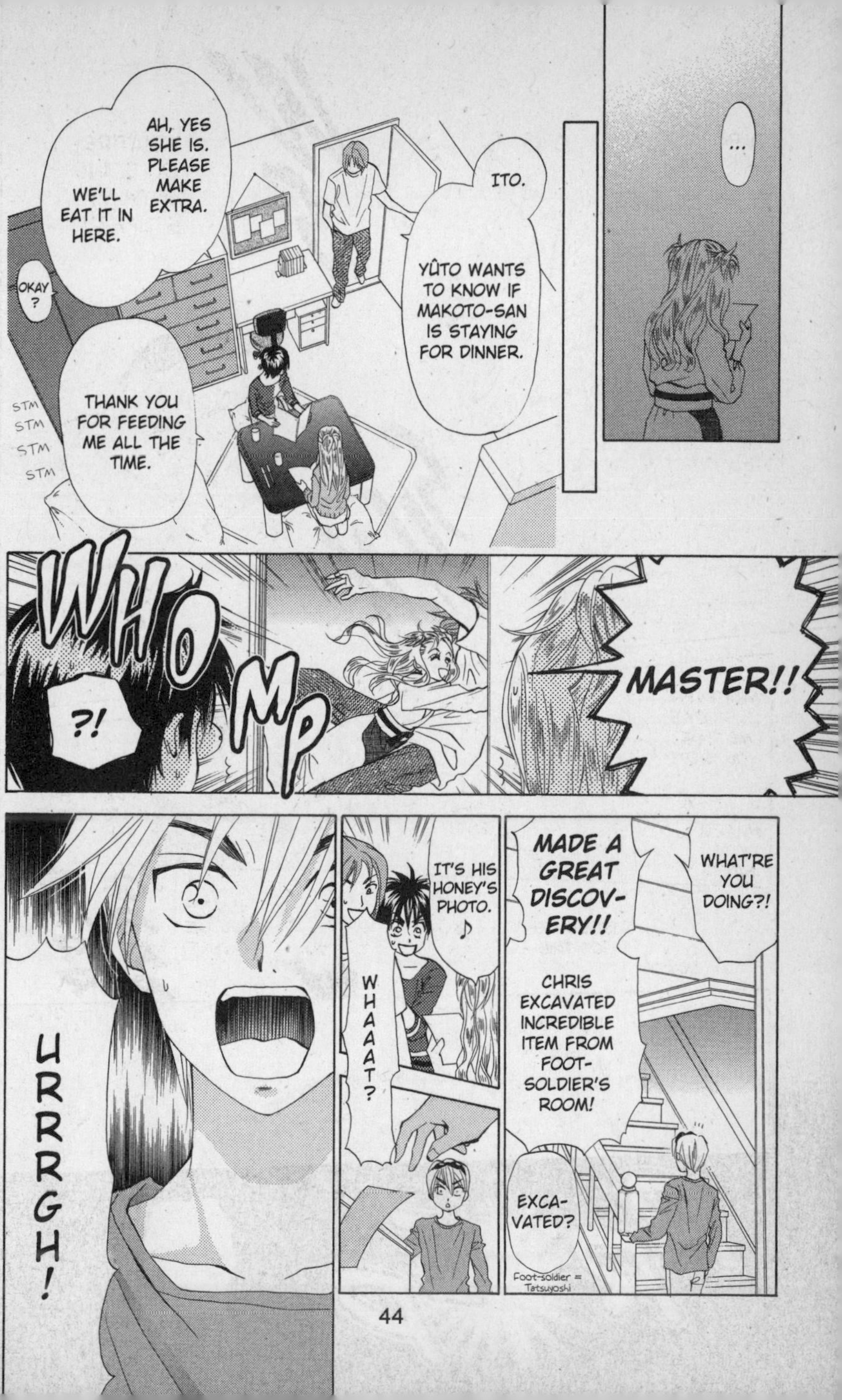
...
ITO.
YÛTO WANTS TO KNOW IF MAKOTO-SAN IS STAYING FOR DINNER.
AH, YES SHE IS. PLEASE MAKE EXTRA.
WE'LL EAT IT IN HERE.
OKAY?
THANK YOU FOR FEEDING ME ALL THE TIME.
STM STM STM STM
MASTER!!
WHOMP
?!
WHAT'RE YOU DOING?!
MADE A GREAT DISCOVERY!!
CHRIS EXCAVATED INCREDIBLE ITEM FROM FOOT-SOLDIER'S ROOM!
EXCAVATED?
Foot-soldier = Tatsuyoshi
IT'S HIS HONEY'S PHOTO. ♪
WHAAAT?
URRRGH!

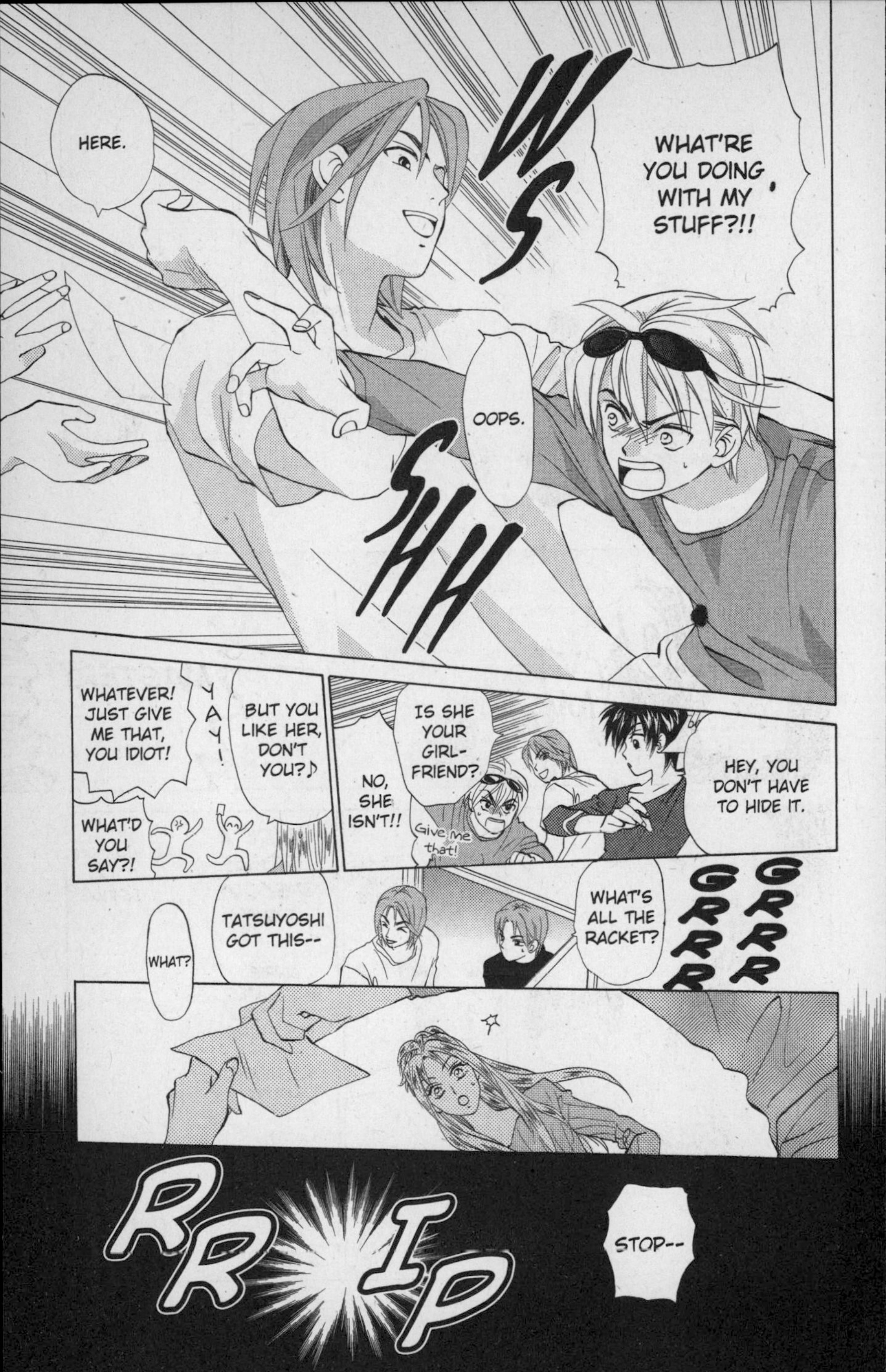
WHAT'RE YOU DOING WITH MY STUFF?!!
WS
HERE.
OOPS.
SHH
HEY, YOU DON'T HAVE TO HIDE IT.
IS SHE YOUR GIRL-FRIEND?
NO, SHE ISN'T!!
Give me that!
BUT YOU LIKE HER, DON'T YOU?♪
YAY!
WHATEVER! JUST GIVE ME THAT, YOU IDIOT!
WHAT'D YOU SAY?!
GRRR GRRR
WHAT'S ALL THE RACKET?
TATSUYOSHI GOT THIS--
WHAT?
STOP--
RRIP

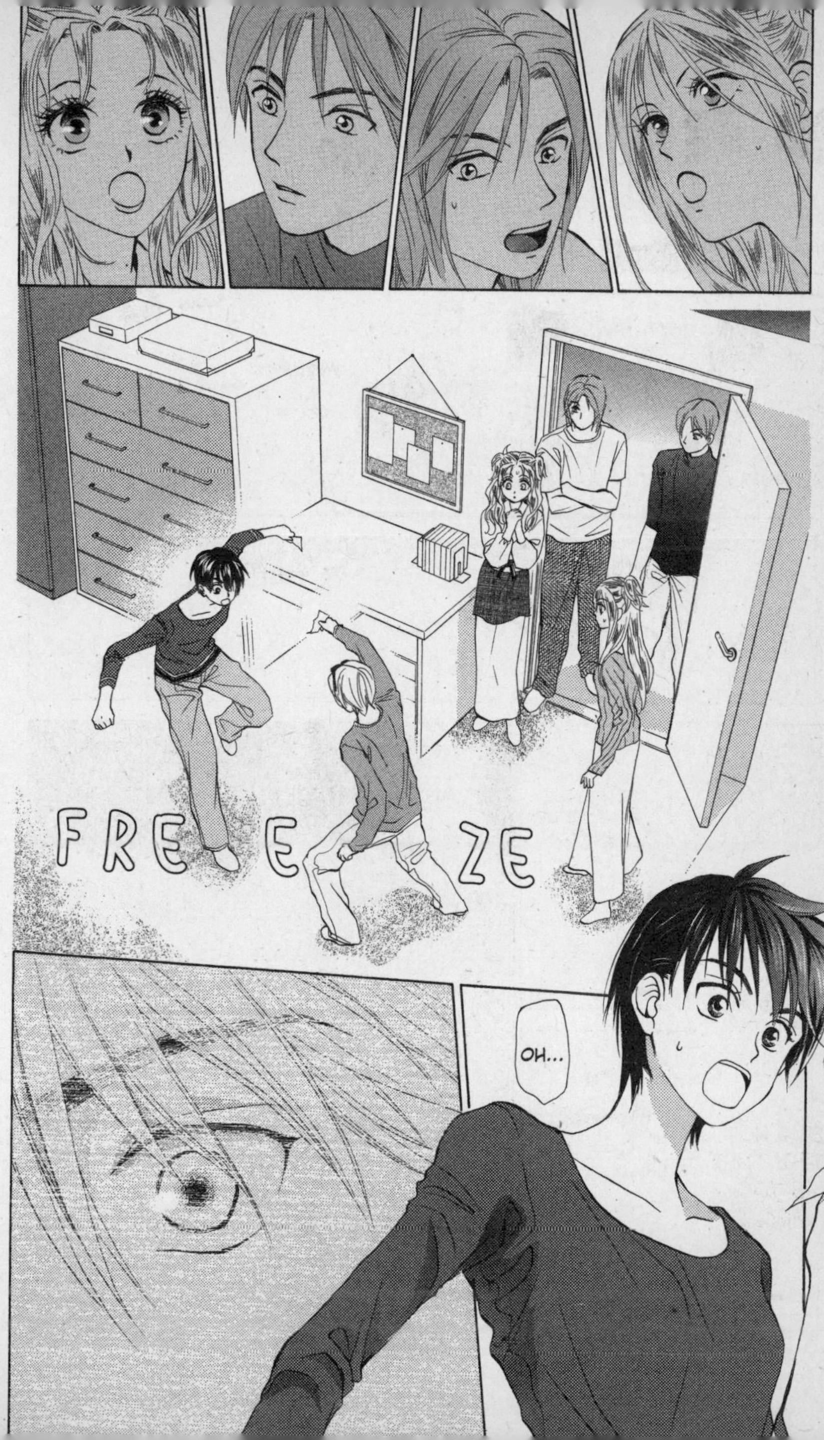
FREEZE
OH...

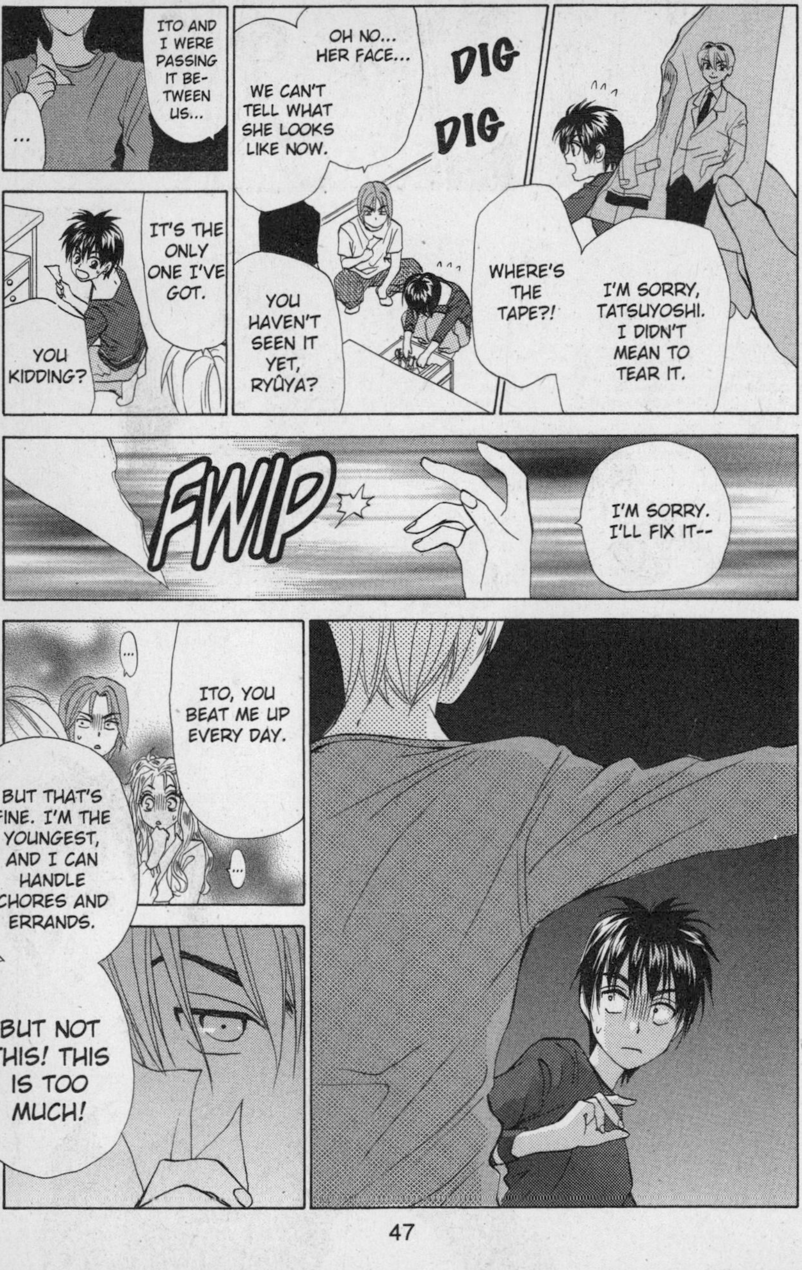
I'M SORRY, TATSUYOSHI. I DIDN'T MEAN TO TEAR IT.
WHERE'S THE TAPE?!
DIG DIG
OH NO... HER FACE...
WE CAN'T TELL WHAT SHE LOOKS LIKE NOW.
YOU HAVEN'T SEEN IT YET, RYÛYA?
ITO AND I WERE PASSING IT BE-TWEEN US...
...
IT'S THE ONLY ONE I'VE GOT.
YOU KIDDING?
I'M SORRY. I'LL FIX IT--
FWIP
ITO, YOU BEAT ME UP EVERY DAY.
...
...
BUT THAT'S FINE. I'M THE YOUNGEST, AND I CAN HANDLE CHORES AND ERRANDS.
BUT NOT THIS! THIS IS TOO MUCH!

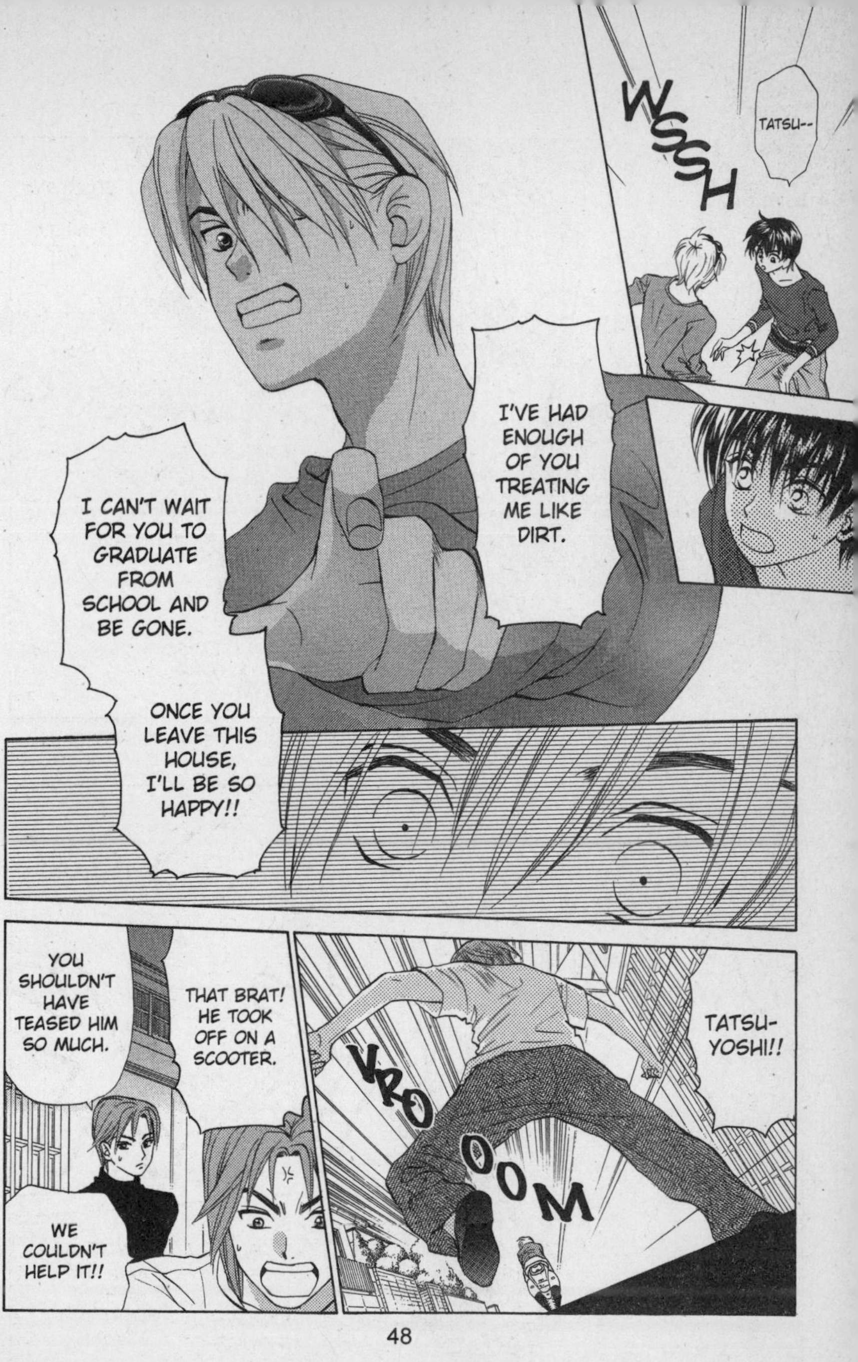
WSSH
TATSU--
I'VE HAD ENOUGH OF YOU TREATING ME LIKE DIRT.
I CAN'T WAIT FOR YOU TO GRADUATE FROM SCHOOL AND BE GONE.
ONCE YOU LEAVE THIS HOUSE, I'LL BE SO HAPPY!!
TATSU-YOSHI!!
VROOOOM
THAT BRAT! HE TOOK OFF ON A SCOOTER.
YOU SHOULDN'T HAVE TEASED HIM SO MUCH.
WE COULDN'T HELP IT!!

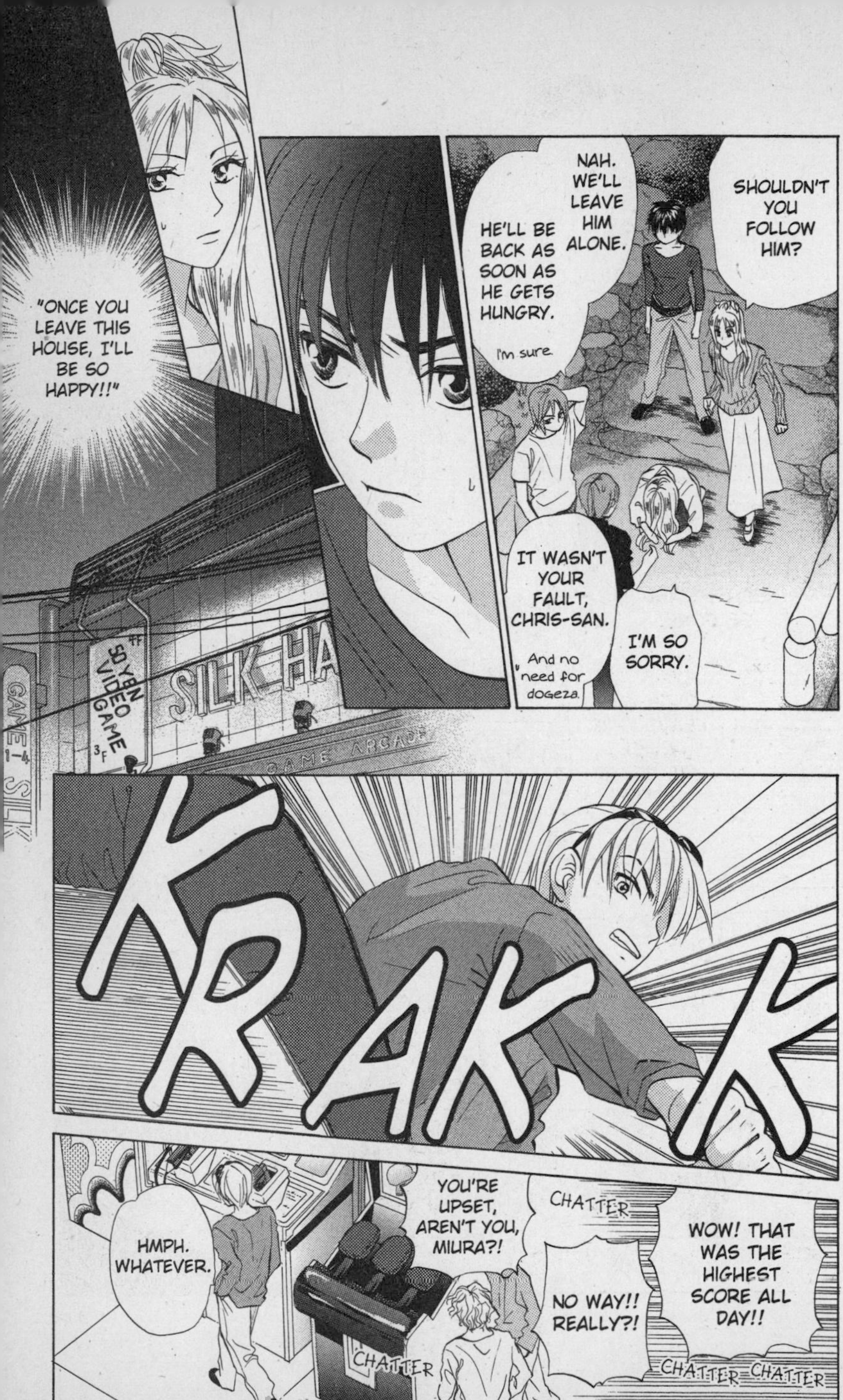
SHOULDN'T YOU FOLLOW HIM?
NAH. WE'LL LEAVE HIM ALONE.
HE'LL BE BACK AS SOON AS HE GETS HUNGRY.
I'm sure.
I'M SO SORRY.
IT WASN'T YOUR FAULT, CHRIS-SAN.
And no need for dogeza.
"ONCE YOU LEAVE THIS HOUSE, I'LL BE SO HAPPY!!"
SILK HA
50 YEN VIDEO GAME
3F
GAME 1-4
SILK
GAME ARCADE
KRAK
WOW! THAT WAS THE HIGHEST SCORE ALL DAY!!
CHATTER
NO WAY!! REALLY?!
YOU'RE UPSET, AREN'T YOU, MIURA?!
HMPH. WHATEVER.
CHATTER CHATTER
CHATTER

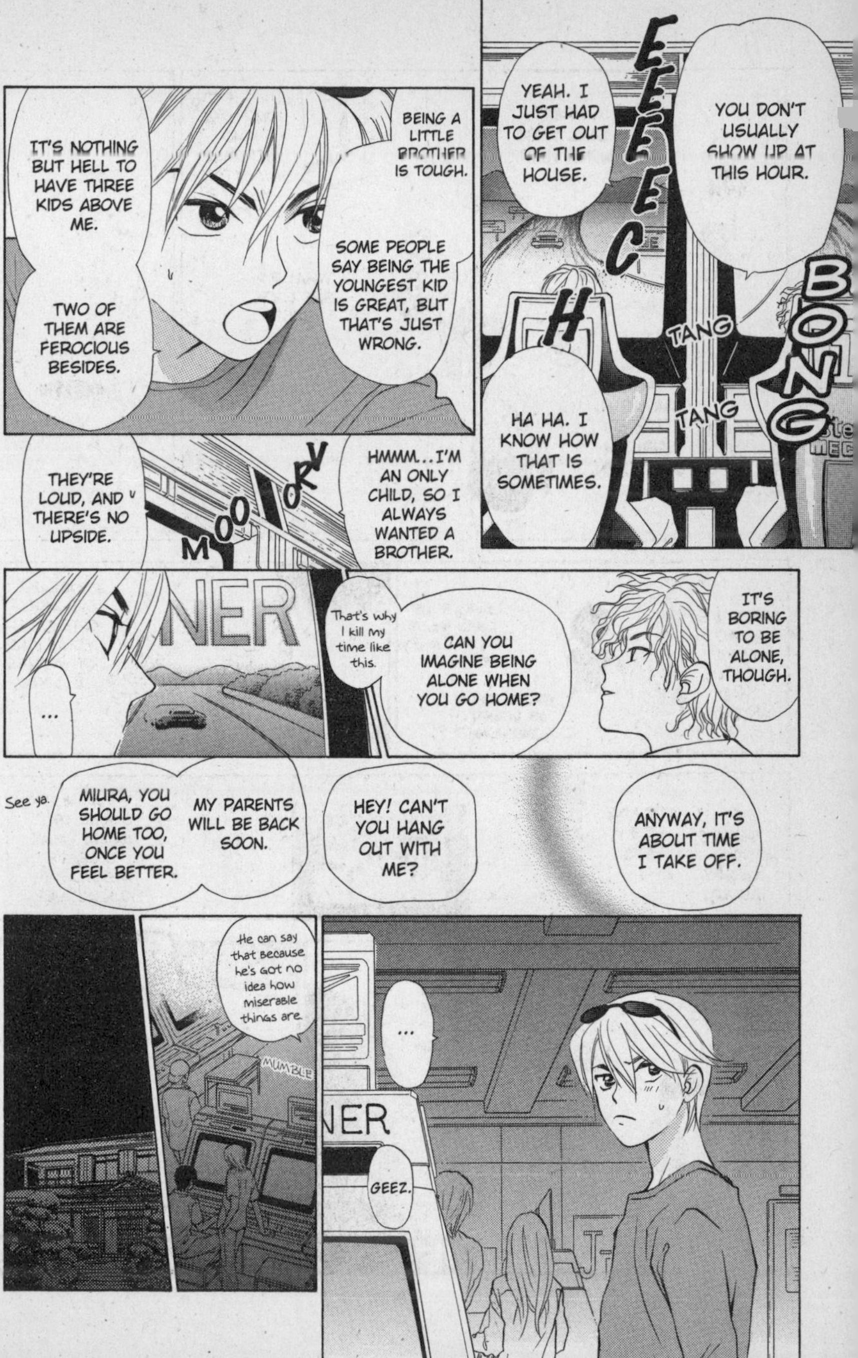
YOU DON'T USUALLY SHOW UP AT THIS HOUR.
YEAH. I JUST HAD TO GET OUT OF THE HOUSE.
EEEECH
BONG
TANG
TANG
HA HA. I KNOW HOW THAT IS SOMETIMES.
BEING A LITTLE BROTHER IS TOUGH.
SOME PEOPLE SAY BEING THE YOUNGEST KID IS GREAT, BUT THAT'S JUST WRONG.
IT'S NOTHING BUT HELL TO HAVE THREE KIDS ABOVE ME.
TWO OF THEM ARE FEROCIOUS BESIDES.
HMMM...I'M AN ONLY CHILD, SO I ALWAYS WANTED A BROTHER.
THEY'RE LOUD, AND THERE'S NO UPSIDE.
IT'S BORING TO BE ALONE, THOUGH.
CAN YOU IMAGINE BEING ALONE WHEN YOU GO HOME?
That's why I kill my time like this.
NER
...
ANYWAY, IT'S ABOUT TIME I TAKE OFF.
HEY! CAN'T YOU HANG OUT WITH ME?
MY PARENTS WILL BE BACK SOON.
MIURA, YOU SHOULD GO HOME TOO, ONCE YOU FEEL BETTER.
See ya.
...
NER
GEEZ.
He can say that because he's got no idea how miserable things are.
MUMBLE

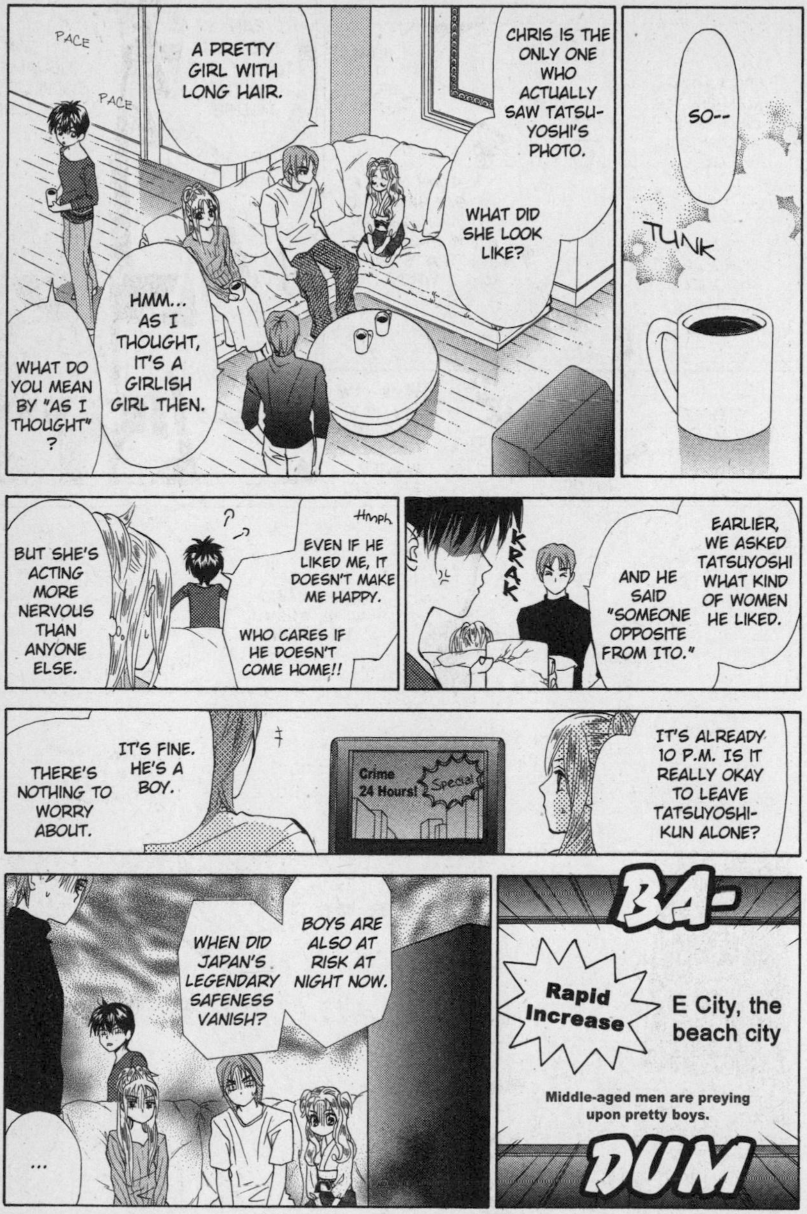
SO--
TUNK
CHRIS IS THE ONLY ONE WHO ACTUALLY SAW TATSUYOSHI'S PHOTO.
WHAT DID SHE LOOK LIKE?
A PRETTY GIRL WITH LONG HAIR.
PACE
PACE
HMM... AS I THOUGHT, IT'S A GIRLISH GIRL THEN.
WHAT DO YOU MEAN BY "AS I THOUGHT"?
EARLIER, WE ASKED TATSUYOSHI WHAT KIND OF WOMEN HE LIKED.
AND HE SAID "SOMEONE OPPOSITE FROM ITO."
KRAK
Hmph.
EVEN IF HE LIKED ME, IT DOESN'T MAKE ME HAPPY.
WHO CARES IF HE DOESN'T COME HOME!!
?
BUT SHE'S ACTING MORE NERVOUS THAN ANYONE ELSE.
IT'S ALREADY 10 P.M. IS IT REALLY OKAY TO LEAVE TATSUYOSHI-KUN ALONE?
Crime 24 Hours! Special
IT'S FINE. HE'S A BOY.
THERE'S NOTHING TO WORRY ABOUT.
BA-
Rapid Increase
E City, the beach city
Middle-aged men are preying upon pretty boys.
DUM
BOYS ARE ALSO AT RISK AT NIGHT NOW.
WHEN DID JAPAN'S LEGENDARY SAFENESS VANISH?
...

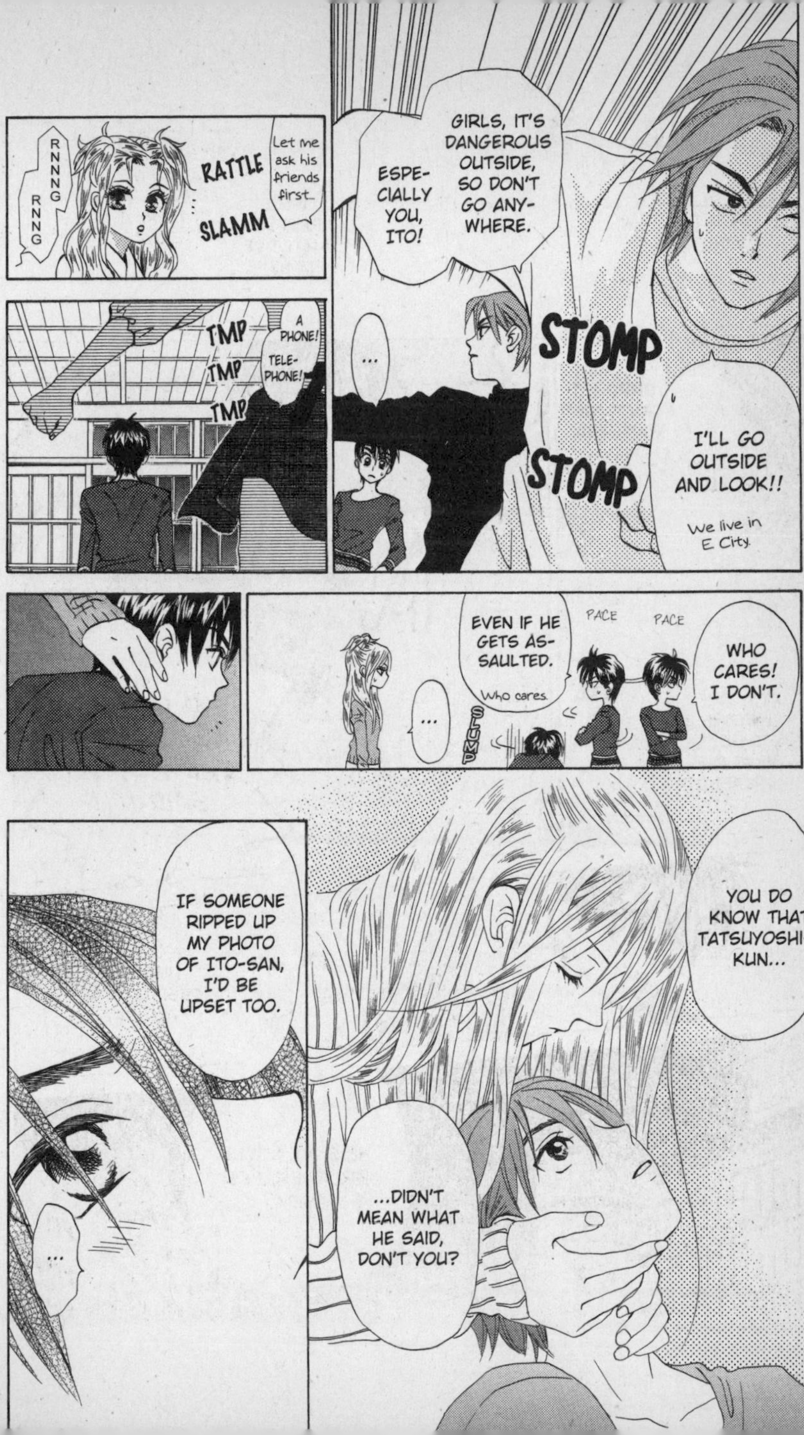
GIRLS, IT'S DANGEROUS OUTSIDE, SO DON'T GO ANYWHERE.
ESPECIALLY YOU, ITO!
STOMP
I'LL GO OUTSIDE AND LOOK!!
We live in E City.
STOMP
...
Let me ask his friends first...
RATTLE
SLAMM
RNNNG
RNNG
A PHONE!
TELEPHONE!
TMP
TMP
TMP
WHO CARES! I DON'T.
PACE
PACE
EVEN IF HE GETS ASSAULTED.
Who cares.
...
SLUMP
YOU DO KNOW THAT TATSUYOSHI-KUN...
...DIDN'T MEAN WHAT HE SAID, DON'T YOU?
IF SOMEONE RIPPED UP MY PHOTO OF ITO-SAN, I'D BE UPSET TOO.
...

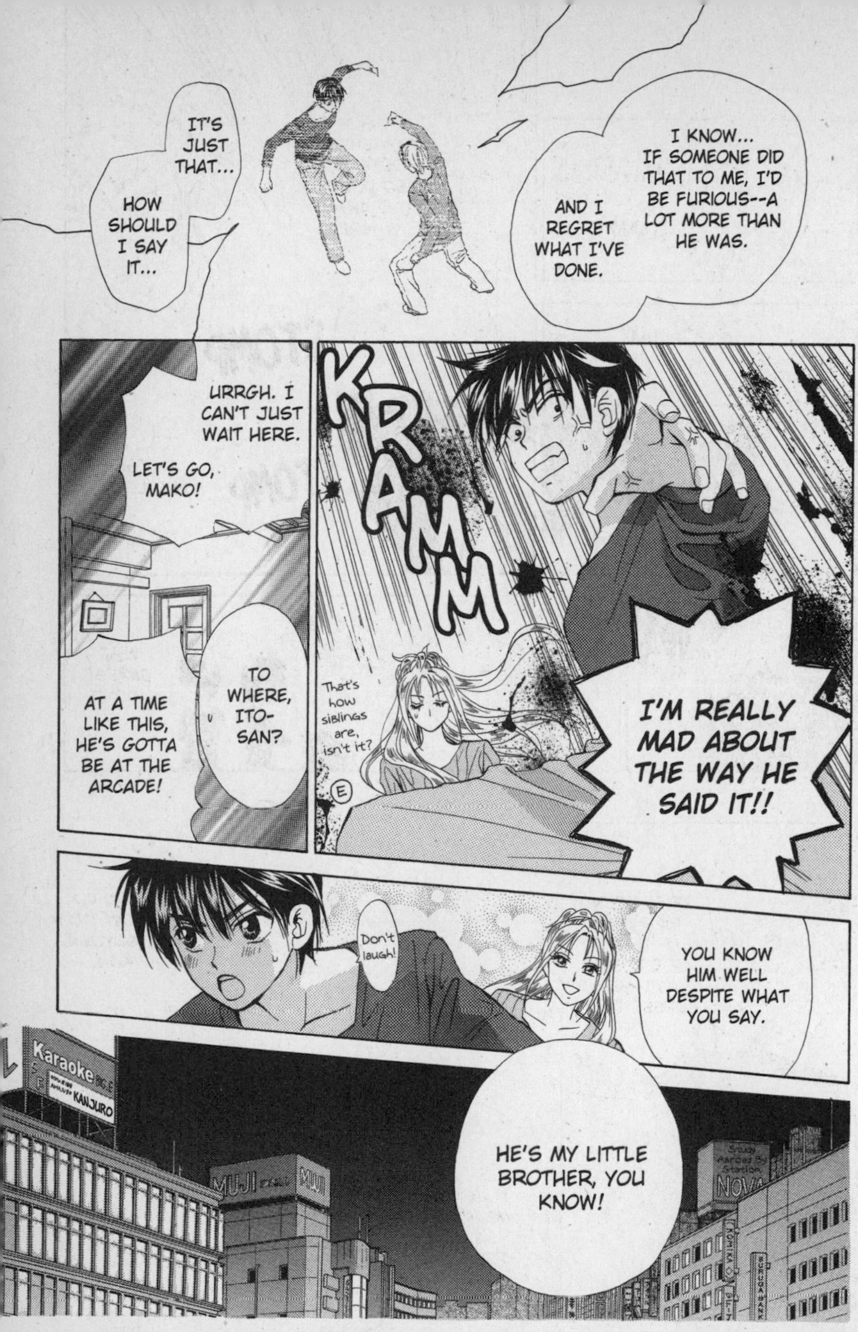
I KNOW... IF SOMEONE DID THAT TO ME, I'D BE FURIOUS--A LOT MORE THAN HE WAS.
AND I REGRET WHAT I'VE DONE.
IT'S JUST THAT...
HOW SHOULD I SAY IT...
KRAMM
I'M REALLY MAD ABOUT THE WAY HE SAID IT!!
That's how siblings are, isn't it?
URRGH. I CAN'T JUST WAIT HERE.
LET'S GO, MAKO!
TO WHERE, ITO-SAN?
AT A TIME LIKE THIS, HE'S GOTTA BE AT THE ARCADE!
YOU KNOW HIM WELL DESPITE WHAT YOU SAY.
Don't laugh!
HE'S MY LITTLE BROTHER, YOU KNOW!
Karaoke
KANJURO
MUJI
NOVA

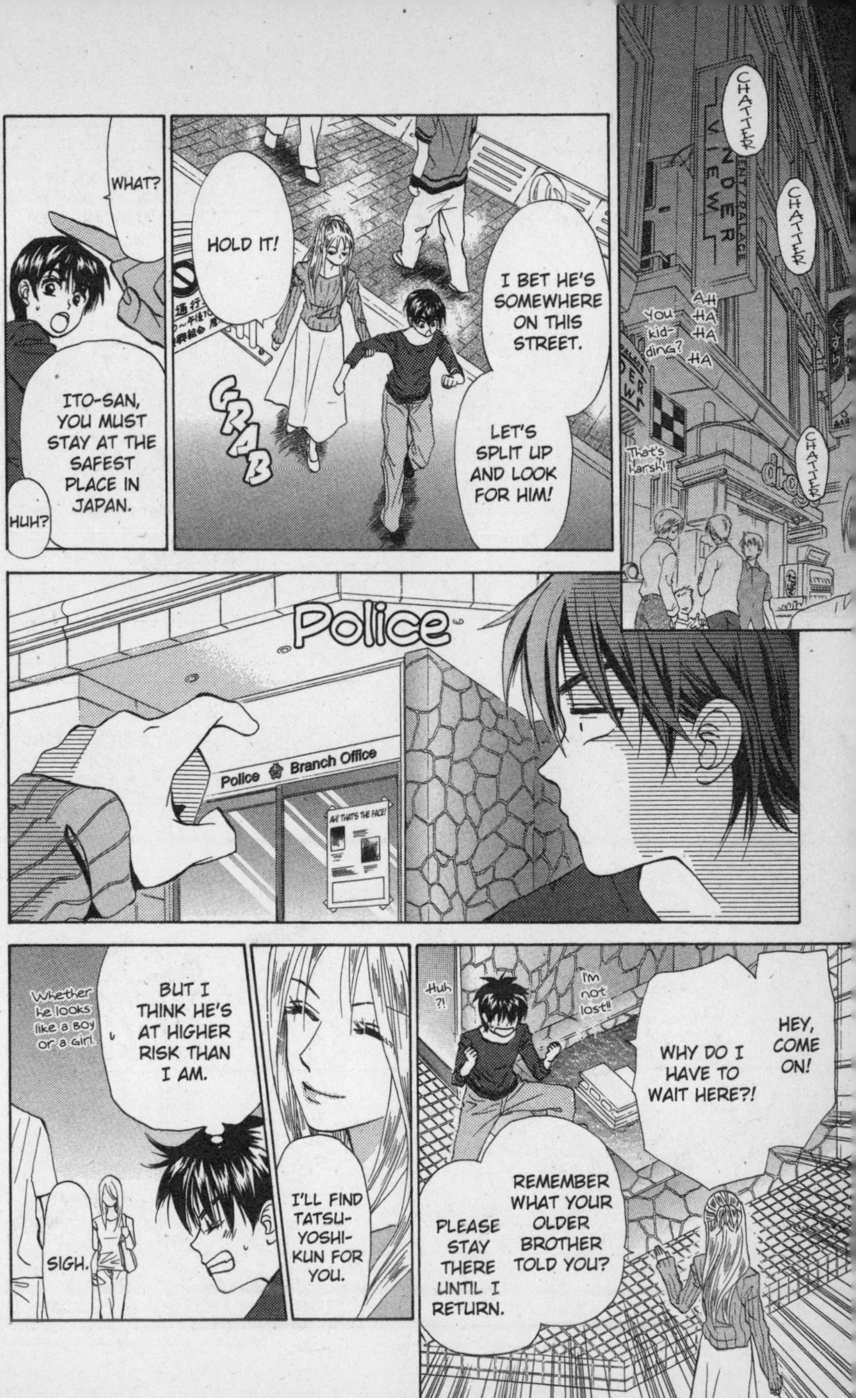
CHATTER
CHATTER
You kid-ding?
AH HA HA HA
That's harsh!
CHATTER
I BET HE'S SOMEWHERE ON THIS STREET.
LET'S SPLIT UP AND LOOK FOR HIM!
HOLD IT!
GRAB
WHAT?
ITO-SAN, YOU MUST STAY AT THE SAFEST PLACE IN JAPAN.
HUH?
Police
Police Branch Office
AH! THAT'S THE FACE!
HEY, COME ON!
WHY DO I HAVE TO WAIT HERE?!
I'm not lost!!
Huh?!
REMEMBER WHAT YOUR OLDER BROTHER TOLD YOU?
PLEASE STAY THERE UNTIL I RETURN.
I'LL FIND TATSU-YOSHI-KUN FOR YOU.
BUT I THINK HE'S AT HIGHER RISK THAN I AM.
Whether he looks like a boy or a girl.
SIGH.

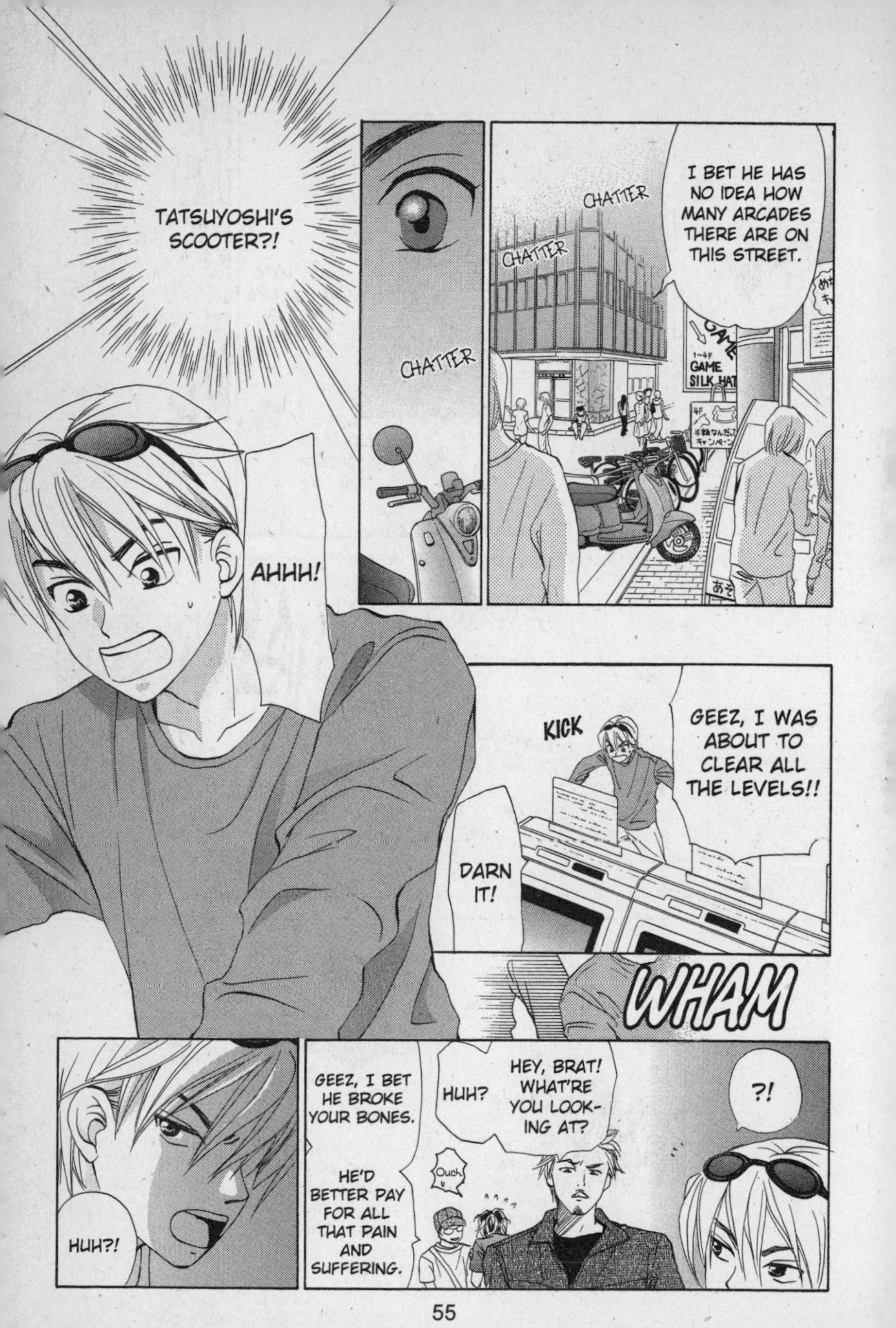
I BET HE HAS NO IDEA HOW MANY ARCADES THERE ARE ON THIS STREET.
CHATTER
CHATTER
GAME
1~4F GAME SILK HAT
CHATTER
GEEZ, I WAS ABOUT TO CLEAR ALL THE LEVELS!!
KICK
DARN IT!
WHAM
TATSUYOSHI'S SCOOTER?!
AHHH!
?!
HEY, BRAT! WHAT'RE YOU LOOKING AT?
HUH?
GEEZ, I BET HE BROKE YOUR BONES.
Ouch
HE'D BETTER PAY FOR ALL THAT PAIN AND SUFFERING.
HUH?!

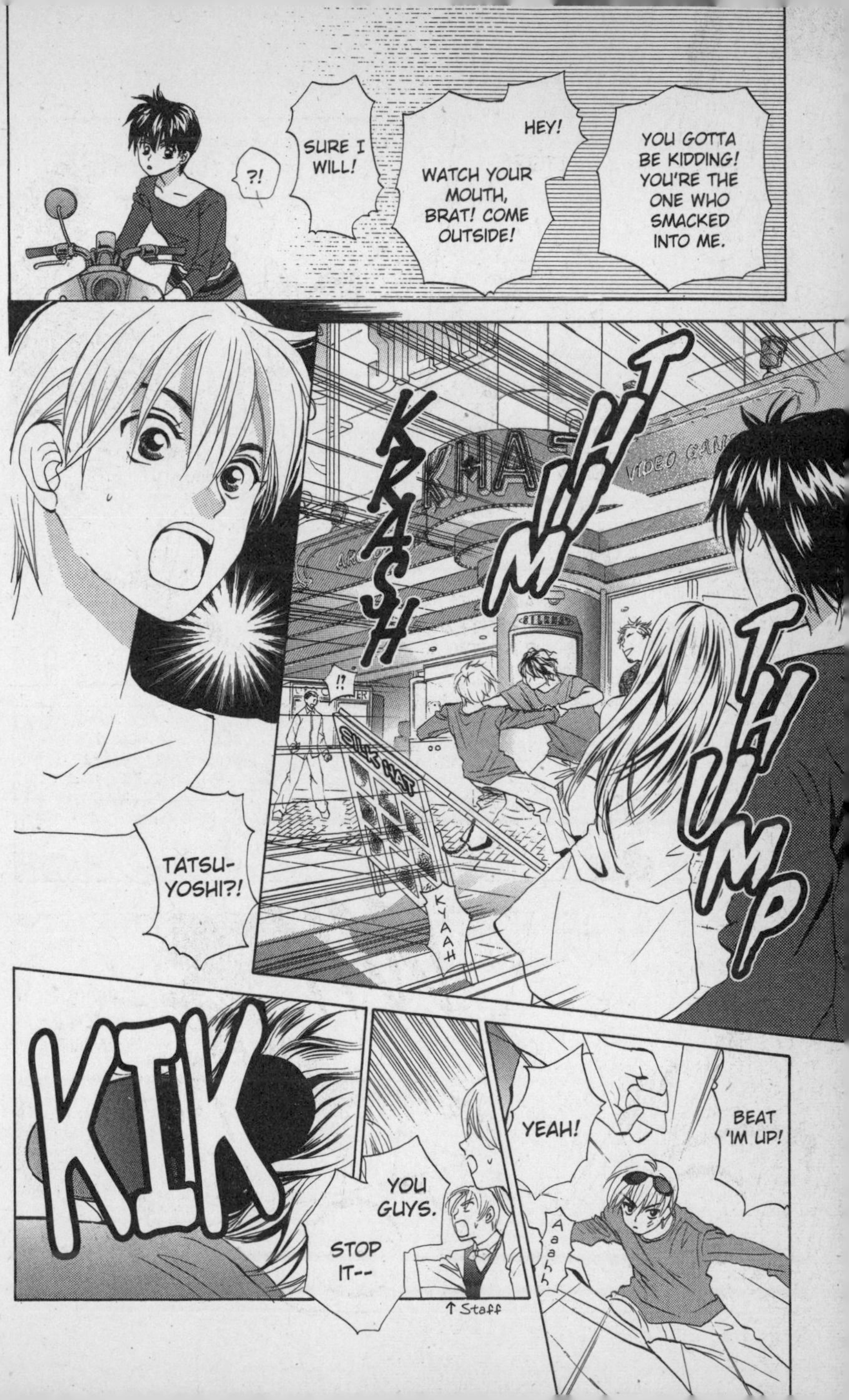
YOU GOTTA BE KIDDING! YOU'RE THE ONE WHO SMACKED INTO ME.
HEY!
WATCH YOUR MOUTH, BRAT! COME OUTSIDE!
SURE I WILL!
?!
THUMP
THUMM
KRASH
!?
KYAAH
SILK HAT
TATSU-YOSHI?!
BEAT 'IM UP!
YEAH!
Aaahh
YOU GUYS.
STOP IT--
↑ Staff
KIK

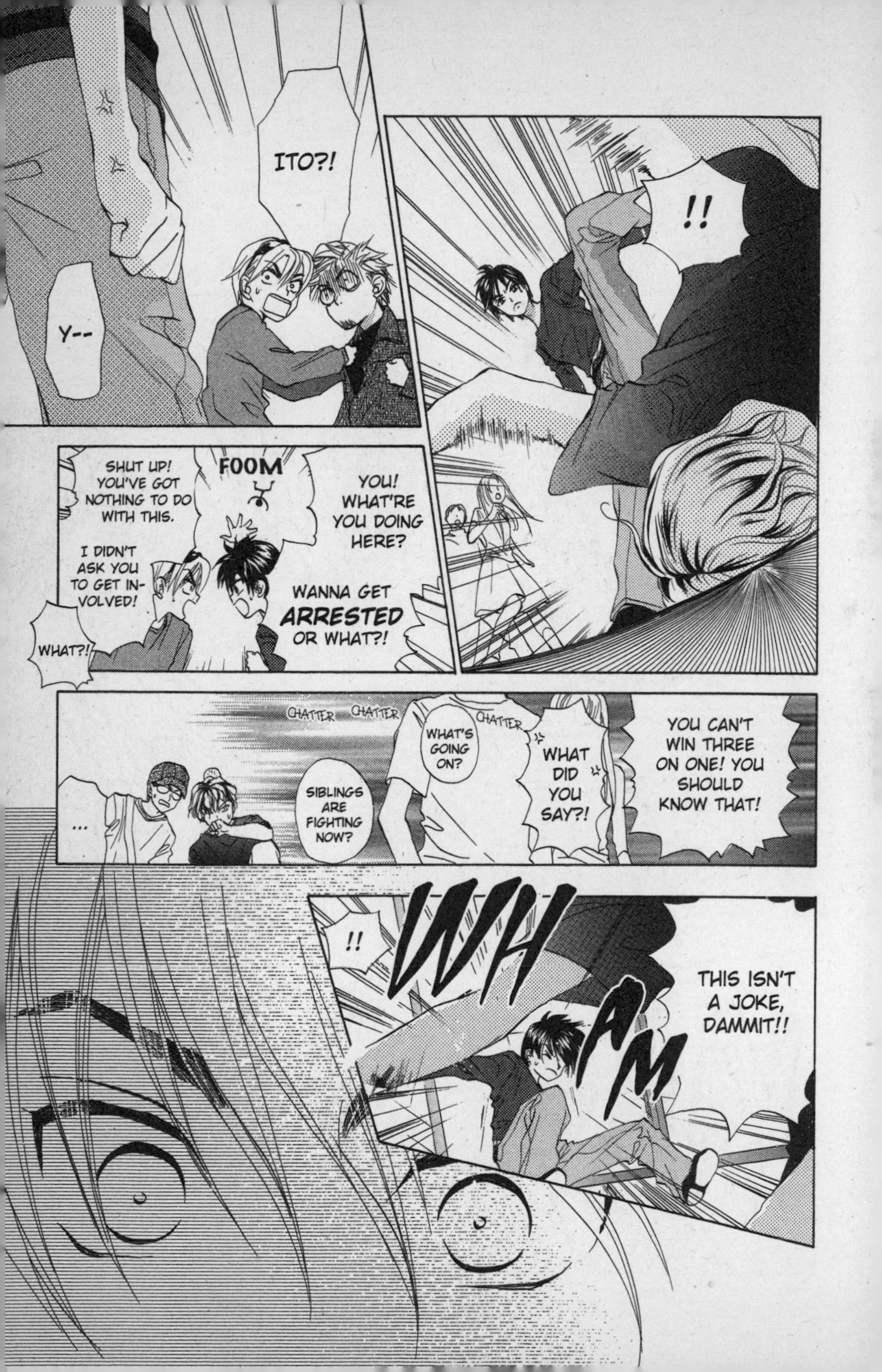
!!
ITO?!
Y--
FOOM
YOU! WHAT'RE YOU DOING HERE?
WANNA GET ARRESTED OR WHAT?!
SHUT UP! YOU'VE GOT NOTHING TO DO WITH THIS.
I DIDN'T ASK YOU TO GET IN-VOLVED!
WHAT?!
YOU CAN'T WIN THREE ON ONE! YOU SHOULD KNOW THAT!
WHAT DID YOU SAY?!
CHATTER CHATTER CHATTER
WHAT'S GOING ON?
SIBLINGS ARE FIGHTING NOW?
...
THIS ISN'T A JOKE, DAMMIT!!
WHAM
!!

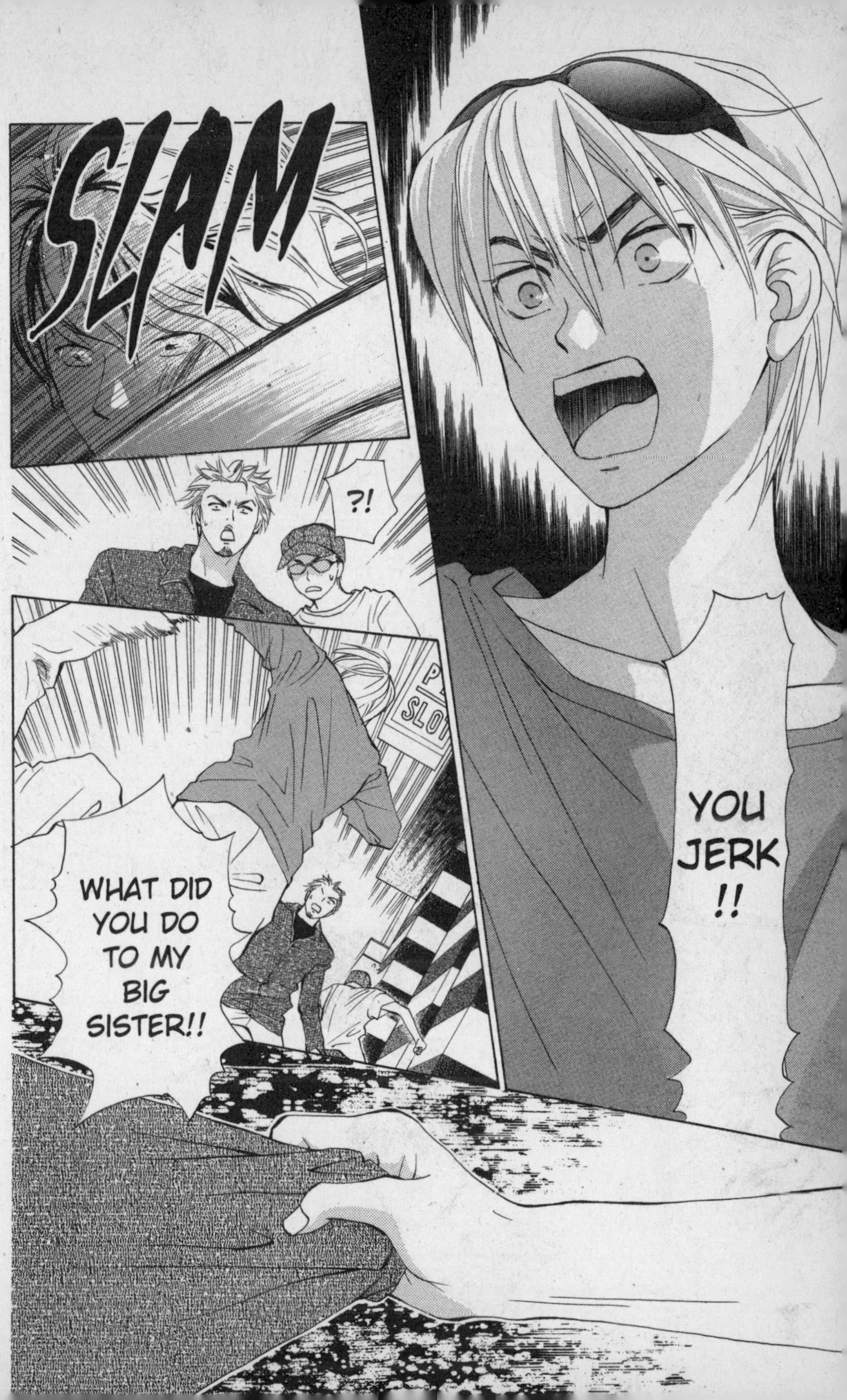
YOU JERK!!
SLAM
?!
WHAT DID YOU DO TO MY BIG SISTER!!

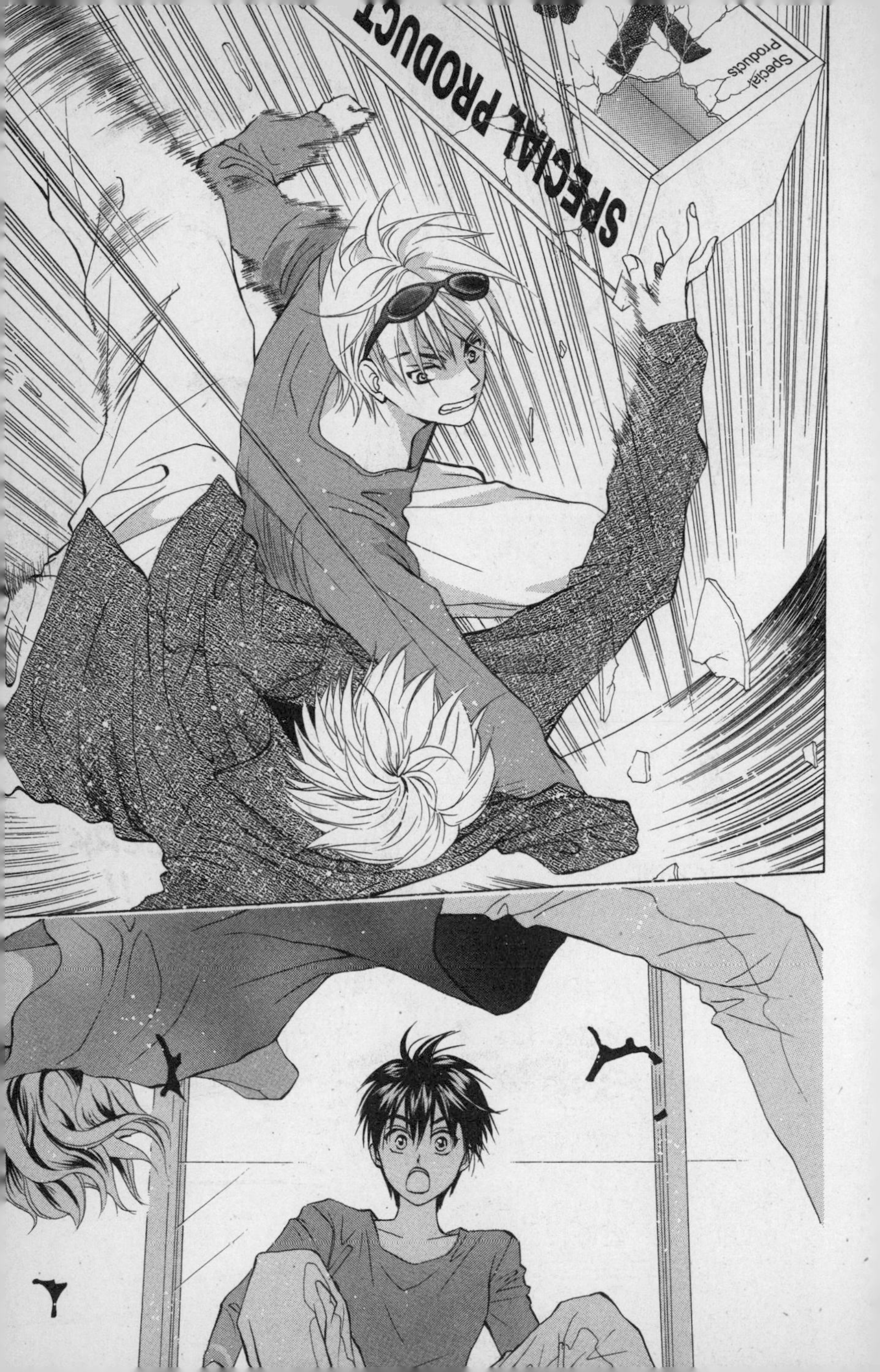
SPECIAL PRODUCT
Special Products

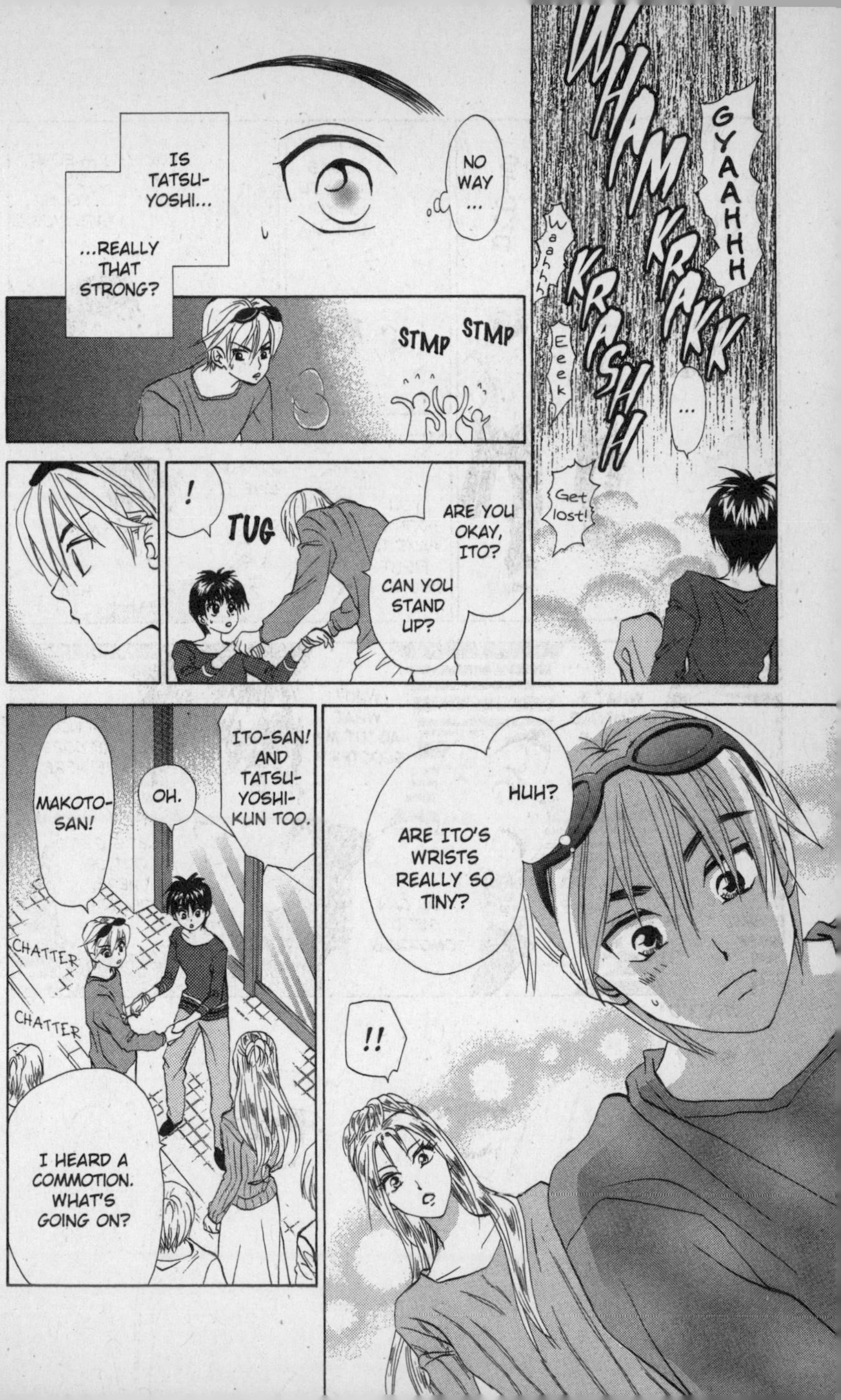
WHAM
KRAKK
KRASHH
GYAAHHH
Waahhh
Eeek
...
Get lost!
NO WAY...
IS TATSU-YOSHI...
...REALLY THAT STRONG?
STMP
STMP
ARE YOU OKAY, ITO?
CAN YOU STAND UP?
TUG
!
HUH?
ARE ITO'S WRISTS REALLY SO TINY?
!!
ITO-SAN! AND TATSU-YOSHI-KUN TOO.
OH.
MAKOTO-SAN!
CHATTER
CHATTER
I HEARD A COMMOTION. WHAT'S GOING ON?

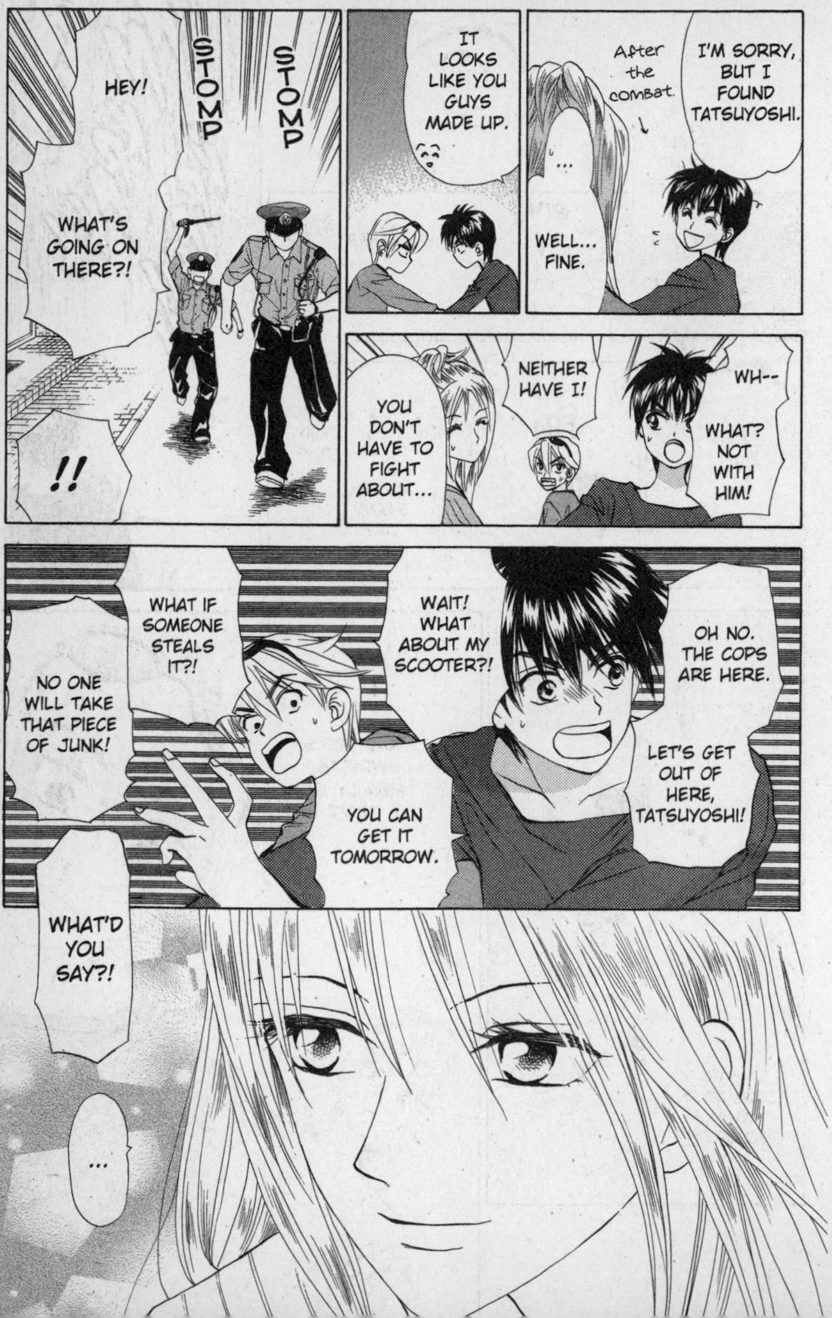
I'M SORRY, BUT I FOUND TATSUYOSHI.
After the combat.
...
WELL... FINE.
IT LOOKS LIKE YOU GUYS MADE UP.
WH-- WHAT? NOT WITH HIM!
NEITHER HAVE I!
YOU DON'T HAVE TO FIGHT ABOUT...
STOMP
STOMP
HEY!
WHAT'S GOING ON THERE?!
!!
OH NO. THE COPS ARE HERE.
LET'S GET OUT OF HERE, TATSUYOSHI!
WAIT! WHAT ABOUT MY SCOOTER?!
YOU CAN GET IT TOMORROW.
WHAT IF SOMEONE STEALS IT?!
NO ONE WILL TAKE THAT PIECE OF JUNK!
WHAT'D YOU SAY?!
...

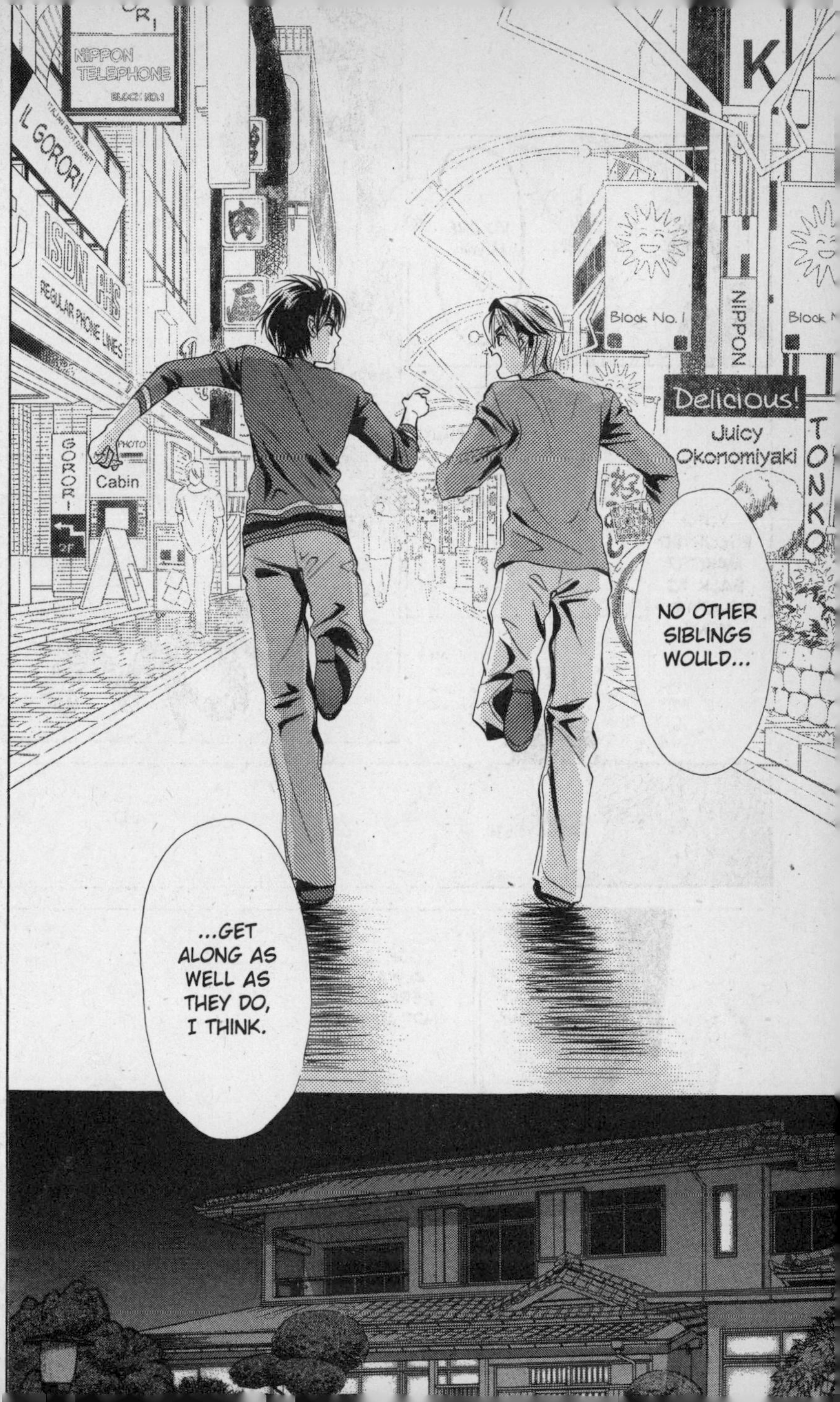
K
Block No. 1
NIPPON
Delicious!
Juicy Okonomiyaki
TONKO
NO OTHER SIBLINGS WOULD...
NIPPON TELEPHONE
BLOCK: NO.1
IL GORORI
ISDN PHS
REGULAR PHONE LINES
GORORI
PHOTO
Cabin
...GET ALONG AS WELL AS THEY DO, I THINK.

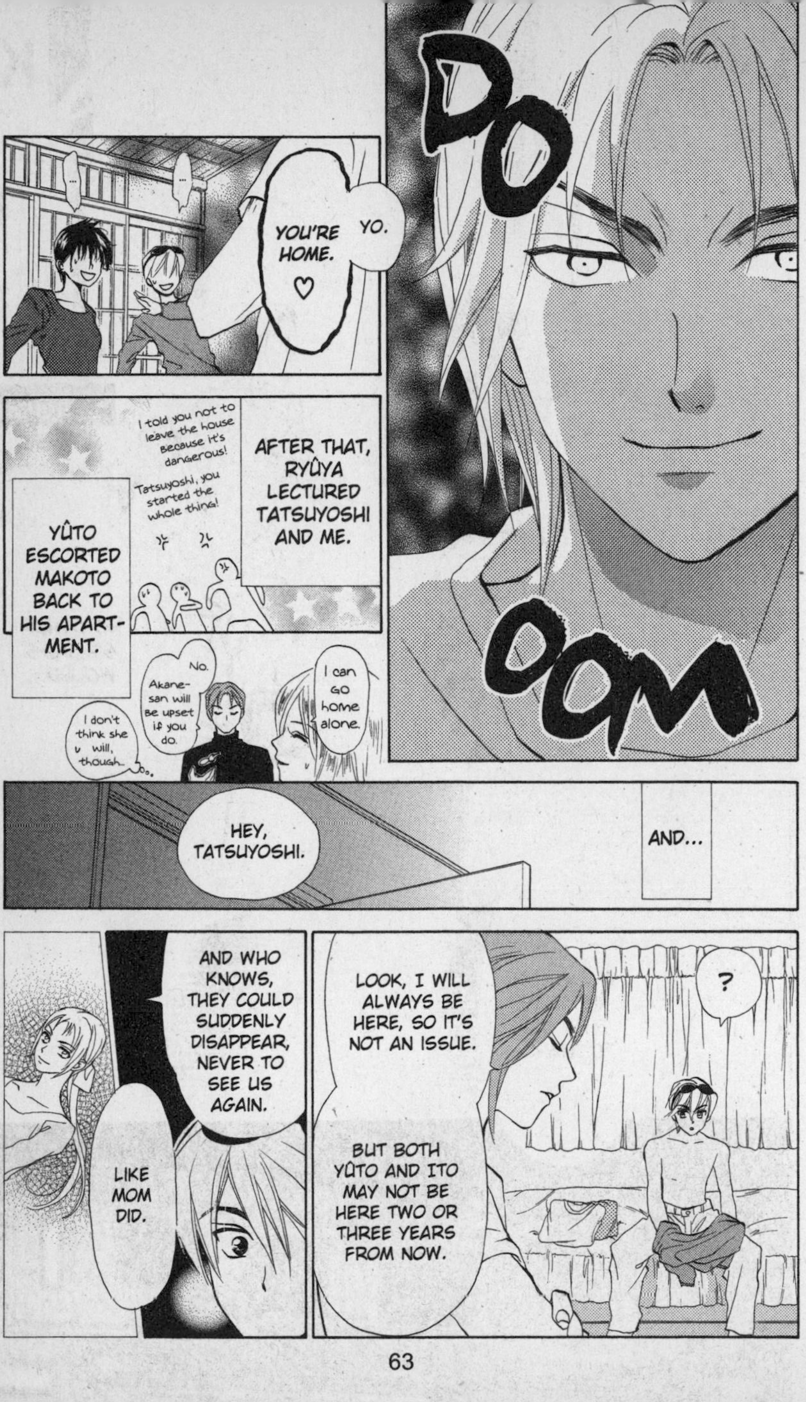
DO
OOM
YO.
YOU'RE HOME. ♡
...
...
AFTER THAT, RYÛYA LECTURED TATSUYOSHI AND ME.
I told you not to leave the house because it's dangerous!
Tatsuyoshi, you started the whole thing!
YÛTO ESCORTED MAKOTO BACK TO HIS APARTMENT.
I can go home alone.
No. Akane-san will be upset if you do.
I don't think she will, though...
AND...
HEY, TATSUYOSHI.
?
LOOK, I WILL ALWAYS BE HERE, SO IT'S NOT AN ISSUE.
BUT BOTH YÛTO AND ITO MAY NOT BE HERE TWO OR THREE YEARS FROM NOW.
AND WHO KNOWS, THEY COULD SUDDENLY DISAPPEAR, NEVER TO SEE US AGAIN.
LIKE MOM DID.

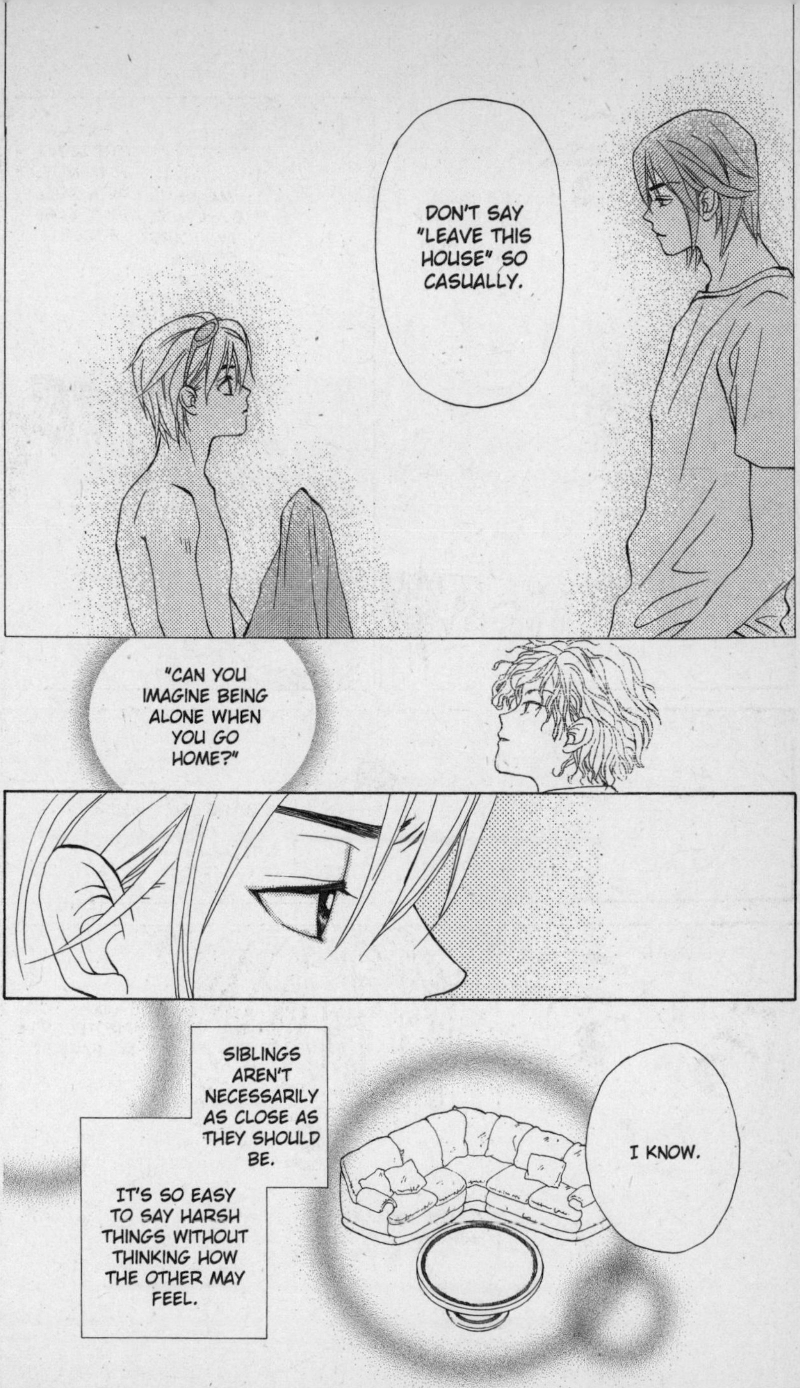
DON'T SAY "LEAVE THIS HOUSE" SO CASUALLY.
"CAN YOU IMAGINE BEING ALONE WHEN YOU GO HOME?"
I KNOW.
SIBLINGS AREN'T NECESSARILY AS CLOSE AS THEY SHOULD BE.
IT'S SO EASY TO SAY HARSH THINGS WITHOUT THINKING HOW THE OTHER MAY FEEL.

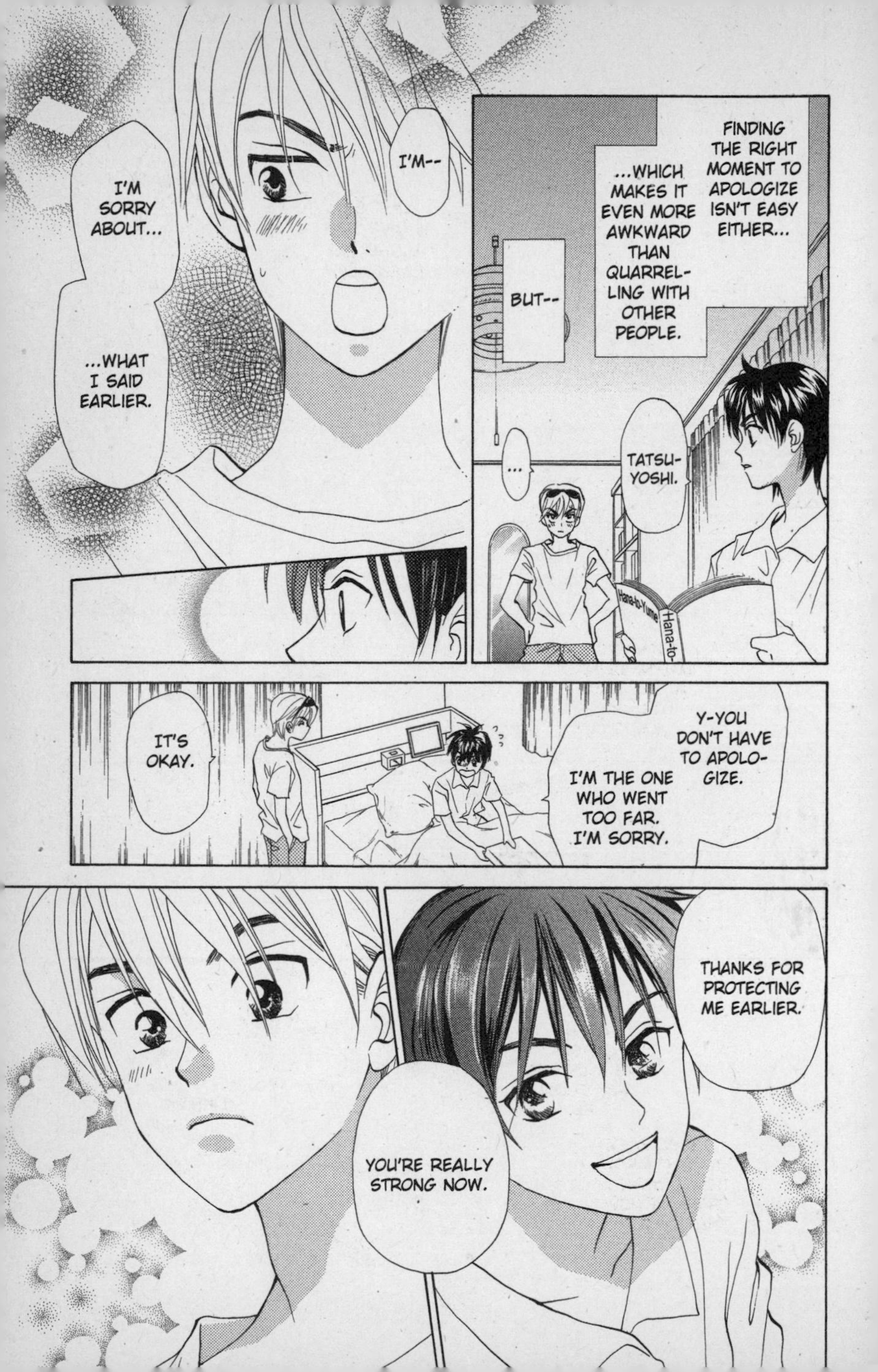
FINDING THE RIGHT MOMENT TO APOLOGIZE ISN'T EASY EITHER...
...WHICH MAKES IT EVEN MORE AWKWARD THAN QUARREL-LING WITH OTHER PEOPLE.
BUT--
TATSU-YOSHI.
...
Hana-to-Yume
I'M--
I'M SORRY ABOUT...
...WHAT I SAID EARLIER.
Y-YOU DON'T HAVE TO APOLO-GIZE.
I'M THE ONE WHO WENT TOO FAR. I'M SORRY.
IT'S OKAY.
THANKS FOR PROTECTING ME EARLIER.
YOU'RE REALLY STRONG NOW.

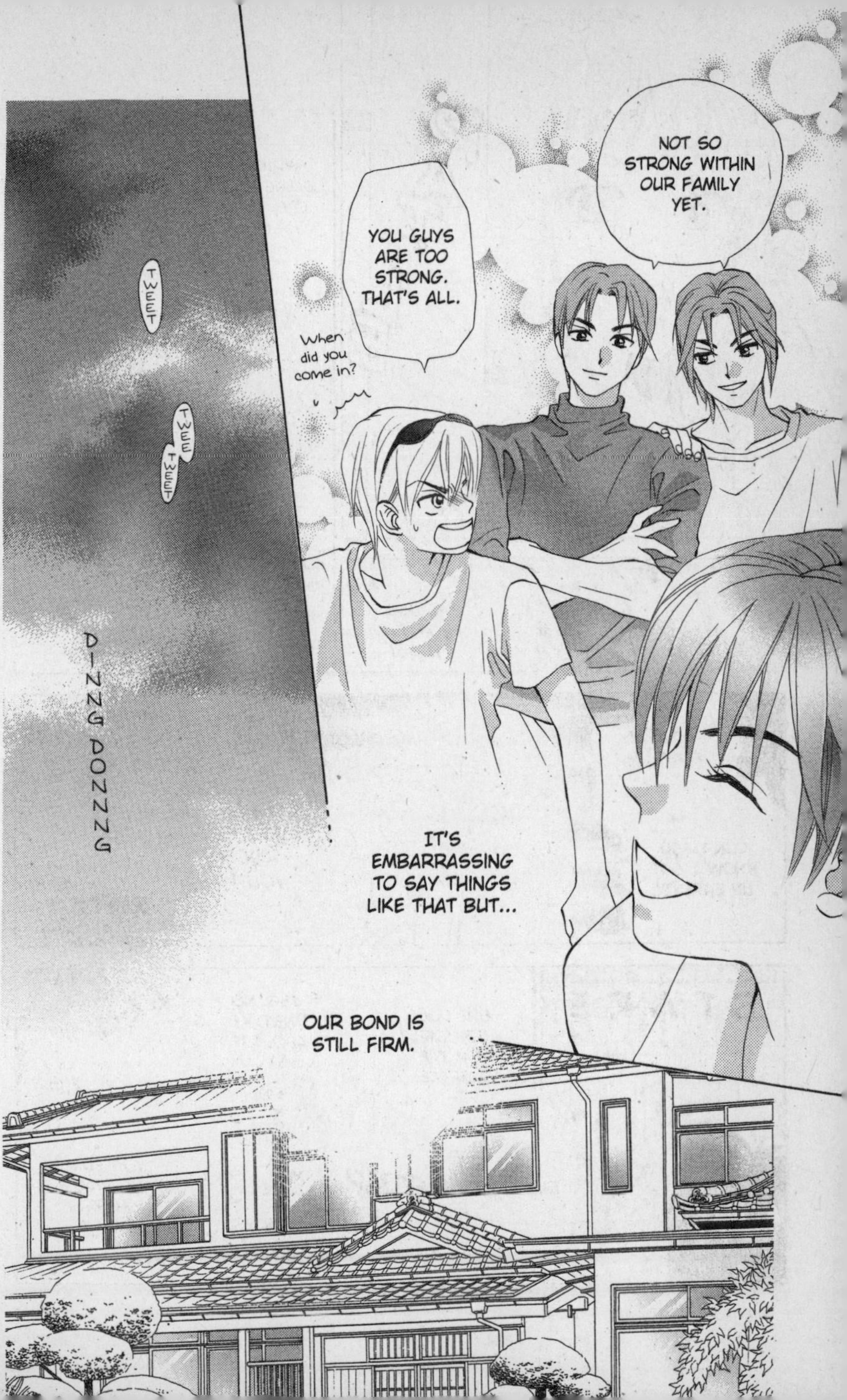
NOT SO STRONG WITHIN OUR FAMILY YET.
YOU GUYS ARE TOO STRONG. THAT'S ALL.
When did you come in?
IT'S EMBARRASSING TO SAY THINGS LIKE THAT BUT...
TWEET
TWEE TWEET
DINNG DONNNG
OUR BOND IS STILL FIRM.

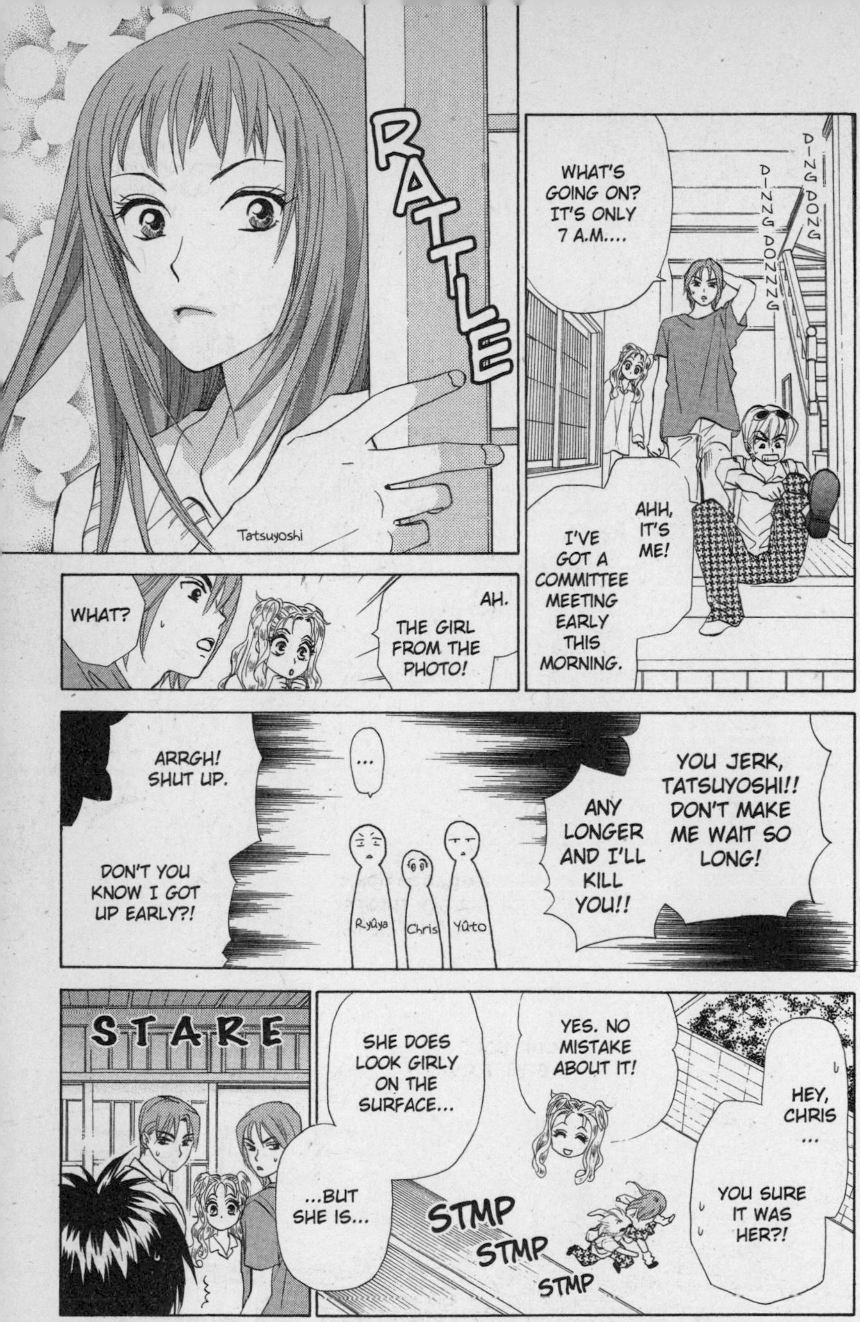
DING DONG
DING DONNG
WHAT'S GOING ON? IT'S ONLY 7 A.M....
AHH, IT'S ME!
I'VE GOT A COMMITTEE MEETING EARLY THIS MORNING.
RATTLE
Tatsuyoshi
AH. THE GIRL FROM THE PHOTO!
WHAT?
YOU JERK, TATSUYOSHI!! DON'T MAKE ME WAIT SO LONG!
ANY LONGER AND I'LL KILL YOU!!
...
Ryûya
Chris
Yûto
ARRGH! SHUT UP.
DON'T YOU KNOW I GOT UP EARLY?!
HEY, CHRIS...
YOU SURE IT WAS HER?!
YES. NO MISTAKE ABOUT IT!
STMP
STMP
STMP
SHE DOES LOOK GIRLY ON THE SURFACE...
...BUT SHE IS...
STARE

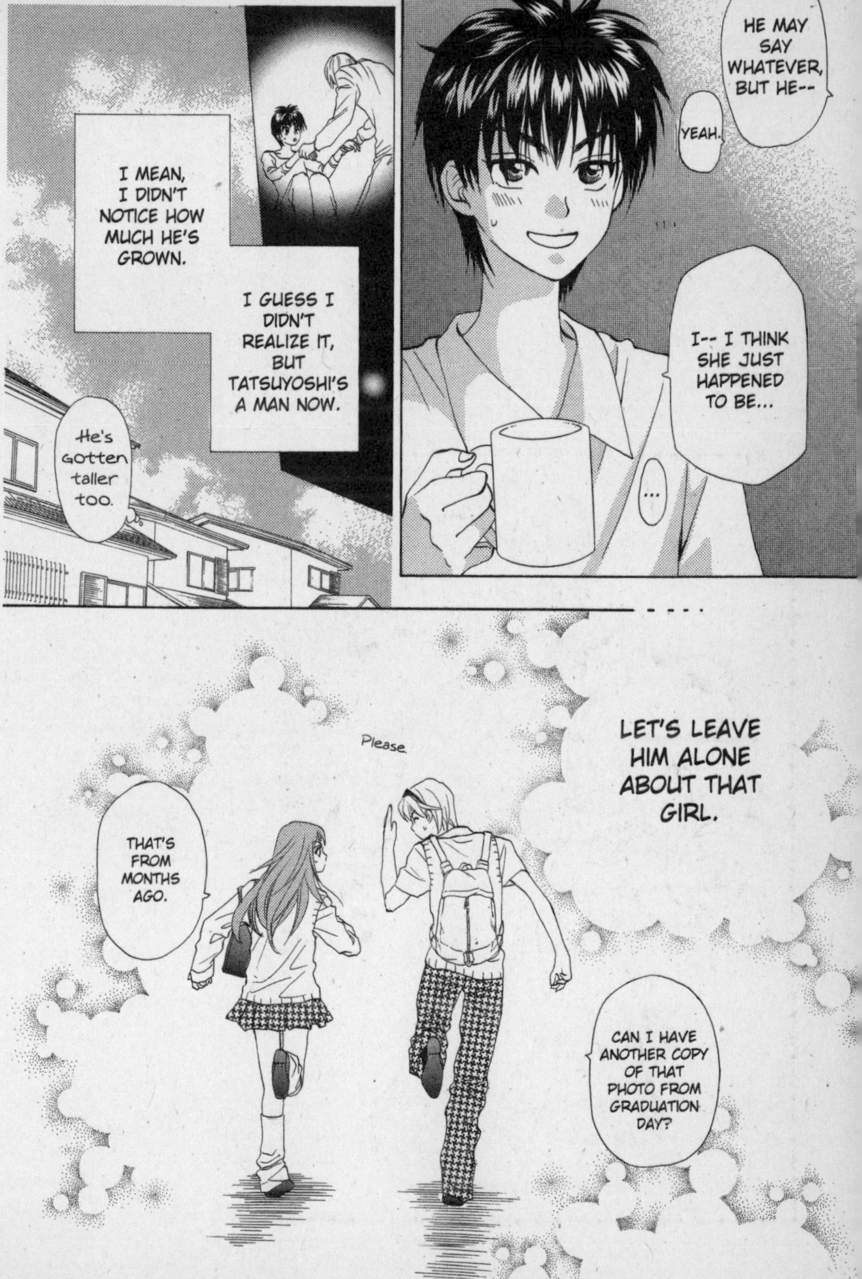
HE MAY SAY WHATEVER, BUT HE--
YEAH.
I-- I THINK SHE JUST HAPPENED TO BE...
...
I MEAN, I DIDN'T NOTICE HOW MUCH HE'S GROWN.
I GUESS I DIDN'T REALIZE IT, BUT TATSUYOSHI'S A MAN NOW.
He's gotten taller too.
LET'S LEAVE HIM ALONE ABOUT THAT GIRL.
CAN I HAVE ANOTHER COPY OF THAT PHOTO FROM GRADUATION DAY?
Please.
THAT'S FROM MONTHS AGO.

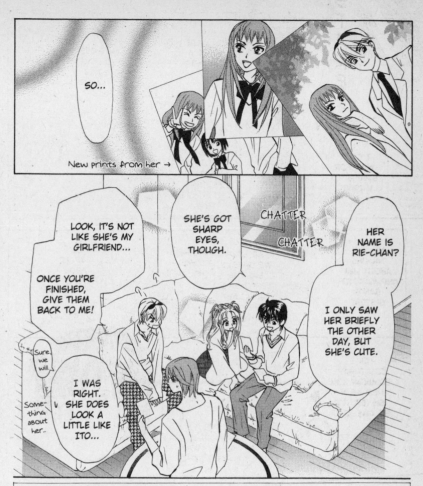

SO...
New prints from her →
HER NAME IS RIE-CHAN?
I ONLY SAW HER BRIEFLY THE OTHER DAY, BUT SHE'S CUTE.
CHATTER
CHATTER
SHE'S GOT SHARP EYES, THOUGH.
LOOK, IT'S NOT LIKE SHE'S MY GIRLFRIEND...
ONCE YOU'RE FINISHED, GIVE THEM BACK TO ME!
I WAS RIGHT. SHE DOES LOOK A LITTLE LIKE ITO...
Sure, we will.
Something about her..

—Behind the Scenes Story ③—

When I was working on the episode where Yûto gets sick, I ended up getting sick too. Before I finished the draft, I had to get an intravenous injection administered. It had been so long since I had it done previously that it made me laugh. (Hey.)

As always, Yûto wouldn't do anything and gave me a lot of trouble. But I'm relieved that somehow they are together now. But yes, I know, having them together is another problem.

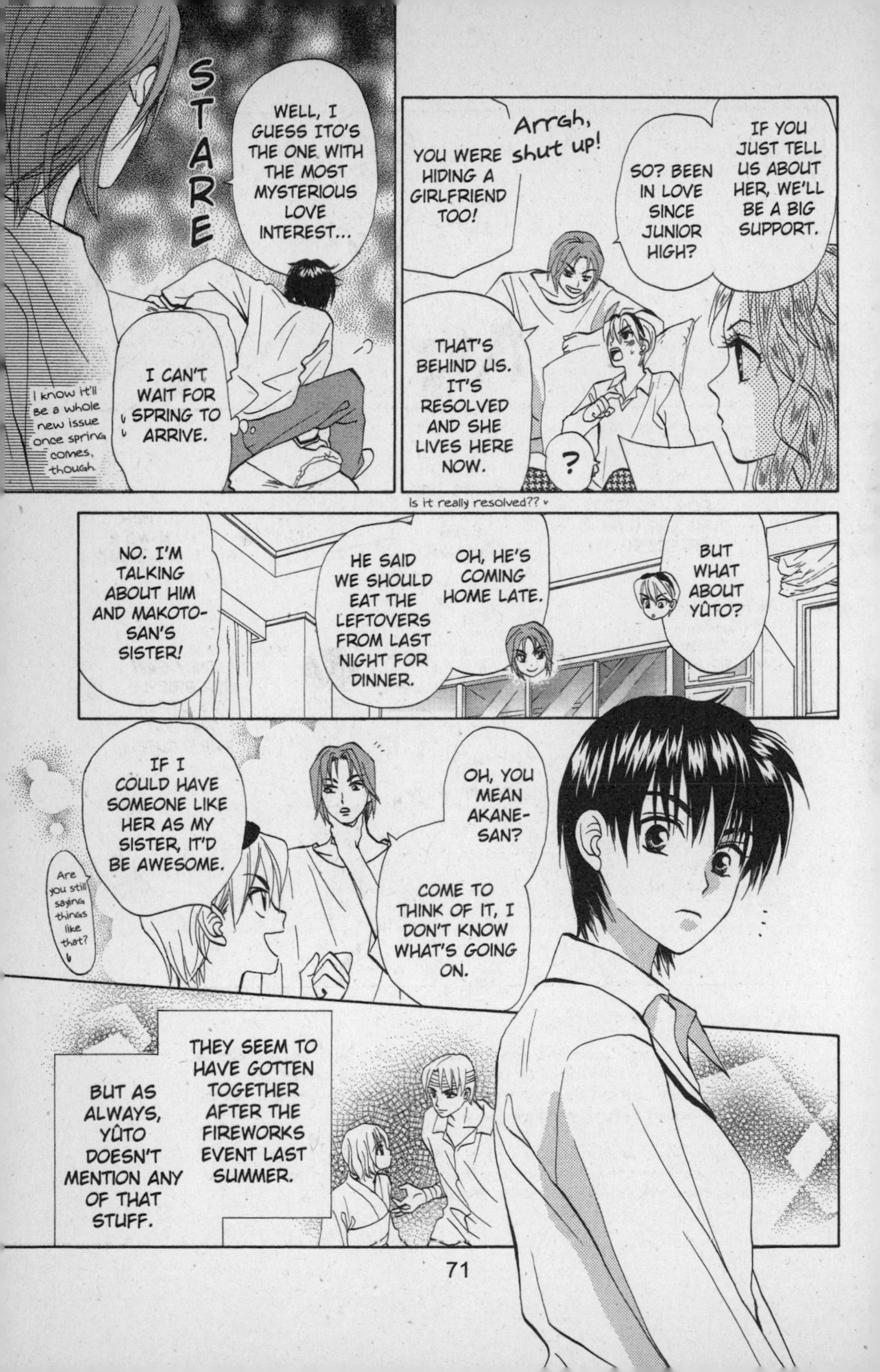
IF YOU JUST TELL US ABOUT HER, WE'LL BE A BIG SUPPORT.
SO? BEEN IN LOVE SINCE JUNIOR HIGH?
YOU WERE HIDING A GIRLFRIEND TOO!
Arrgh, shut up!
THAT'S BEHIND US. IT'S RESOLVED AND SHE LIVES HERE NOW.
?
Is it really resolved??
STARE
WELL, I GUESS ITO'S THE ONE WITH THE MOST MYSTERIOUS LOVE INTEREST...
I CAN'T WAIT FOR SPRING TO ARRIVE.
I know it'll be a whole new issue once spring comes, though.
BUT WHAT ABOUT YÛTO?
OH, HE'S COMING HOME LATE.
HE SAID WE SHOULD EAT THE LEFTOVERS FROM LAST NIGHT FOR DINNER.
NO. I'M TALKING ABOUT HIM AND MAKOTO-SAN'S SISTER!
OH, YOU MEAN AKANE-SAN?
COME TO THINK OF IT, I DON'T KNOW WHAT'S GOING ON.
IF I COULD HAVE SOMEONE LIKE HER AS MY SISTER, IT'D BE AWESOME.
Are you still saying things like that?
THEY SEEM TO HAVE GOTTEN TOGETHER AFTER THE FIREWORKS EVENT LAST SUMMER.
BUT AS ALWAYS, YÛTO DOESN'T MENTION ANY OF THAT STUFF.

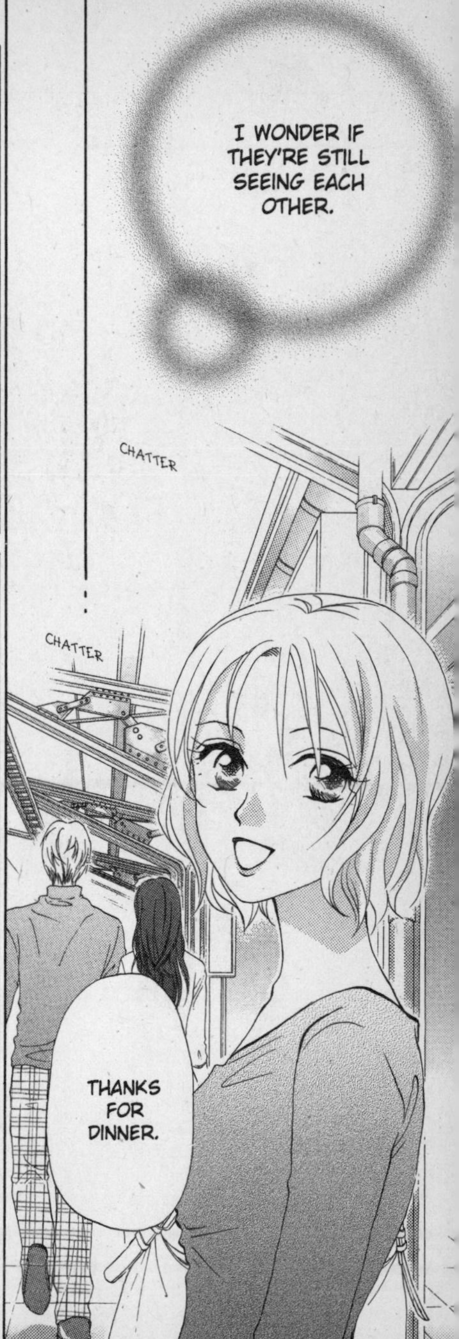
I WONDER IF THEY'RE STILL SEEING EACH OTHER.
CHATTER
CHATTER
THANKS FOR DINNER.

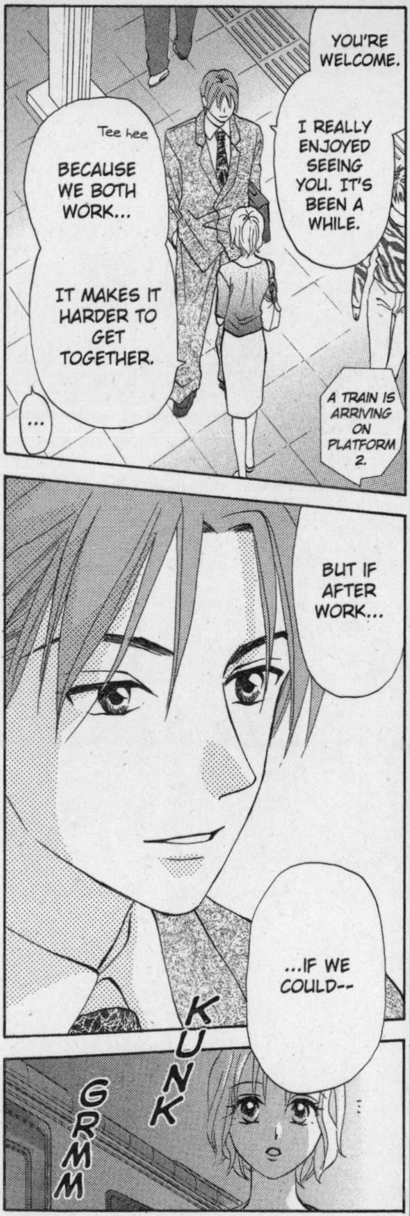
YOU'RE WELCOME.
I REALLY ENJOYED SEEING YOU. IT'S BEEN A WHILE.
Tee hee
BECAUSE WE BOTH WORK...
IT MAKES IT HARDER TO GET TOGETHER.
A TRAIN IS ARRIVING ON PLATFORM 2.
...
BUT IF AFTER WORK...
...IF WE COULD--
KUNK
GRMM

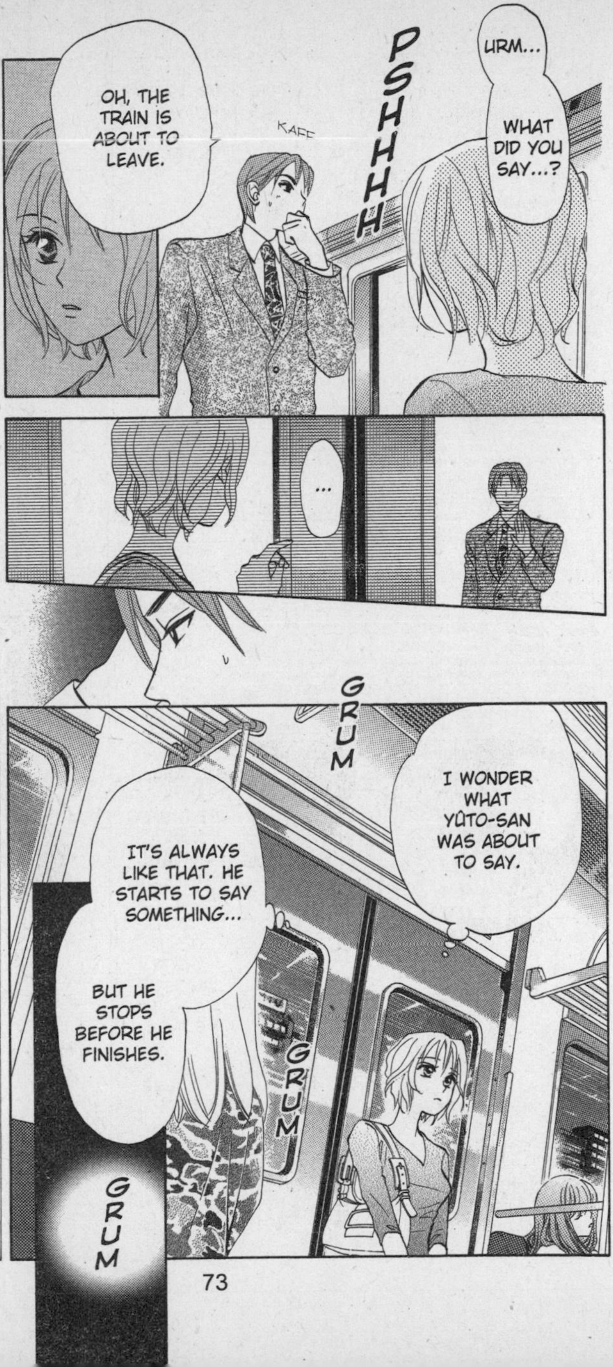
URM...
WHAT DID YOU SAY...?
PSHHHH
KAFF
OH, THE TRAIN IS ABOUT TO LEAVE.
...
GRUM
I WONDER WHAT YÛTO-SAN WAS ABOUT TO SAY.
IT'S ALWAYS LIKE THAT. HE STARTS TO SAY SOMETHING...
BUT HE STOPS BEFORE HE FINISHES.
GRUM
GRUM

Pen Tip

G-pen from Nikko
(Chrome color)

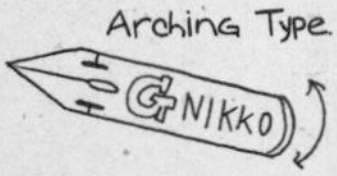
Arching Type.
NIKKO

Because it's soft, you can draw both thick and thin lines with it! Until last summer, I used **Kabura pen from Zebra (Tama-pen).** But compared with G-Pen, it's much harder.

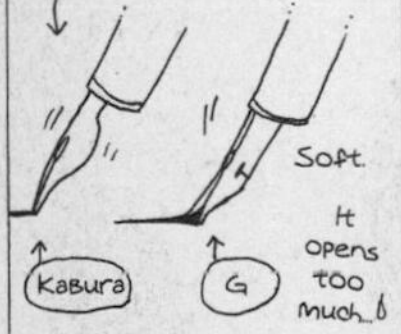
Soft.
Kabura
G
It opens too much

It lets you draw fast with strong pen pressure, but I switched to G-Pen after I hurt my wrist. I've gotten pretty used to it now.

And **Maru-pen from Zebra.** It's thin and round.

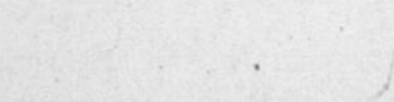
Backside

I use this to draw Mako's hair and other characters with fine details.

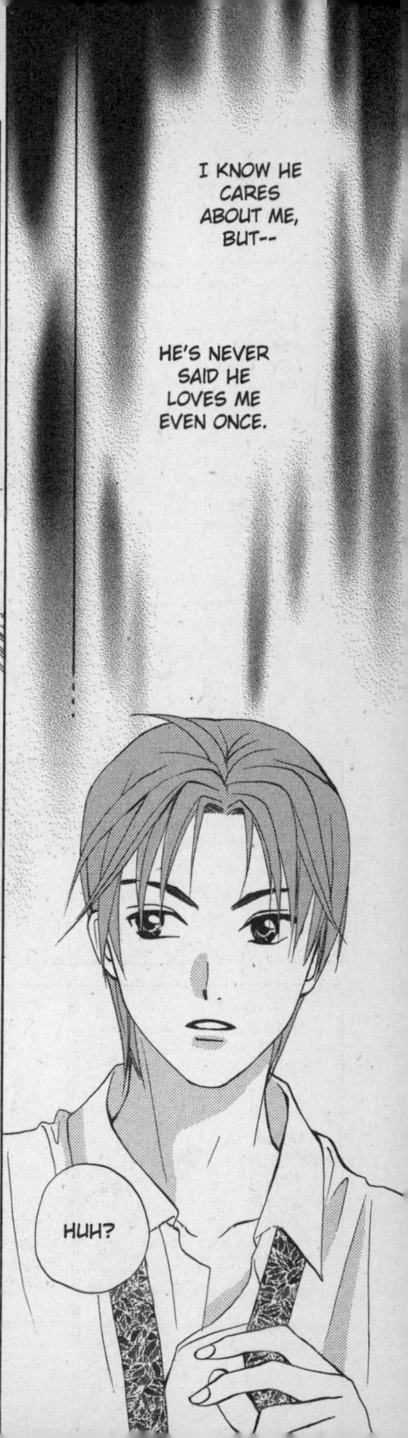
I KNOW HE CARES ABOUT ME, BUT--
HE'S NEVER SAID HE LOVES ME EVEN ONCE.
HUH?

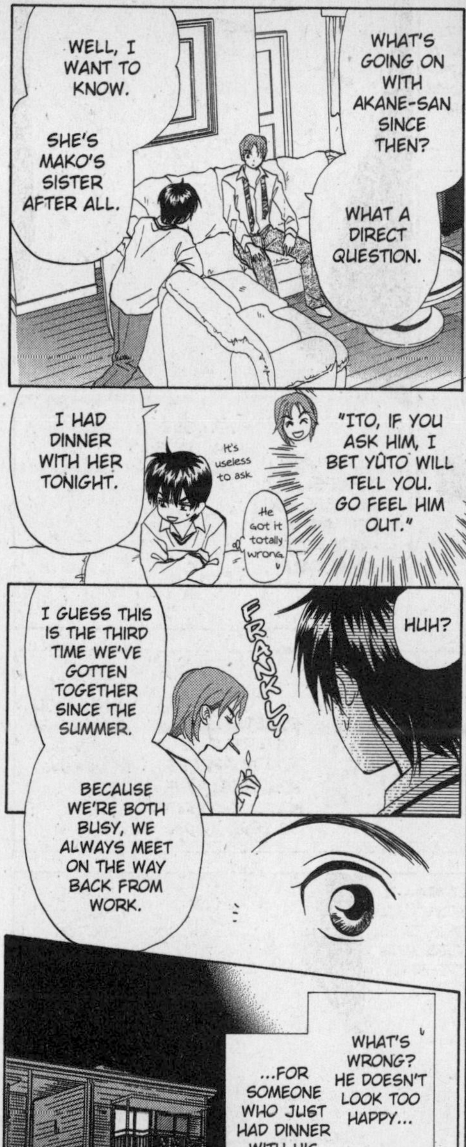
WHAT'S GOING ON WITH AKANE-SAN SINCE THEN?
WELL, I WANT TO KNOW.
SHE'S MAKO'S SISTER AFTER ALL.
WHAT A DIRECT QUESTION.
"ITO, IF YOU ASK HIM, I BET YÛTO WILL TELL YOU. GO FEEL HIM OUT."
It's useless to ask
He got it totally wrong.
I HAD DINNER WITH HER TONIGHT.
HUH?
FRANKLY
I GUESS THIS IS THE THIRD TIME WE'VE GOTTEN TOGETHER SINCE THE SUMMER.
BECAUSE WE'RE BOTH BUSY, WE ALWAYS MEET ON THE WAY BACK FROM WORK.
WHAT'S WRONG? HE DOESN'T LOOK TOO HAPPY...
...FOR SOMEONE WHO JUST HAD DINNER WITH HIS GIRLFRIEND.

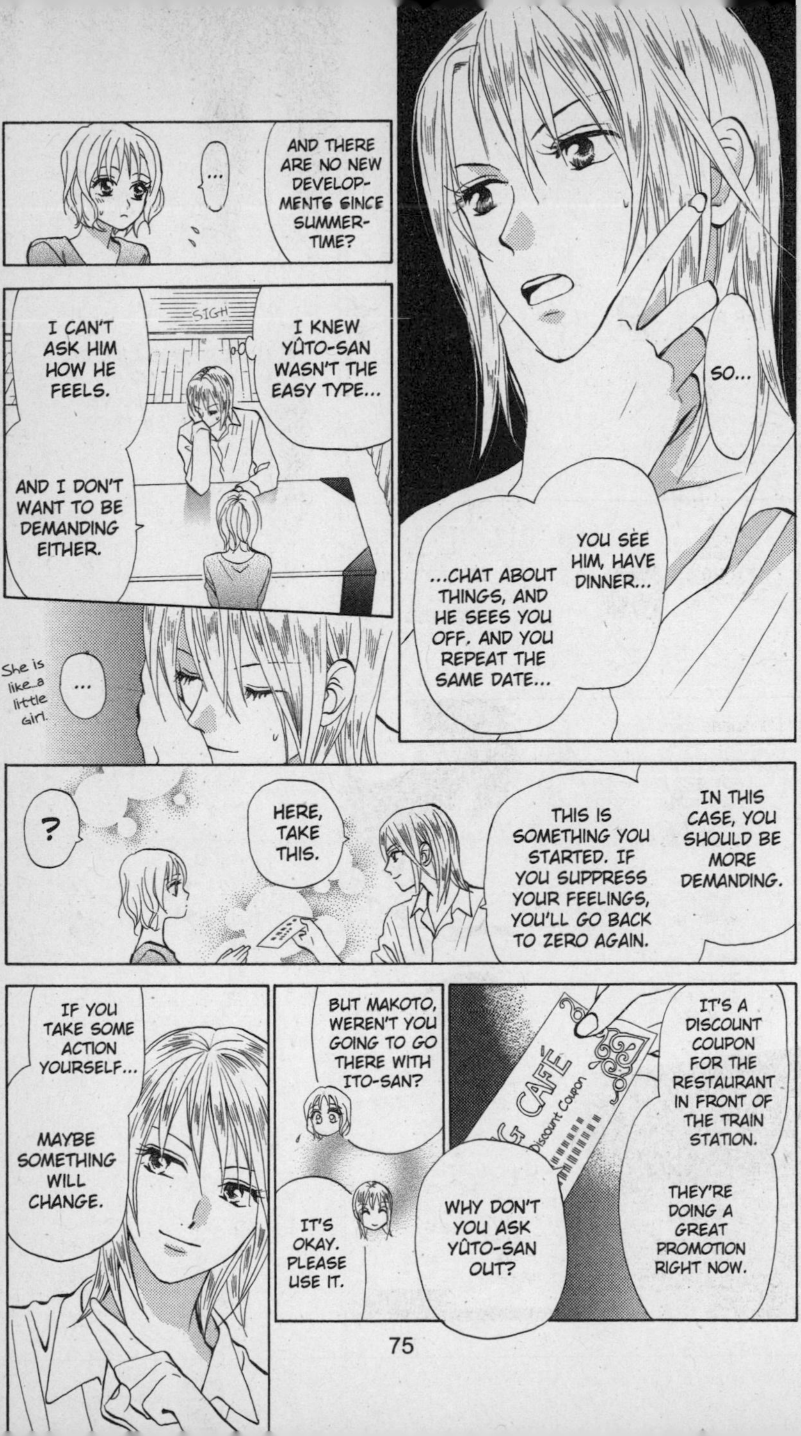
SO...
YOU SEE HIM, HAVE DINNER...
...CHAT ABOUT THINGS, AND HE SEES YOU OFF. AND YOU REPEAT THE SAME DATE...
AND THERE ARE NO NEW DEVELOPMENTS SINCE SUMMERTIME?
...
I KNEW YÛTO-SAN WASN'T THE EASY TYPE...
SIGH
I CAN'T ASK HIM HOW HE FEELS.
AND I DON'T WANT TO BE DEMANDING EITHER.
...
She is like a little girl.
IN THIS CASE, YOU SHOULD BE MORE DEMANDING.
THIS IS SOMETHING YOU STARTED. IF YOU SUPPRESS YOUR FEELINGS, YOU'LL GO BACK TO ZERO AGAIN.
HERE, TAKE THIS.
?
IT'S A DISCOUNT COUPON FOR THE RESTAURANT IN FRONT OF THE TRAIN STATION.
THEY'RE DOING A GREAT PROMOTION RIGHT NOW.
CAFÉ
Discount Coupon
WHY DON'T YOU ASK YÛTO-SAN OUT?
BUT MAKOTO, WEREN'T YOU GOING TO GO THERE WITH ITO-SAN?
IT'S OKAY. PLEASE USE IT.
IF YOU TAKE SOME ACTION YOURSELF...
MAYBE SOMETHING WILL CHANGE.

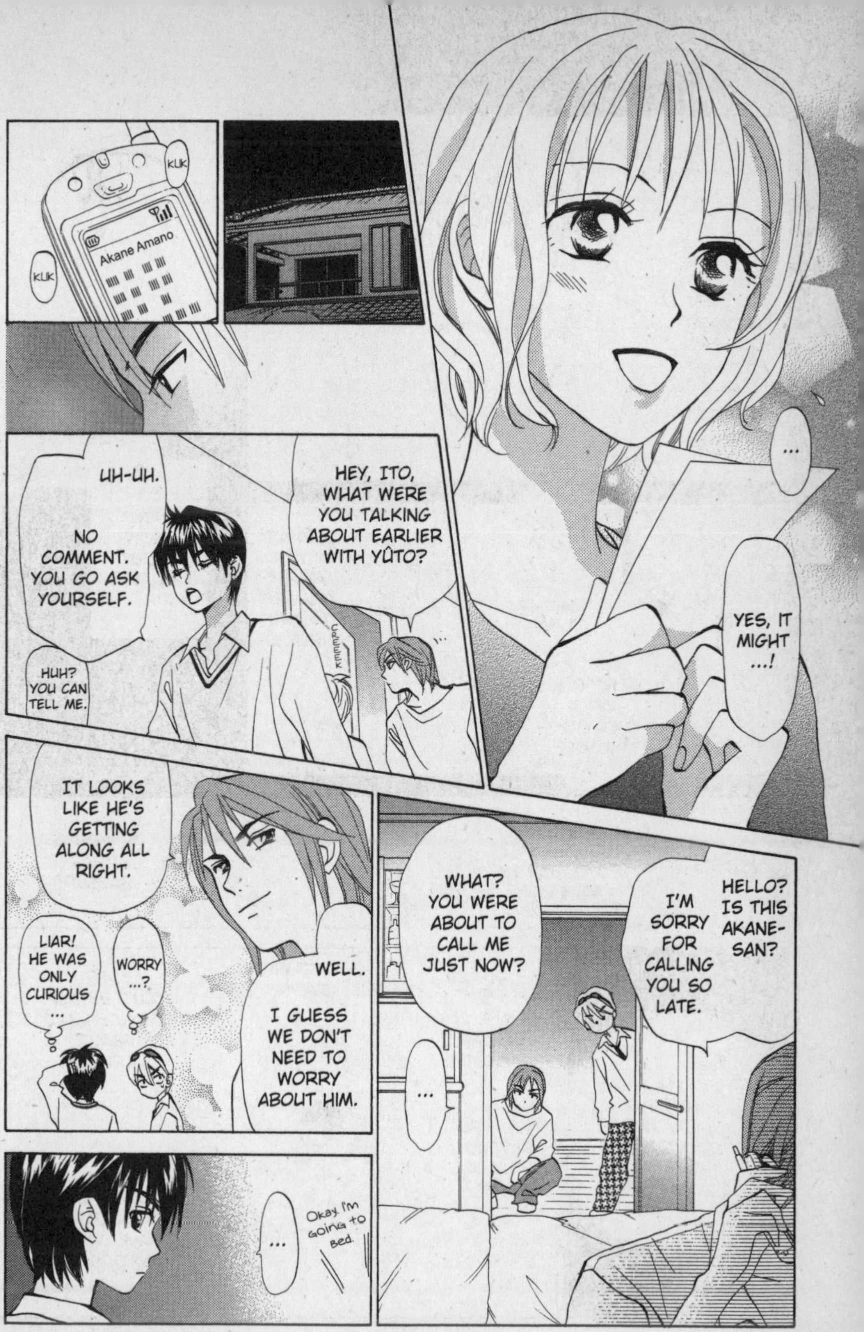
...
YES, IT MIGHT ...!
KUK
KUK
Akane Amano
HEY, ITO, WHAT WERE YOU TALKING ABOUT EARLIER WITH YÛTO?
...
UH-UH.
NO COMMENT. YOU GO ASK YOURSELF.
HUH? YOU CAN TELL ME.
HELLO? IS THIS AKANE-SAN?
I'M SORRY FOR CALLING YOU SO LATE.
WHAT? YOU WERE ABOUT TO CALL ME JUST NOW?
...
IT LOOKS LIKE HE'S GETTING ALONG ALL RIGHT.
WELL.
I GUESS WE DON'T NEED TO WORRY ABOUT HIM.
WORRY ...?
LIAR! HE WAS ONLY CURIOUS ...
Okay. I'm going to bed.
...

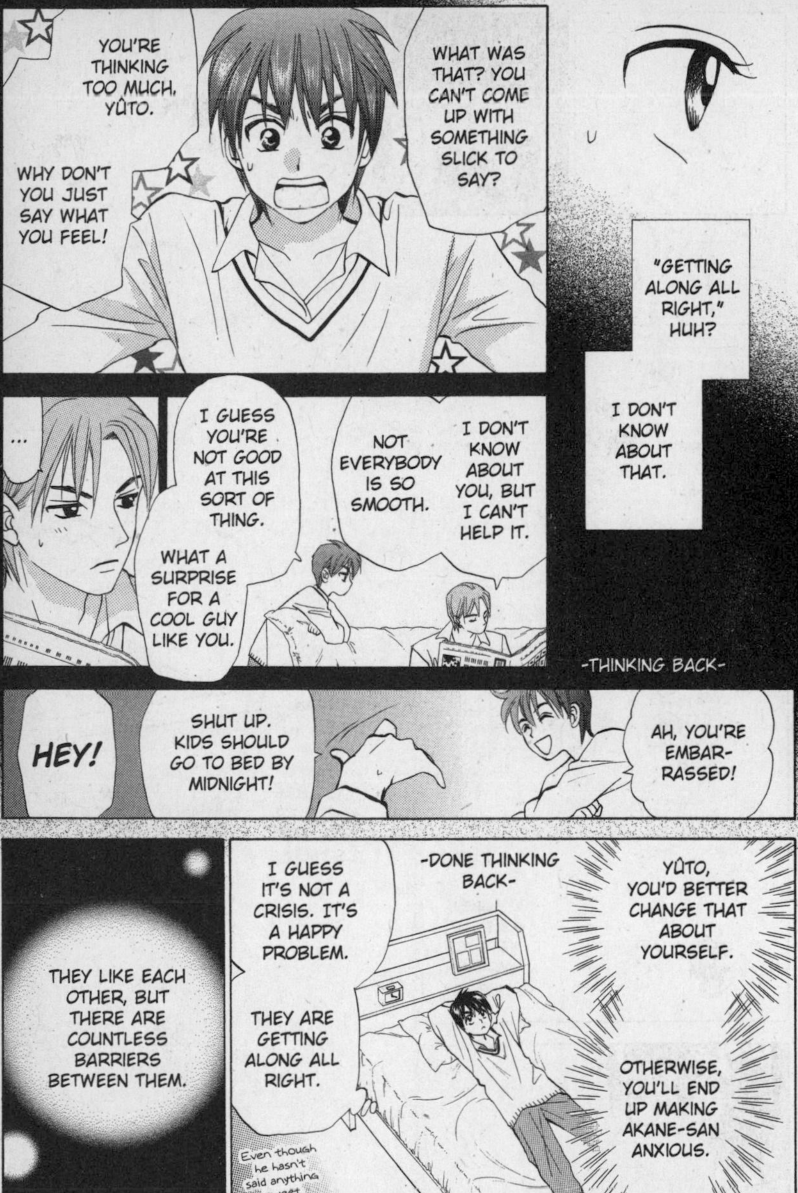
"GETTING ALONG ALL RIGHT," HUH?
I DON'T KNOW ABOUT THAT.
WHAT WAS THAT? YOU CAN'T COME UP WITH SOMETHING SLICK TO SAY?
YOU'RE THINKING TOO MUCH, YÛTO.
WHY DON'T YOU JUST SAY WHAT YOU FEEL!
I DON'T KNOW ABOUT YOU, BUT I CAN'T HELP IT.
NOT EVERYBODY IS SO SMOOTH.
I GUESS YOU'RE NOT GOOD AT THIS SORT OF THING.
WHAT A SURPRISE FOR A COOL GUY LIKE YOU.
...
-THINKING BACK-
AH, YOU'RE EMBARRASSED!
SHUT UP. KIDS SHOULD GO TO BED BY MIDNIGHT!
HEY!
YÛTO, YOU'D BETTER CHANGE THAT ABOUT YOURSELF.
-DONE THINKING BACK-
I GUESS IT'S NOT A CRISIS. IT'S A HAPPY PROBLEM.
OTHERWISE, YOU'LL END UP MAKING AKANE-SAN ANXIOUS.
THEY ARE GETTING ALONG ALL RIGHT.
Even though he hasn't said anything sweet.
THEY LIKE EACH OTHER, BUT THERE ARE COUNTLESS BARRIERS BETWEEN THEM.

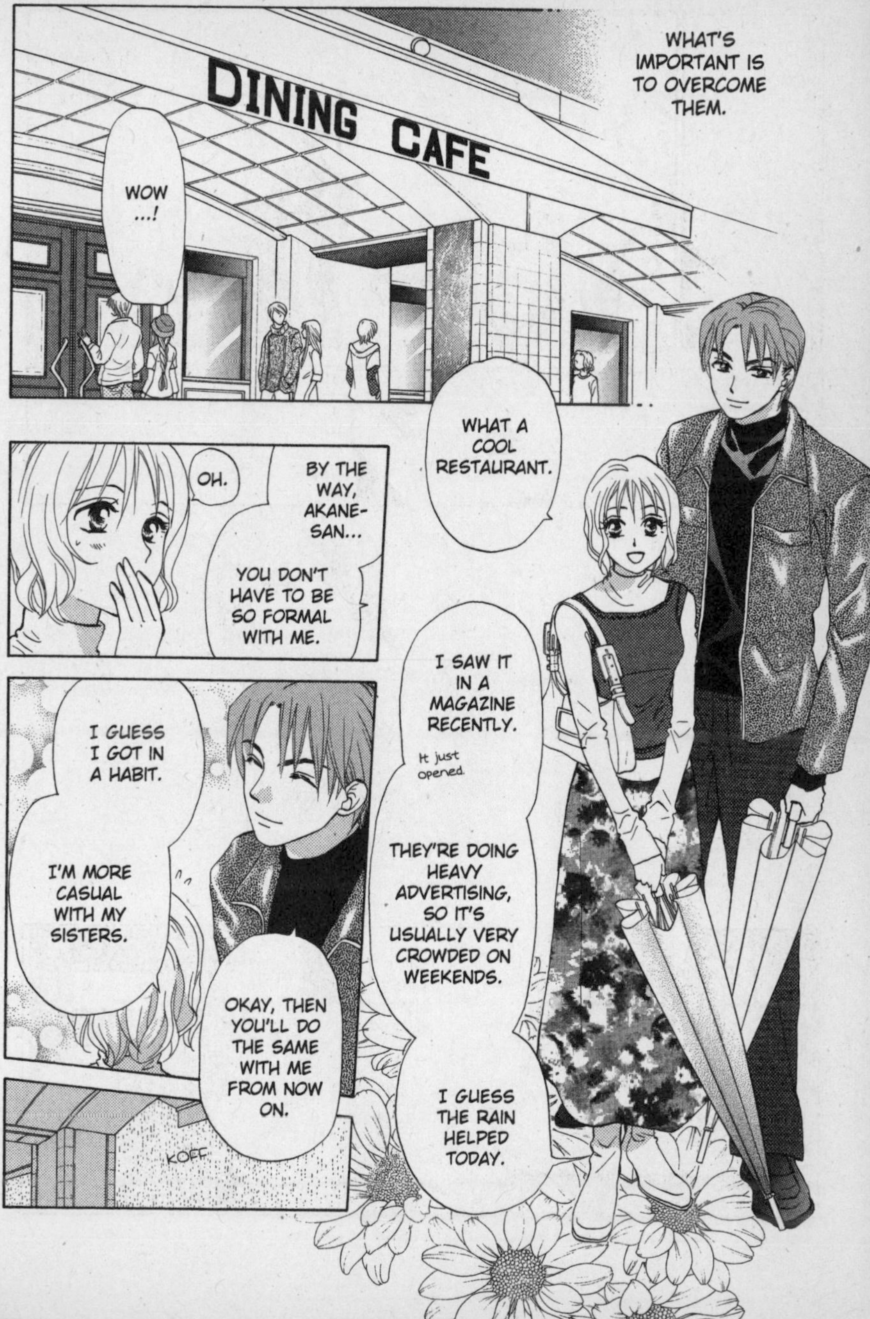
WHAT'S IMPORTANT IS TO OVERCOME THEM.
DINING CAFE
WOW ...!
WHAT A COOL RESTAURANT.
I SAW IT IN A MAGAZINE RECENTLY.
It just opened.
THEY'RE DOING HEAVY ADVERTISING, SO IT'S USUALLY VERY CROWDED ON WEEKENDS.
I GUESS THE RAIN HELPED TODAY.
OH.
BY THE WAY, AKANE-SAN...
YOU DON'T HAVE TO BE SO FORMAL WITH ME.
I GUESS I GOT IN A HABIT.
I'M MORE CASUAL WITH MY SISTERS.
OKAY, THEN YOU'LL DO THE SAME WITH ME FROM NOW ON.
KOFF

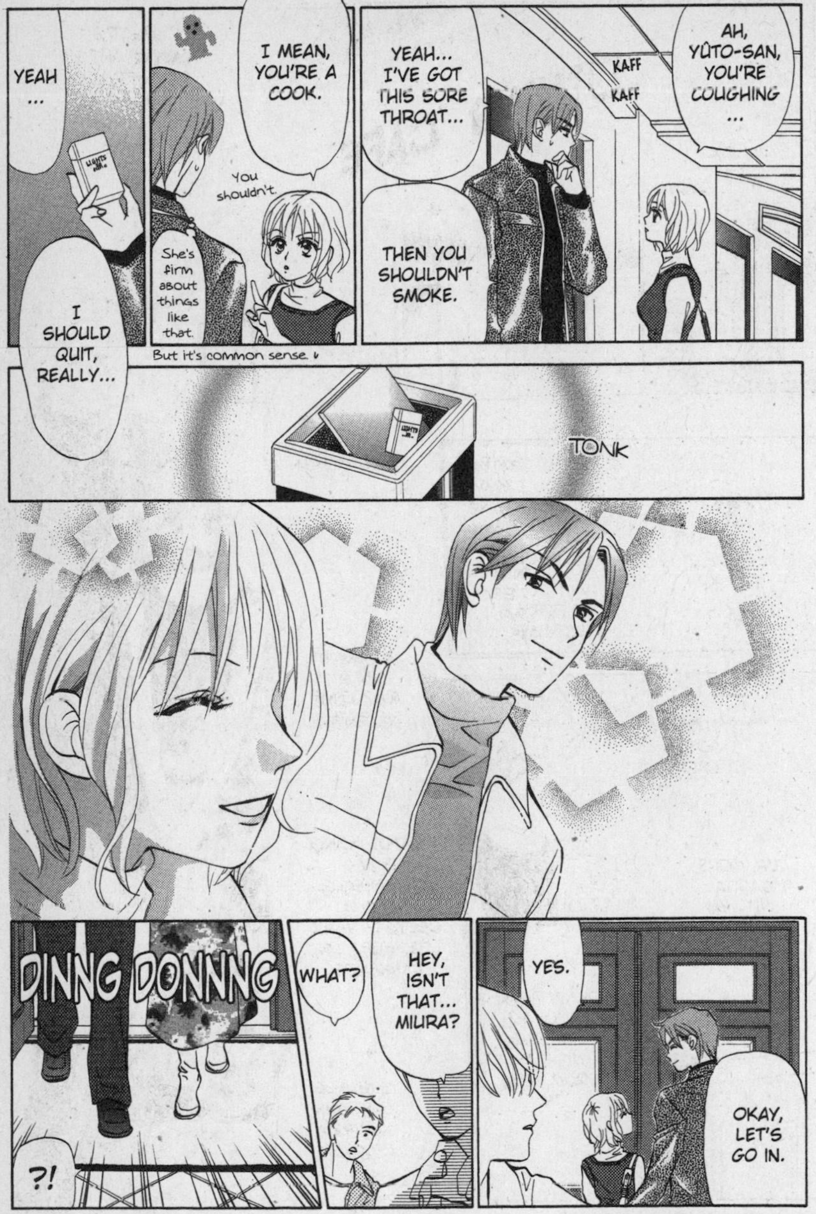
AH, YÛTO-SAN, YOU'RE COUGHING ...
KAFF KAFF
YEAH... I'VE GOT THIS SORE THROAT...
THEN YOU SHOULDN'T SMOKE.
I MEAN, YOU'RE A COOK.
You shouldn't.
She's firm about things like that.
But it's common sense.
YEAH ...
I SHOULD QUIT, REALLY...
TONK
YES.
OKAY, LET'S GO IN.
HEY, ISN'T THAT... MIURA?
WHAT?
DINNG DONNNG
?!

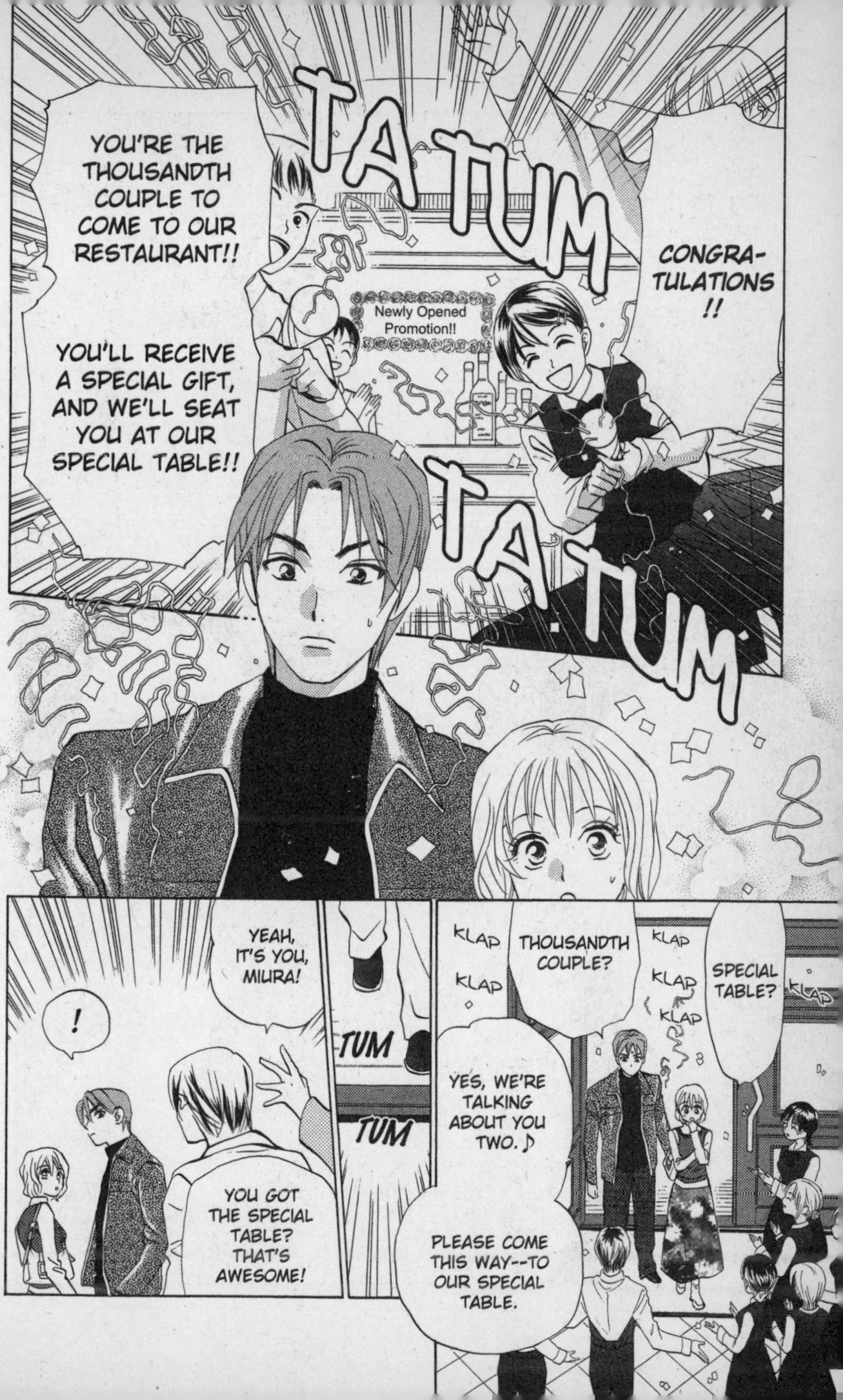
CONGRA-
TULATIONS
!!
TA TUM
YOU'RE THE THOUSANDTH COUPLE TO COME TO OUR RESTAURANT!!
Newly Opened Promotion!!
YOU'LL RECEIVE A SPECIAL GIFT, AND WE'LL SEAT YOU AT OUR SPECIAL TABLE!!
TA TUM
SPECIAL TABLE?
KLAP
KLAP
KLAP
KLAP
THOUSANDTH COUPLE?
KLAP
KLAP
YES, WE'RE TALKING ABOUT YOU TWO.♪
PLEASE COME THIS WAY--TO OUR SPECIAL TABLE.
TUM
TUM
YEAH, IT'S YOU, MIURA!
!
YOU GOT THE SPECIAL TABLE? THAT'S AWESOME!

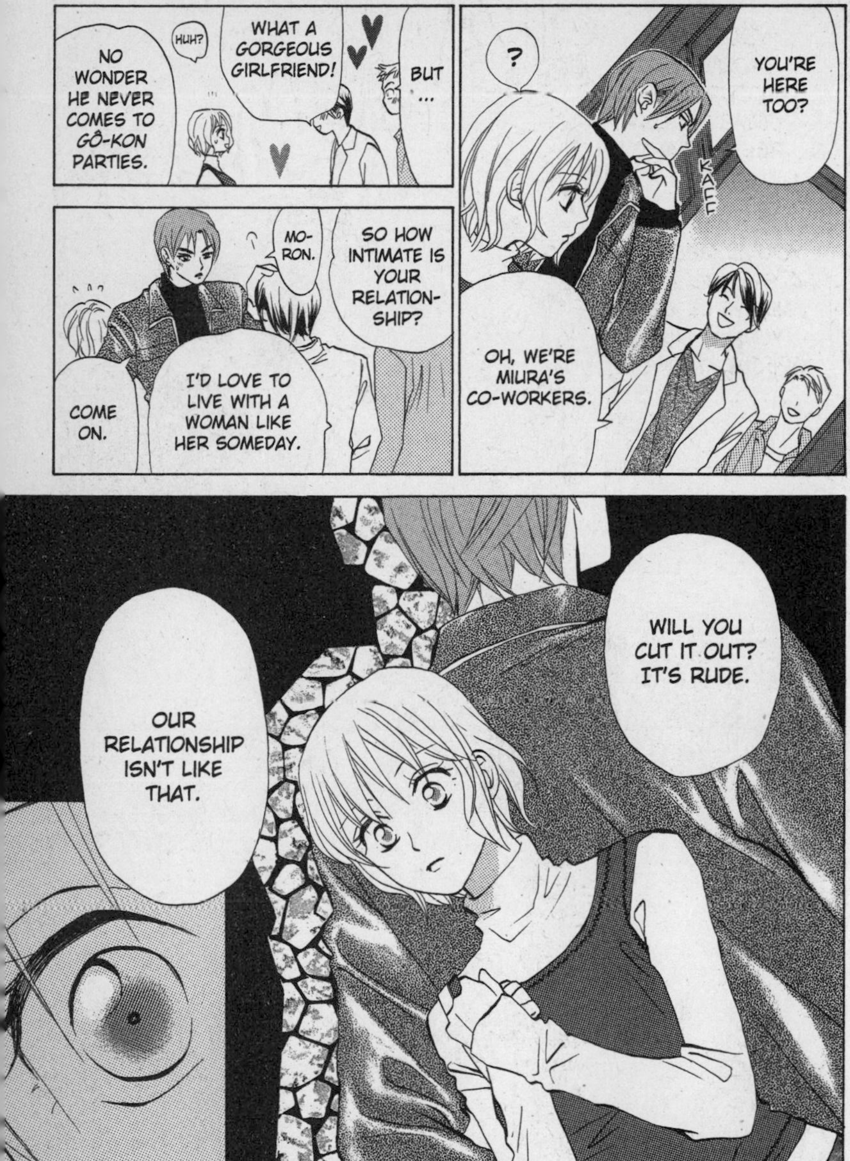
?
YOU'RE HERE TOO?
KAFF
OH, WE'RE MIURA'S CO-WORKERS.
BUT ...
WHAT A GORGEOUS GIRLFRIEND!
HUH?
NO WONDER HE NEVER COMES TO GÔ-KON PARTIES.
SO HOW INTIMATE IS YOUR RELATIONSHIP?
MO-RON.
I'D LOVE TO LIVE WITH A WOMAN LIKE HER SOMEDAY.
COME ON.
WILL YOU CUT IT OUT? IT'S RUDE.
OUR RELATIONSHIP ISN'T LIKE THAT.

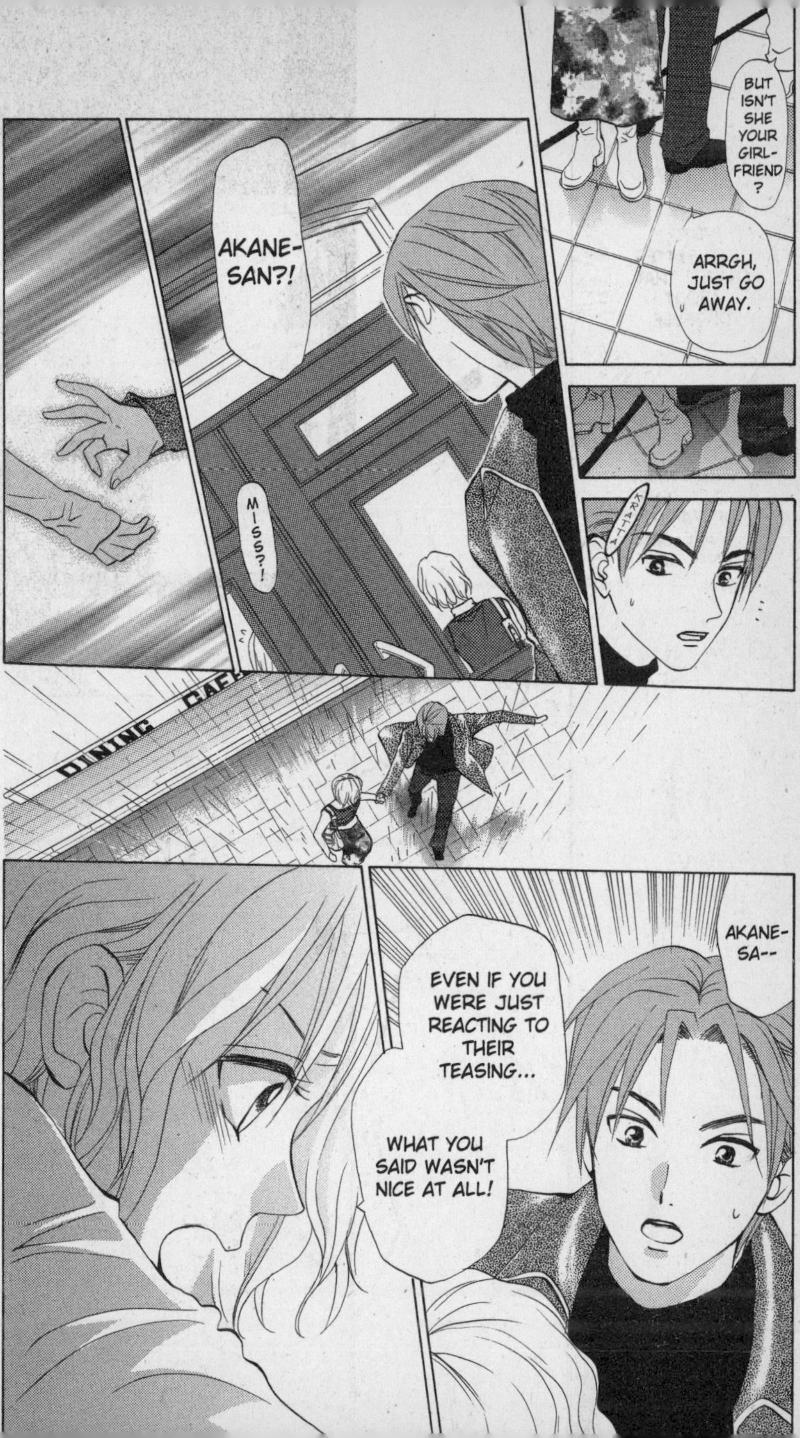
BUT ISN'T SHE YOUR GIRL-FRIEND?
ARRGH, JUST GO AWAY.
KRATTA
AKANE-SAN?!
MISS?!
DINING CAF
AKANE-SA--
EVEN IF YOU WERE JUST REACTING TO THEIR TEASING...
WHAT YOU SAID WASN'T NICE AT ALL!

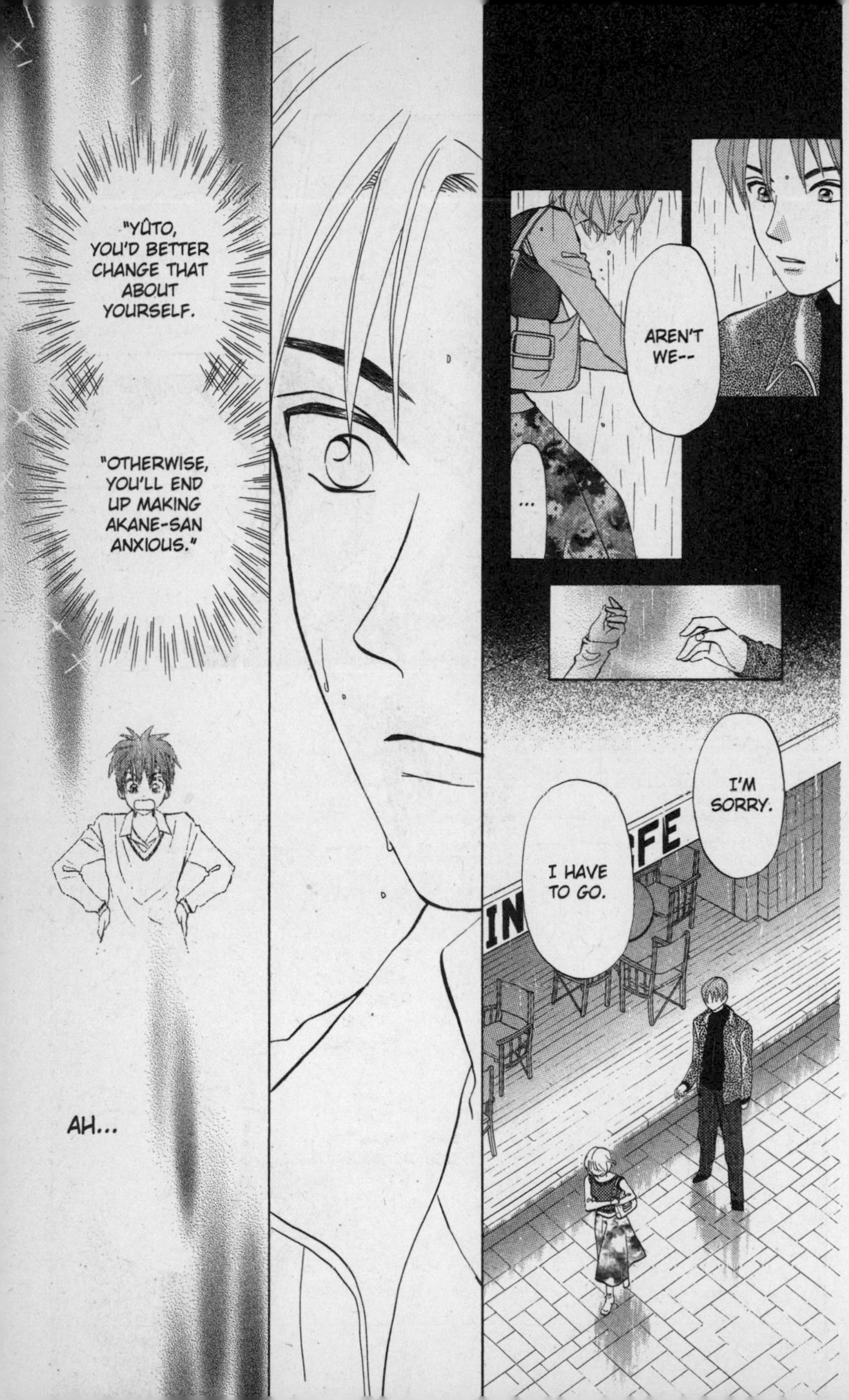
AREN'T WE--
...
I'M SORRY.
I HAVE TO GO.
"YÛTO, YOU'D BETTER CHANGE THAT ABOUT YOURSELF.
"OTHERWISE, YOU'LL END UP MAKING AKANE-SAN ANXIOUS."
AH...

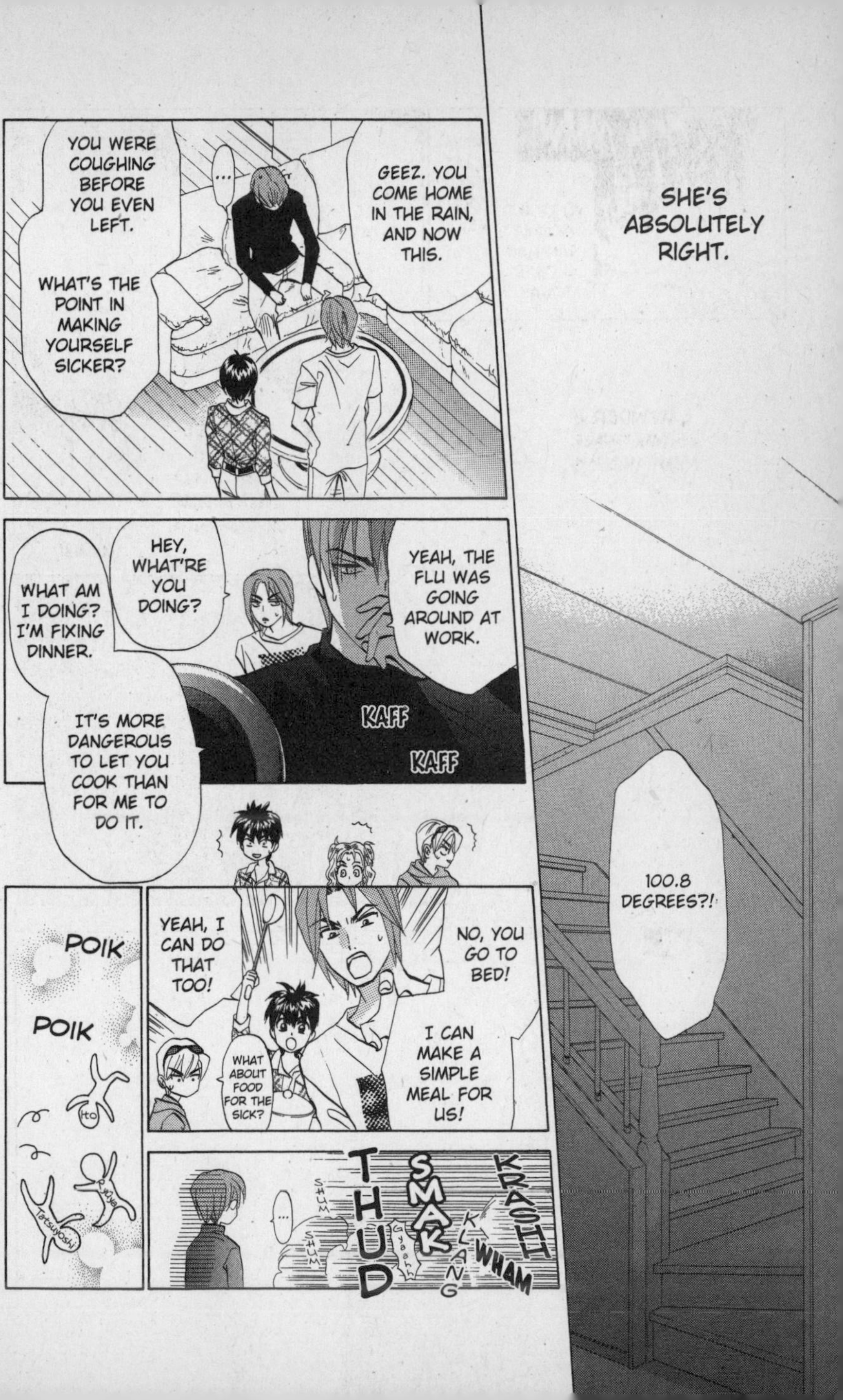
SHE'S ABSOLUTELY RIGHT.
100.8 DEGREES?!
GEEZ. YOU COME HOME IN THE RAIN, AND NOW THIS.
...
YOU WERE COUGHING BEFORE YOU EVEN LEFT.
WHAT'S THE POINT IN MAKING YOURSELF SICKER?
YEAH, THE FLU WAS GOING AROUND AT WORK.
KAFF
KAFF
HEY, WHAT'RE YOU DOING?
WHAT AM I DOING? I'M FIXING DINNER.
IT'S MORE DANGEROUS TO LET YOU COOK THAN FOR ME TO DO IT.
NO, YOU GO TO BED!
I CAN MAKE A SIMPLE MEAL FOR US!
YEAH, I CAN DO THAT TOO!
WHAT ABOUT FOOD FOR THE SICK?
KRASHH
WHAM
KLANG
SMAK
THUD
Gyaahh
SHUM
SHUM
...
POIK
POIK
Ito
Ryuya
Tatsuyoshi

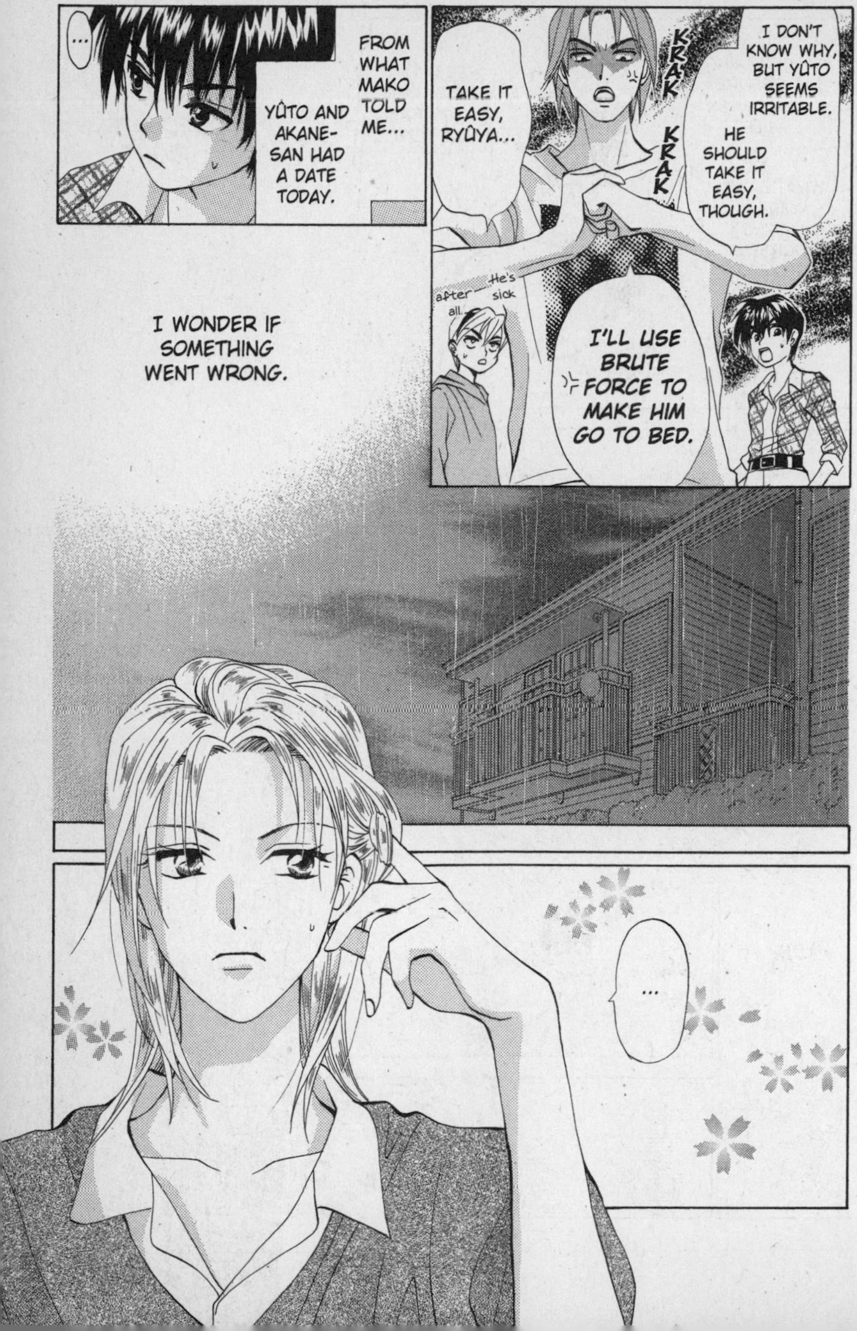
I DON'T KNOW WHY, BUT YÛTO SEEMS IRRITABLE.
HE SHOULD TAKE IT EASY, THOUGH.
KRAK
KRAK
TAKE IT EASY, RYÛYA...
I'LL USE BRUTE FORCE TO MAKE HIM GO TO BED.
He's sick after all...
...
FROM WHAT MAKO TOLD ME...
YÛTO AND AKANE-SAN HAD A DATE TODAY.
I WONDER IF SOMETHING WENT WRONG.
...

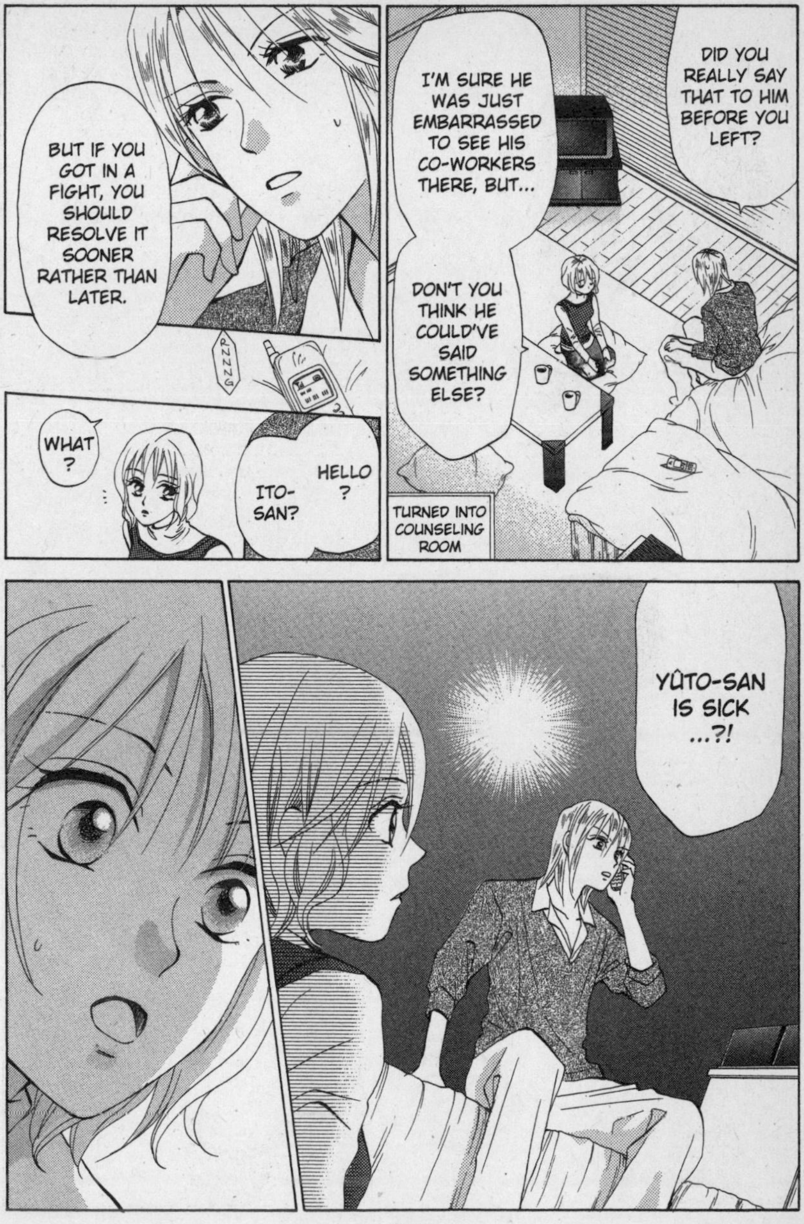
DID YOU REALLY SAY THAT TO HIM BEFORE YOU LEFT?
I'M SURE HE WAS JUST EMBARRASSED TO SEE HIS CO-WORKERS THERE, BUT...
DON'T YOU THINK HE COULD'VE SAID SOMETHING ELSE?
TURNED INTO COUNSELING ROOM
BUT IF YOU GOT IN A FIGHT, YOU SHOULD RESOLVE IT SOONER RATHER THAN LATER.
RNNG
HELLO?
ITO-SAN?
WHAT?
YÛTO-SAN IS SICK ...?!

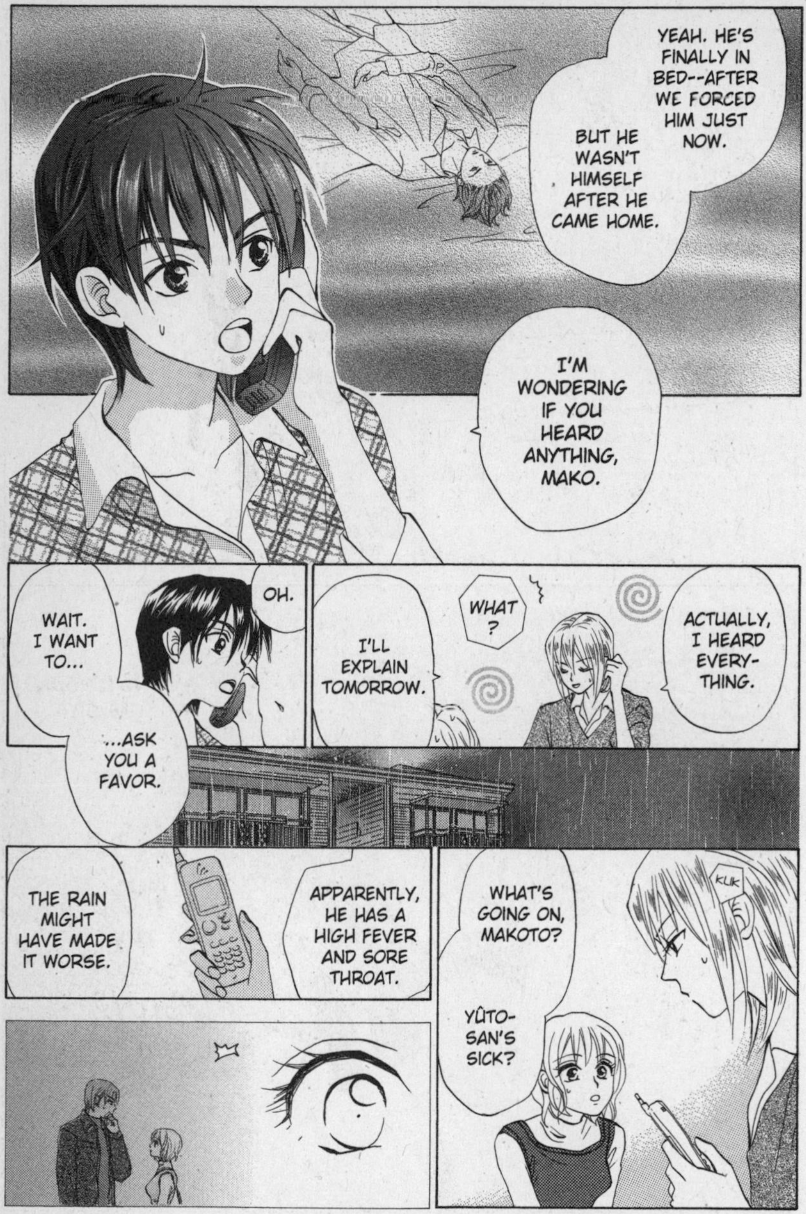
YEAH. HE'S FINALLY IN BED--AFTER WE FORCED HIM JUST NOW.
BUT HE WASN'T HIMSELF AFTER HE CAME HOME.
I'M WONDERING IF YOU HEARD ANYTHING, MAKO.
ACTUALLY, I HEARD EVERY-THING.
WHAT?
I'LL EXPLAIN TOMORROW.
OH.
WAIT. I WANT TO...
...ASK YOU A FAVOR.
KLIK
WHAT'S GOING ON, MAKOTO?
YÛTO-SAN'S SICK?
APPARENTLY, HE HAS A HIGH FEVER AND SORE THROAT.
THE RAIN MIGHT HAVE MADE IT WORSE.

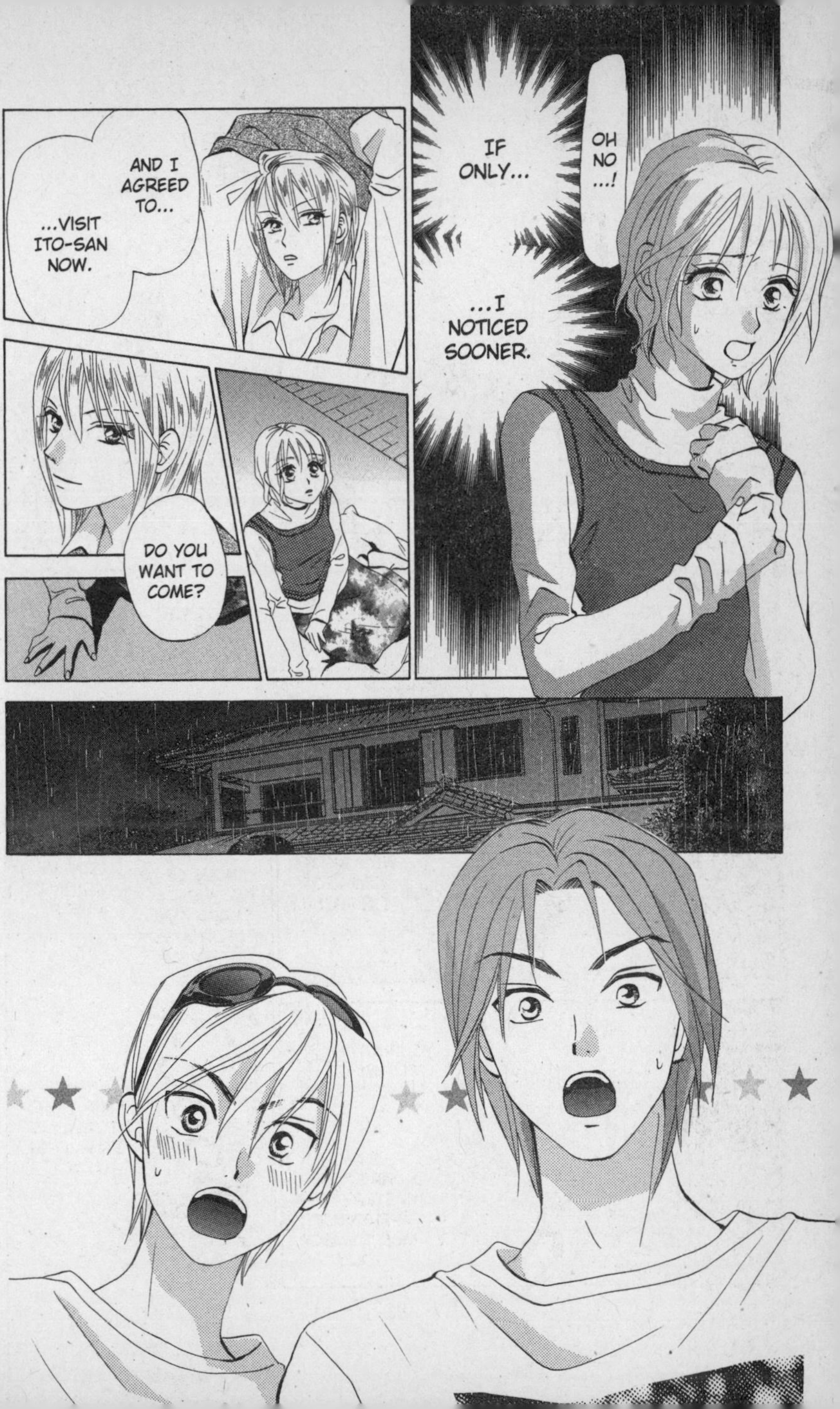
OH NO ...!
IF ONLY...
...I NOTICED SOONER.
AND I AGREED TO...
...VISIT ITO-SAN NOW.
DO YOU WANT TO COME?

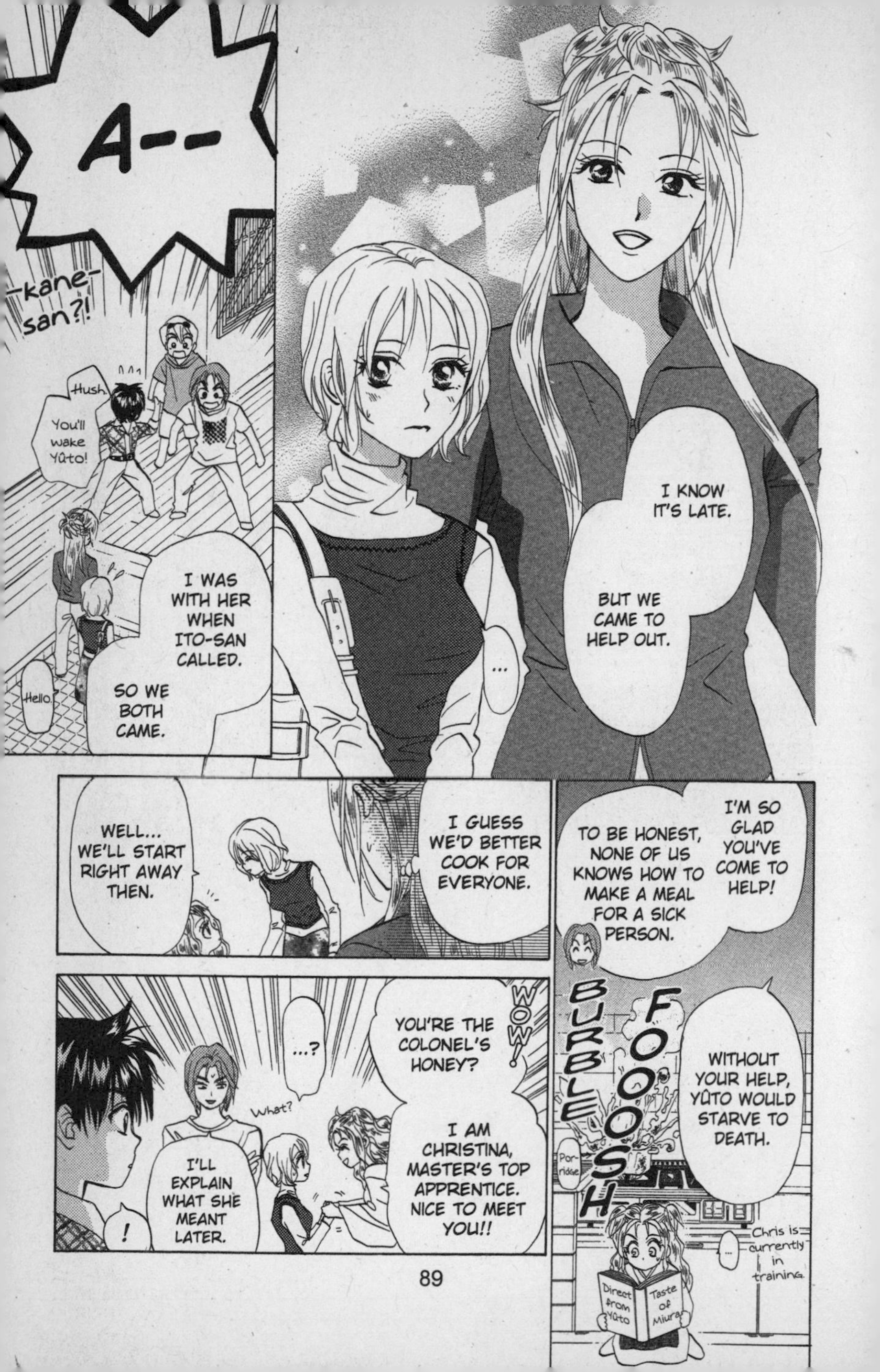
I KNOW IT'S LATE.
BUT WE CAME TO HELP OUT.
...
A--
-kane-san?!
Hush.
You'll wake Yûto!
I WAS WITH HER WHEN ITO-SAN CALLED.
SO WE BOTH CAME.
Hello.
I'M SO GLAD YOU'VE COME TO HELP!
TO BE HONEST, NONE OF US KNOWS HOW TO MAKE A MEAL FOR A SICK PERSON.
BURBLE
FOOOOSH
WITHOUT YOUR HELP, YÛTO WOULD STARVE TO DEATH.
Porridge
...
Chris is currently in training.
Direct from Yûto
Taste of Miura
I GUESS WE'D BETTER COOK FOR EVERYONE.
WELL... WE'LL START RIGHT AWAY THEN.
WOW!
YOU'RE THE COLONEL'S HONEY?
...?
I AM CHRISTINA, MASTER'S TOP APPRENTICE. NICE TO MEET YOU!!
What?
I'LL EXPLAIN WHAT SHE MEANT LATER.
!

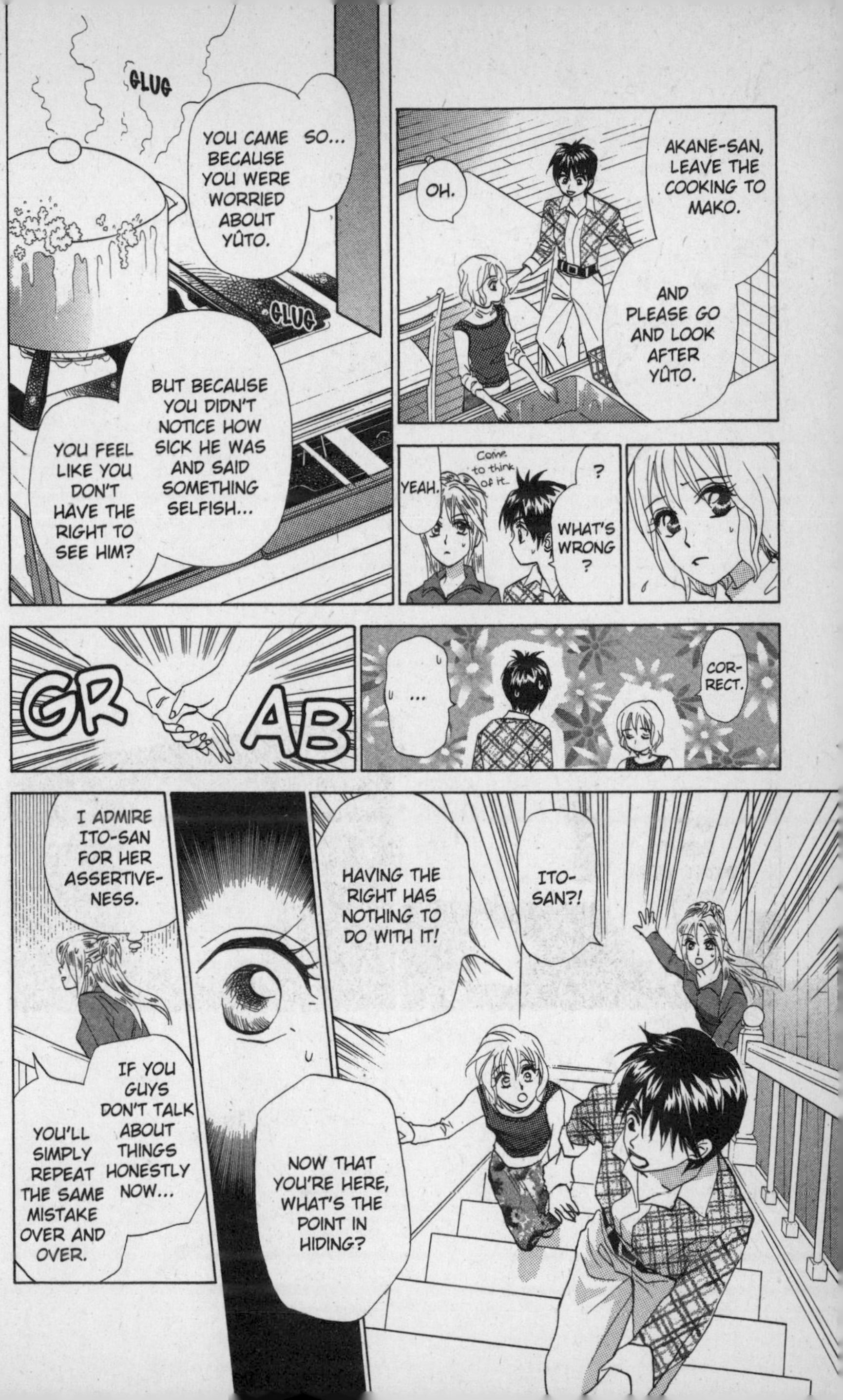
AKANE-SAN, LEAVE THE COOKING TO MAKO.
AND PLEASE GO AND LOOK AFTER YÛTO.
OH.
? WHAT'S WRONG?
Come to think of it..
YEAH.
GLUG
SO... YOU CAME BECAUSE YOU WERE WORRIED ABOUT YÛTO.
GLUG
BUT BECAUSE YOU DIDN'T NOTICE HOW SICK HE WAS AND SAID SOMETHING SELFISH...
YOU FEEL LIKE YOU DON'T HAVE THE RIGHT TO SEE HIM?
COR-RECT.
...
GR AB
ITO-SAN?!
HAVING THE RIGHT HAS NOTHING TO DO WITH IT!
NOW THAT YOU'RE HERE, WHAT'S THE POINT IN HIDING?
I ADMIRE ITO-SAN FOR HER ASSERTIVE-NESS.
IF YOU GUYS DON'T TALK ABOUT THINGS HONESTLY NOW...
YOU'LL SIMPLY REPEAT THE SAME MISTAKE OVER AND OVER.

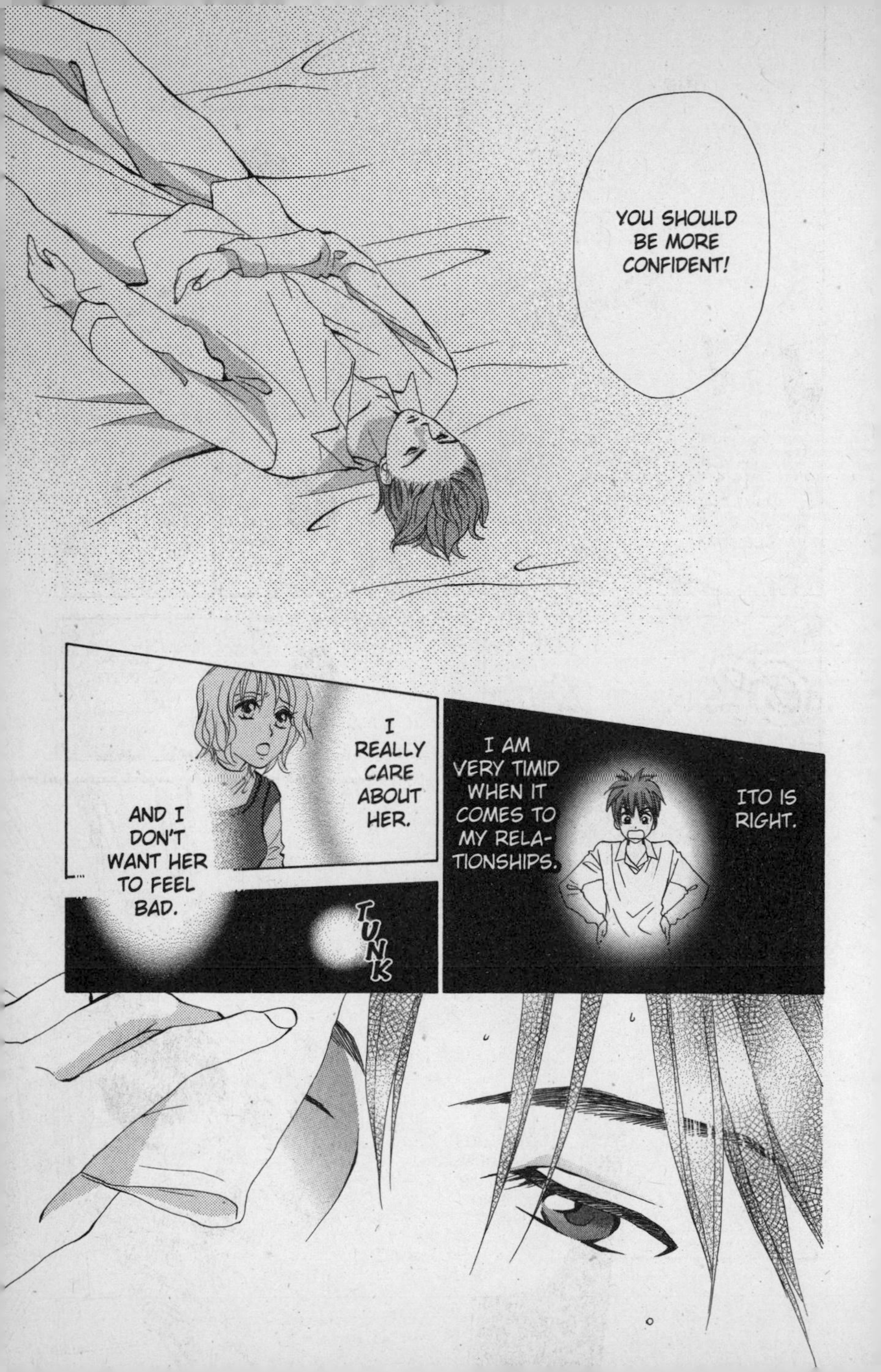
YOU SHOULD BE MORE CONFIDENT!
ITO IS RIGHT.
I AM VERY TIMID WHEN IT COMES TO MY RELA-TIONSHIPS.
I REALLY CARE ABOUT HER.
AND I DON'T WANT HER TO FEEL BAD.
TUNK

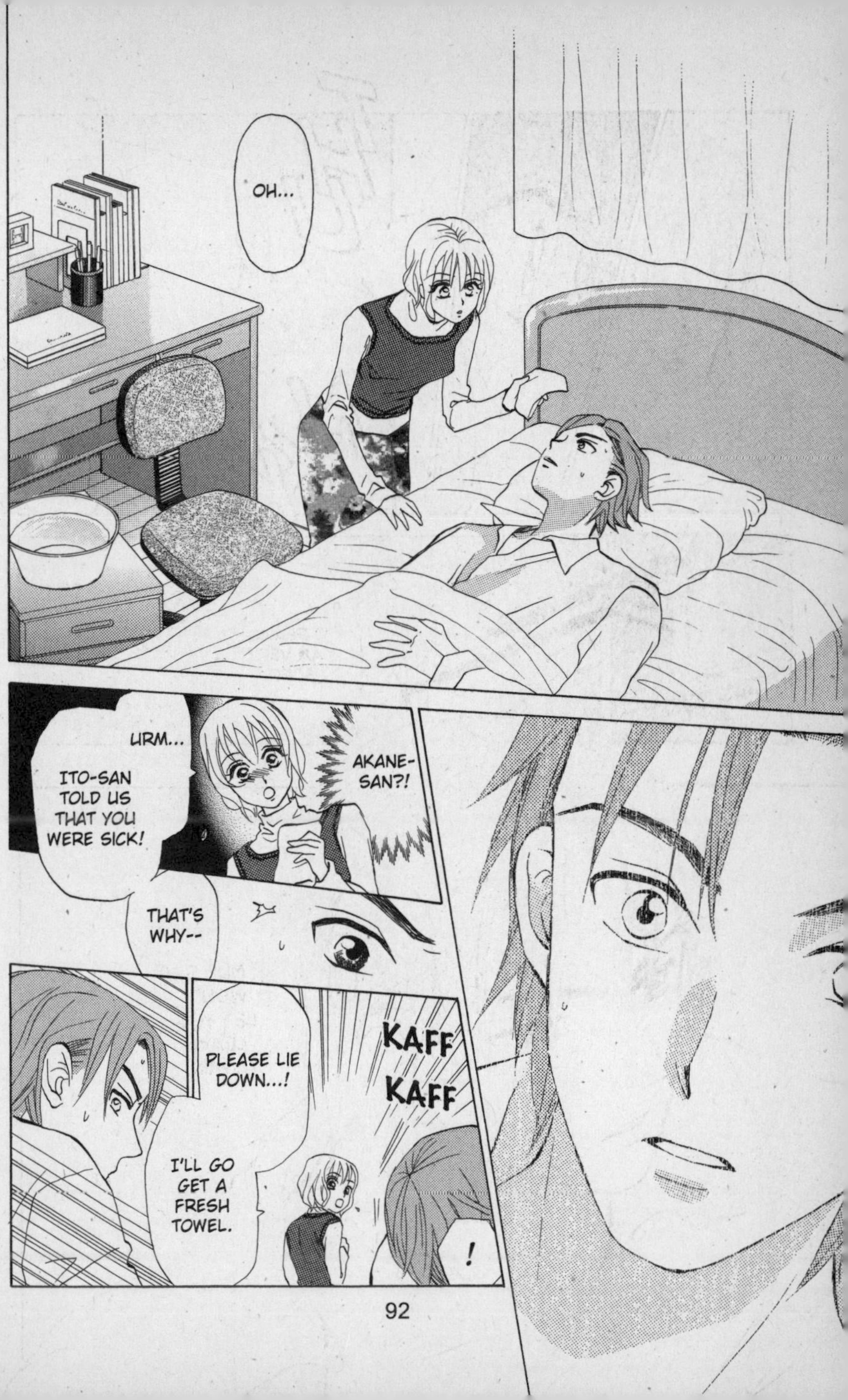
OH...
AKANE-SAN?!
URM...
ITO-SAN TOLD US THAT YOU WERE SICK!
THAT'S WHY--
KAFF KAFF
PLEASE LIE DOWN...!
I'LL GO GET A FRESH TOWEL.
!

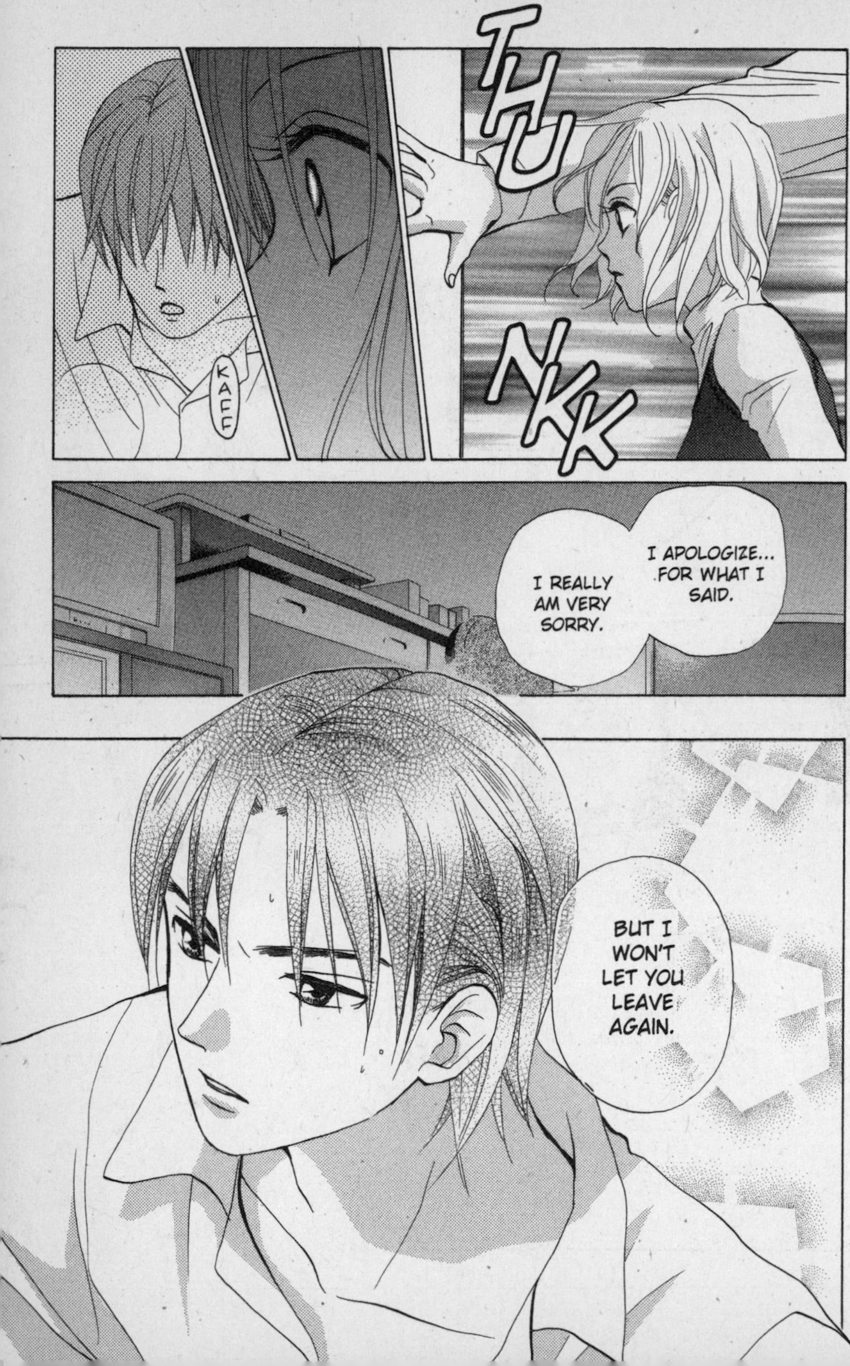
THUNKK
KAFF
I APOLOGIZE... FOR WHAT I SAID.
I REALLY AM VERY SORRY.
BUT I WON'T LET YOU LEAVE AGAIN.

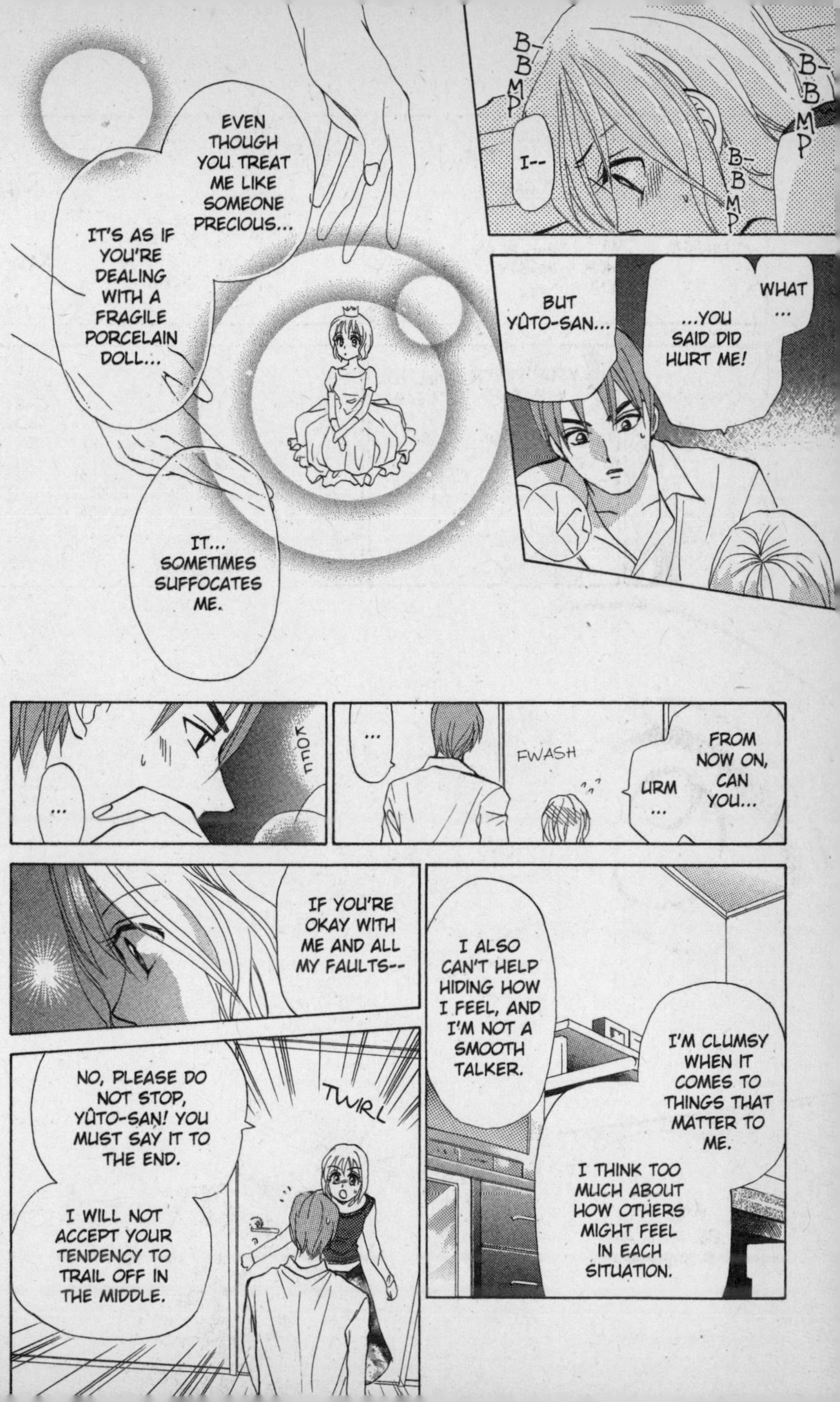
B-B-MP
B-B-MP
B-B-MP
I--
WHAT...
...YOU SAID DID HURT ME!
BUT YÛTO-SAN...
EVEN THOUGH YOU TREAT ME LIKE SOMEONE PRECIOUS...
IT'S AS IF YOU'RE DEALING WITH A FRAGILE PORCELAIN DOLL...
IT... SOMETIMES SUFFOCATES ME.
FROM NOW ON, CAN YOU...
URM...
FWASH
...
KOFF
...
I ALSO CAN'T HELP HIDING HOW I FEEL, AND I'M NOT A SMOOTH TALKER.
I'M CLUMSY WHEN IT COMES TO THINGS THAT MATTER TO ME.
I THINK TOO MUCH ABOUT HOW OTHERS MIGHT FEEL IN EACH SITUATION.
IF YOU'RE OKAY WITH ME AND ALL MY FAULTS--
TWIRL
NO, PLEASE DO NOT STOP, YÛTO-SAN! YOU MUST SAY IT TO THE END.
I WILL NOT ACCEPT YOUR TENDENCY TO TRAIL OFF IN THE MIDDLE.

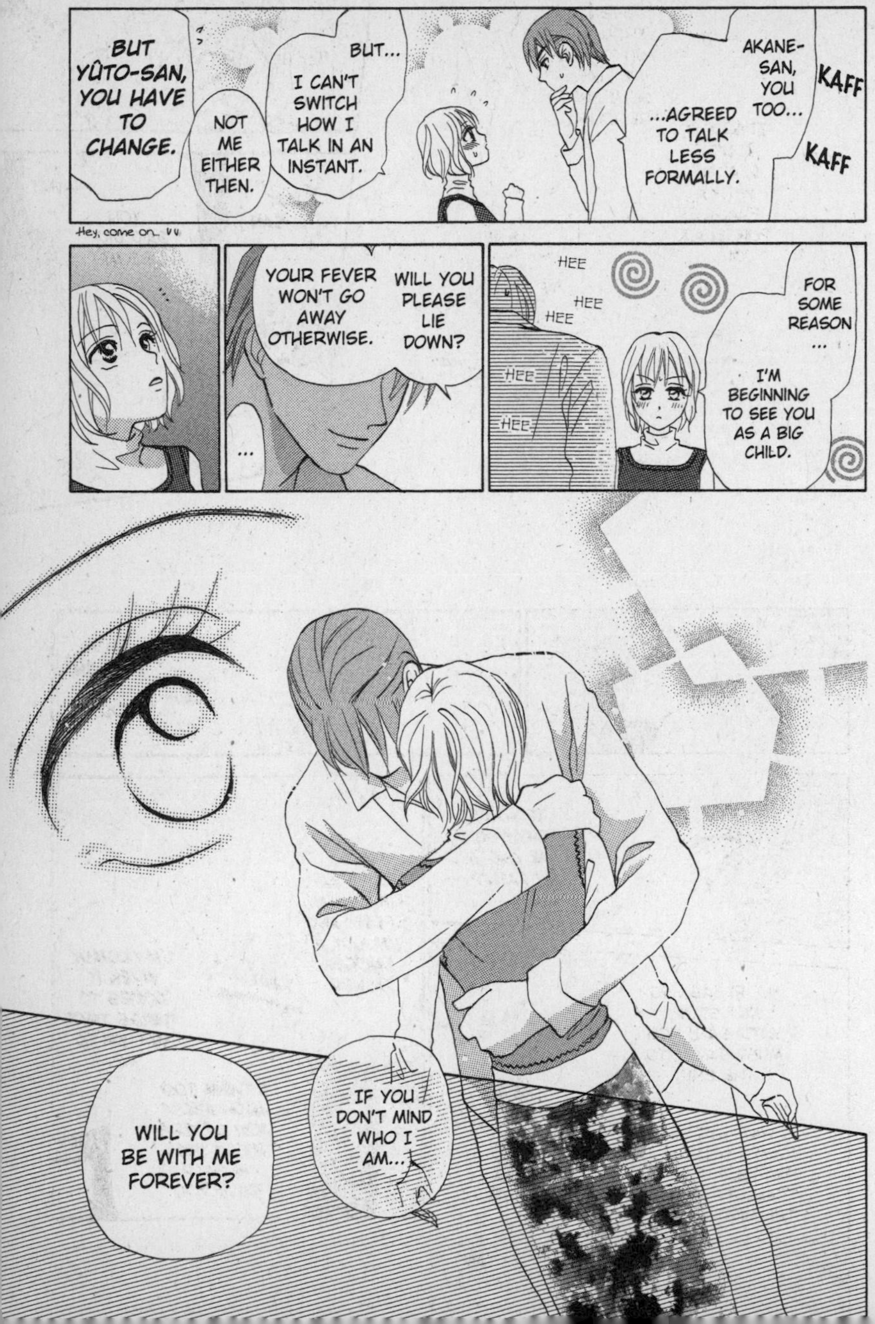
KAFF
KAFF
AKANE-SAN, YOU TOO...
...AGREED TO TALK LESS FORMALLY.
BUT...
I CAN'T SWITCH HOW I TALK IN AN INSTANT.
NOT ME EITHER THEN.
BUT YÛTO-SAN, YOU HAVE TO CHANGE.
Hey, come on..
FOR SOME REASON...
I'M BEGINNING TO SEE YOU AS A BIG CHILD.
HEE
HEE
HEE
HEE
HEE
WILL YOU PLEASE LIE DOWN?
YOUR FEVER WON'T GO AWAY OTHERWISE.
...
IF YOU DON'T MIND WHO I AM...
WILL YOU BE WITH ME FOREVER?

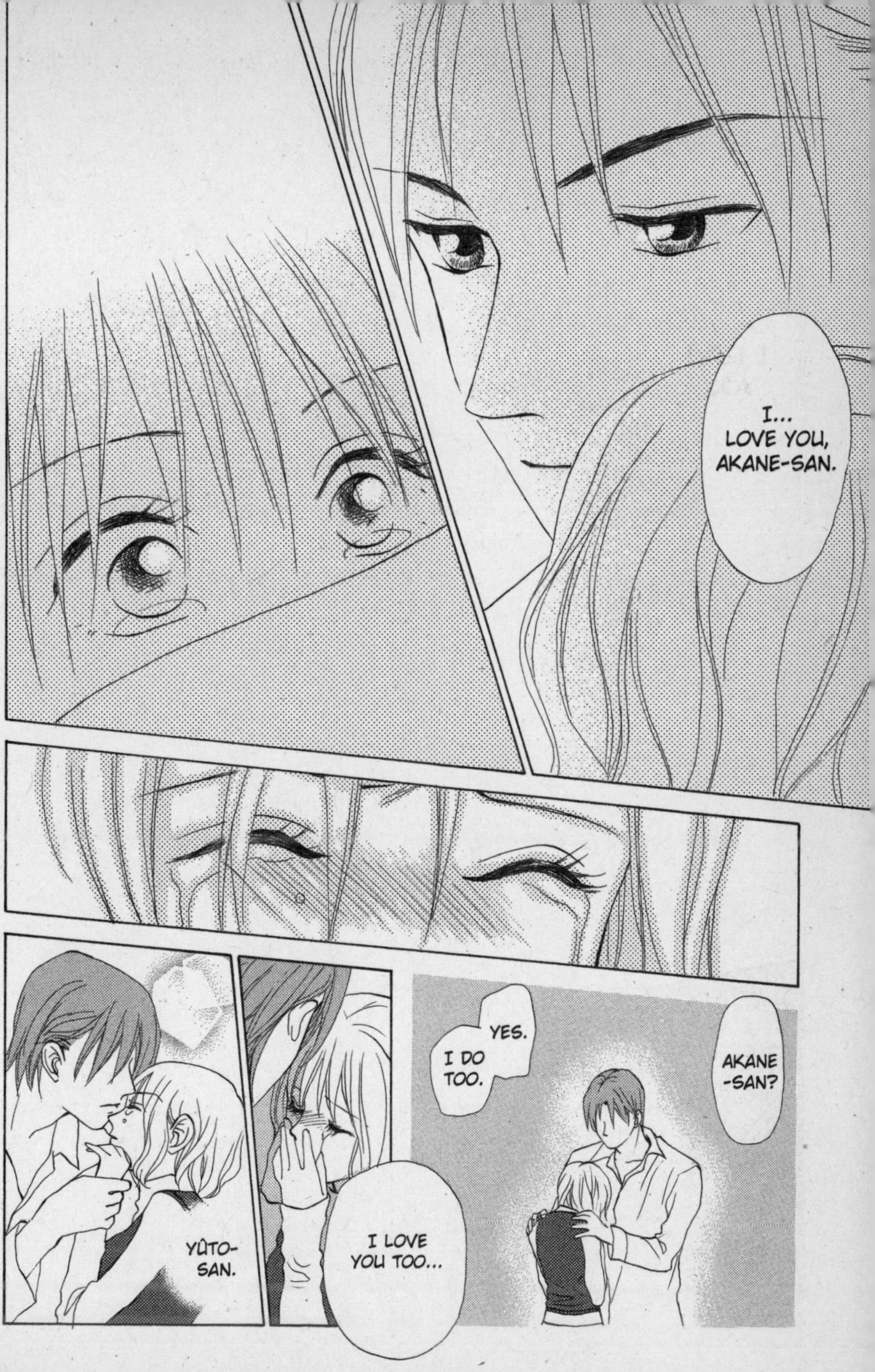
I... LOVE YOU, AKANE-SAN.
AKANE-SAN?
YES. I DO TOO.
I LOVE YOU TOO...
YÛTO-SAN.

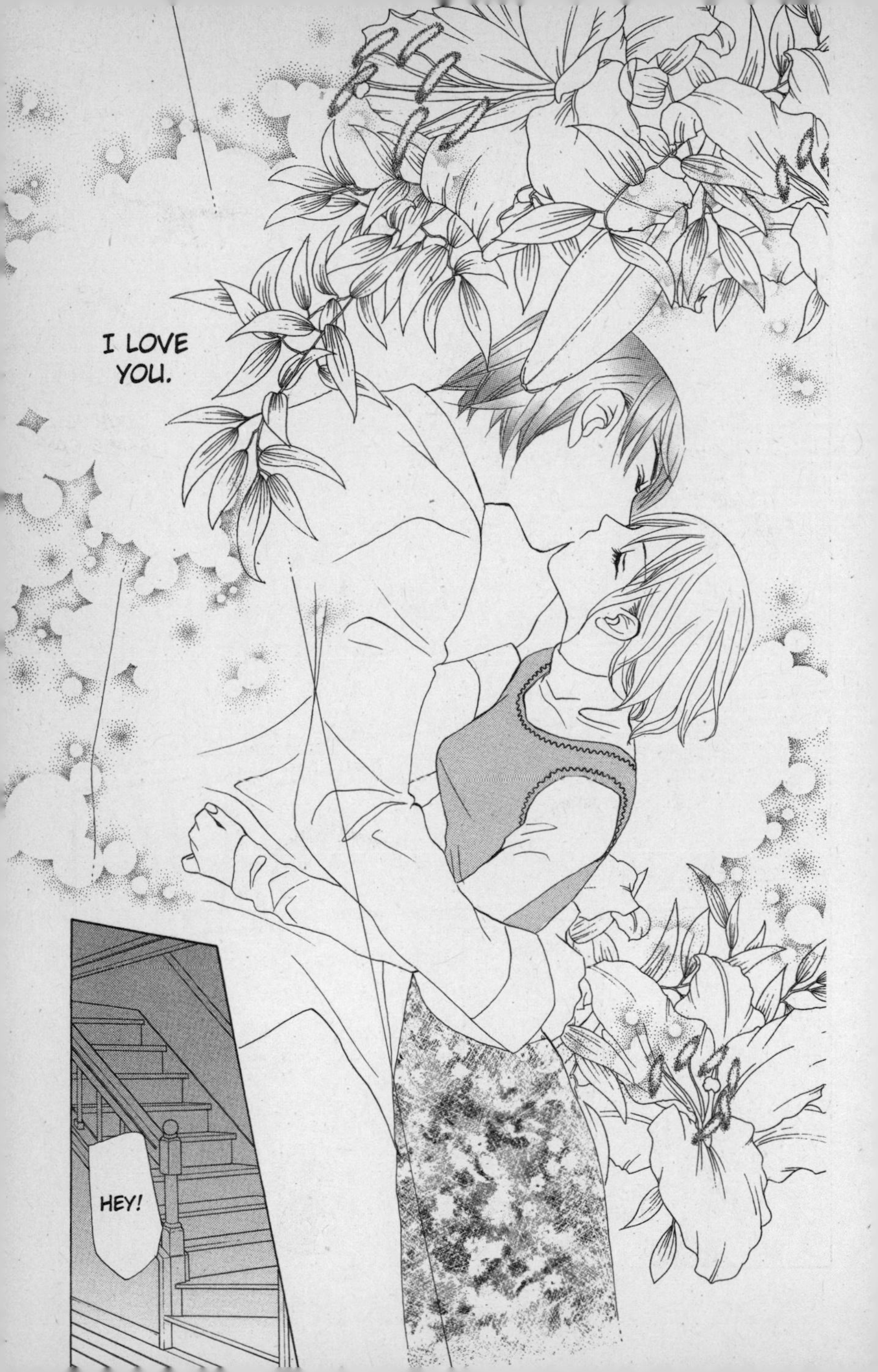
I LOVE YOU.
HEY!

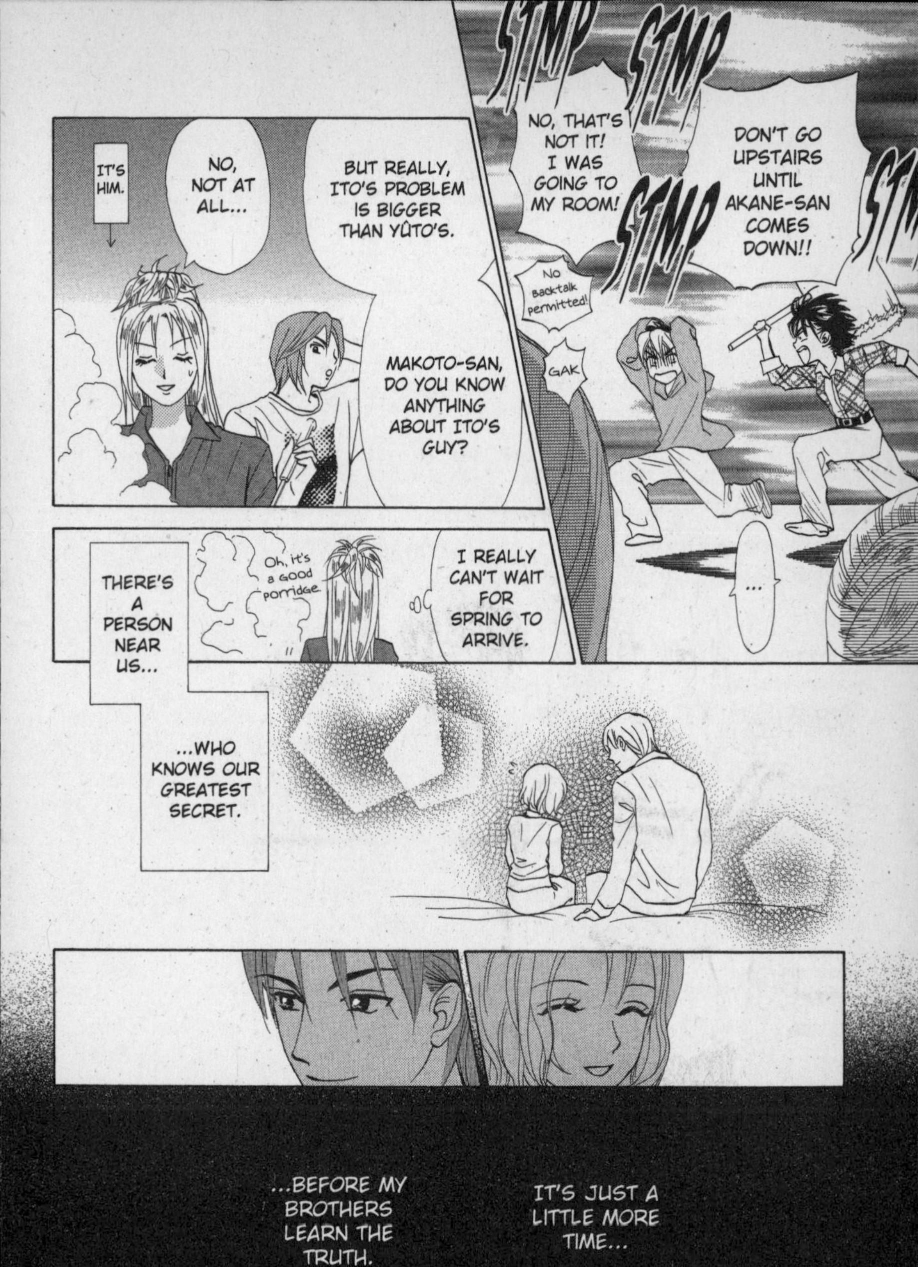
STMP STMP
NO, THAT'S NOT IT! I WAS GOING TO MY ROOM!
DON'T GO UPSTAIRS UNTIL AKANE-SAN COMES DOWN!!
STMP STMP
No backtalk permitted!
GAK
...
BUT REALLY, ITO'S PROBLEM IS BIGGER THAN YÛTO'S.
MAKOTO-SAN, DO YOU KNOW ANYTHING ABOUT ITO'S GUY?
NO, NOT AT ALL...
IT'S HIM.
I REALLY CAN'T WAIT FOR SPRING TO ARRIVE.
Oh, it's a good porridge.
THERE'S A PERSON NEAR US...
...WHO KNOWS OUR GREATEST SECRET.
IT'S JUST A LITTLE MORE TIME...
...BEFORE MY BROTHERS LEARN THE TRUTH.

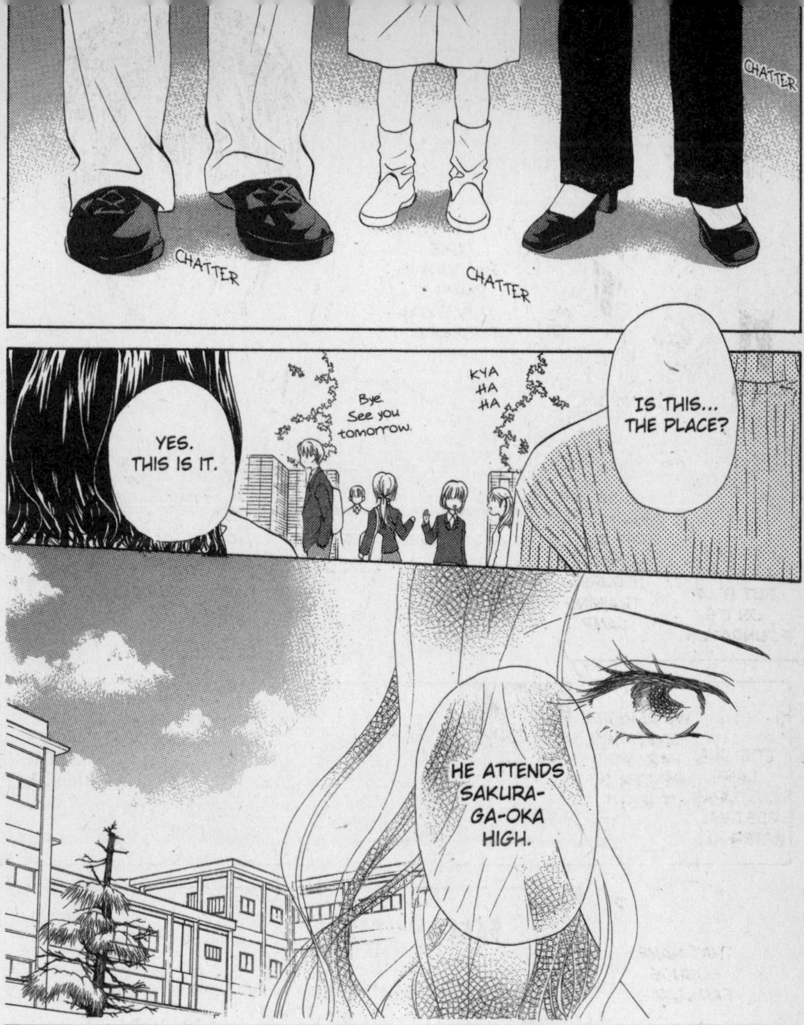
CHATTER
CHATTER
CHATTER
IS THIS... THE PLACE?
KYA HA HA
Bye. See you tomorrow.
YES. THIS IS IT.
HE ATTENDS SAKURA-GA-OKA HIGH.

—Behind the Scenes Story ④—

Sakura-chan makes her appearance again after a long absence! Yes, I enjoyed painting her hair! And Risa, the mother and real backbone of the Narita family, explodes. (Laugh) I really wanted to draw her sweet smiling face. People who can show their real strength at crucial moments are great. I admire that. ♪

She might be reserved most of the time, but she has a hidden strength. A strong person. I bet Mako's father fell in love with that part of her.

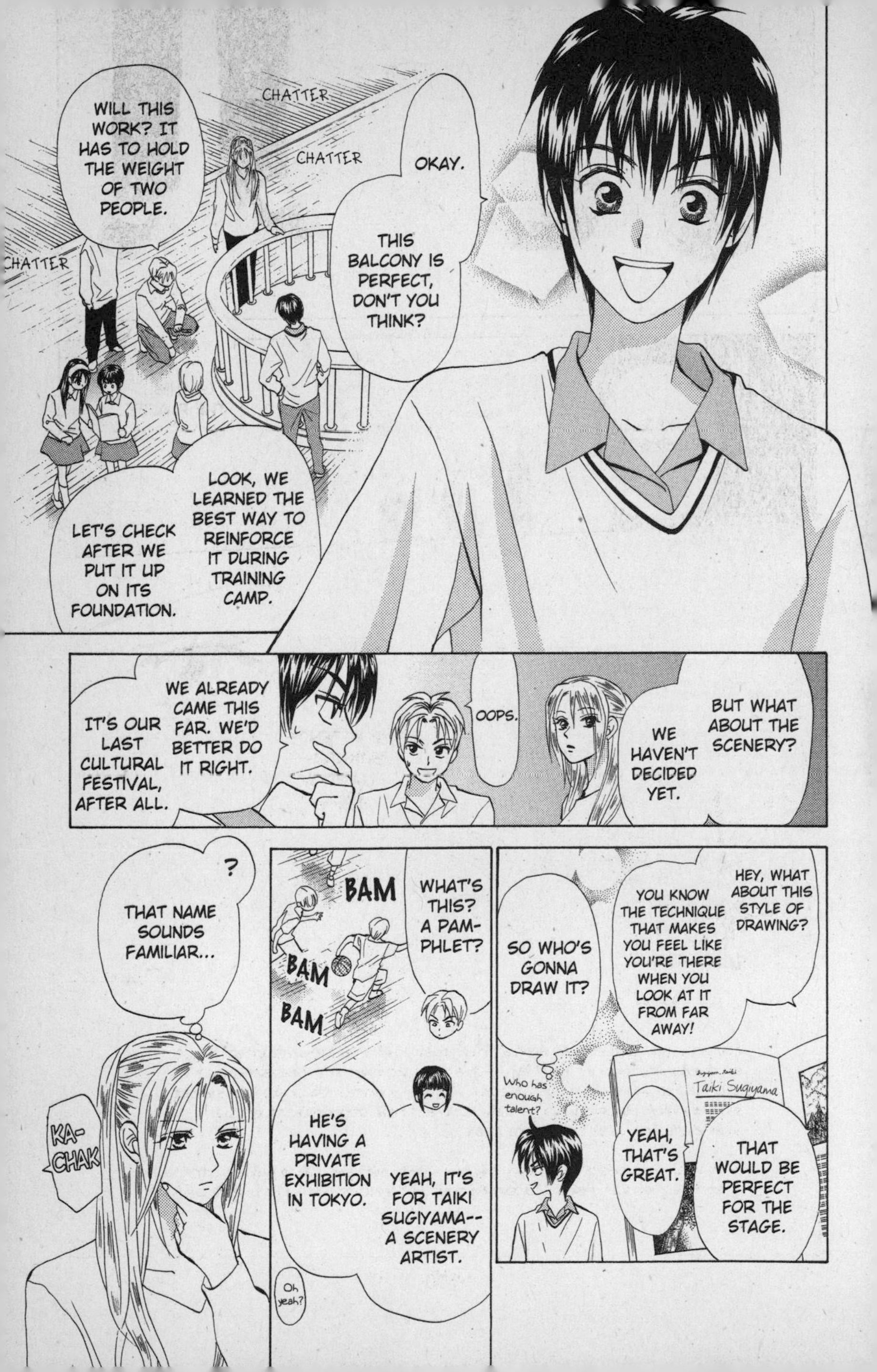
OKAY.
THIS BALCONY IS PERFECT, DON'T YOU THINK?
CHATTER
CHATTER
WILL THIS WORK? IT HAS TO HOLD THE WEIGHT OF TWO PEOPLE.
CHATTER
LOOK, WE LEARNED THE BEST WAY TO REINFORCE IT DURING TRAINING CAMP.
LET'S CHECK AFTER WE PUT IT UP ON ITS FOUNDATION.
BUT WHAT ABOUT THE SCENERY?
WE HAVEN'T DECIDED YET.
OOPS.
WE ALREADY CAME THIS FAR. WE'D BETTER DO IT RIGHT.
IT'S OUR LAST CULTURAL FESTIVAL, AFTER ALL.
HEY, WHAT ABOUT THIS STYLE OF DRAWING?
YOU KNOW THE TECHNIQUE THAT MAKES YOU FEEL LIKE YOU'RE THERE WHEN YOU LOOK AT IT FROM FAR AWAY!
SO WHO'S GONNA DRAW IT?
Who has enough talent?
Taiki Sugiyama
THAT WOULD BE PERFECT FOR THE STAGE.
YEAH, THAT'S GREAT.
BAM
WHAT'S THIS? A PAMPHLET?
BAM
BAM
YEAH, IT'S FOR TAIKI SUGIYAMA--A SCENERY ARTIST.
HE'S HAVING A PRIVATE EXHIBITION IN TOKYO.
Oh yeah?
?
THAT NAME SOUNDS FAMILIAR...
KA-CHAK

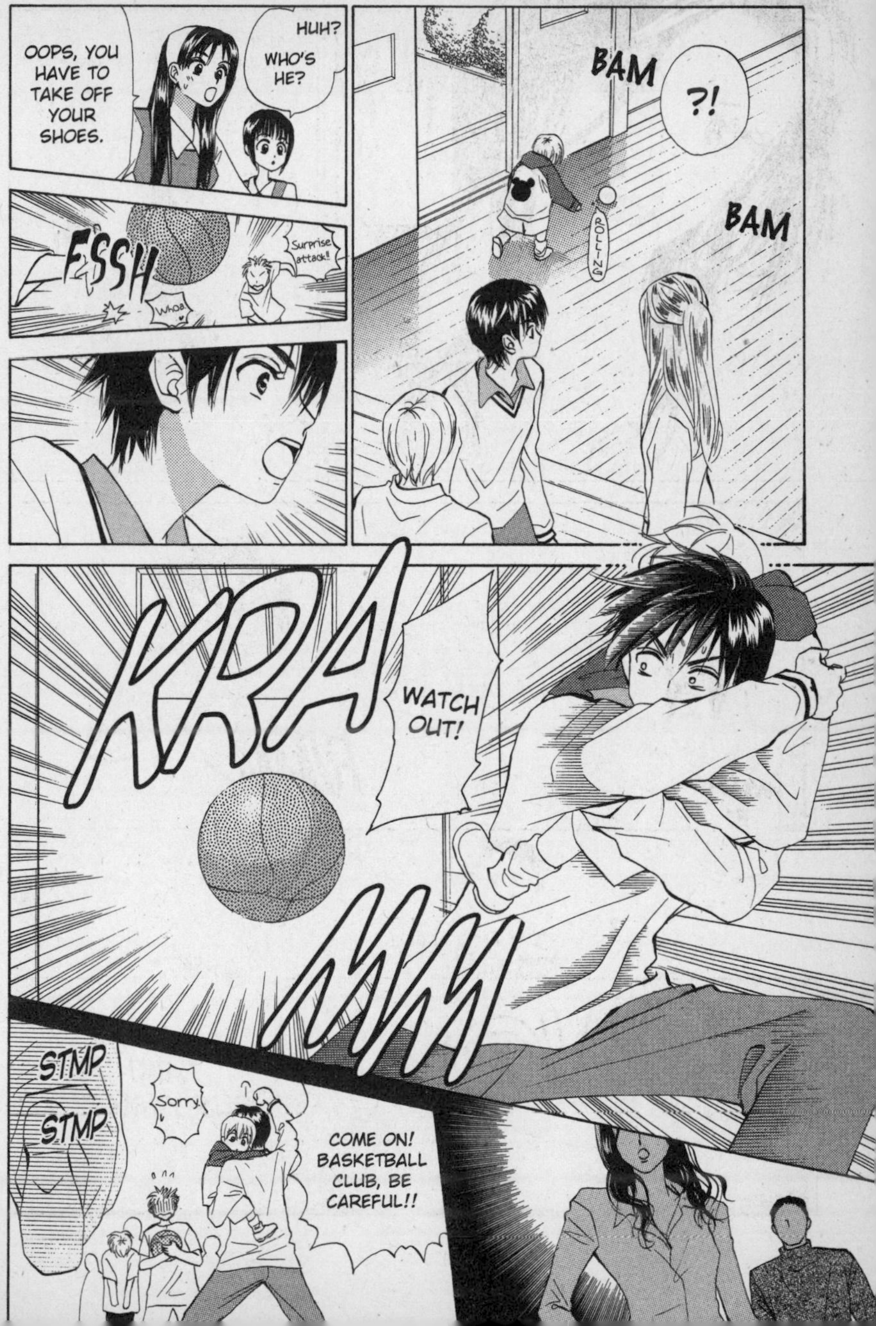
BAM
?!
ROLLING
BAM
HUH?
WHO'S HE?
OOPS, YOU HAVE TO TAKE OFF YOUR SHOES.
Surprise attack!!
FSSH
Whoa
WATCH OUT!
KRA
MMM
COME ON! BASKETBALL CLUB, BE CAREFUL!!
Sorry.
STMP
STMP

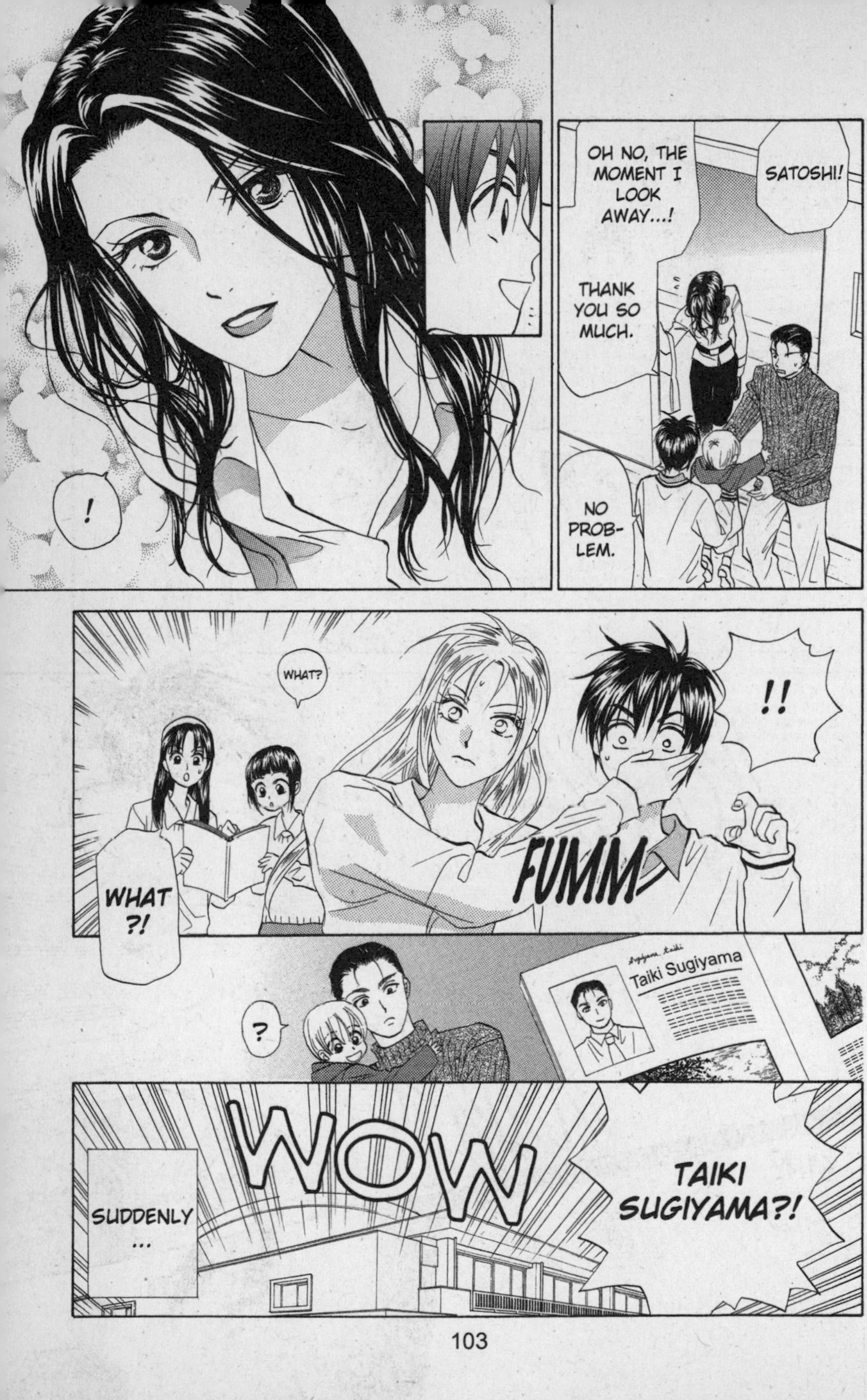
SATOSHI!
OH NO, THE MOMENT I LOOK AWAY...!
THANK YOU SO MUCH.
NO PROBLEM.
!
!!
WHAT?
FUMM
WHAT ?!
Taiki Sugiyama
?
TAIKI SUGIYAMA?!
WOW
SUDDENLY ...

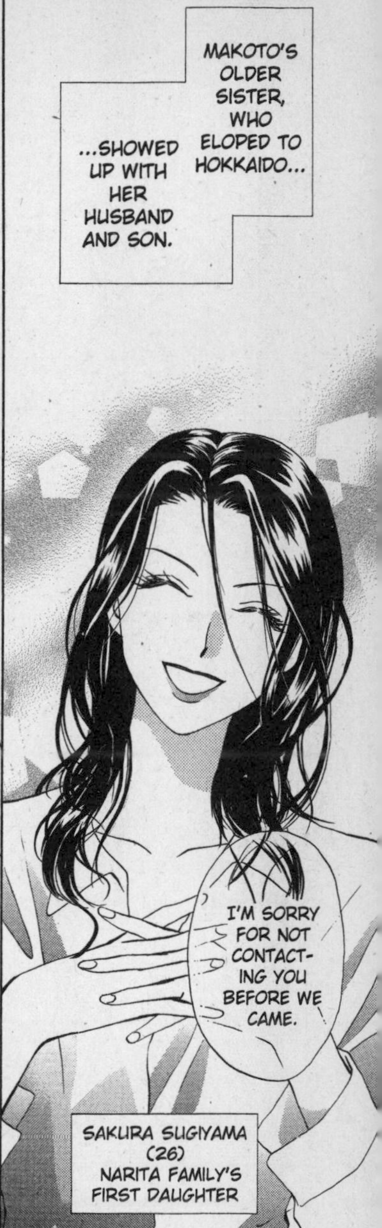
MAKOTO'S OLDER SISTER, WHO ELOPED TO HOKKAIDO...
...SHOWED UP WITH HER HUSBAND AND SON.
I'M SORRY FOR NOT CONTACTING YOU BEFORE WE CAME.
SAKURA SUGIYAMA (26) NARITA FAMILY'S FIRST DAUGHTER

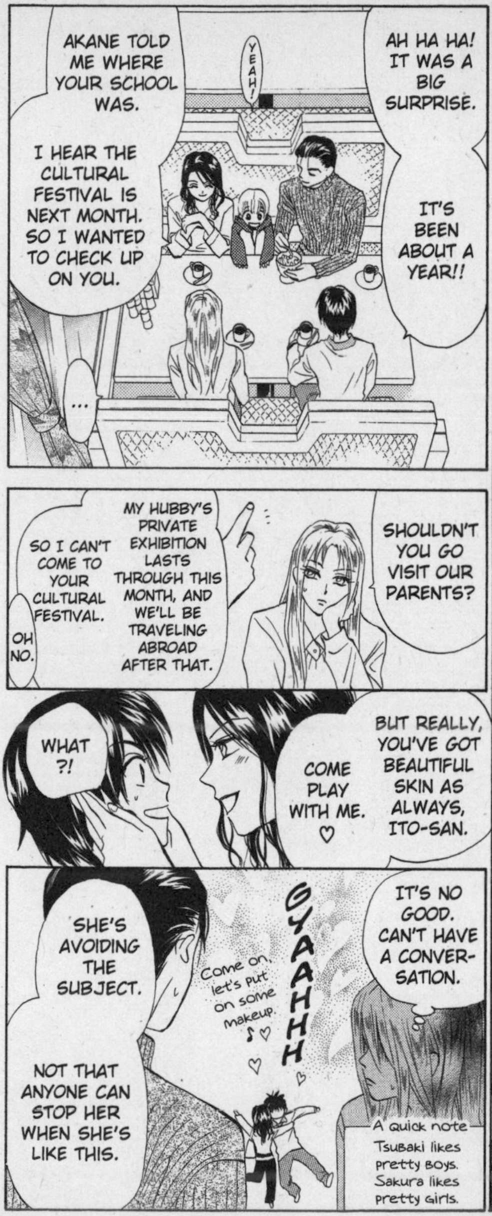
AH HA HA! IT WAS A BIG SURPRISE.
IT'S BEEN ABOUT A YEAR!!
YEAH!
AKANE TOLD ME WHERE YOUR SCHOOL WAS.
I HEAR THE CULTURAL FESTIVAL IS NEXT MONTH. SO I WANTED TO CHECK UP ON YOU.
...
SHOULDN'T YOU GO VISIT OUR PARENTS?
MY HUBBY'S PRIVATE EXHIBITION LASTS THROUGH THIS MONTH, AND WE'LL BE TRAVELING ABROAD AFTER THAT.
SO I CAN'T COME TO YOUR CULTURAL FESTIVAL.
OH NO.
BUT REALLY, YOU'VE GOT BEAUTIFUL SKIN AS ALWAYS, ITO-SAN.
COME PLAY WITH ME. ♡
WHAT?!
IT'S NO GOOD. CAN'T HAVE A CONVERSATION.
GYAAHHH
Come on, let's put on some makeup. ♪♡
SHE'S AVOIDING THE SUBJECT.
NOT THAT ANYONE CAN STOP HER WHEN SHE'S LIKE THIS.
A quick note
Tsubaki likes pretty boys. Sakura likes pretty girls.

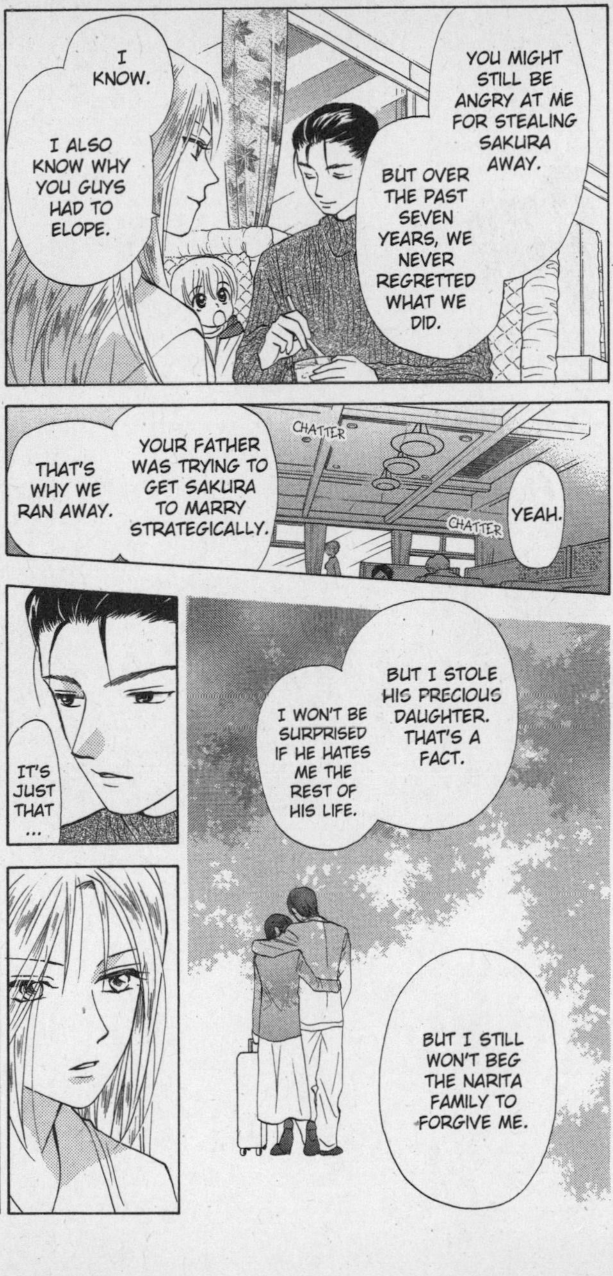
YOU MIGHT STILL BE ANGRY AT ME FOR STEALING SAKURA AWAY.
BUT OVER THE PAST SEVEN YEARS, WE NEVER REGRETTED WHAT WE DID.
I KNOW.
I ALSO KNOW WHY YOU GUYS HAD TO ELOPE.
CHATTER
YEAH.
CHATTER
YOUR FATHER WAS TRYING TO GET SAKURA TO MARRY STRATEGICALLY.
THAT'S WHY WE RAN AWAY.
BUT I STOLE HIS PRECIOUS DAUGHTER. THAT'S A FACT.
I WON'T BE SURPRISED IF HE HATES ME THE REST OF HIS LIFE.
BUT I STILL WON'T BEG THE NARITA FAMILY TO FORGIVE ME.
IT'S JUST THAT ...

When I paint, I use a water soluble pen from Pigma or a Kuretake fountain brush pen. ← Brush pen

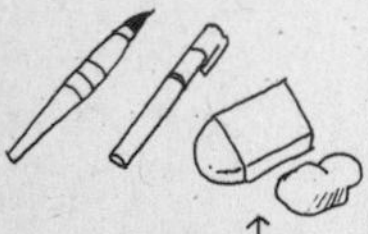

For the eraser I use Nondust and kneaded eraser from Mono.

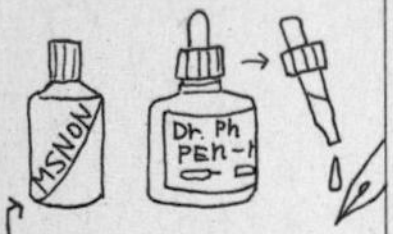
MISNON
Dr. Ph PEN-

For the white liquid paper, I use MISNON (rapid dry type), A-20 and Dr. Martin's Pen White. As for the ink, I use "Sumi no Hana" from Kaimei.

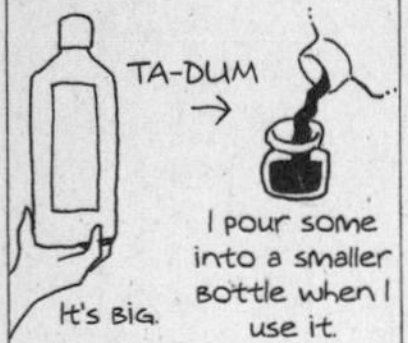
TA-DUM →

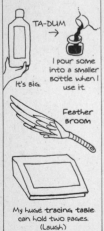

It's big.

I pour some into a smaller bottle when I use it.

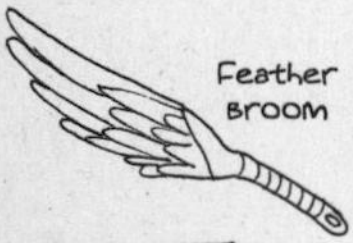

Feather Broom

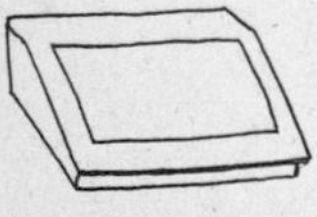

My huge tracing table can hold two pages. (Laugh)

And there's some good extra space on top.

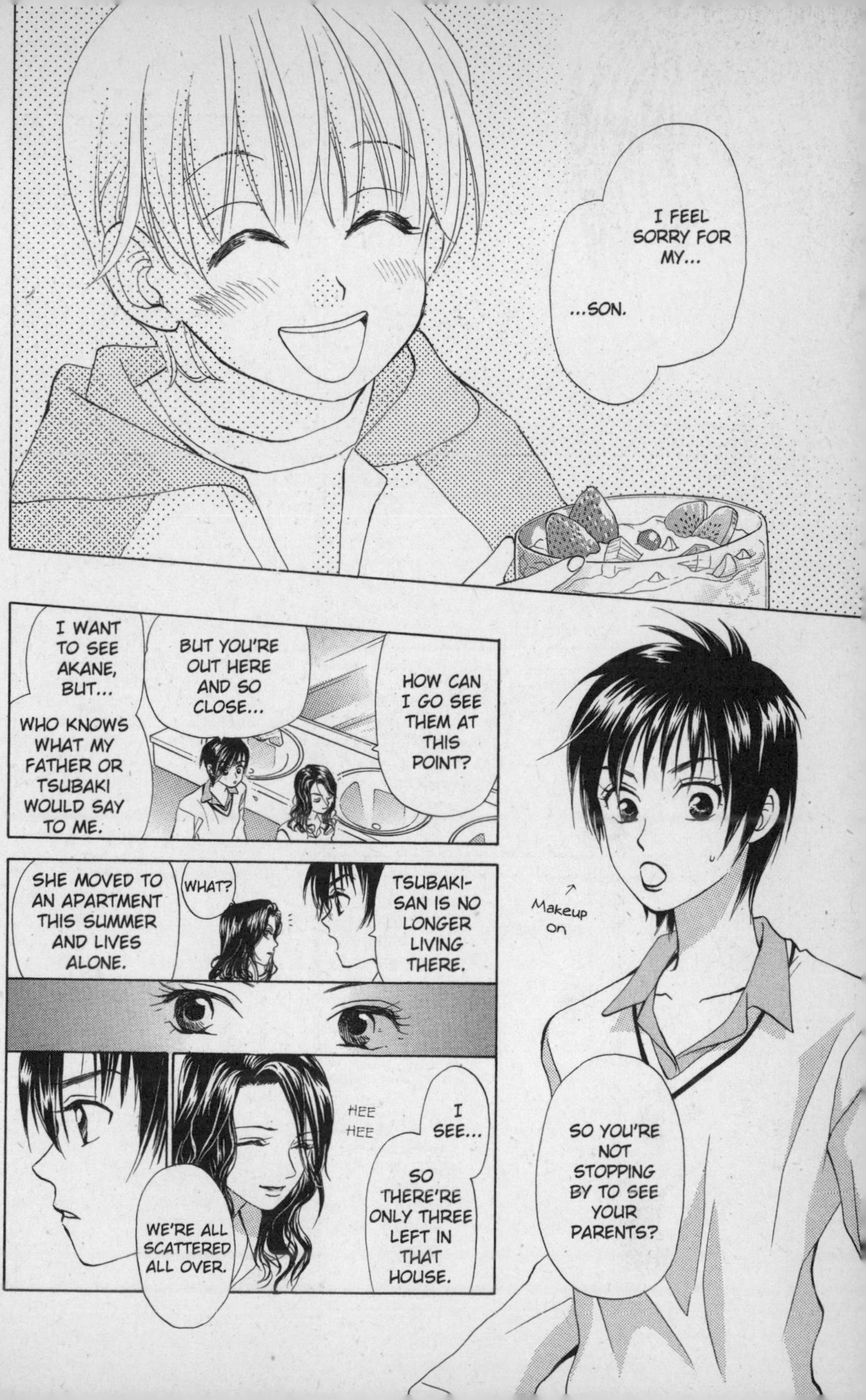
I FEEL SORRY FOR MY...
...SON.
Makeup on
SO YOU'RE NOT STOPPING BY TO SEE YOUR PARENTS?
HOW CAN I GO SEE THEM AT THIS POINT?
BUT YOU'RE OUT HERE AND SO CLOSE...
I WANT TO SEE AKANE, BUT...
WHO KNOWS WHAT MY FATHER OR TSUBAKI WOULD SAY TO ME.
TSUBAKI-SAN IS NO LONGER LIVING THERE.
WHAT?
SHE MOVED TO AN APARTMENT THIS SUMMER AND LIVES ALONE.
I SEE...
SO THERE'RE ONLY THREE LEFT IN THAT HOUSE.
HEE HEE
WE'RE ALL SCATTERED ALL OVER.

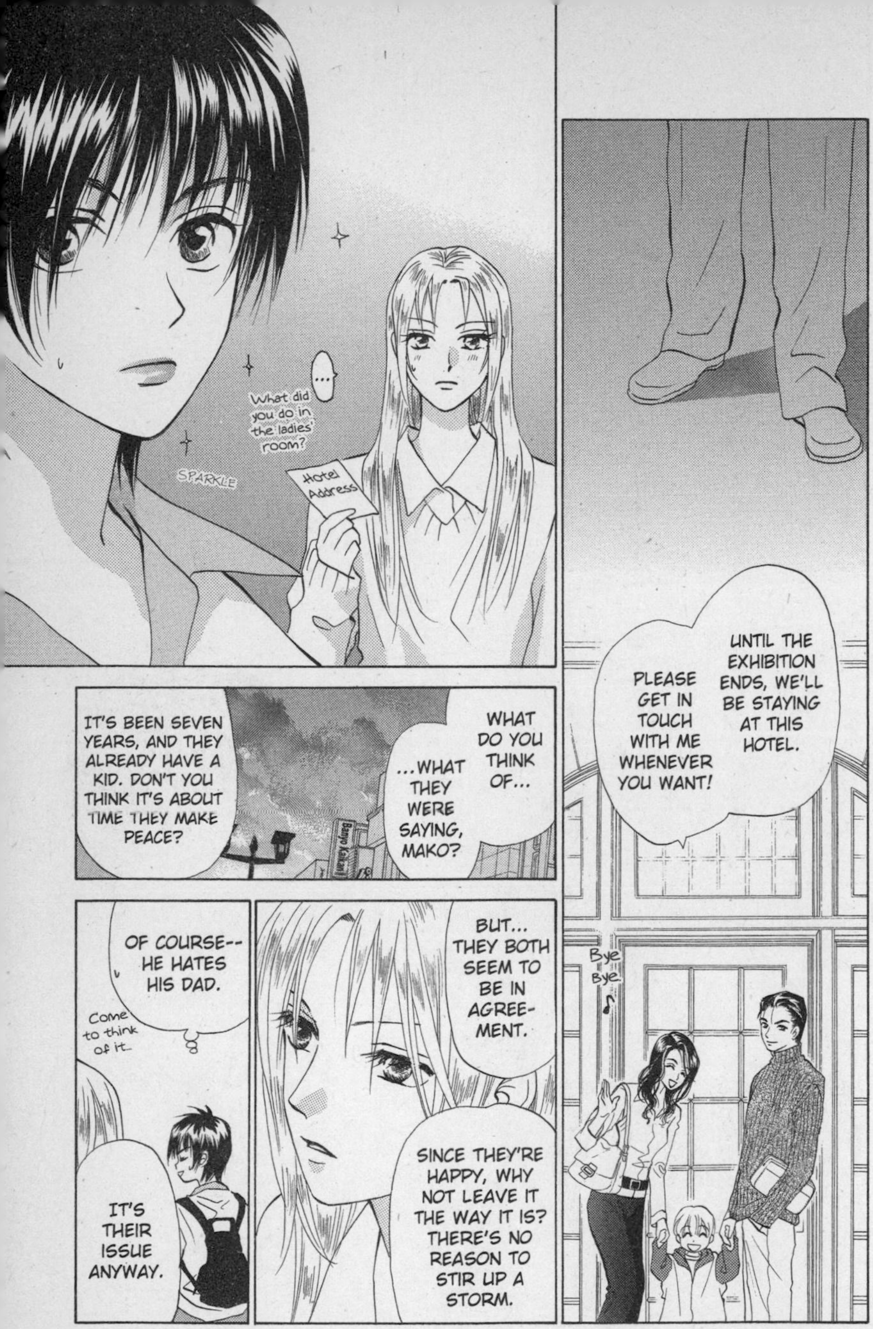
UNTIL THE EXHIBITION ENDS, WE'LL BE STAYING AT THIS HOTEL.
PLEASE GET IN TOUCH WITH ME WHENEVER YOU WANT!
Bye Bye
...
What did you do in the ladies' room?
SPARKLE
Hotel Address
WHAT DO YOU THINK OF...
...WHAT THEY WERE SAYING, MAKO?
IT'S BEEN SEVEN YEARS, AND THEY ALREADY HAVE A KID. DON'T YOU THINK IT'S ABOUT TIME THEY MAKE PEACE?
BUT... THEY BOTH SEEM TO BE IN AGREE-MENT.
SINCE THEY'RE HAPPY, WHY NOT LEAVE IT THE WAY IT IS? THERE'S NO REASON TO STIR UP A STORM.
OF COURSE-- HE HATES HIS DAD.
Come to think of it...
IT'S THEIR ISSUE ANYWAY.

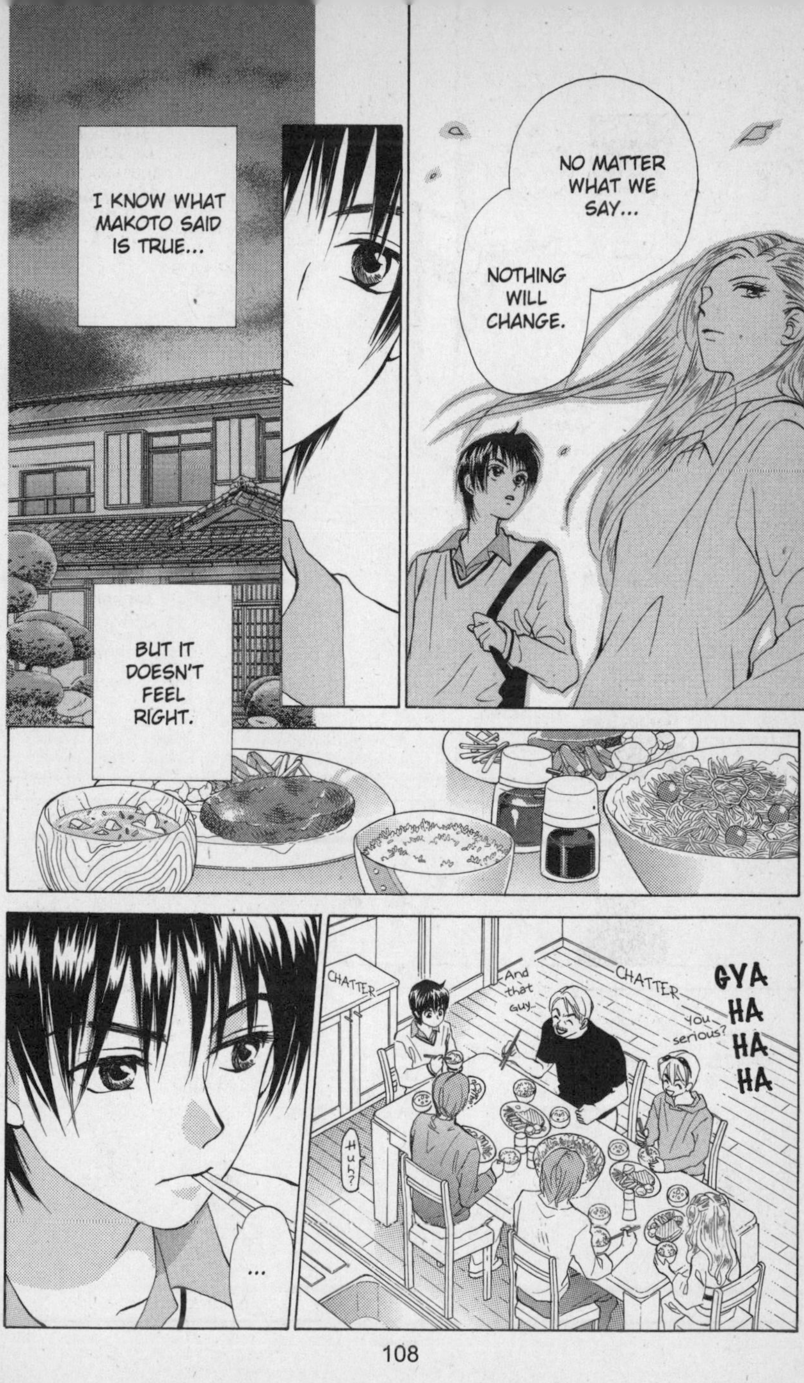
NO MATTER WHAT WE SAY...
NOTHING WILL CHANGE.
I KNOW WHAT MAKOTO SAID IS TRUE...
BUT IT DOESN'T FEEL RIGHT.
GYA HA HA HA
CHATTER
You serious?
And that guy...
CHATTER
Huh?
...

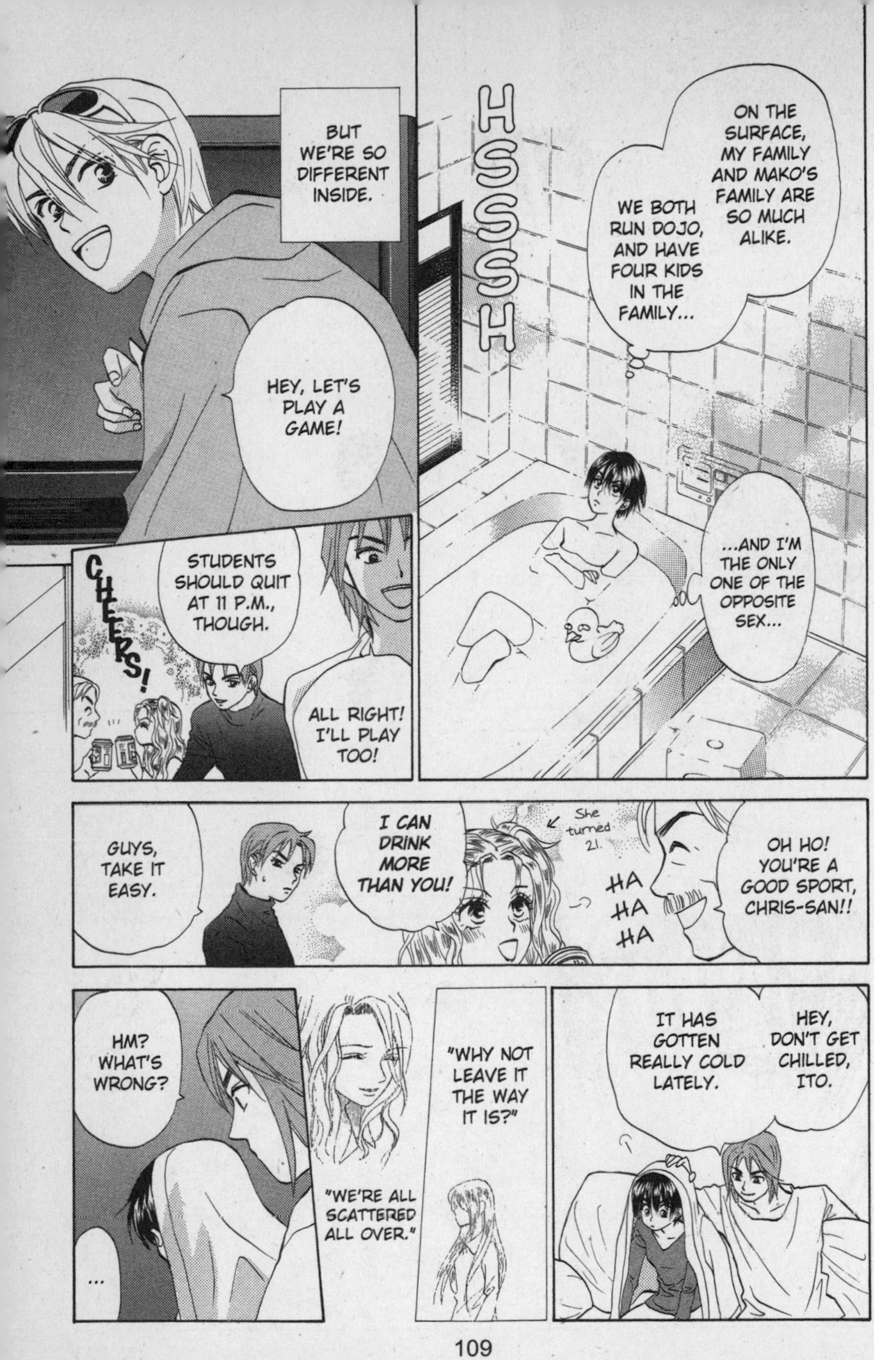
HSSSH
ON THE SURFACE, MY FAMILY AND MAKO'S FAMILY ARE SO MUCH ALIKE.
WE BOTH RUN DOJO, AND HAVE FOUR KIDS IN THE FAMILY...
...AND I'M THE ONLY ONE OF THE OPPOSITE SEX...
BUT WE'RE SO DIFFERENT INSIDE.
HEY, LET'S PLAY A GAME!
STUDENTS SHOULD QUIT AT 11 P.M., THOUGH.
ALL RIGHT! I'LL PLAY TOO!
CHEERS!
OH HO! YOU'RE A GOOD SPORT, CHRIS-SAN!!
HA HA HA
She turned 21.
I CAN DRINK MORE THAN YOU!
GUYS, TAKE IT EASY.
HEY, DON'T GET CHILLED, ITO.
IT HAS GOTTEN REALLY COLD LATELY.
"WHY NOT LEAVE IT THE WAY IT IS?"
"WE'RE ALL SCATTERED ALL OVER."
HM? WHAT'S WRONG?
...

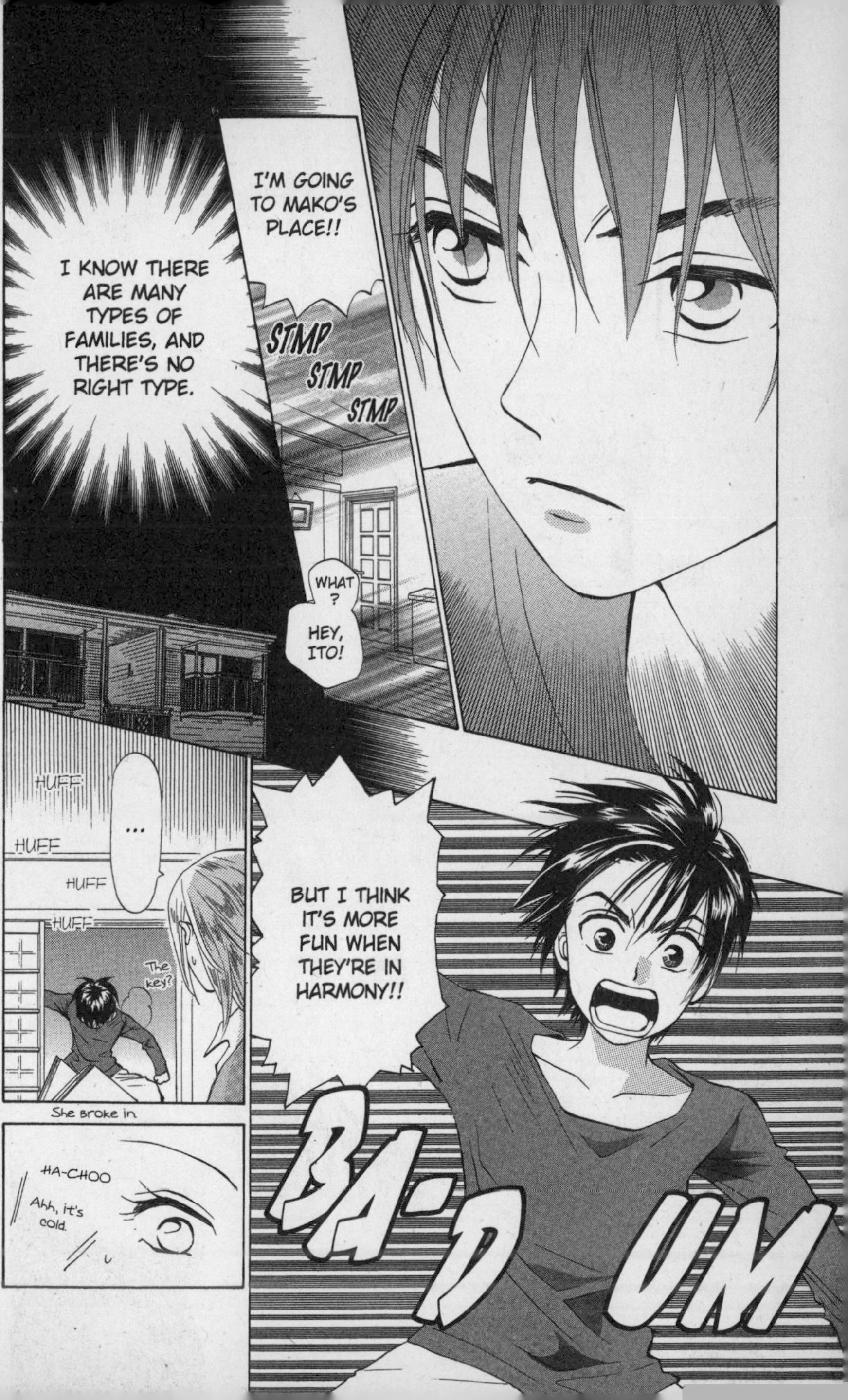
I'M GOING TO MAKO'S PLACE!!
STMP STMP STMP
WHAT?
HEY, ITO!
I KNOW THERE ARE MANY TYPES OF FAMILIES, AND THERE'S NO RIGHT TYPE.
BUT I THINK IT'S MORE FUN WHEN THEY'RE IN HARMONY!!
BA-DUM
HUFF HUFF HUFF HUFF
...
The key?
She broke in.
HA-CHOO
Ahh, it's cold.

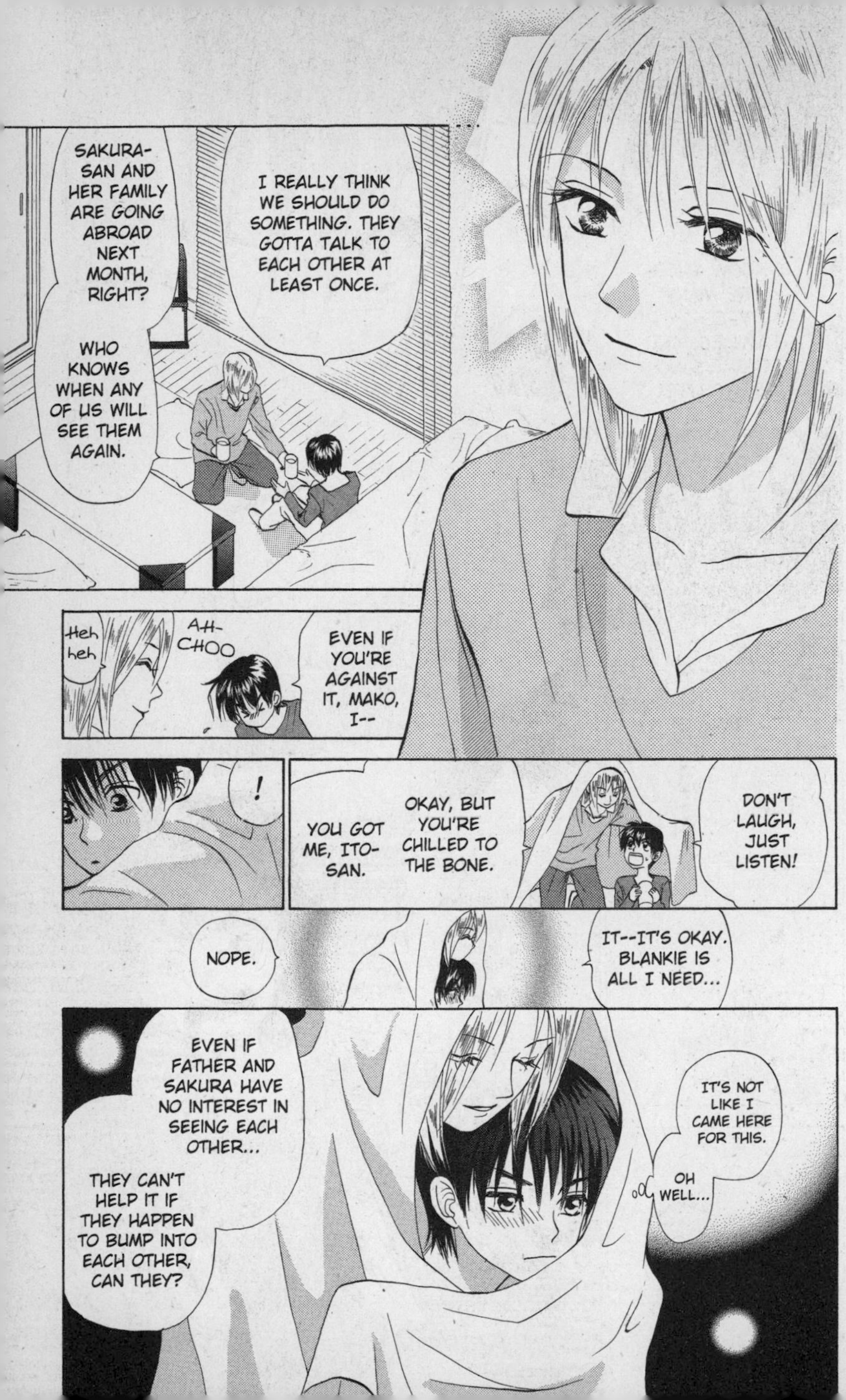
...
I REALLY THINK WE SHOULD DO SOMETHING. THEY GOTTA TALK TO EACH OTHER AT LEAST ONCE.
SAKURA-SAN AND HER FAMILY ARE GOING ABROAD NEXT MONTH, RIGHT?
WHO KNOWS WHEN ANY OF US WILL SEE THEM AGAIN.
EVEN IF YOU'RE AGAINST IT, MAKO, I--
AH-CHOO
Heh heh
DON'T LAUGH, JUST LISTEN!
OKAY, BUT YOU'RE CHILLED TO THE BONE.
YOU GOT ME, ITO-SAN.
!
IT--IT'S OKAY. BLANKIE IS ALL I NEED...
NOPE.
IT'S NOT LIKE I CAME HERE FOR THIS.
OH WELL...
EVEN IF FATHER AND SAKURA HAVE NO INTEREST IN SEEING EACH OTHER...
THEY CAN'T HELP IT IF THEY HAPPEN TO BUMP INTO EACH OTHER, CAN THEY?

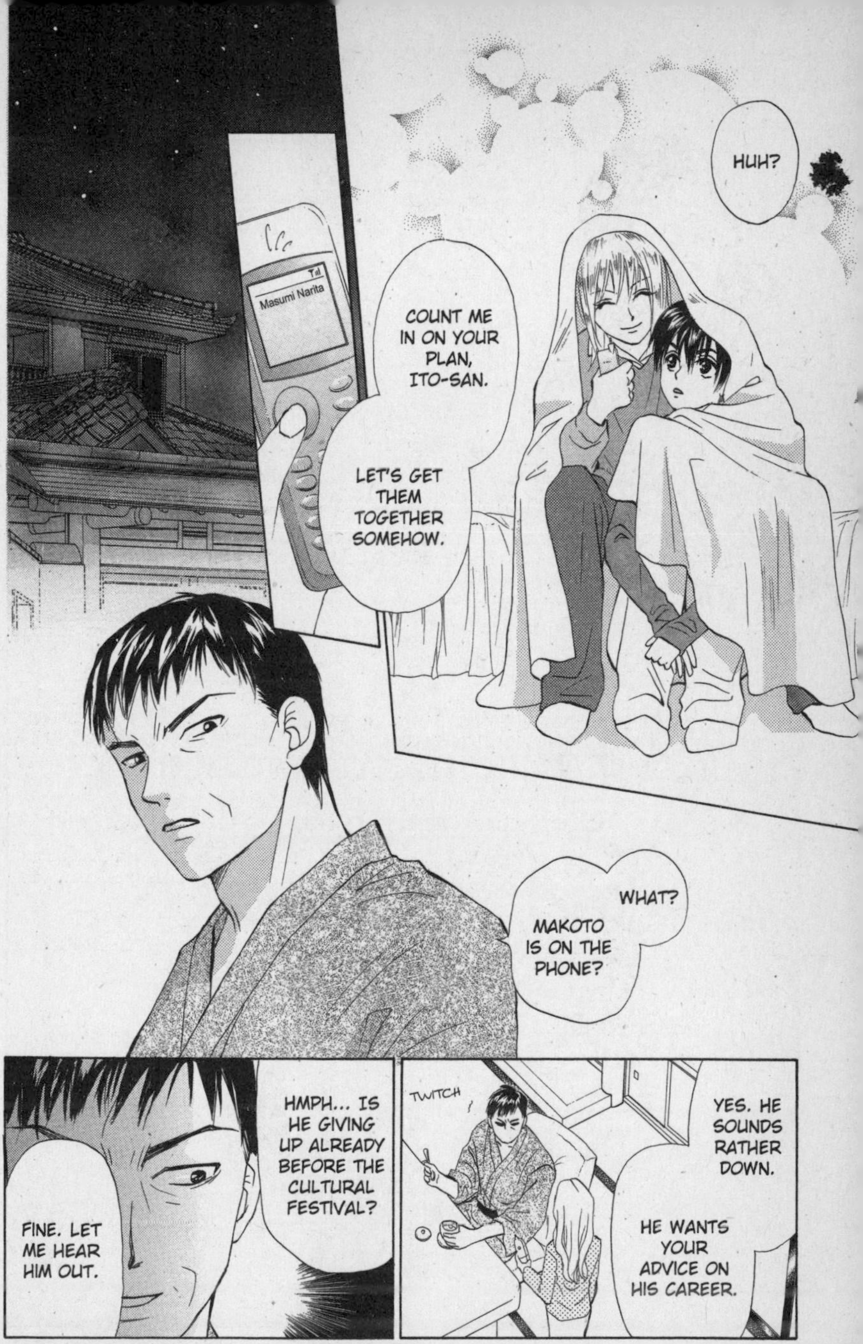
HUH?
COUNT ME IN ON YOUR PLAN, ITO-SAN.
LET'S GET THEM TOGETHER SOMEHOW.
Masumi Narita
WHAT? MAKOTO IS ON THE PHONE?
YES. HE SOUNDS RATHER DOWN.
HE WANTS YOUR ADVICE ON HIS CAREER.
TWITCH
HMPH... IS HE GIVING UP ALREADY BEFORE THE CULTURAL FESTIVAL?
FINE. LET ME HEAR HIM OUT.

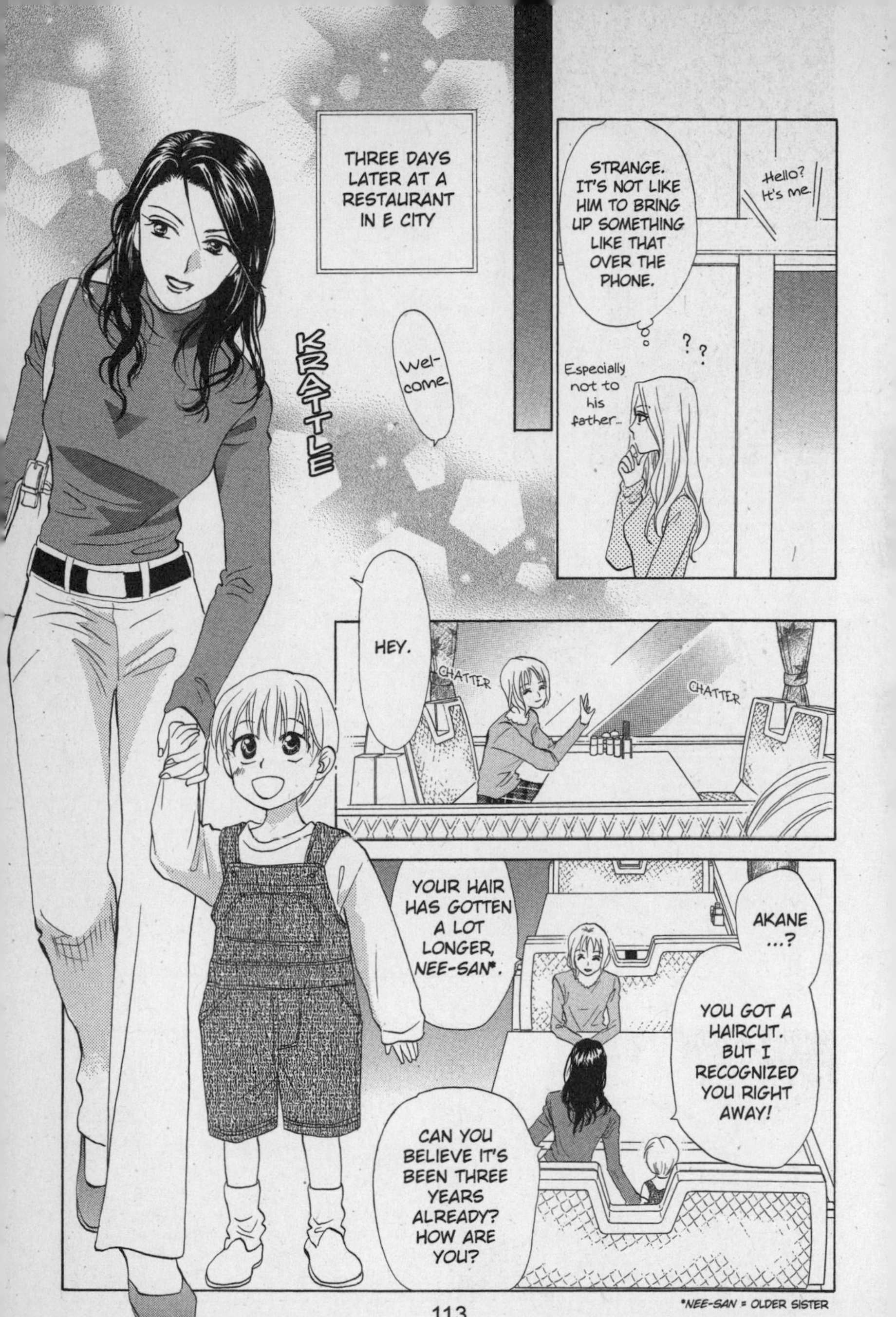
Hello? It's me.
STRANGE. IT'S NOT LIKE HIM TO BRING UP SOMETHING LIKE THAT OVER THE PHONE.
? ?
Especially not to his father...
THREE DAYS LATER AT A RESTAURANT IN E CITY
Wel-come.
KRATTLE
HEY.
CHATTER
CHATTER
AKANE ...?
YOU GOT A HAIRCUT. BUT I RECOGNIZED YOU RIGHT AWAY!
YOUR HAIR HAS GOTTEN A LOT LONGER, NEE-SAN*.
CAN YOU BELIEVE IT'S BEEN THREE YEARS ALREADY? HOW ARE YOU?

*NEE-SAN = OLDER SISTER

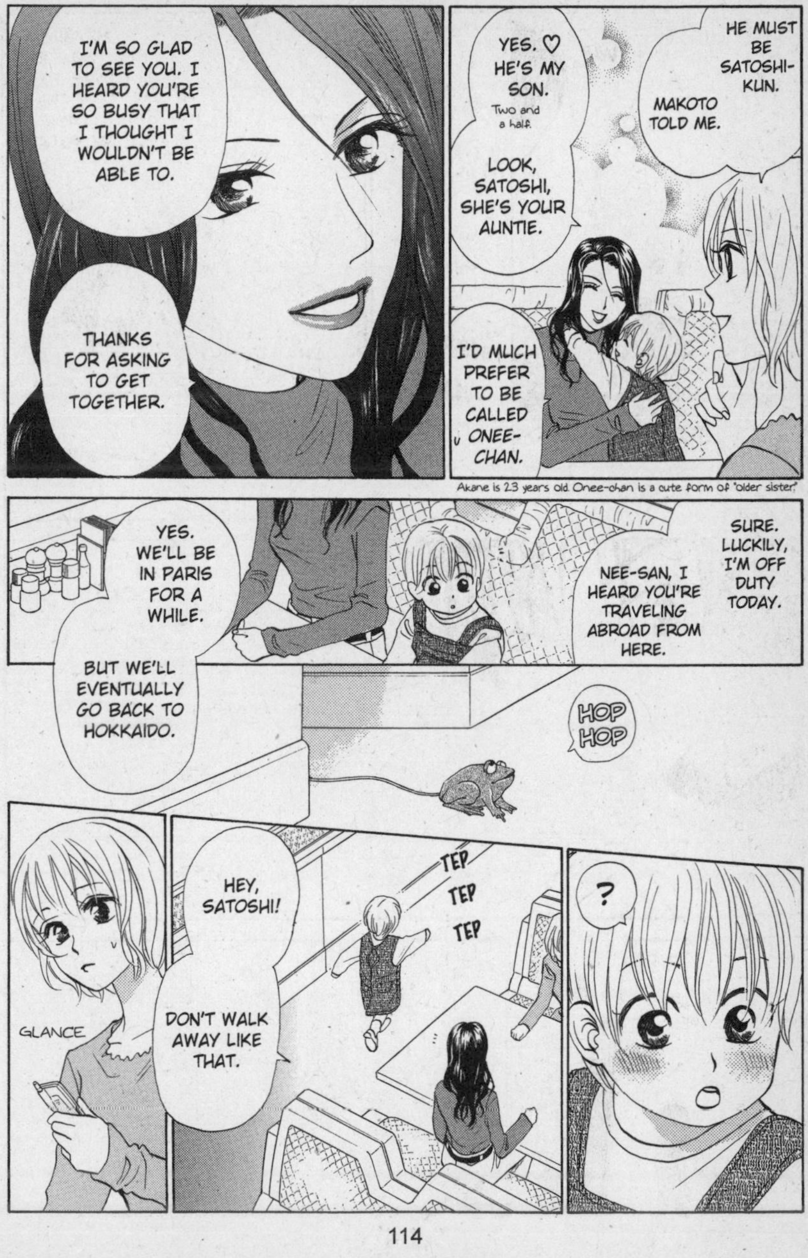
HE MUST BE SATOSHI-KUN.
MAKOTO TOLD ME.
YES. ♡ HE'S MY SON.
Two and a half.
LOOK, SATOSHI, SHE'S YOUR AUNTIE.
I'D MUCH PREFER TO BE CALLED ONEE-CHAN.
I'M SO GLAD TO SEE YOU. I HEARD YOU'RE SO BUSY THAT I THOUGHT I WOULDN'T BE ABLE TO.
THANKS FOR ASKING TO GET TOGETHER.
SURE. LUCKILY, I'M OFF DUTY TODAY.
NEE-SAN, I HEARD YOU'RE TRAVELING ABROAD FROM HERE.
YES. WE'LL BE IN PARIS FOR A WHILE.
BUT WE'LL EVENTUALLY GO BACK TO HOKKAIDO.
HOP HOP
?
TEP TEP TEP
HEY, SATOSHI!
DON'T WALK AWAY LIKE THAT.
GLANCE

Akane is 23 years old. Onee-chan is a cute form of "older sister."

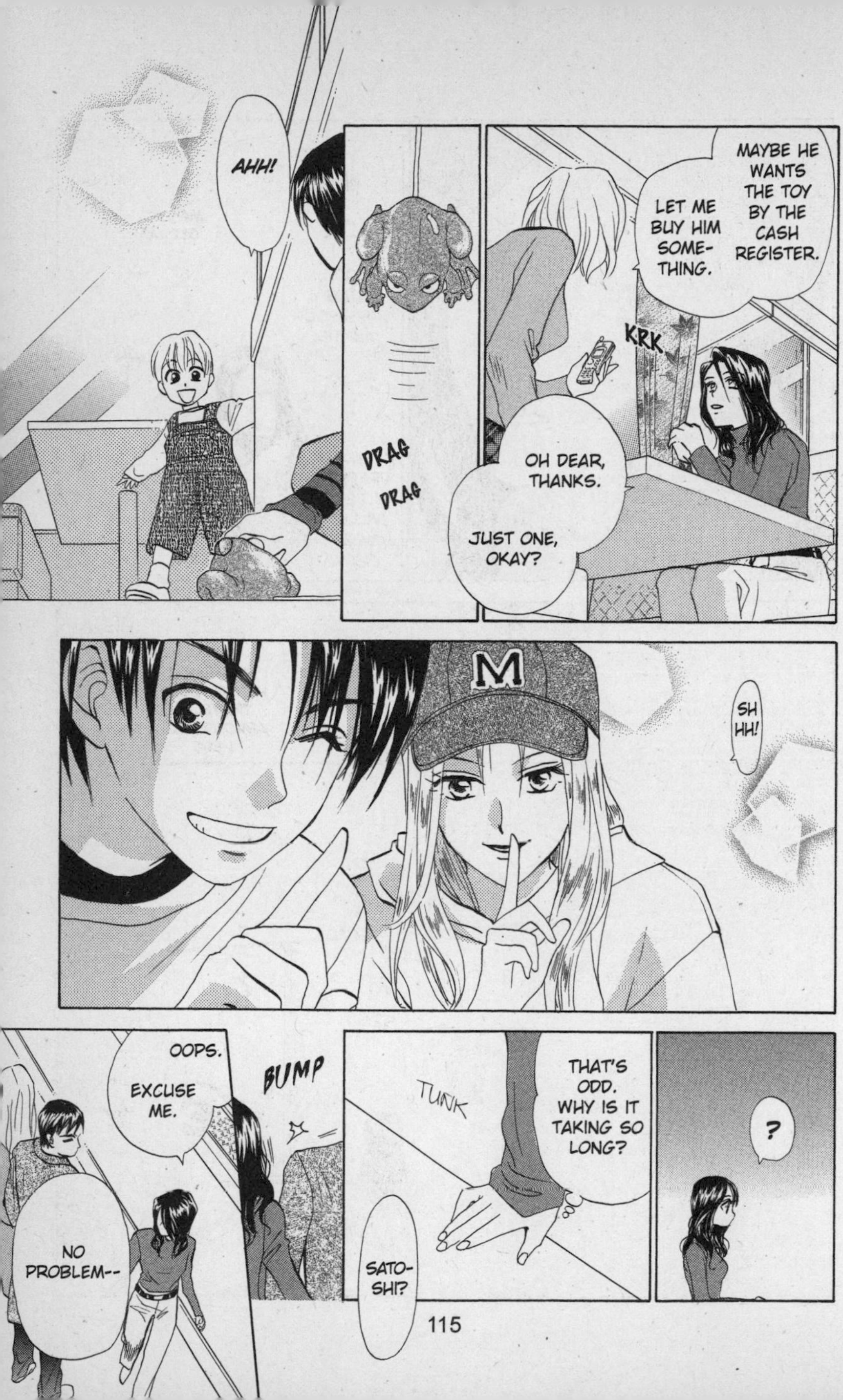
MAYBE HE WANTS THE TOY BY THE CASH REGISTER.
LET ME BUY HIM SOME-THING.
KRK
OH DEAR, THANKS.
JUST ONE, OKAY?
DRAG
DRAG
AHH!
SHHH!
?
THAT'S ODD. WHY IS IT TAKING SO LONG?
TUNK
SATO-SHI?
OOPS.
EXCUSE ME.
BUMP
NO PROBLEM--

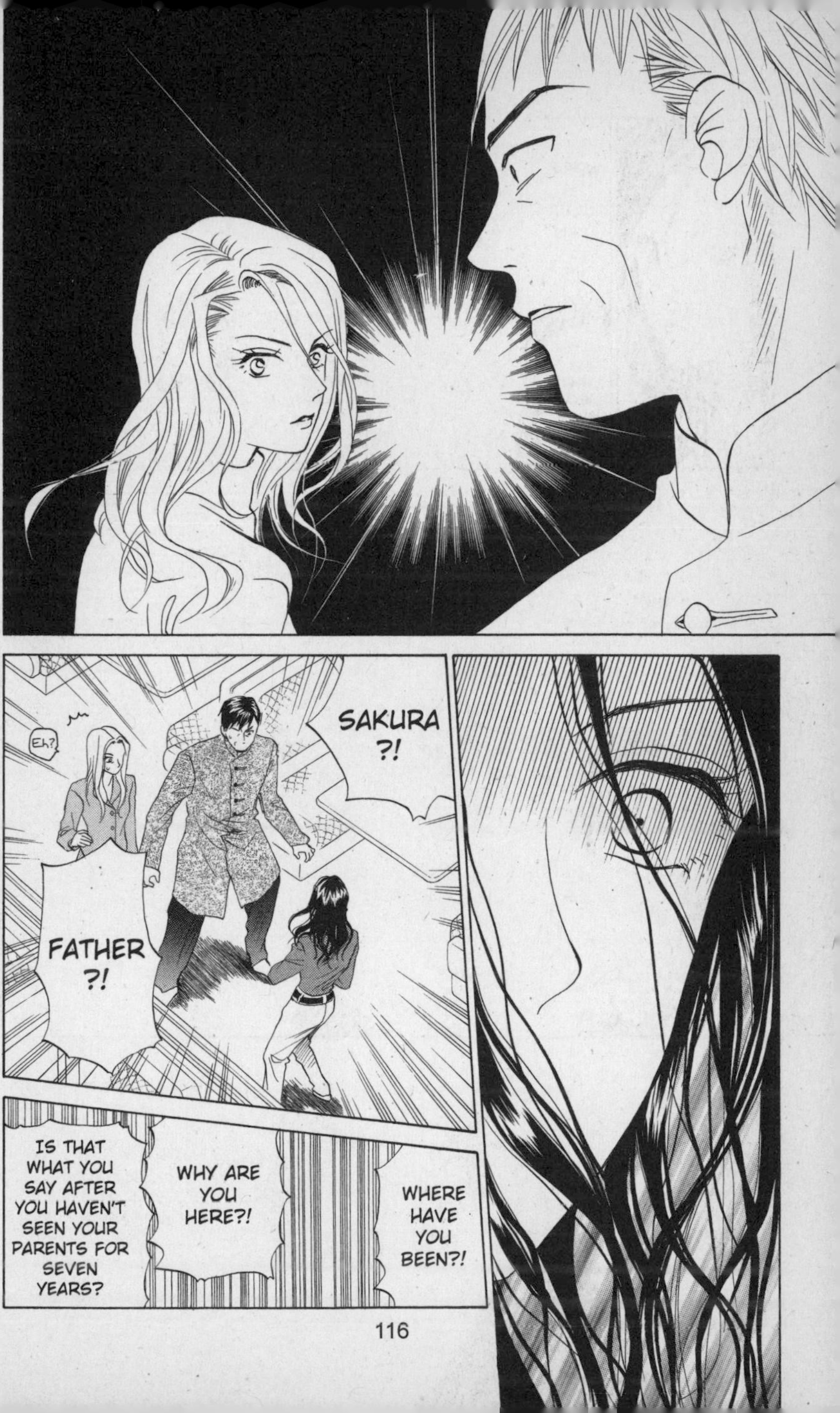
SAKURA ?!
Eh?
FATHER ?!
WHERE HAVE YOU BEEN?!
WHY ARE YOU HERE?!
IS THAT WHAT YOU SAY AFTER YOU HAVEN'T SEEN YOUR PARENTS FOR SEVEN YEARS?

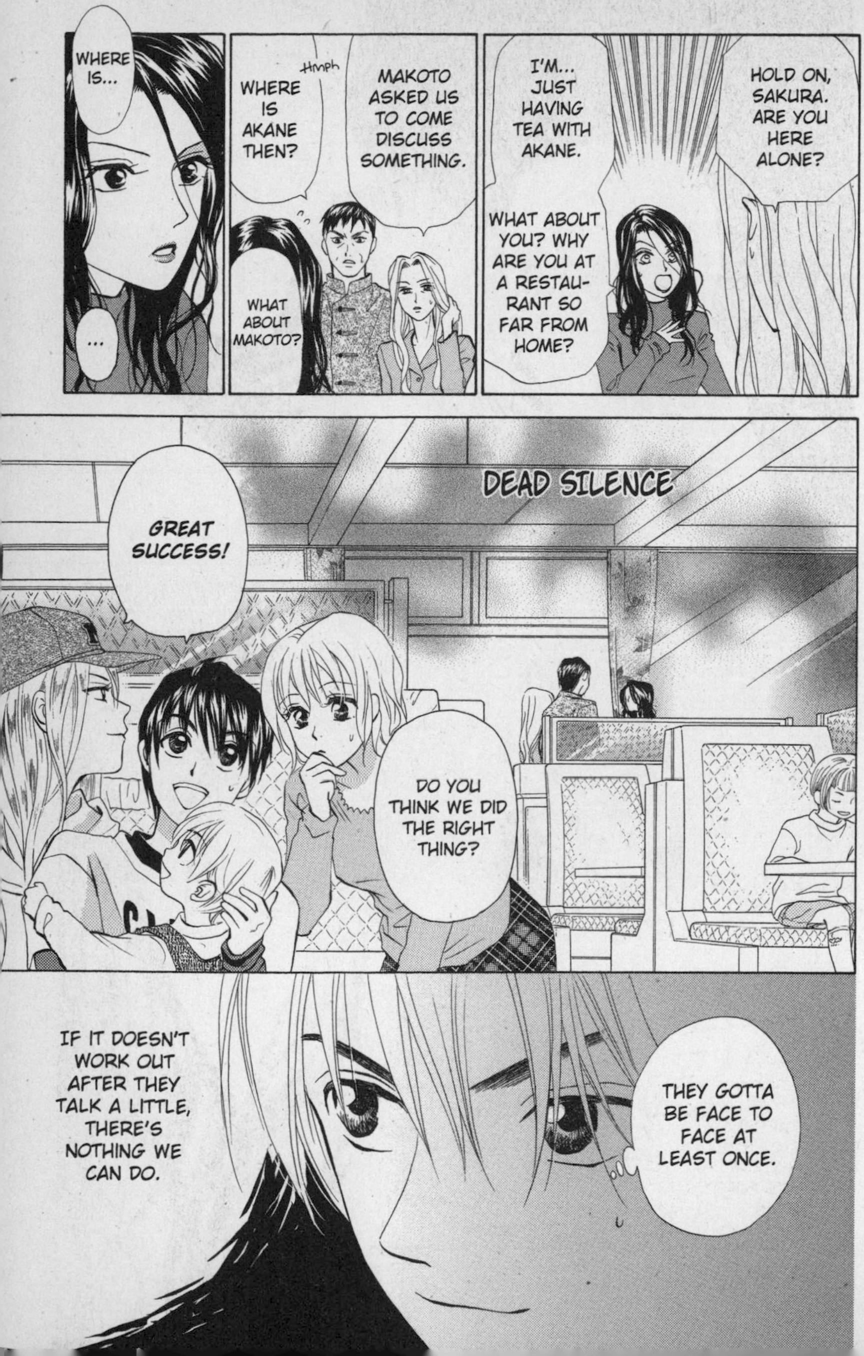
HOLD ON, SAKURA. ARE YOU HERE ALONE?
I'M... JUST HAVING TEA WITH AKANE.
WHAT ABOUT YOU? WHY ARE YOU AT A RESTAURANT SO FAR FROM HOME?
MAKOTO ASKED US TO COME DISCUSS SOMETHING.
Hmph
WHERE IS AKANE THEN?
WHAT ABOUT MAKOTO?
WHERE IS...
...
DEAD SILENCE
DO YOU THINK WE DID THE RIGHT THING?
GREAT SUCCESS!
THEY GOTTA BE FACE TO FACE AT LEAST ONCE.
IF IT DOESN'T WORK OUT AFTER THEY TALK A LITTLE, THERE'S NOTHING WE CAN DO.

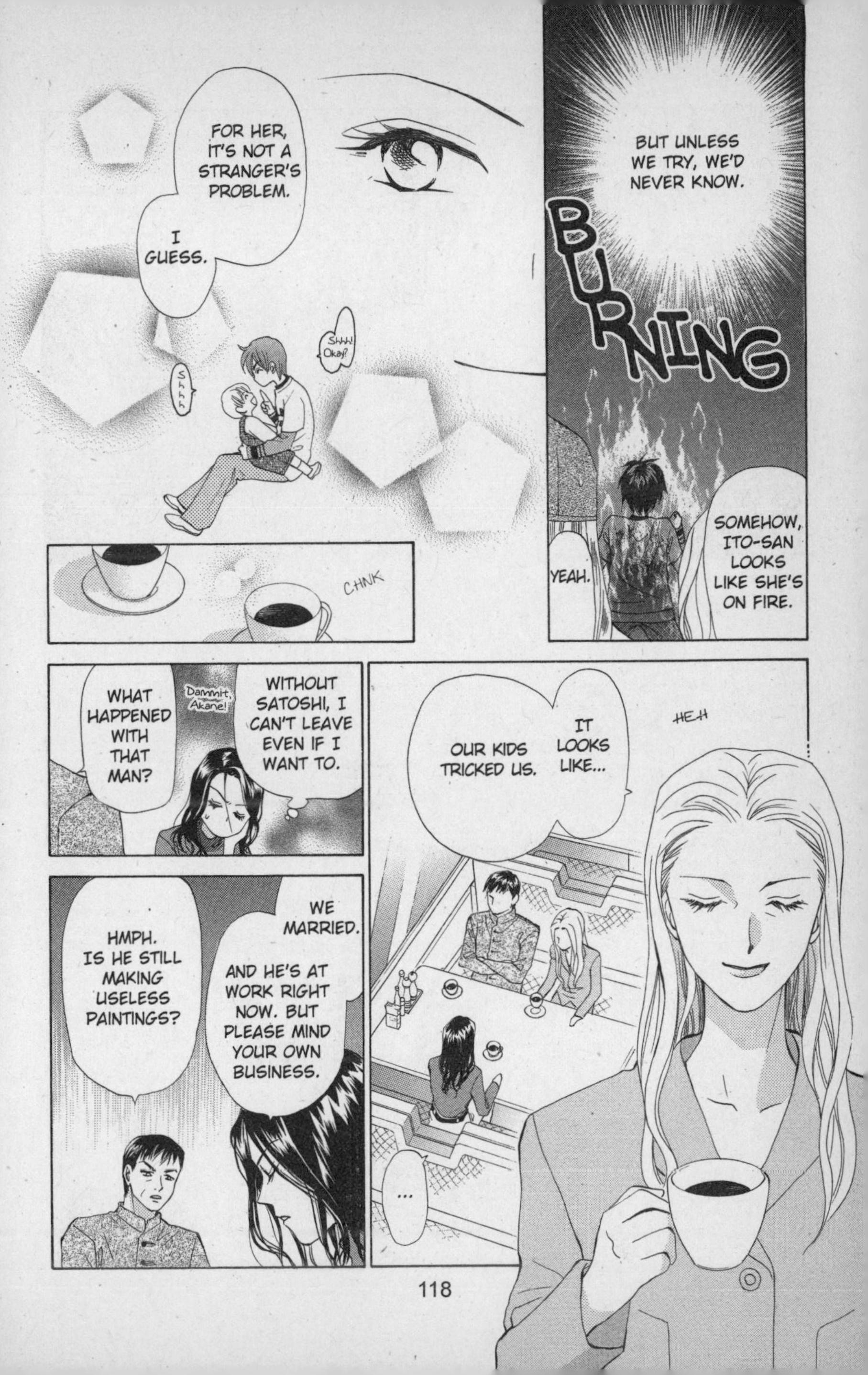
BUT UNLESS WE TRY, WE'D NEVER KNOW.
BURNING
SOMEHOW, ITO-SAN LOOKS LIKE SHE'S ON FIRE.
YEAH.
FOR HER, IT'S NOT A STRANGER'S PROBLEM.
I GUESS.
Shhh! Okay?
Shhh
CHNK
IT LOOKS LIKE...
OUR KIDS TRICKED US.
HEH
...
WITHOUT SATOSHI, I CAN'T LEAVE EVEN IF I WANT TO.
Dammit, Akane!
WHAT HAPPENED WITH THAT MAN?
WE MARRIED.
AND HE'S AT WORK RIGHT NOW. BUT PLEASE MIND YOUR OWN BUSINESS.
HMPH. IS HE STILL MAKING USELESS PAINTINGS?

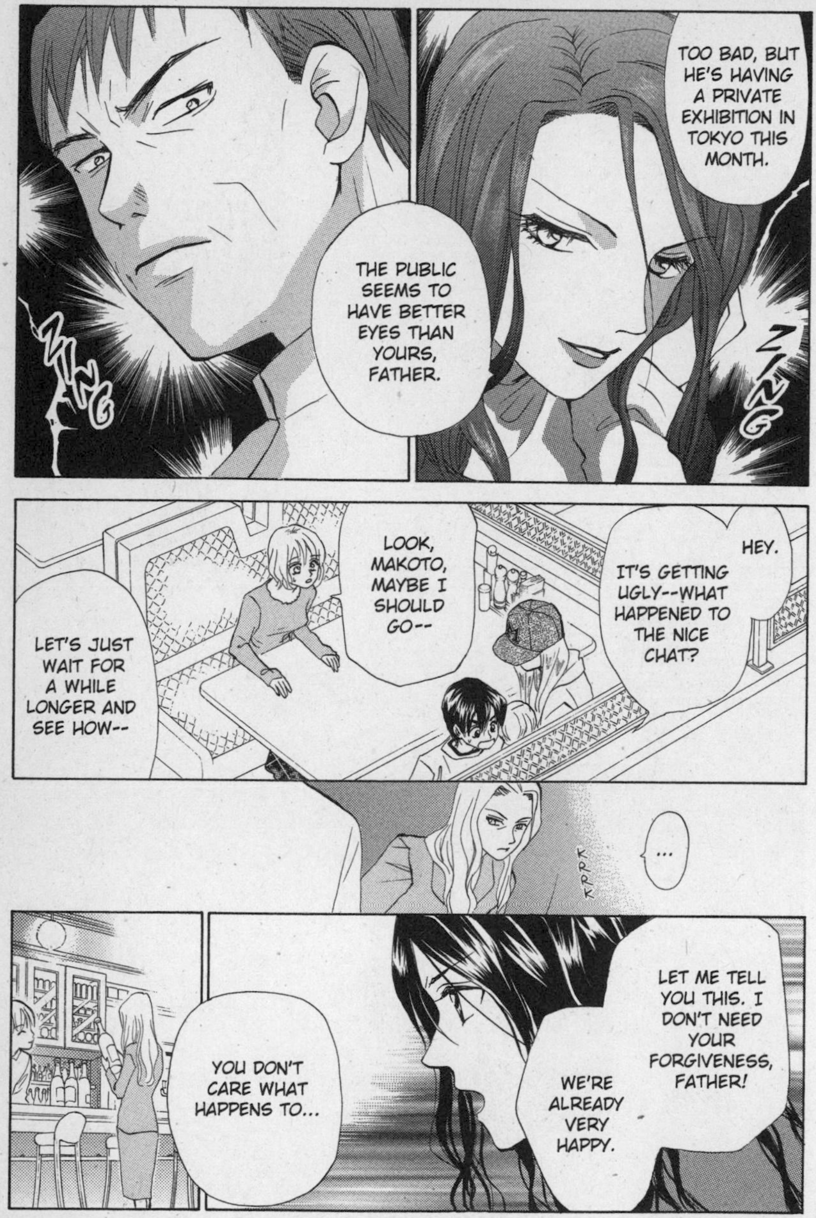
TOO BAD, BUT HE'S HAVING A PRIVATE EXHIBITION IN TOKYO THIS MONTH.
THE PUBLIC SEEMS TO HAVE BETTER EYES THAN YOURS, FATHER.
ZING
ZING
HEY.
IT'S GETTING UGLY--WHAT HAPPENED TO THE NICE CHAT?
LOOK, MAKOTO, MAYBE I SHOULD GO--
LET'S JUST WAIT FOR A WHILE LONGER AND SEE HOW--
...
KRRK
LET ME TELL YOU THIS. I DON'T NEED YOUR FORGIVENESS, FATHER!
WE'RE ALREADY VERY HAPPY.
YOU DON'T CARE WHAT HAPPENS TO...

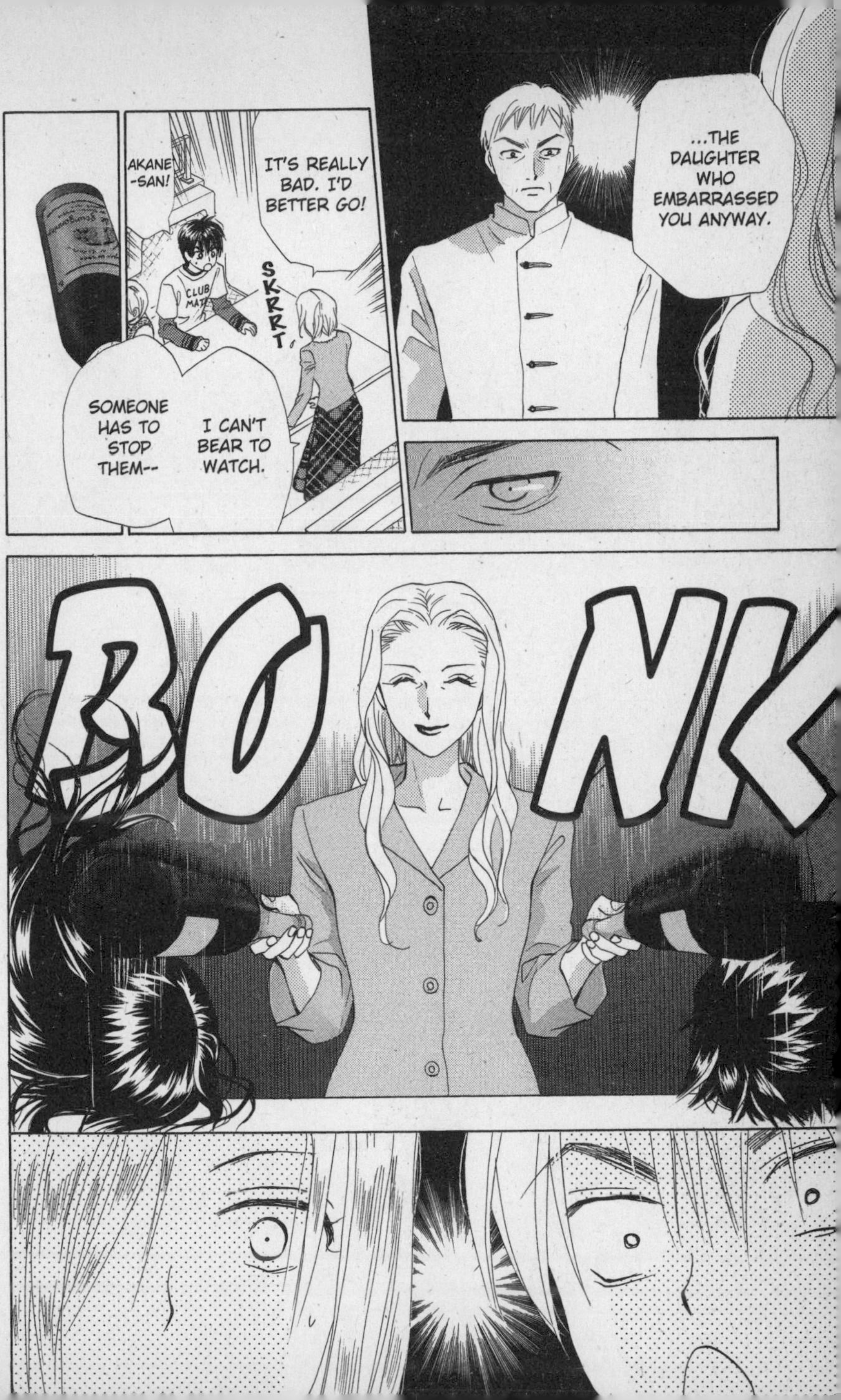
...THE DAUGHTER WHO EMBARRASSED YOU ANYWAY.
IT'S REALLY BAD. I'D BETTER GO!
SKRRT
AKANE-SAN!
I CAN'T BEAR TO WATCH.
SOMEONE HAS TO STOP THEM--
BONK

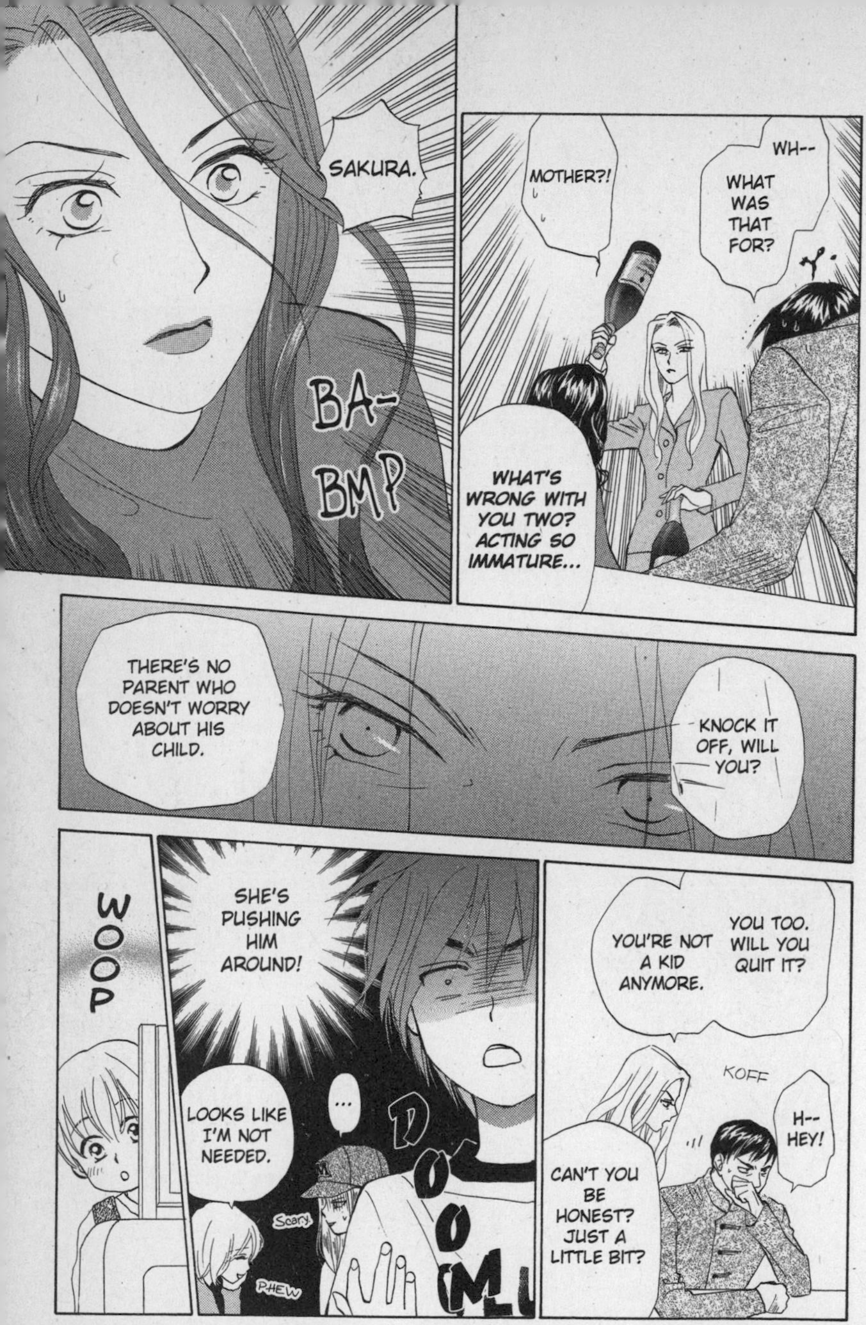
WH--
WHAT WAS THAT FOR?
MOTHER?!
WHAT'S WRONG WITH YOU TWO? ACTING SO IMMATURE...
SAKURA.
BA-BMP
KNOCK IT OFF, WILL YOU?
THERE'S NO PARENT WHO DOESN'T WORRY ABOUT HIS CHILD.
YOU TOO. WILL YOU QUIT IT?
YOU'RE NOT A KID ANYMORE.
KOFF
H-- HEY!
CAN'T YOU BE HONEST? JUST A LITTLE BIT?
SHE'S PUSHING HIM AROUND!
...
DOOM
LOOKS LIKE I'M NOT NEEDED.
Scary.
PHEW
WOOOP

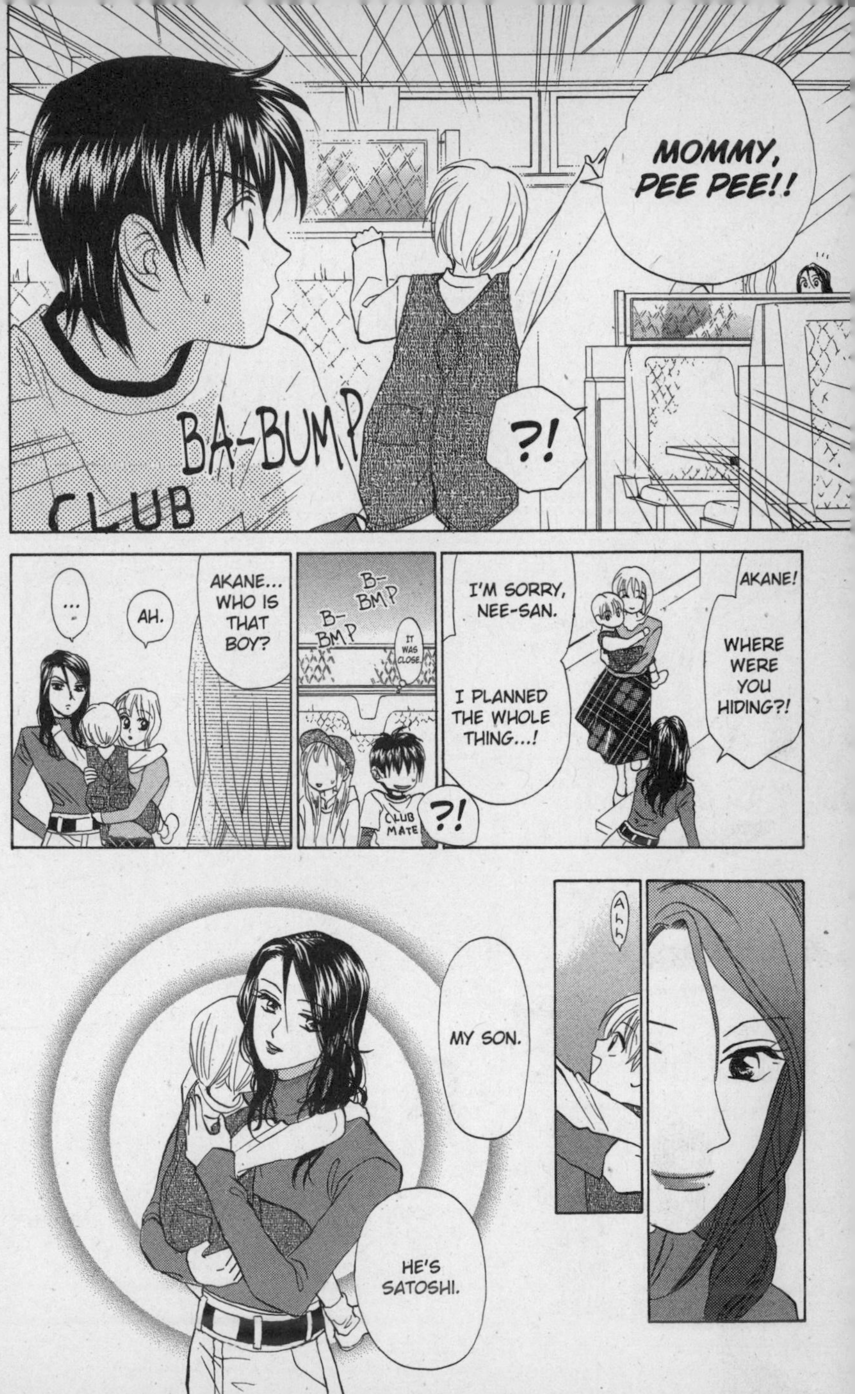
MOMMY, PEE PEE!!
?!
BA-BUMP
CLUB
AKANE!
WHERE WERE YOU HIDING?!
I'M SORRY, NEE-SAN.
I PLANNED THE WHOLE THING...!
B-BMP
B-BMP
IT WAS CLOSE.
CLUB MATE
?!
AKANE... WHO IS THAT BOY?
AH.
...
Ahh
MY SON.
HE'S SATOSHI.

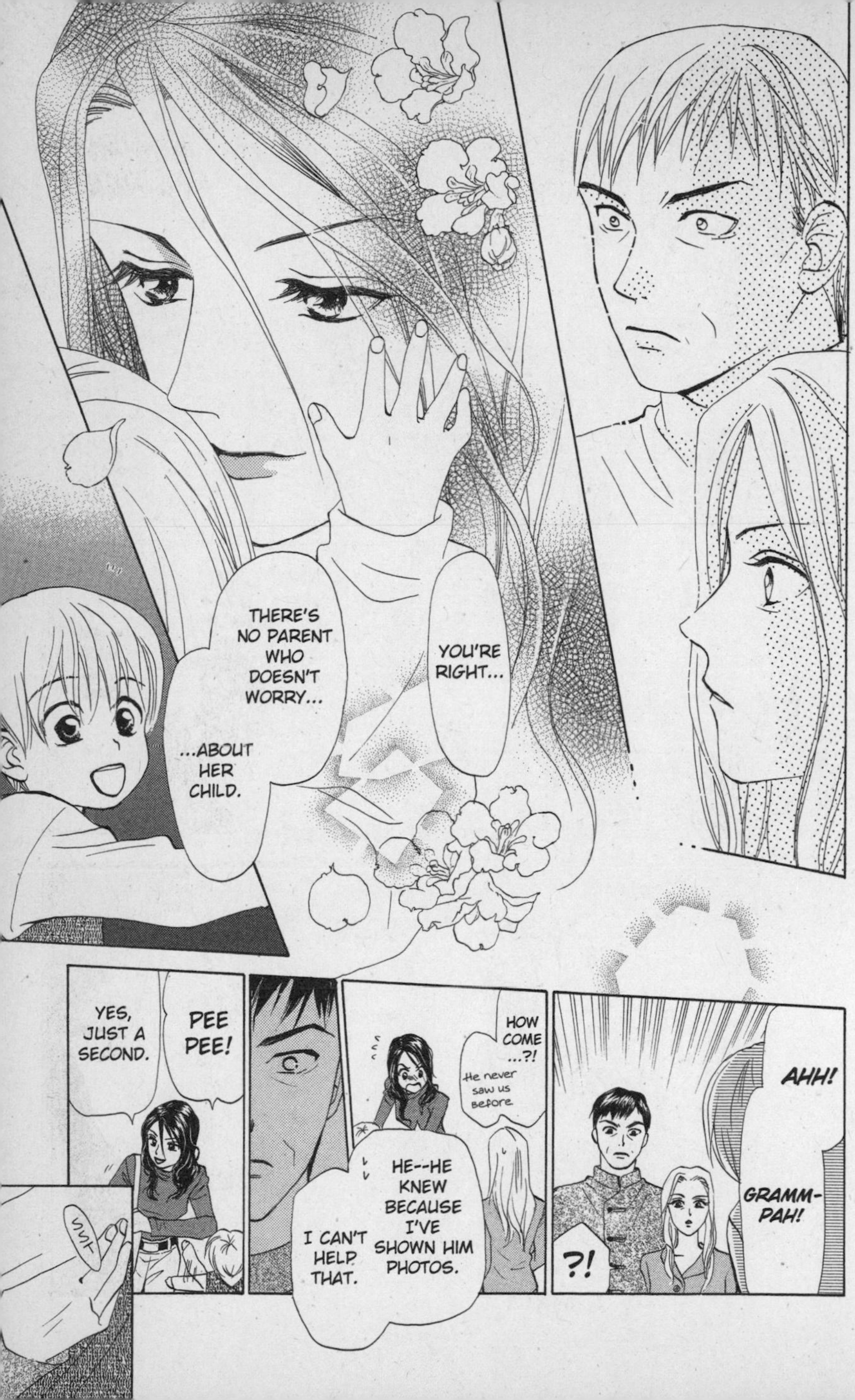
YOU'RE RIGHT...
THERE'S NO PARENT WHO DOESN'T WORRY...
...ABOUT HER CHILD.
AHH!
GRAMM-PAH!
?!
HOW COME ...?!
He never saw us before
HE--HE KNEW BECAUSE I'VE SHOWN HIM PHOTOS.
I CAN'T HELP THAT.
PEE PEE!
YES, JUST A SECOND.

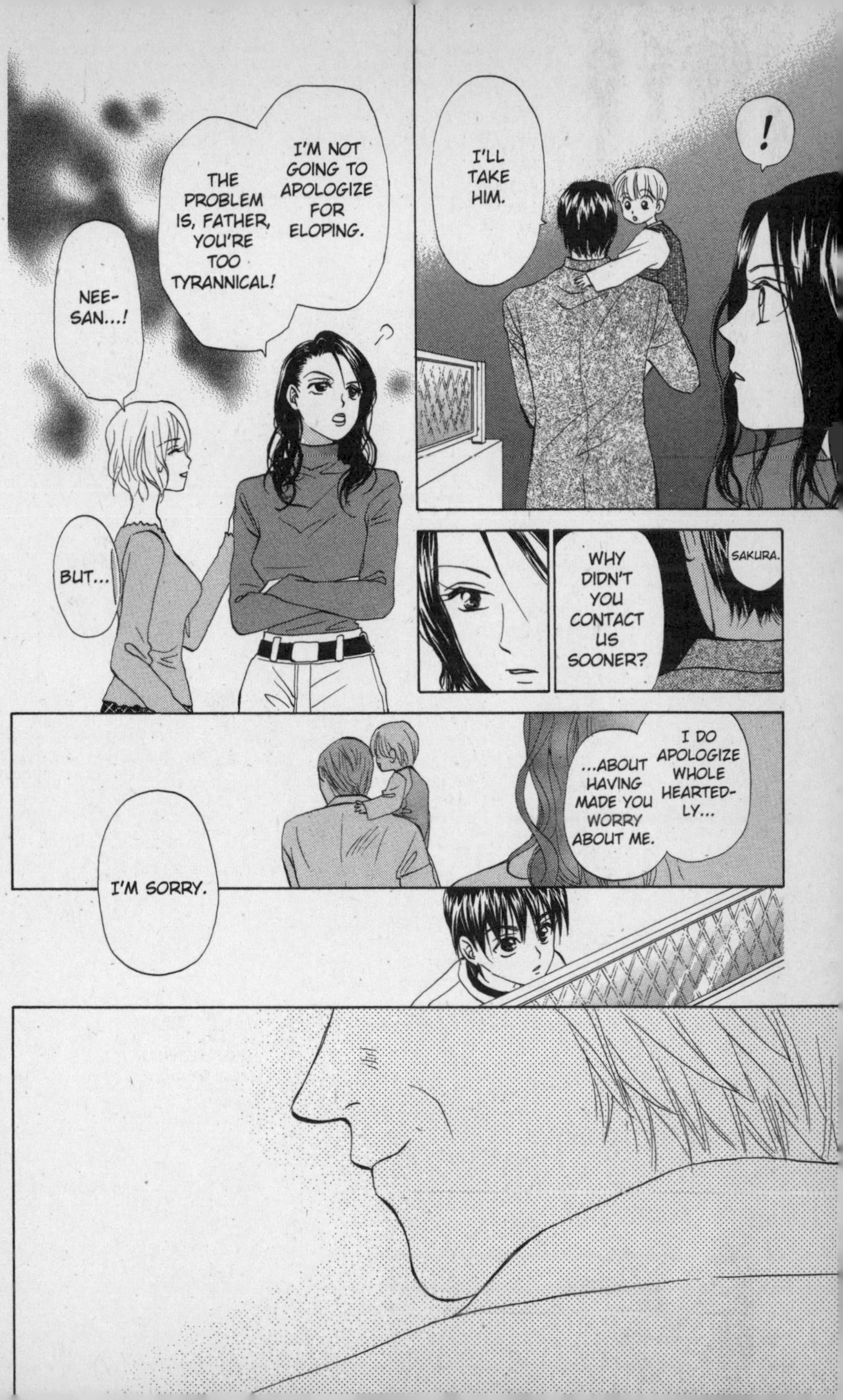
!
I'LL TAKE HIM.
SAKURA.
WHY DIDN'T YOU CONTACT US SOONER?
I'M NOT GOING TO APOLOGIZE FOR ELOPING.
THE PROBLEM IS, FATHER, YOU'RE TOO TYRANNICAL!
NEE-SAN...!
BUT...
I DO APOLOGIZE WHOLE HEARTED-LY...
...ABOUT HAVING MADE YOU WORRY ABOUT ME.
I'M SORRY.

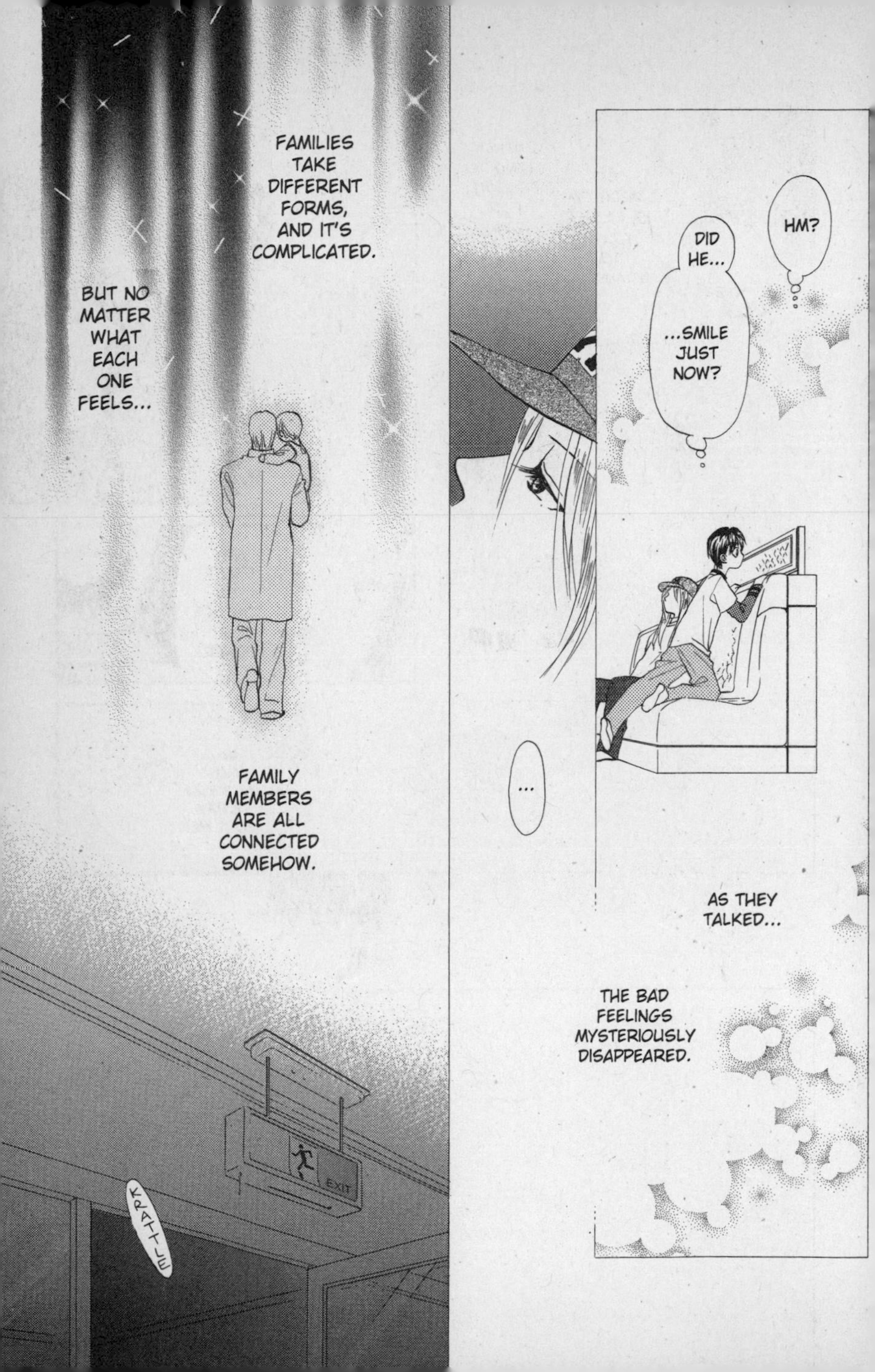
HM?
DID HE... ...SMILE JUST NOW?
...
AS THEY TALKED...
THE BAD FEELINGS MYSTERIOUSLY DISAPPEARED.
FAMILIES TAKE DIFFERENT FORMS, AND IT'S COMPLICATED.
BUT NO MATTER WHAT EACH ONE FEELS...
FAMILY MEMBERS ARE ALL CONNECTED SOMEHOW.
EXIT
KRATTLE

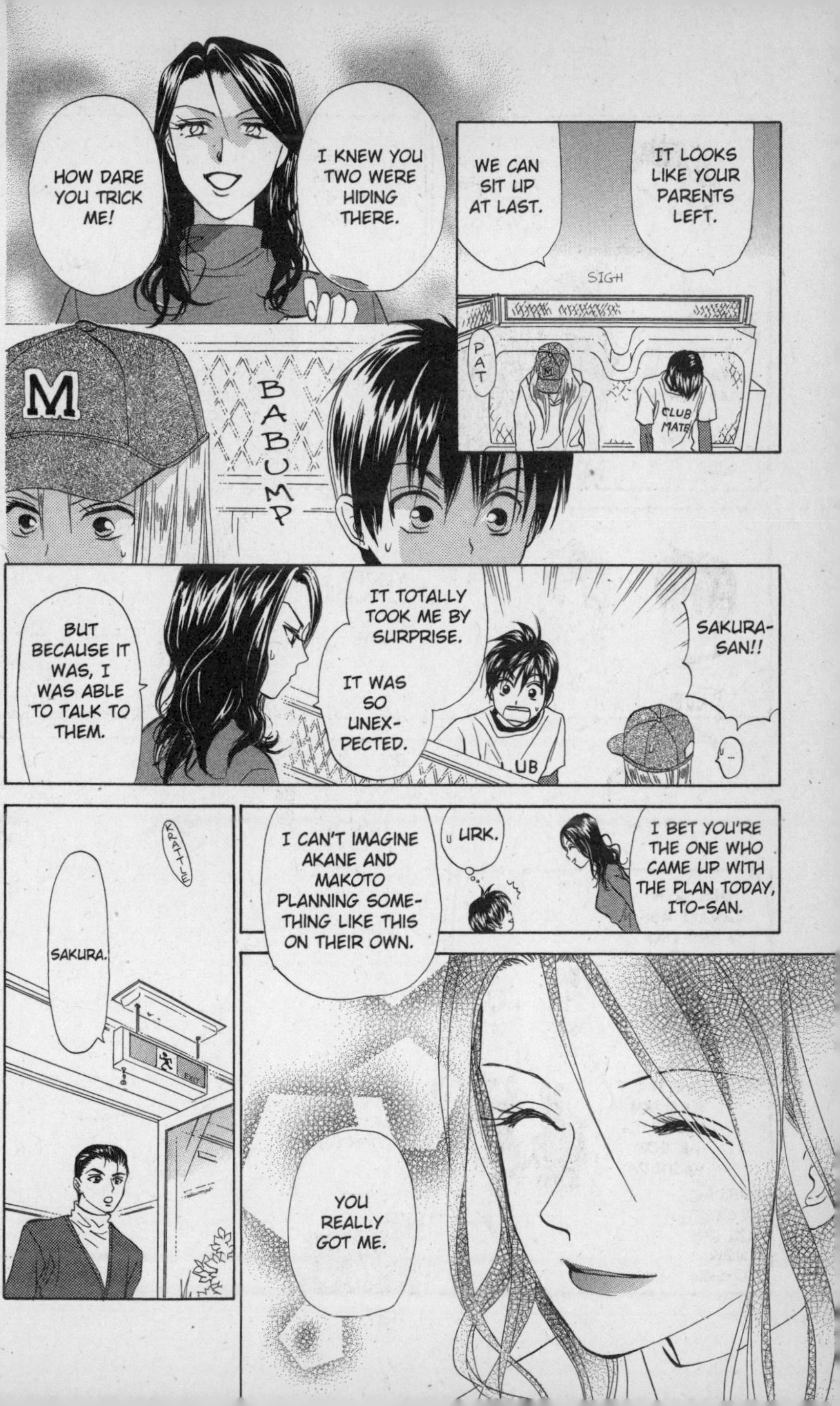
IT LOOKS LIKE YOUR PARENTS LEFT.
WE CAN SIT UP AT LAST.
SIGH
PAT
I KNEW YOU TWO WERE HIDING THERE.
HOW DARE YOU TRICK ME!
BABUMP
SAKURA-SAN!!
...
IT TOTALLY TOOK ME BY SURPRISE.
IT WAS SO UNEXPECTED.
BUT BECAUSE IT WAS, I WAS ABLE TO TALK TO THEM.
I BET YOU'RE THE ONE WHO CAME UP WITH THE PLAN TODAY, ITO-SAN.
URK.
I CAN'T IMAGINE AKANE AND MAKOTO PLANNING SOME-THING LIKE THIS ON THEIR OWN.
YOU REALLY GOT ME.
KRATTLE
SAKURA.

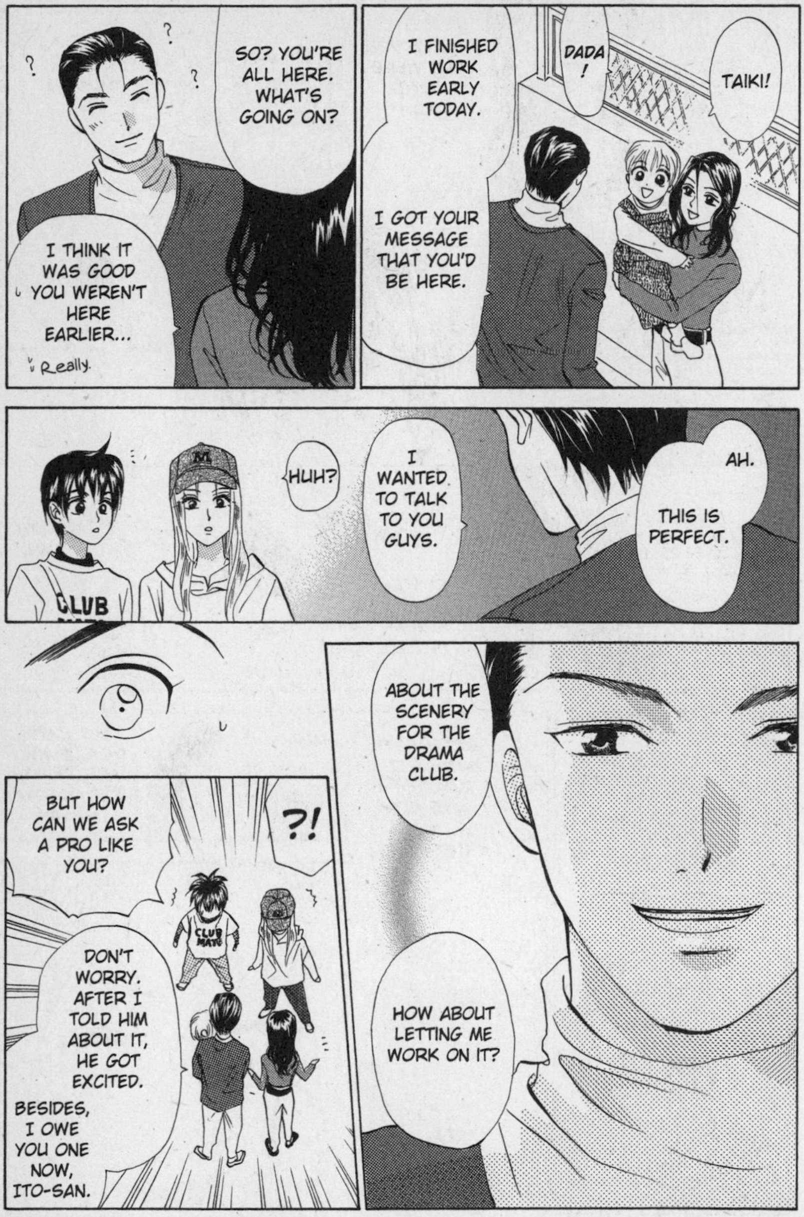
TAIKI!
DADA!
I FINISHED WORK EARLY TODAY.
I GOT YOUR MESSAGE THAT YOU'D BE HERE.
SO? YOU'RE ALL HERE. WHAT'S GOING ON?
I THINK IT WAS GOOD YOU WEREN'T HERE EARLIER...
Really.
AH.
THIS IS PERFECT.
I WANTED TO TALK TO YOU GUYS.
HUH?
CLUB
ABOUT THE SCENERY FOR THE DRAMA CLUB.
HOW ABOUT LETTING ME WORK ON IT?
?!
BUT HOW CAN WE ASK A PRO LIKE YOU?
DON'T WORRY. AFTER I TOLD HIM ABOUT IT, HE GOT EXCITED.
BESIDES, I OWE YOU ONE NOW, ITO-SAN.

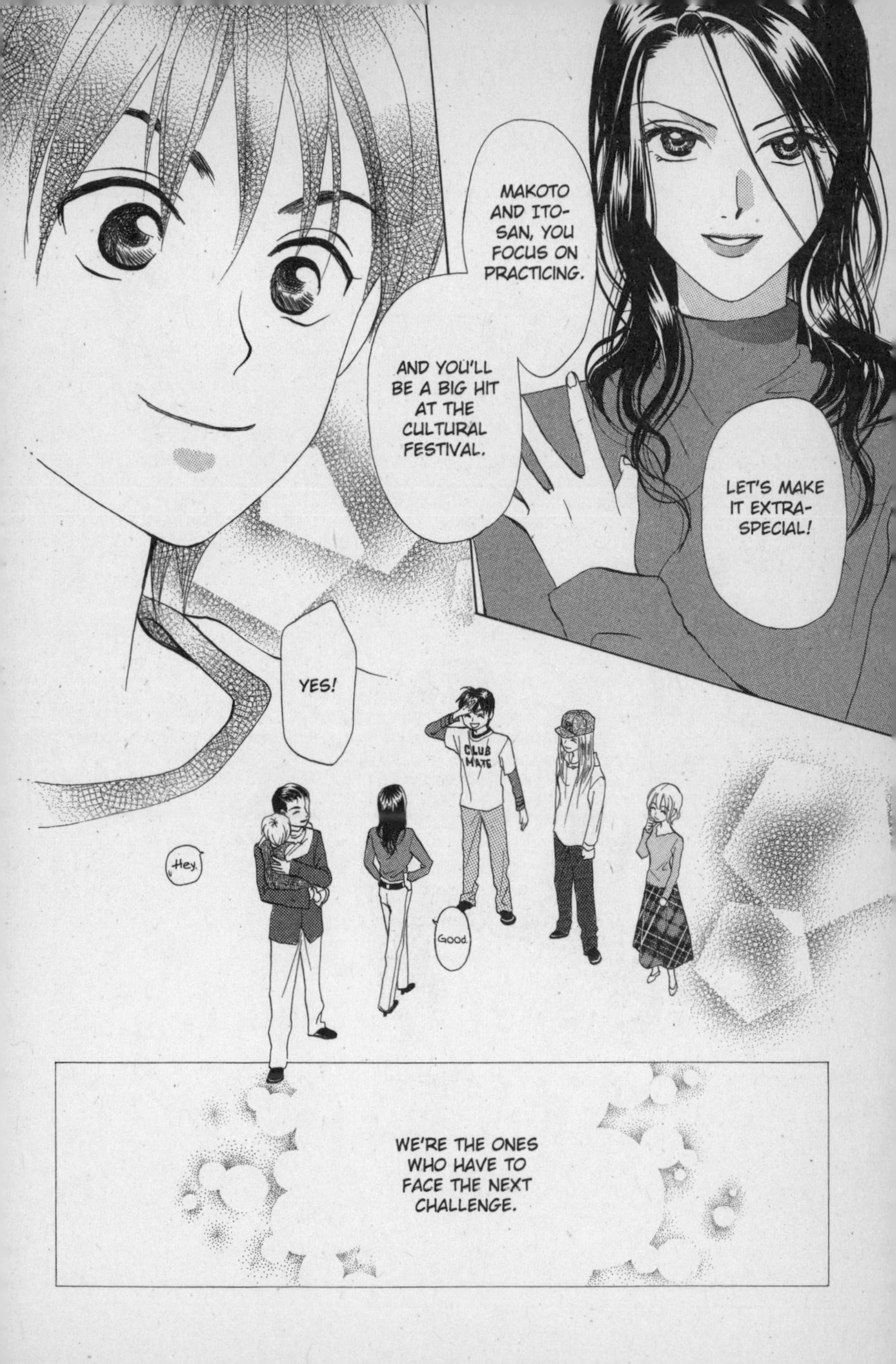
MAKOTO AND ITO-SAN, YOU FOCUS ON PRACTICING.
AND YOU'LL BE A BIG HIT AT THE CULTURAL FESTIVAL.
LET'S MAKE IT EXTRA-SPECIAL!
YES!
Good.
Hey.
WE'RE THE ONES WHO HAVE TO FACE THE NEXT CHALLENGE.

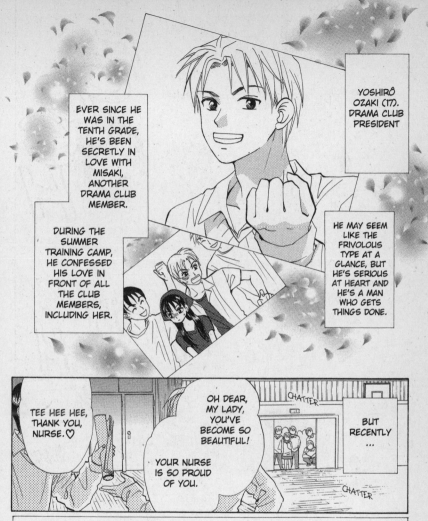

YOSHIRÔ OZAKI (17). DRAMA CLUB PRESIDENT
EVER SINCE HE WAS IN THE TENTH GRADE, HE'S BEEN SECRETLY IN LOVE WITH MISAKI, ANOTHER DRAMA CLUB MEMBER.
HE MAY SEEM LIKE THE FRIVOLOUS TYPE AT A GLANCE, BUT HE'S SERIOUS AT HEART AND HE'S A MAN WHO GETS THINGS DONE.
DURING THE SUMMER TRAINING CAMP, HE CONFESSED HIS LOVE IN FRONT OF ALL THE CLUB MEMBERS, INCLUDING HER.
BUT RECENTLY ...
CHATTER
OH DEAR, MY LADY, YOU'VE BECOME SO BEAUTIFUL!
YOUR NURSE IS SO PROUD OF YOU.
TEE HEE HEE, THANK YOU, NURSE.♡
CHATTER

—Behind the Scenes Story ⑤—

This is an episode I wanted to draw for a long time. There are hardly any male-female friends who get along so well as Ito and Yoshirô.

Regarding Mako's famous sayings (page 141), my assistant picked them out from the comics, and we had a big laugh at work. (laugh) Thank you so much, Sano-san. ♪

But you know, it embarrasses me whenever I re-read them. Besides, it's not done yet! I know there are more to come. :

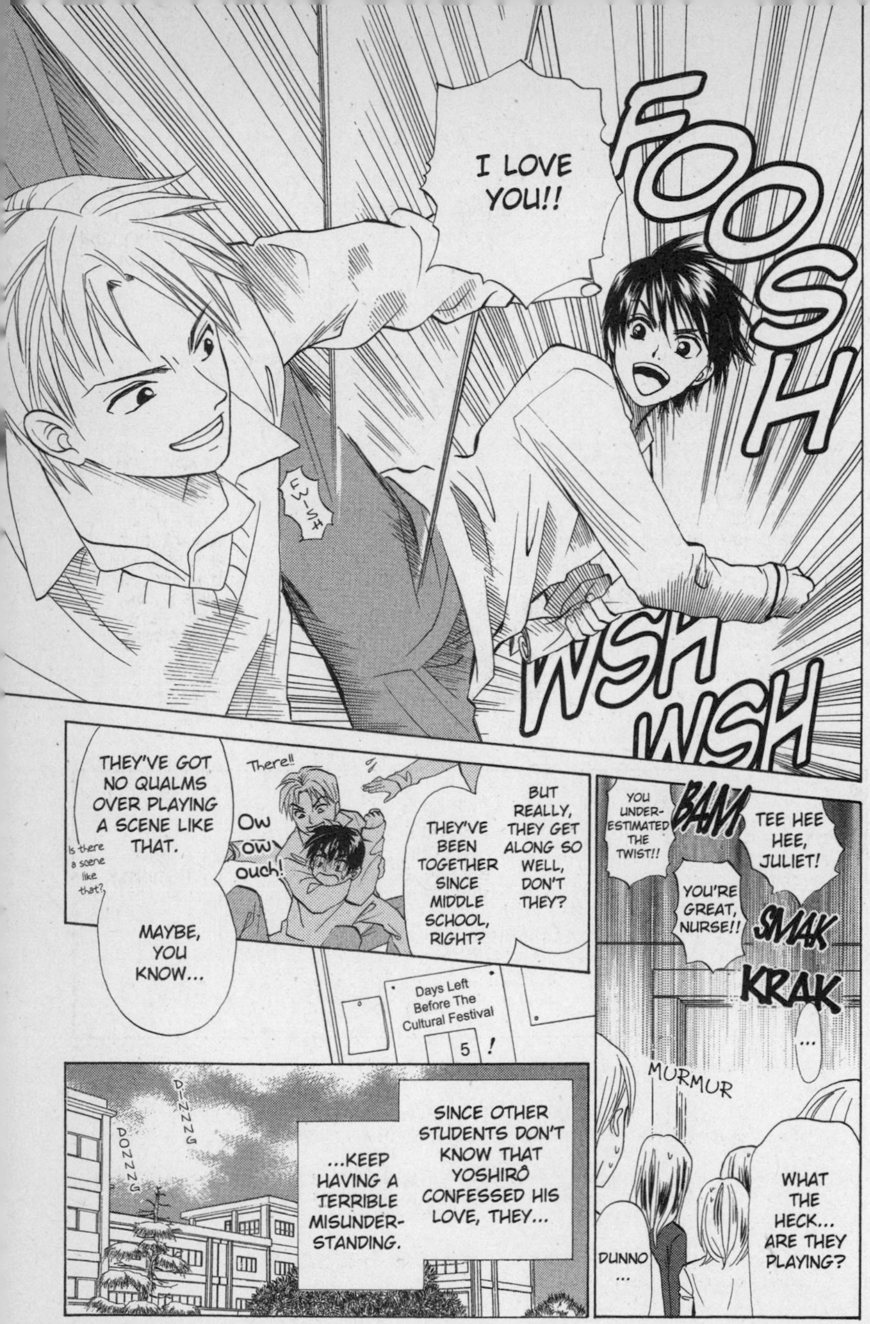
I LOVE YOU!!
FOOSH
FWISH
WSH WSH
YOU UNDER-ESTIMATED THE TWIST!!
BAM
TEE HEE HEE, JULIET!
YOU'RE GREAT, NURSE!!
SMAK
KRAK
...
MURMUR
WHAT THE HECK... ARE THEY PLAYING?
DUNNO ...
BUT REALLY, THEY GET ALONG SO WELL, DON'T THEY?
THEY'VE BEEN TOGETHER SINCE MIDDLE SCHOOL, RIGHT?
There!!
Ow ow ouch!
THEY'VE GOT NO QUALMS OVER PLAYING A SCENE LIKE THAT.
Is there a scene like that?
MAYBE, YOU KNOW...
Days Left Before The Cultural Festival
5 !
SINCE OTHER STUDENTS DON'T KNOW THAT YOSHIRÔ CONFESSED HIS LOVE, THEY...
...KEEP HAVING A TERRIBLE MISUNDER-STANDING.
DINNNG
DONNNG

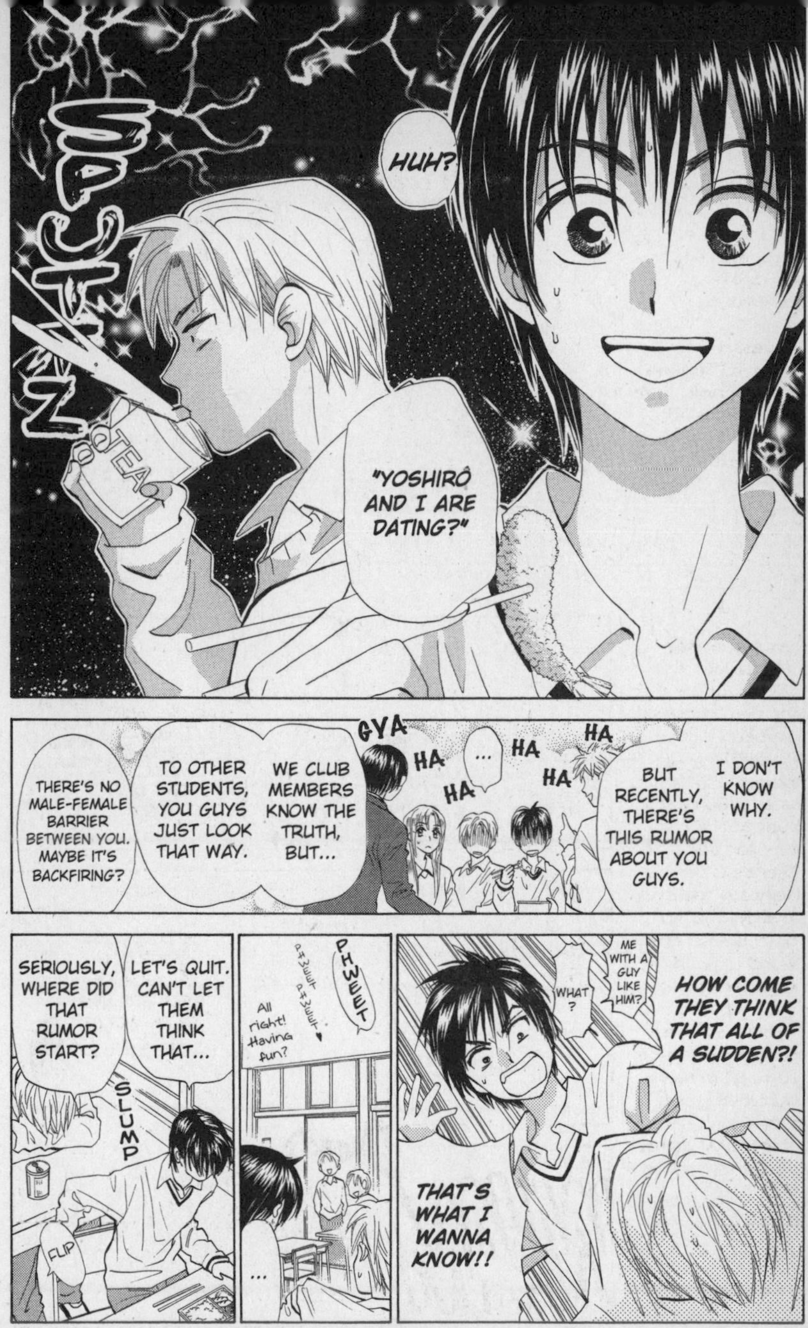
HUH?
"YOSHIRÔ AND I ARE DATING?"
TEA
I DON'T KNOW WHY.
BUT RECENTLY, THERE'S THIS RUMOR ABOUT YOU GUYS.
HA
HA
HA
HA
...
GYA
WE CLUB MEMBERS KNOW THE TRUTH, BUT...
TO OTHER STUDENTS, YOU GUYS JUST LOOK THAT WAY.
THERE'S NO MALE-FEMALE BARRIER BETWEEN YOU. MAYBE IT'S BACKFIRING?
HOW COME THEY THINK THAT ALL OF A SUDDEN?!
ME WITH A GUY LIKE HIM?
WHAT?
THAT'S WHAT I WANNA KNOW!!
PHWEET
PHWEET PHWEET
All right! Having fun?
...
LET'S QUIT. CAN'T LET THEM THINK THAT...
SERIOUSLY, WHERE DID THAT RUMOR START?
SLUMP
FLIP

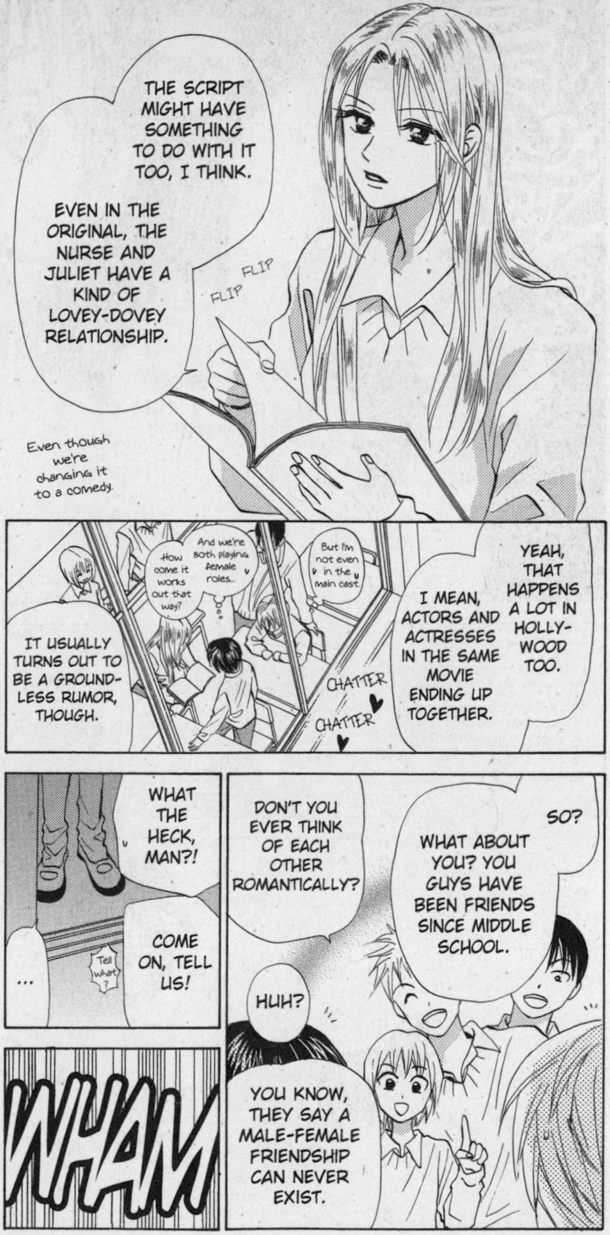
THE SCRIPT MIGHT HAVE SOMETHING TO DO WITH IT TOO, I THINK.
EVEN IN THE ORIGINAL, THE NURSE AND JULIET HAVE A KIND OF LOVEY-DOVEY RELATIONSHIP.
FLIP
FLIP
Even though we're changing it to a comedy.
YEAH, THAT HAPPENS A LOT IN HOLLYWOOD TOO.
I MEAN, ACTORS AND ACTRESSES IN THE SAME MOVIE ENDING UP TOGETHER.
But I'm not even in the main cast.
CHATTER
CHATTER
And we're both playing female roles...
How come it works out that way?
IT USUALLY TURNS OUT TO BE A GROUNDLESS RUMOR, THOUGH.
SO?
WHAT ABOUT YOU? YOU GUYS HAVE BEEN FRIENDS SINCE MIDDLE SCHOOL.
DON'T YOU EVER THINK OF EACH OTHER ROMANTICALLY?
HUH?
YOU KNOW, THEY SAY A MALE-FEMALE FRIENDSHIP CAN NEVER EXIST.
WHAT THE HECK, MAN?!
COME ON, TELL US!
Tell what?
...
WHAM

I do panel lines using 0.5 Rotring with three rulers --45 cm, 30 cm, and 15 cm respectively.

...I guess that's about it? Talking about pencils, I use a regular ¥100 sharp pencil with 0.5 mm lead.

Let me change the subject and talk about another request. I've been receiving letters inquiring if I'd set up a home page. Well, I have no plan for doing it. There's 0% chance. When I already have no time, I'll lose even more! ...I mean, it frightens me. The Internet --once started, there'll be no end to it. I'm happy that there are people who have started **W Juliet** sites. I appreciate that.

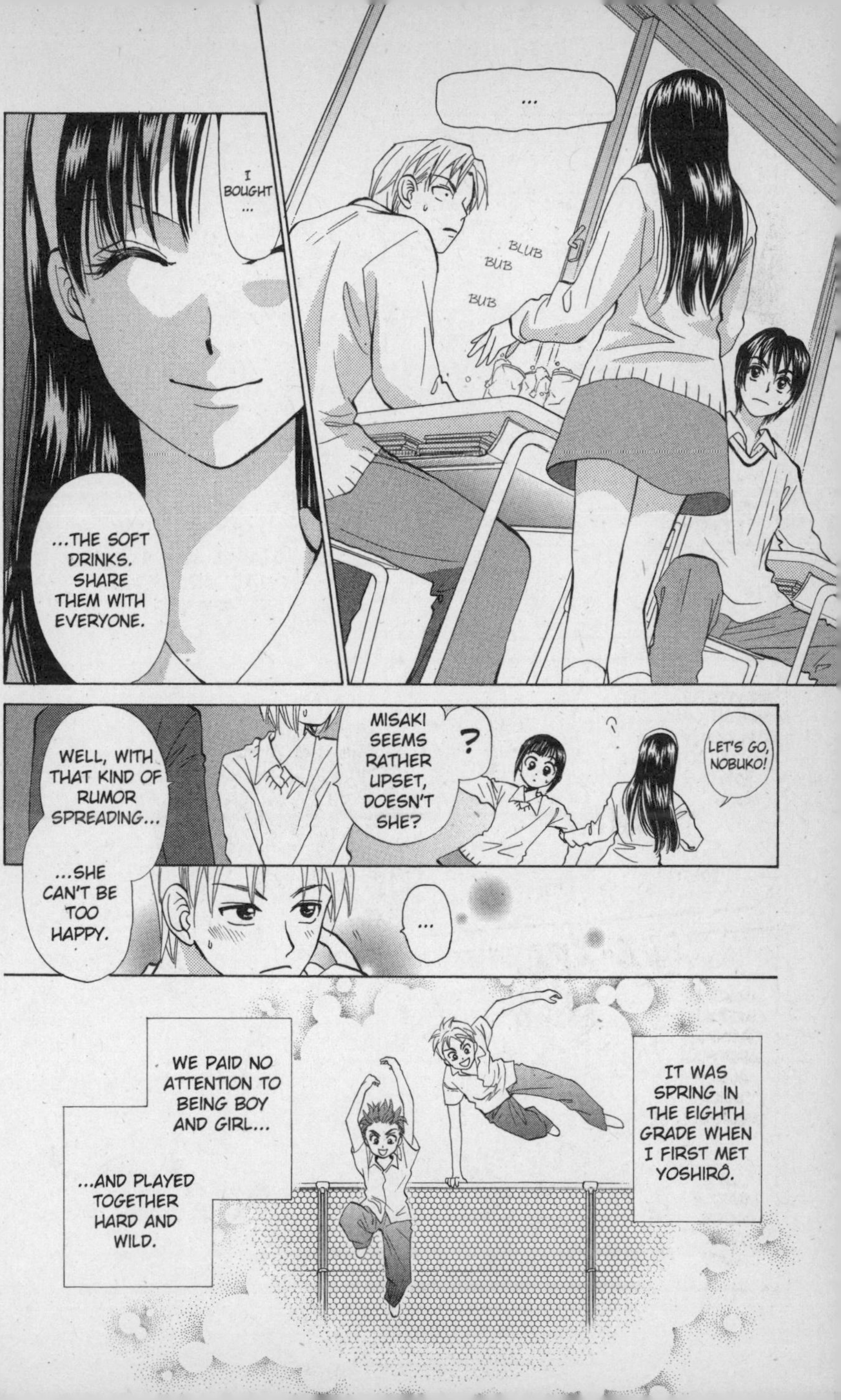
...
I BOUGHT ...
BLUB
BUB
BUB
...THE SOFT DRINKS. SHARE THEM WITH EVERYONE.
LET'S GO, NOBUKO!
?
MISAKI SEEMS RATHER UPSET, DOESN'T SHE?
WELL, WITH THAT KIND OF RUMOR SPREADING...
...SHE CAN'T BE TOO HAPPY.
...
IT WAS SPRING IN THE EIGHTH GRADE WHEN I FIRST MET YOSHIRÔ.
WE PAID NO ATTENTION TO BEING BOY AND GIRL...
...AND PLAYED TOGETHER HARD AND WILD.

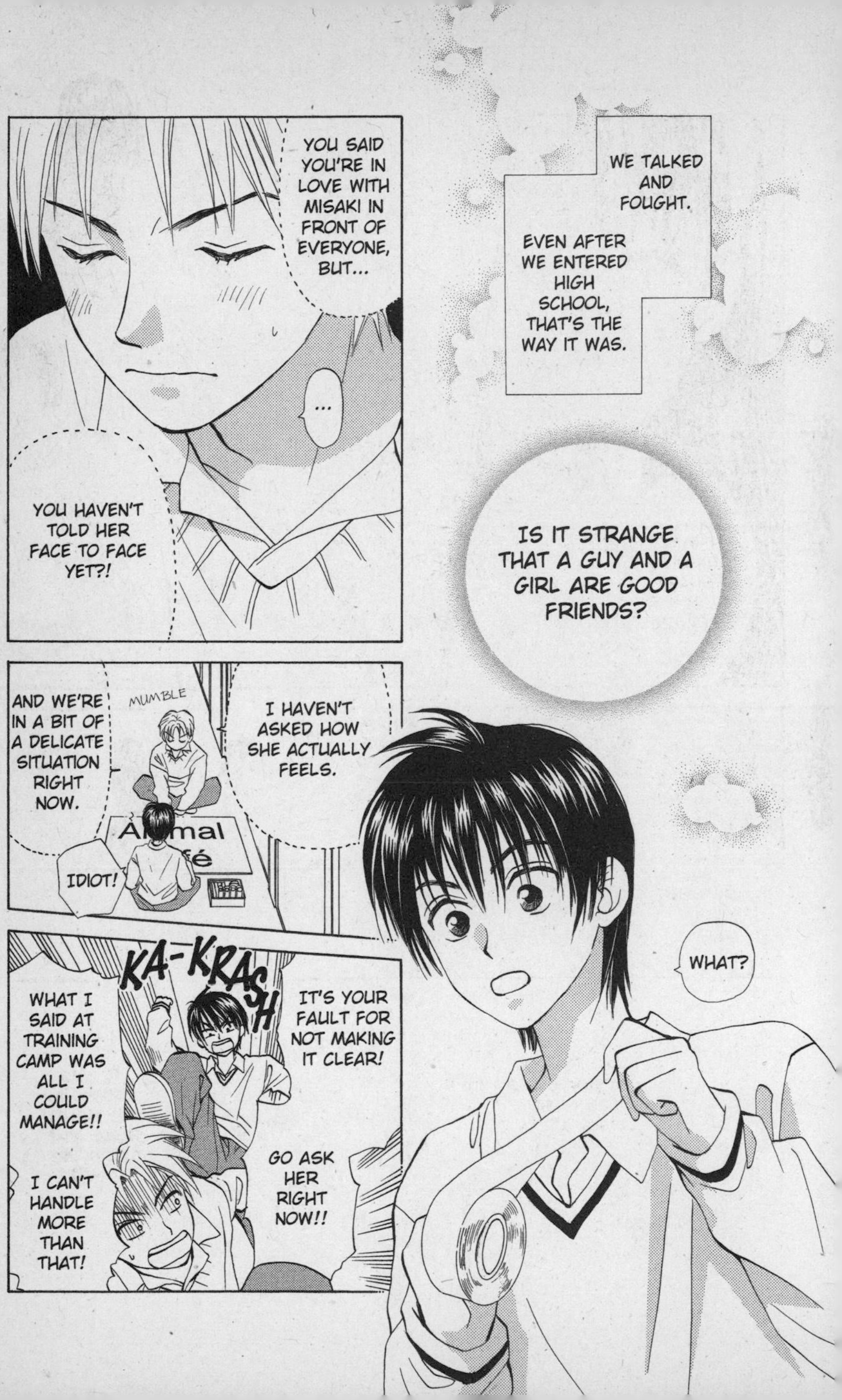
WE TALKED AND FOUGHT.
EVEN AFTER WE ENTERED HIGH SCHOOL, THAT'S THE WAY IT WAS.
IS IT STRANGE THAT A GUY AND A GIRL ARE GOOD FRIENDS?
WHAT?
YOU SAID YOU'RE IN LOVE WITH MISAKI IN FRONT OF EVERYONE, BUT...
...
YOU HAVEN'T TOLD HER FACE TO FACE YET?!
I HAVEN'T ASKED HOW SHE ACTUALLY FEELS.
AND WE'RE IN A BIT OF A DELICATE SITUATION RIGHT NOW.
MUMBLE
IDIOT!
KA-KRASH
IT'S YOUR FAULT FOR NOT MAKING IT CLEAR!
WHAT I SAID AT TRAINING CAMP WAS ALL I COULD MANAGE!!
GO ASK HER RIGHT NOW!!
I CAN'T HANDLE MORE THAN THAT!

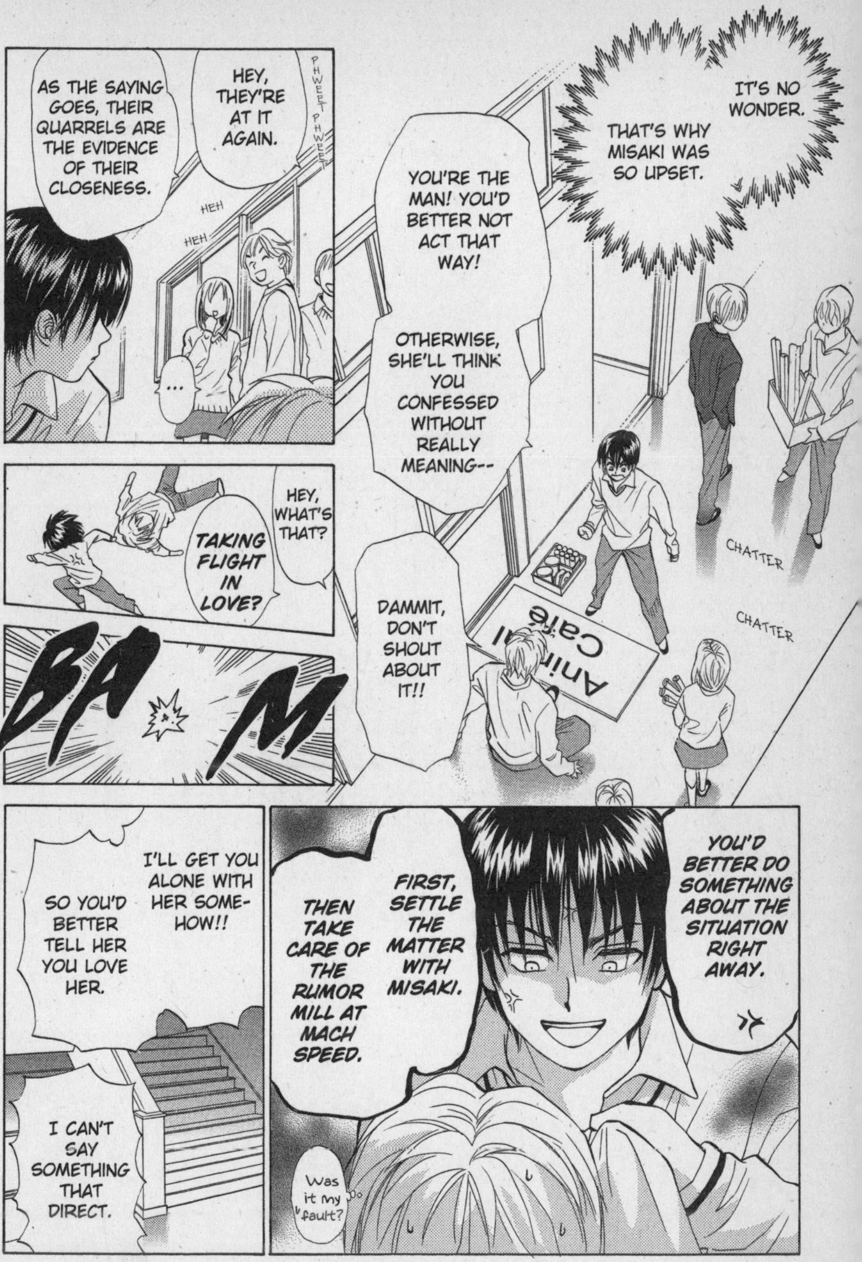
IT'S NO WONDER.
THAT'S WHY MISAKI WAS SO UPSET.
YOU'RE THE MAN! YOU'D BETTER NOT ACT THAT WAY!
OTHERWISE, SHE'LL THINK YOU CONFESSED WITHOUT REALLY MEANING--
CHATTER
CHATTER
DAMMIT, DON'T SHOUT ABOUT IT!!
HEY, THEY'RE AT IT AGAIN.
PHWEET PHWEET
AS THE SAYING GOES, THEIR QUARRELS ARE THE EVIDENCE OF THEIR CLOSENESS.
HEH
HEH
...
HEY, WHAT'S THAT?
TAKING FLIGHT IN LOVE?
BAM
YOU'D BETTER DO SOMETHING ABOUT THE SITUATION RIGHT AWAY.
FIRST, SETTLE THE MATTER WITH MISAKI.
THEN TAKE CARE OF THE RUMOR MILL AT MACH SPEED.
Was it my fault?
I'LL GET YOU ALONE WITH HER SOMEHOW!!
SO YOU'D BETTER TELL HER YOU LOVE HER.
I CAN'T SAY SOMETHING THAT DIRECT.

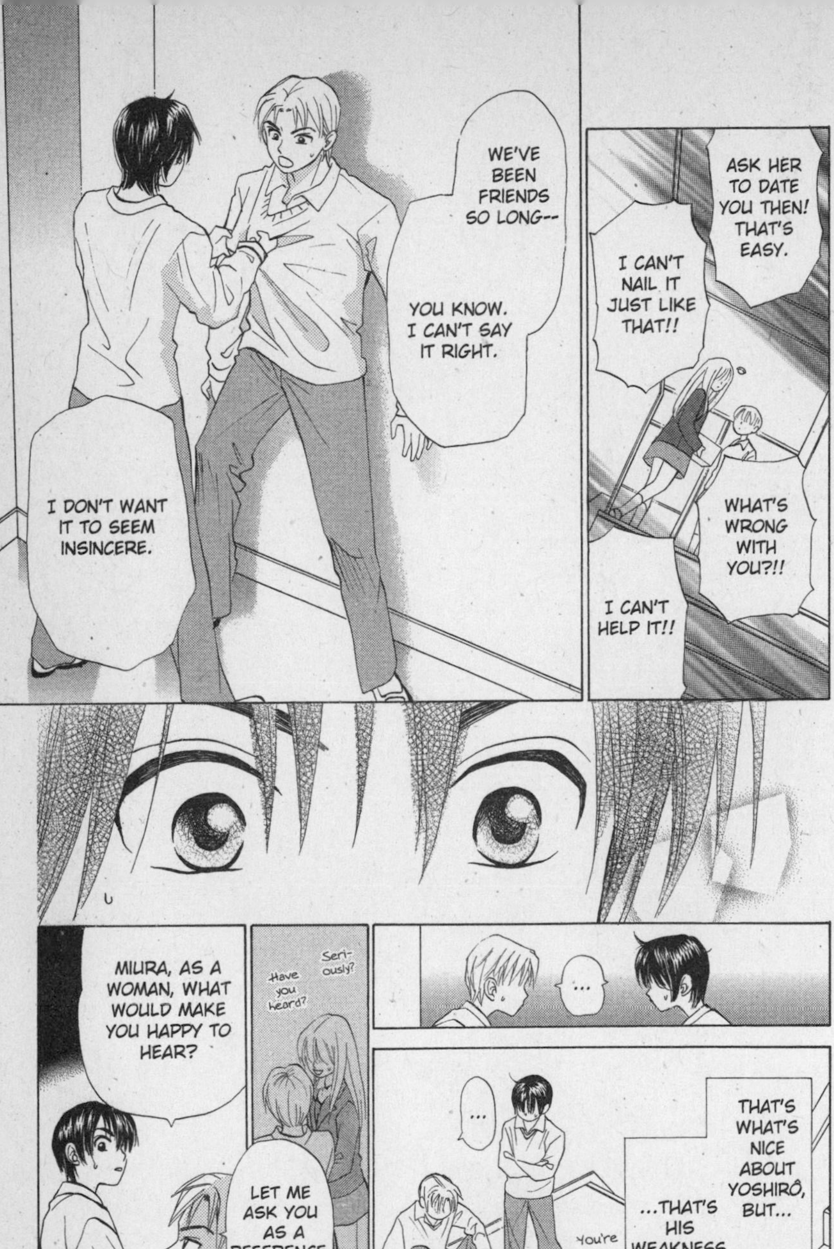
ASK HER TO DATE YOU THEN! THAT'S EASY.
I CAN'T NAIL IT JUST LIKE THAT!!
WHAT'S WRONG WITH YOU?!!
I CAN'T HELP IT!!
WE'VE BEEN FRIENDS SO LONG--
YOU KNOW. I CAN'T SAY IT RIGHT.
I DON'T WANT IT TO SEEM INSINCERE.
...
...
THAT'S WHAT'S NICE ABOUT YOSHIRÔ, BUT...
...THAT'S HIS WEAKNESS TOO.
You're so wishy-washy!
Seri-ously?
Have you heard?
LET ME ASK YOU AS A REFERENCE.
MIURA, AS A WOMAN, WHAT WOULD MAKE YOU HAPPY TO HEAR?
HUH?

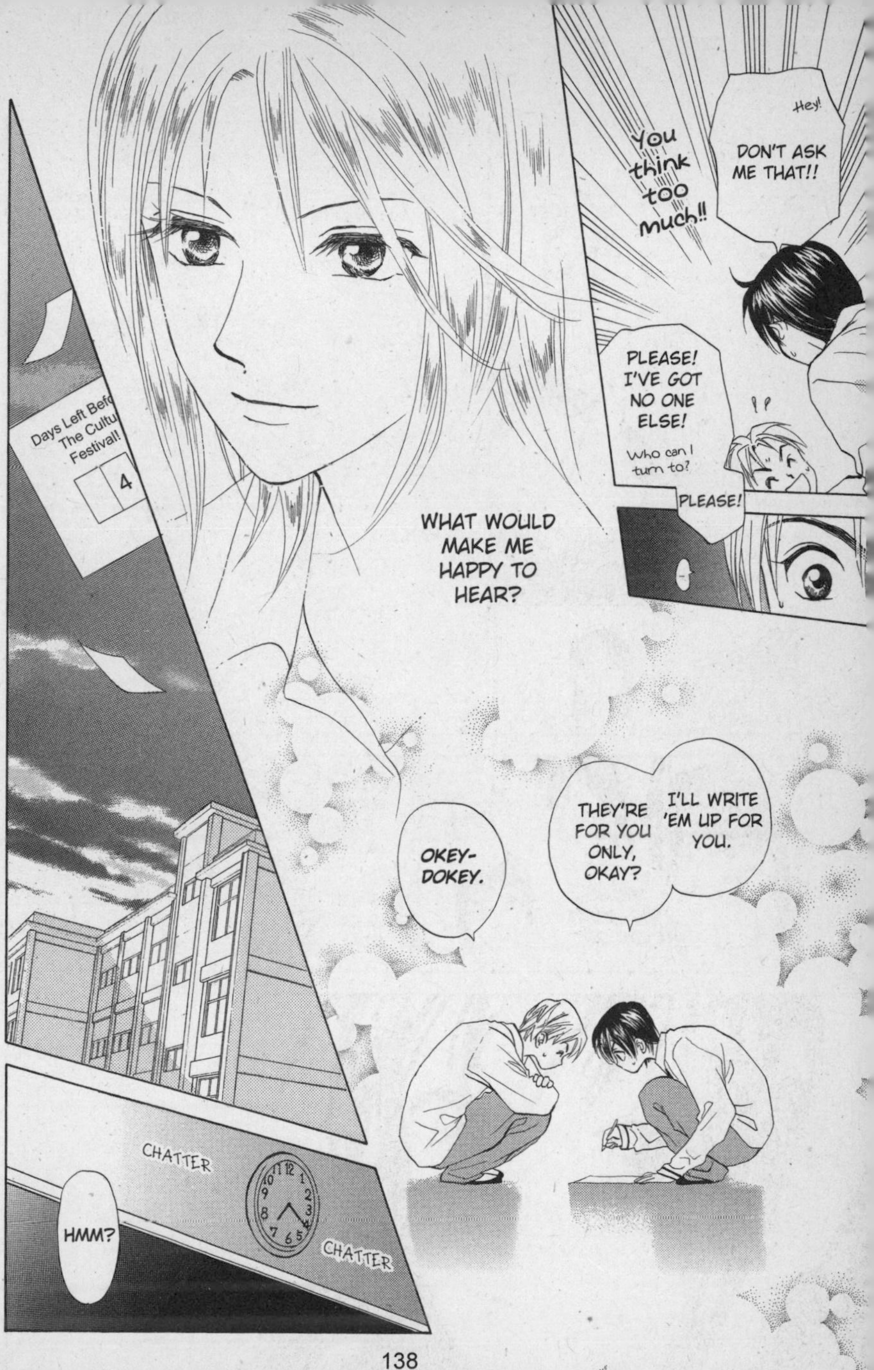
Hey!
DON'T ASK ME THAT!!
You think too much!!
PLEASE! I'VE GOT NO ONE ELSE!
Who can I turn to?
PLEASE!
WHAT WOULD MAKE ME HAPPY TO HEAR?
Days Left Befo
The Cultu
Festival!
4
I'LL WRITE 'EM UP FOR YOU.
THEY'RE FOR YOU ONLY, OKAY?
OKEY-DOKEY.
CHATTER
CHATTER
HMM?

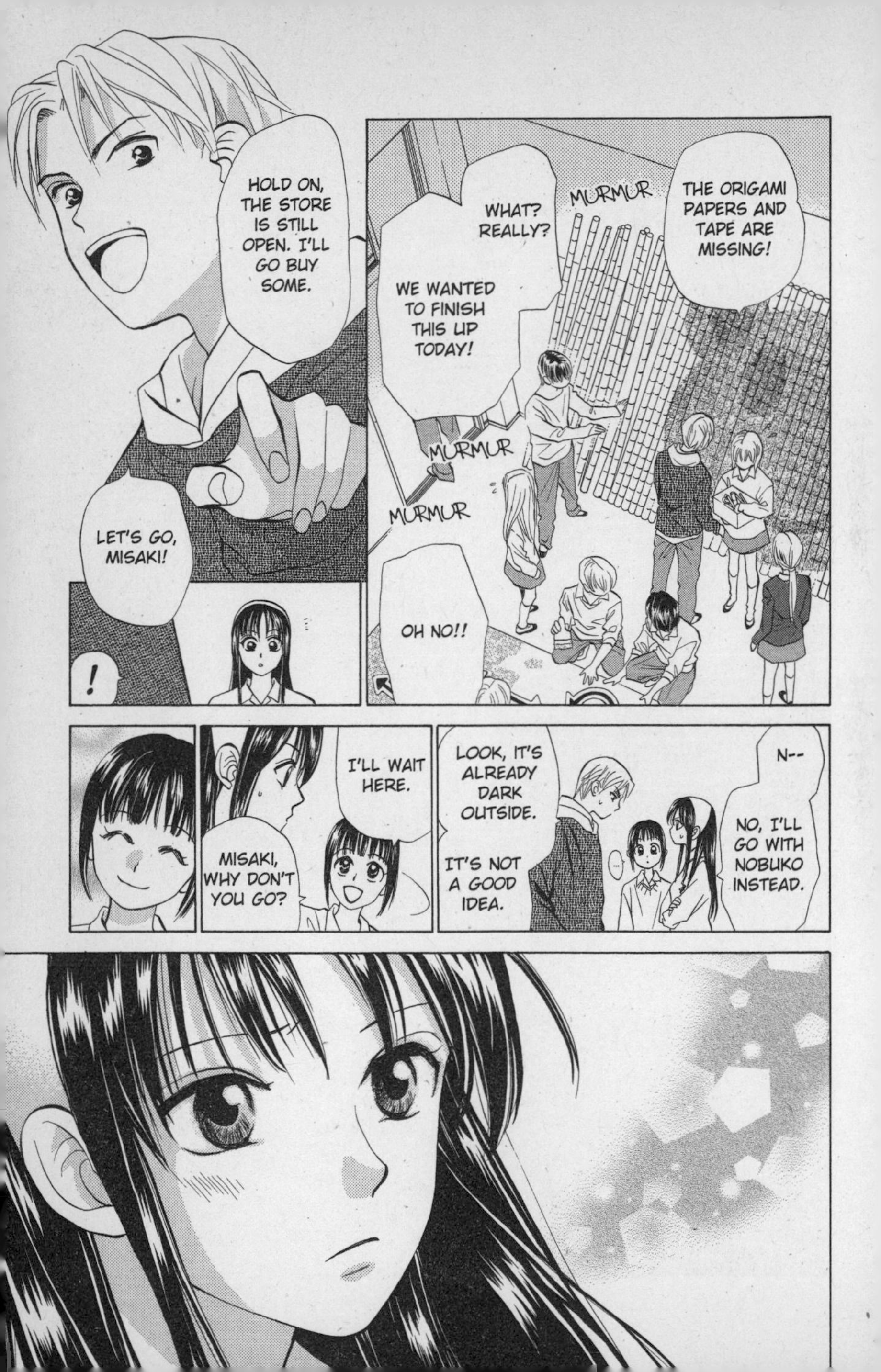
THE ORIGAMI PAPERS AND TAPE ARE MISSING!
MURMUR
WHAT? REALLY?
WE WANTED TO FINISH THIS UP TODAY!
MURMUR
MURMUR
OH NO!!
HOLD ON, THE STORE IS STILL OPEN. I'LL GO BUY SOME.
LET'S GO, MISAKI!
!
N--
NO, I'LL GO WITH NOBUKO INSTEAD.
LOOK, IT'S ALREADY DARK OUTSIDE.
IT'S NOT A GOOD IDEA.
I'LL WAIT HERE.
MISAKI, WHY DON'T YOU GO?

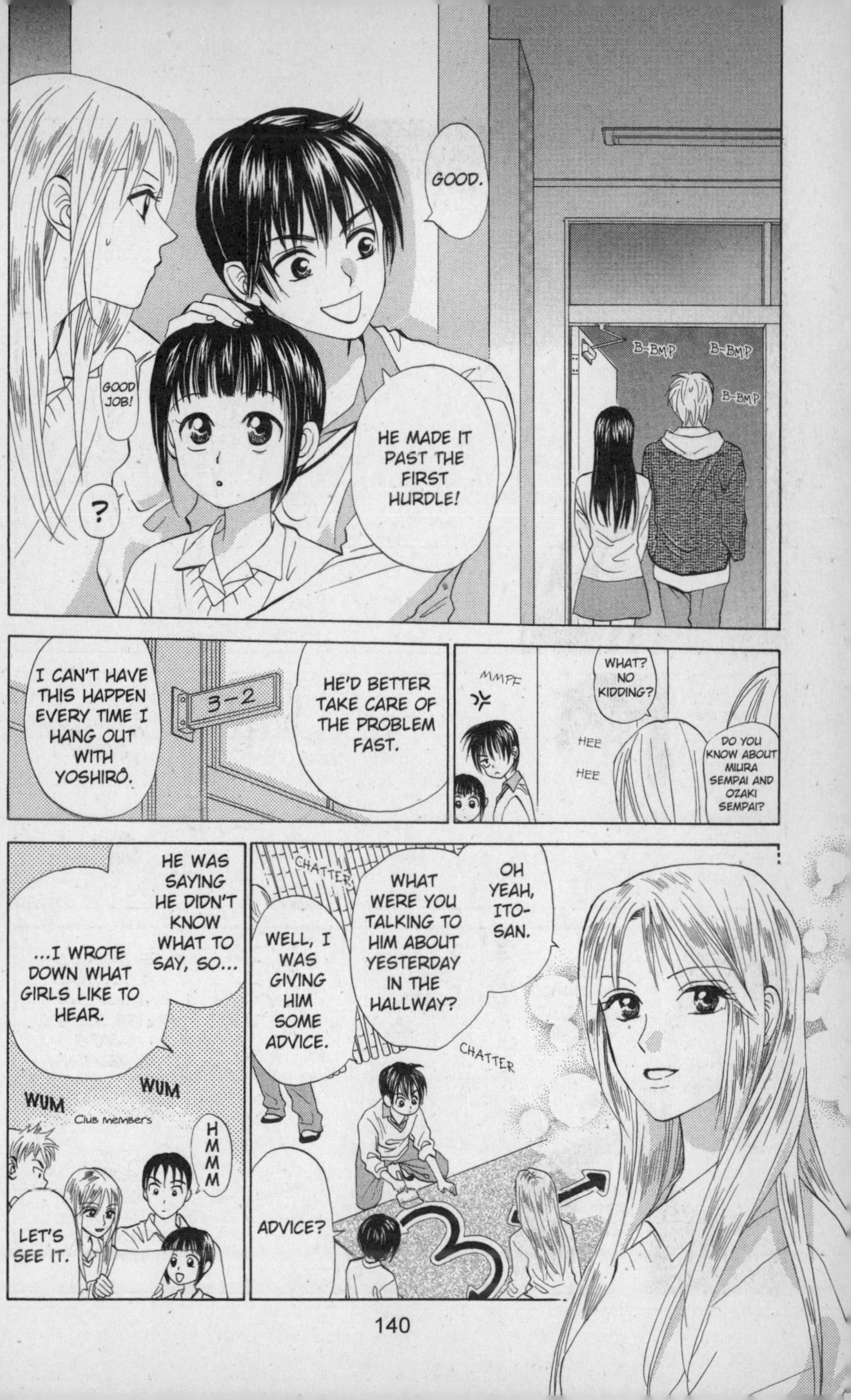
B-BMP
B-BMP
B-BMP
GOOD.
HE MADE IT PAST THE FIRST HURDLE!
GOOD JOB!
?
WHAT? NO KIDDING?
DO YOU KNOW ABOUT MIURA SEMPAI AND OZAKI SEMPAI?
HEE
HEE
MMPF
HE'D BETTER TAKE CARE OF THE PROBLEM FAST.
3-2
I CAN'T HAVE THIS HAPPEN EVERY TIME I HANG OUT WITH YOSHIRÔ.
OH YEAH, ITO-SAN.
WHAT WERE YOU TALKING TO HIM ABOUT YESTERDAY IN THE HALLWAY?
CHATTER
WELL, I WAS GIVING HIM SOME ADVICE.
CHATTER
ADVICE?
HE WAS SAYING HE DIDN'T KNOW WHAT TO SAY, SO...
...I WROTE DOWN WHAT GIRLS LIKE TO HEAR.
WUM
WUM
HMMM
Club members
LET'S SEE IT.

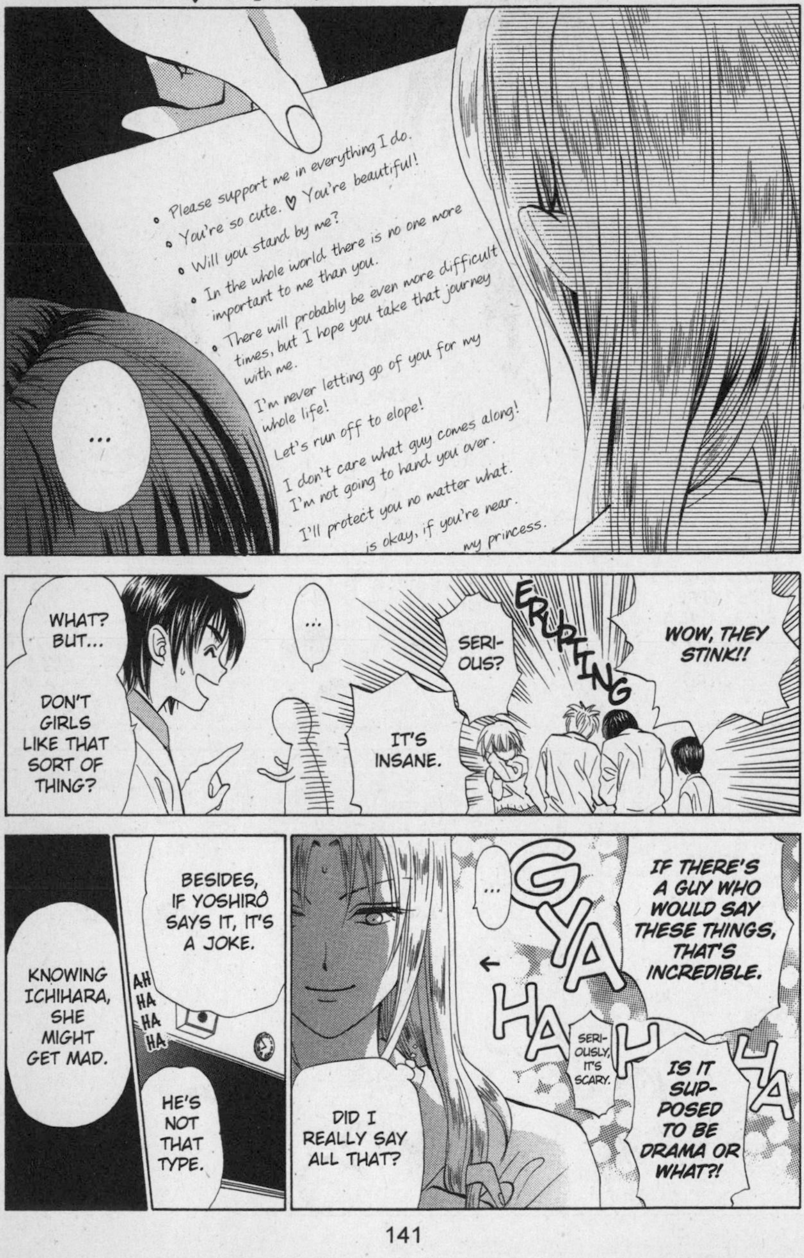

Please support me in everything I do.
You're so cute. ♥ You're beautiful!
Will you stand by me?
In the whole world there is no one more important to me than you.
There will probably be even more difficult times, but I hope you take that journey with me.
I'm never letting go of you for my whole life!
Let's run off to elope!
I don't care what guy comes along! I'm not going to hand you over.
I'll protect you no matter what.
is okay, if you're near.
my princess.
...
WOW, THEY STINK!!
ERUPTING
SERI-OUS?
IT'S INSANE.
...
WHAT? BUT...
DON'T GIRLS LIKE THAT SORT OF THING?
IF THERE'S A GUY WHO WOULD SAY THESE THINGS, THAT'S INCREDIBLE.
GYAHAHAHAHA
...
SERI-OUSLY, IT'S SCARY.
IS IT SUP-POSED TO BE DRAMA OR WHAT?!
DID I REALLY SAY ALL THAT?
BESIDES, IF YOSHIRÔ SAYS IT, IT'S A JOKE.
AH HA HA HA
HE'S NOT THAT TYPE.
KNOWING ICHIHARA, SHE MIGHT GET MAD.

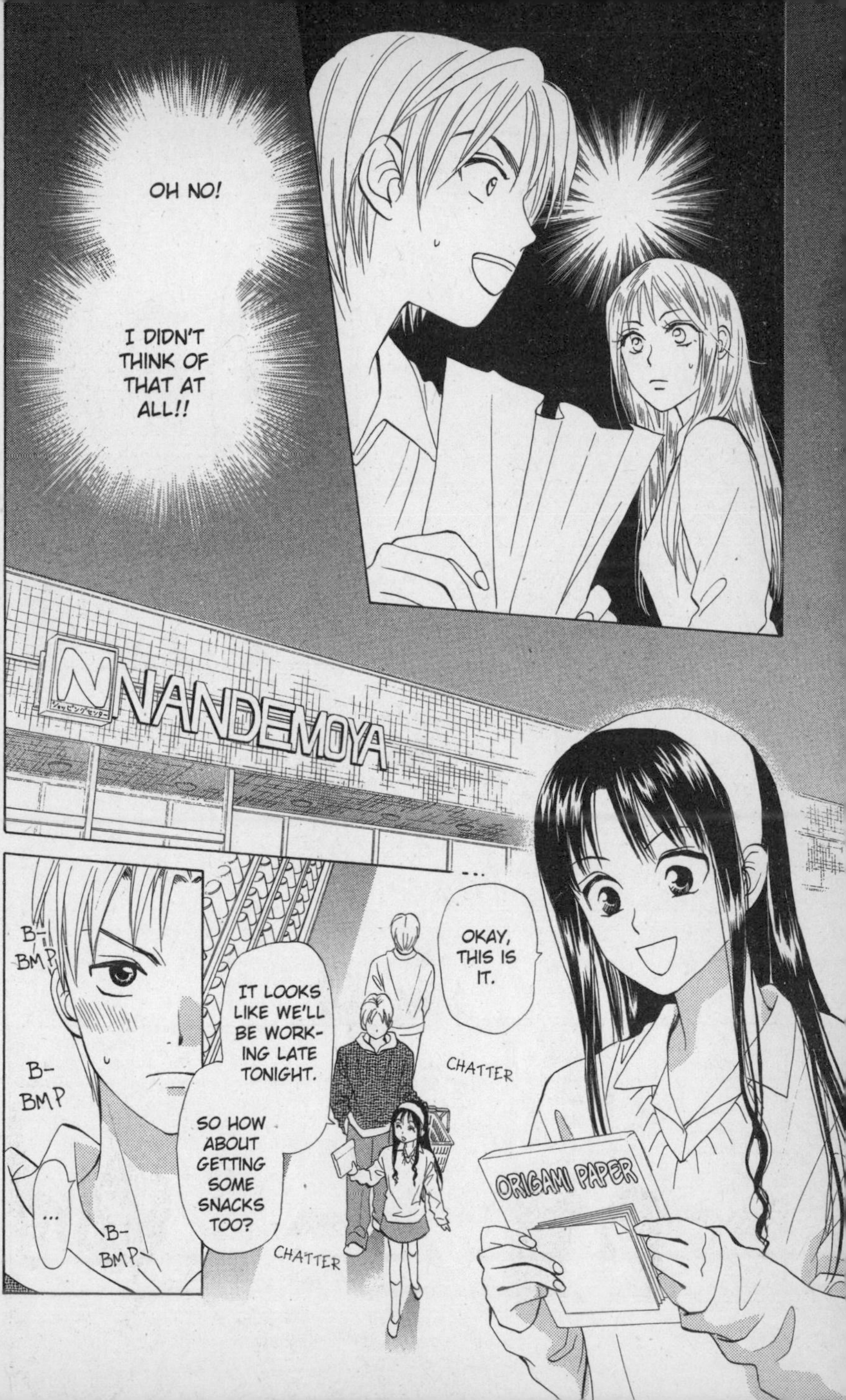
OH NO!
I DIDN'T THINK OF THAT AT ALL!!
NANDEMOYA
...
OKAY, THIS IS IT.
IT LOOKS LIKE WE'LL BE WORKING LATE TONIGHT.
SO HOW ABOUT GETTING SOME SNACKS TOO?
CHATTER
CHATTER
ORIGAMI PAPER
B-BMP
B-BMP
...
B-BMP

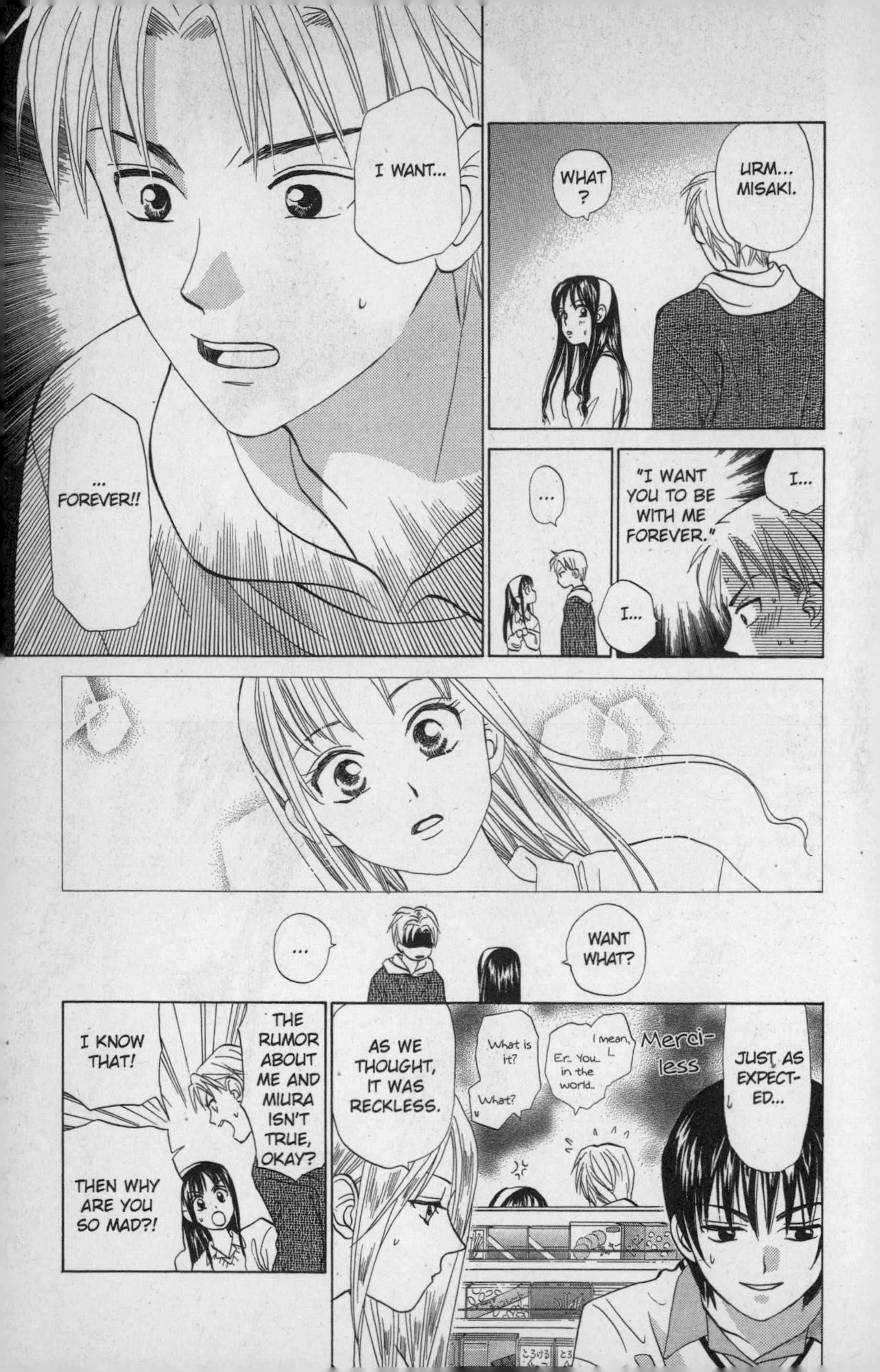
URM... MISAKI.
WHAT?
I...
"I WANT YOU TO BE WITH ME FOREVER."
I...
...
I WANT...
... FOREVER!!
WANT WHAT?
...
JUST AS EXPECTED...
Merciless
I mean, I..
Er.. You.. in the world..
What is it?
What?
AS WE THOUGHT, IT WAS RECKLESS.
THE RUMOR ABOUT ME AND MIURA ISN'T TRUE, OKAY?
I KNOW THAT!
THEN WHY ARE YOU SO MAD?!

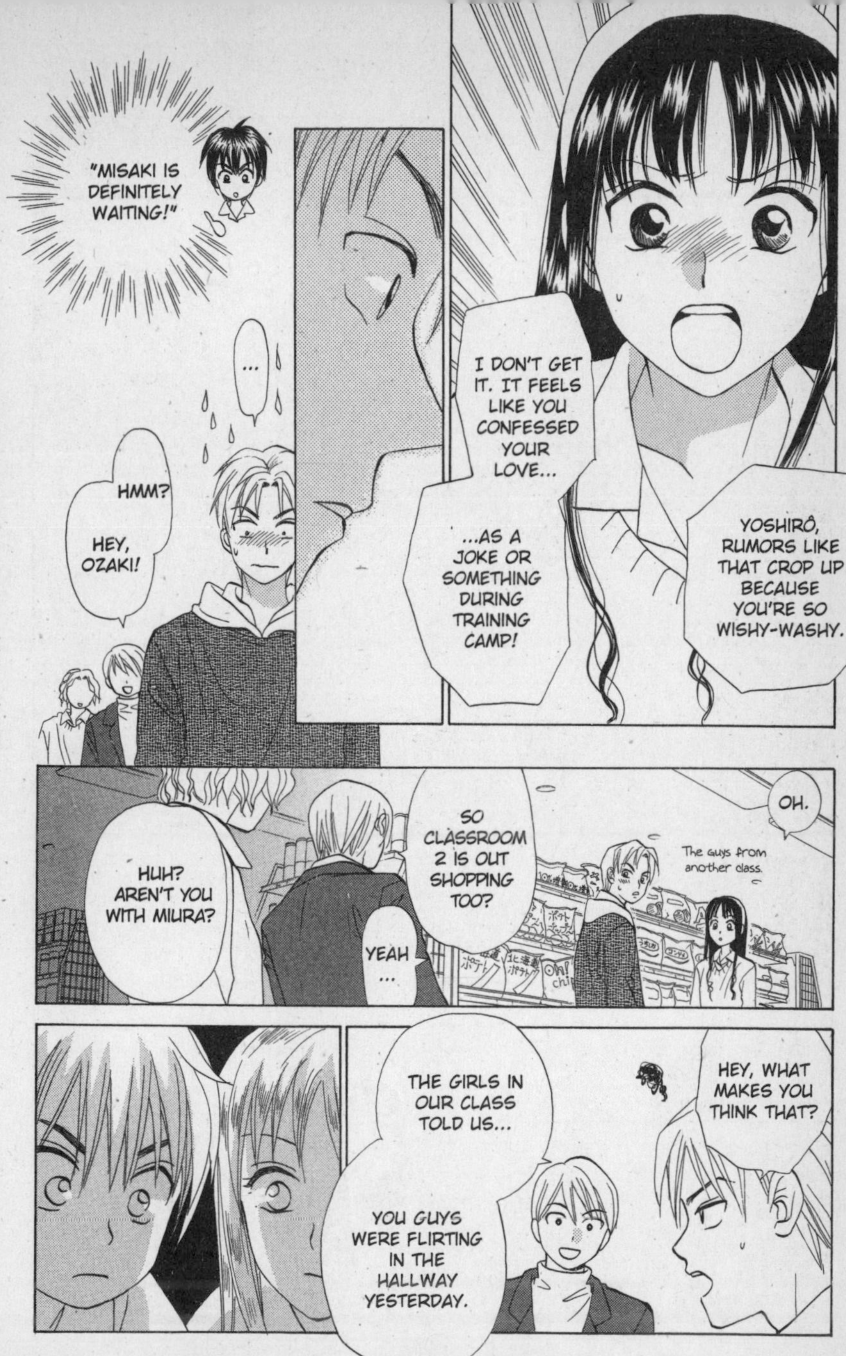
YOSHIRÔ, RUMORS LIKE THAT CROP UP BECAUSE YOU'RE SO WISHY-WASHY.
I DON'T GET IT. IT FEELS LIKE YOU CONFESSED YOUR LOVE...
...AS A JOKE OR SOMETHING DURING TRAINING CAMP!
...
"MISAKI IS DEFINITELY WAITING!"
HMM?
HEY, OZAKI!
OH.
The guys from another class.
SO CLASSROOM 2 IS OUT SHOPPING TOO?
YEAH...
HUH? AREN'T YOU WITH MIURA?
HEY, WHAT MAKES YOU THINK THAT?
THE GIRLS IN OUR CLASS TOLD US...
YOU GUYS WERE FLIRTING IN THE HALLWAY YESTERDAY.

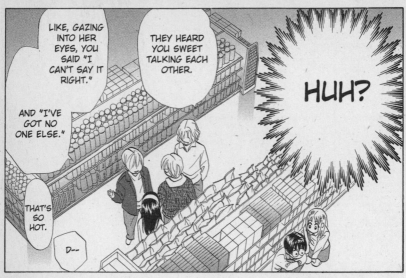

HUH?
THEY HEARD YOU SWEET TALKING EACH OTHER.
LIKE, GAZING INTO HER EYES, YOU SAID "I CAN'T SAY IT RIGHT."
AND "I'VE GOT NO ONE ELSE."
THAT'S SO HOT.
D--
DAMMIT! YOU GOT IT WRONG!
WELL, I CAN'T WAIT TO SEE ALL THIS LOVEY STUFF PLAYED OUT AT THE CULTURAL FESTIVAL!
...
Oh no.
SEE YA!
HA HA HA HA
SILENCE
...
GEEZ, THEY'RE COMING UP WITH THEIR OWN STORY.
NOW WE'VE GOT ANOTHER WEIRD MISUNDER-STANDING.
HA HA
...
SNAP
IF IT BOTHERS YOU, WHY DON'T YOU TELL THEM?!
HUH?

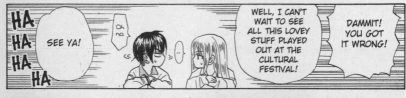

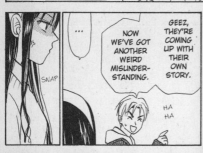

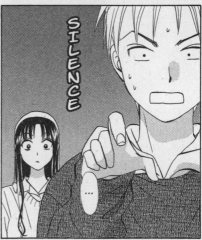

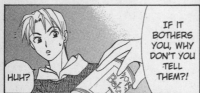

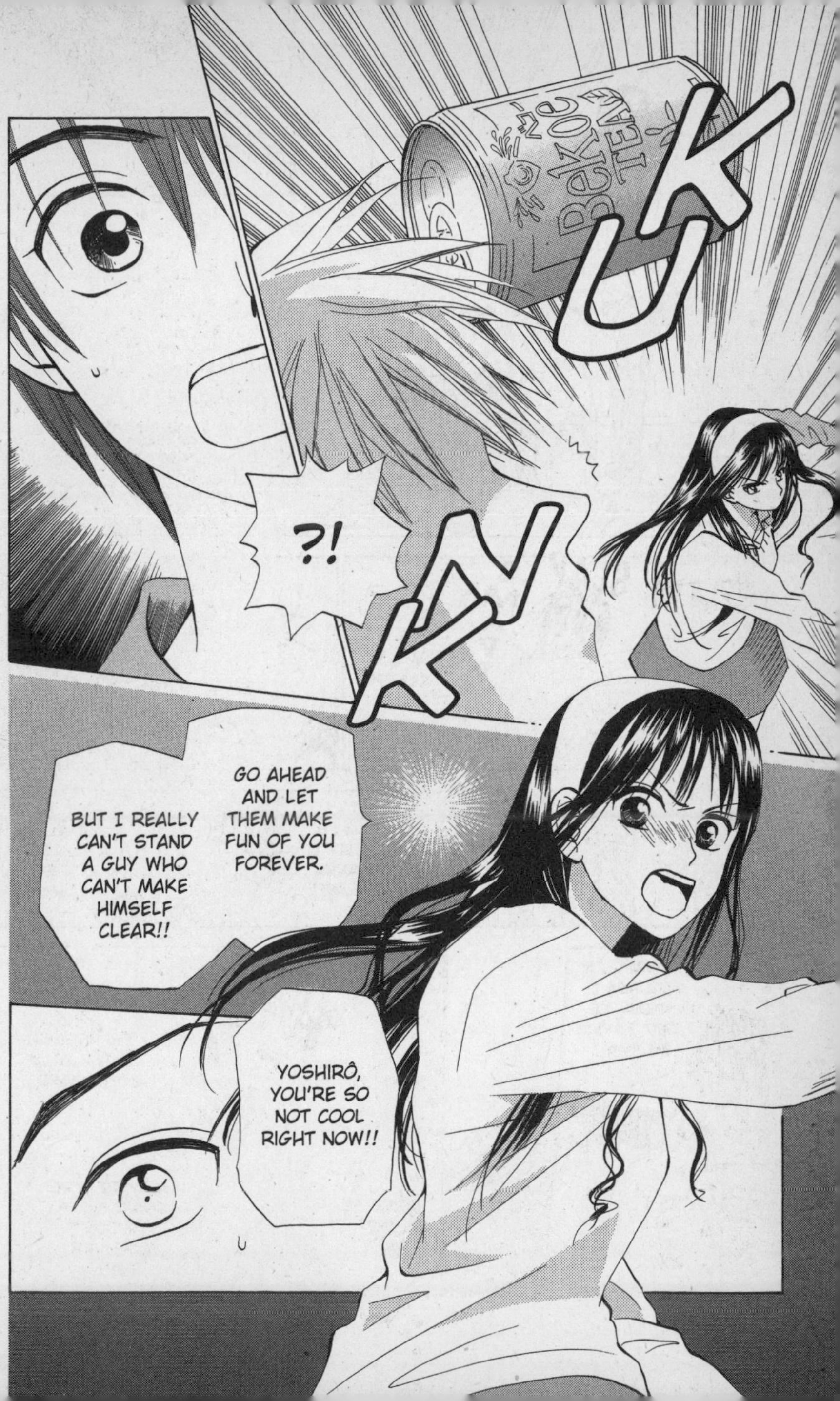
?!
GO AHEAD AND LET THEM MAKE FUN OF YOU FOREVER.
BUT I REALLY CAN'T STAND A GUY WHO CAN'T MAKE HIMSELF CLEAR!!
YOSHIRÔ, YOU'RE SO NOT COOL RIGHT NOW!!

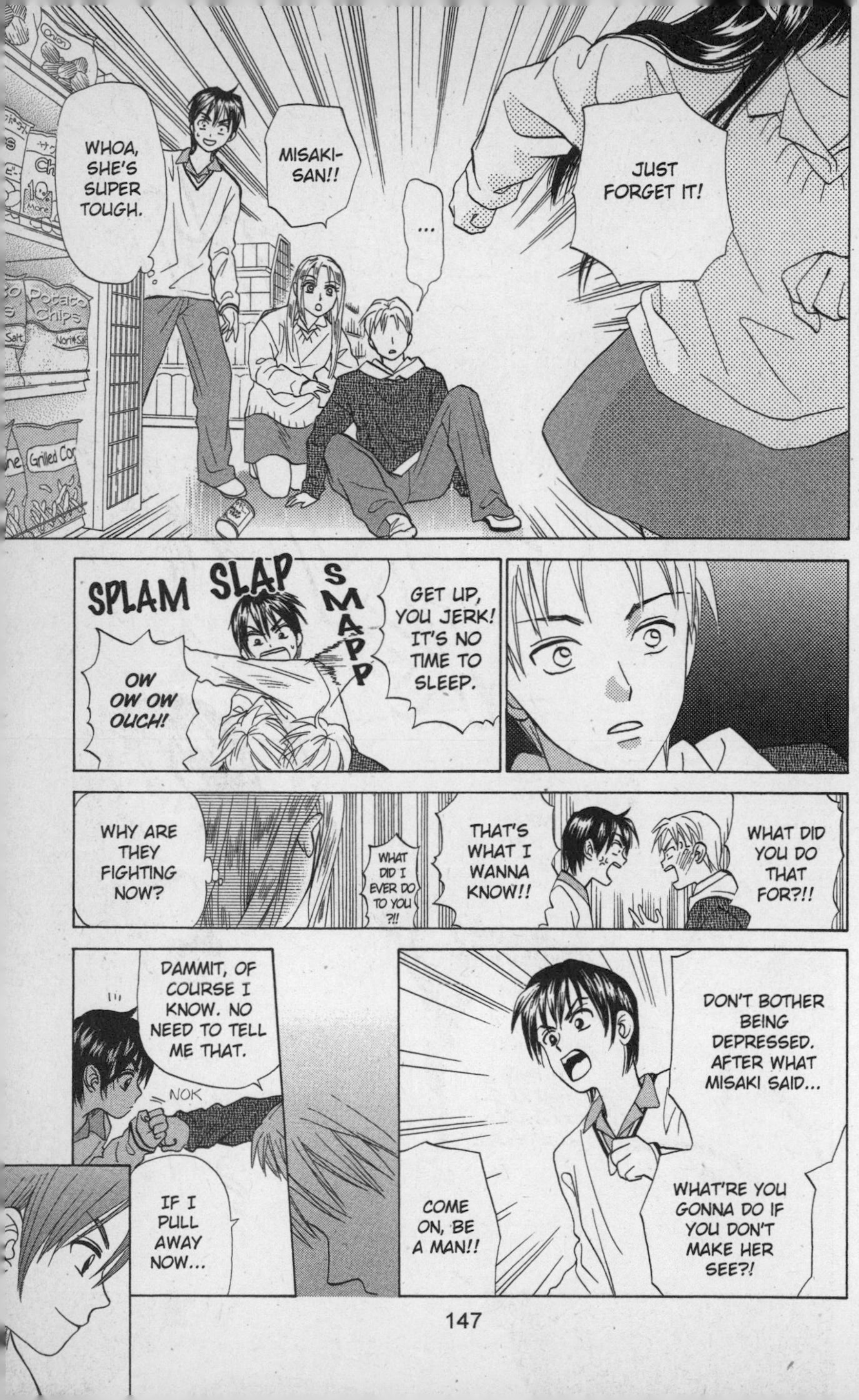
JUST FORGET IT!
...
MISAKI-SAN!!
WHOA, SHE'S SUPER TOUGH.
GET UP, YOU JERK! IT'S NO TIME TO SLEEP.
SMAPP
SLAP
SPLAM
OW OW OW OUCH!
WHAT DID YOU DO THAT FOR?!!
THAT'S WHAT I WANNA KNOW!!
WHAT DID I EVER DO TO YOU ?!!
WHY ARE THEY FIGHTING NOW?
DON'T BOTHER BEING DEPRESSED. AFTER WHAT MISAKI SAID...
WHAT'RE YOU GONNA DO IF YOU DON'T MAKE HER SEE?!
COME ON, BE A MAN!!
DAMMIT, OF COURSE I KNOW. NO NEED TO TELL ME THAT.
NOK
IF I PULL AWAY NOW...

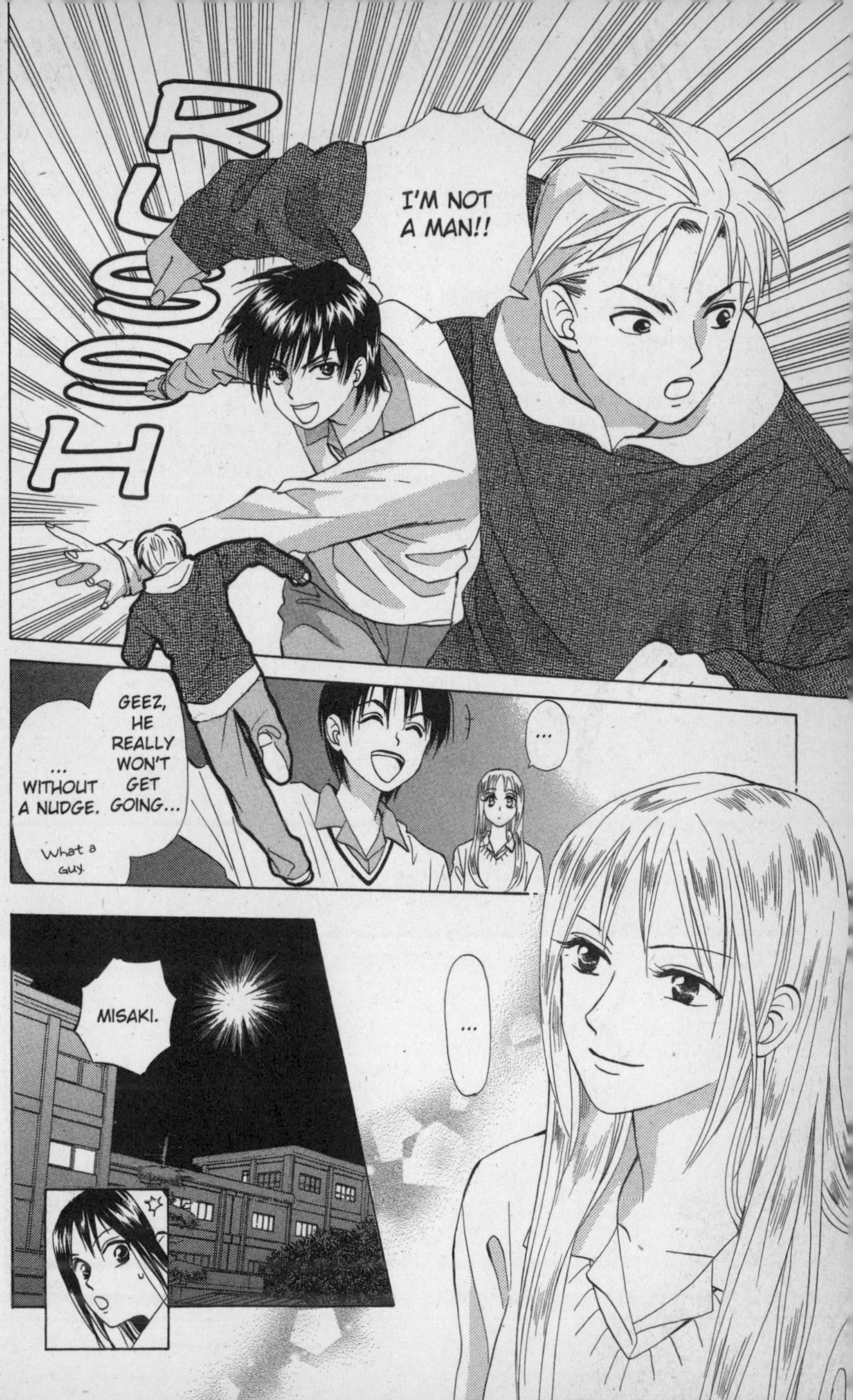
RUSH
I'M NOT A MAN!!
...
GEEZ, HE REALLY WON'T GET GOING...
... WITHOUT A NUDGE.
What a guy.
...
MISAKI.

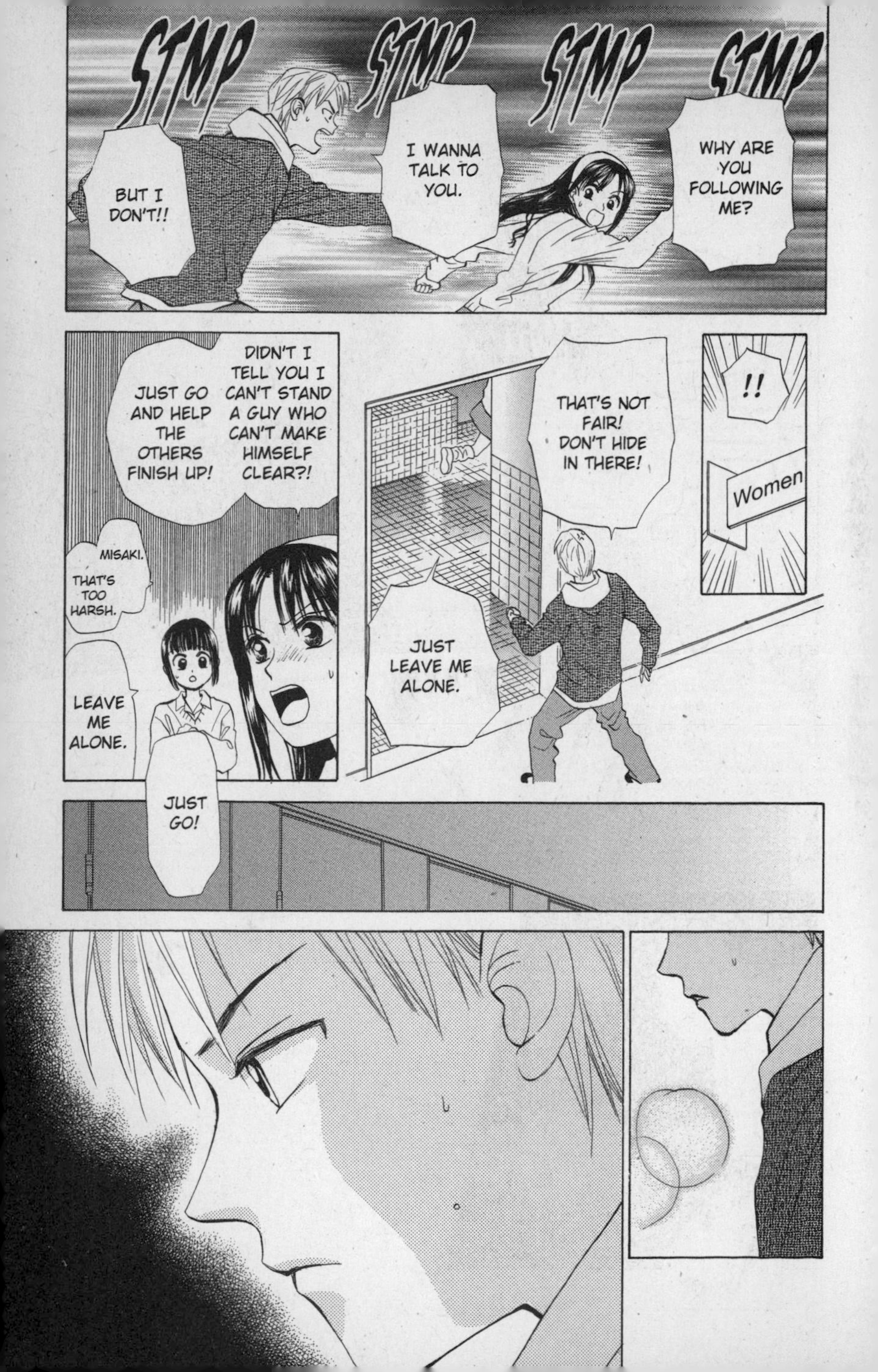
STMP
STMP
STMP
STMP
WHY ARE YOU FOLLOWING ME?
I WANNA TALK TO YOU.
BUT I DON'T!!
!!
Women
THAT'S NOT FAIR! DON'T HIDE IN THERE!
JUST LEAVE ME ALONE.
DIDN'T I TELL YOU I CAN'T STAND A GUY WHO CAN'T MAKE HIMSELF CLEAR?!
JUST GO AND HELP THE OTHERS FINISH UP!
MISAKI.
THAT'S TOO HARSH.
LEAVE ME ALONE.
JUST GO!

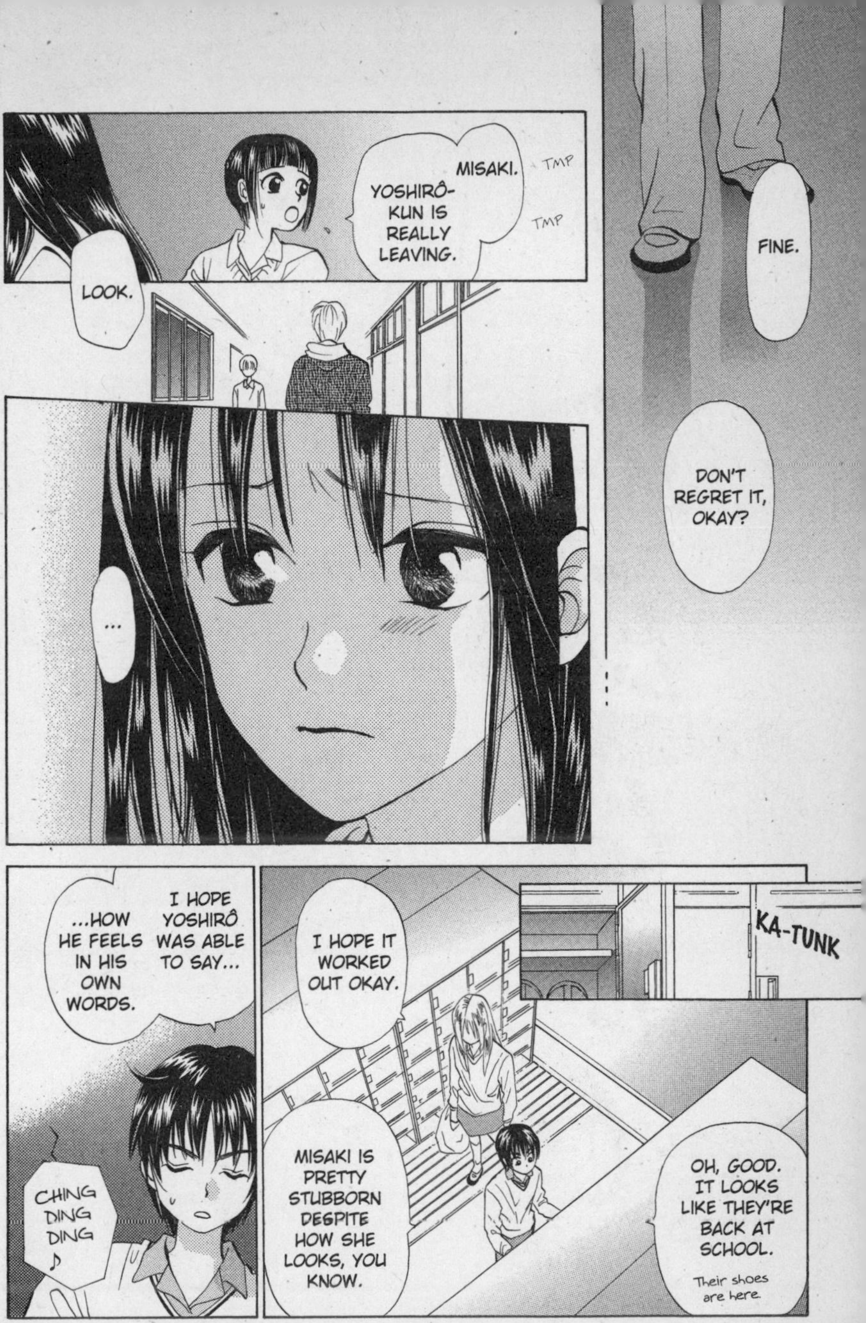
FINE.
DON'T REGRET IT, OKAY?
...
MISAKI.
YOSHIRÔ-KUN IS REALLY LEAVING.
TMP
TMP
LOOK.
...
KA-TUNK
OH, GOOD. IT LOOKS LIKE THEY'RE BACK AT SCHOOL.
Their shoes are here.
I HOPE IT WORKED OUT OKAY.
MISAKI IS PRETTY STUBBORN DESPITE HOW SHE LOOKS, YOU KNOW.
I HOPE YOSHIRÔ WAS ABLE TO SAY...
...HOW HE FEELS IN HIS OWN WORDS.
CHING DING DING ♪

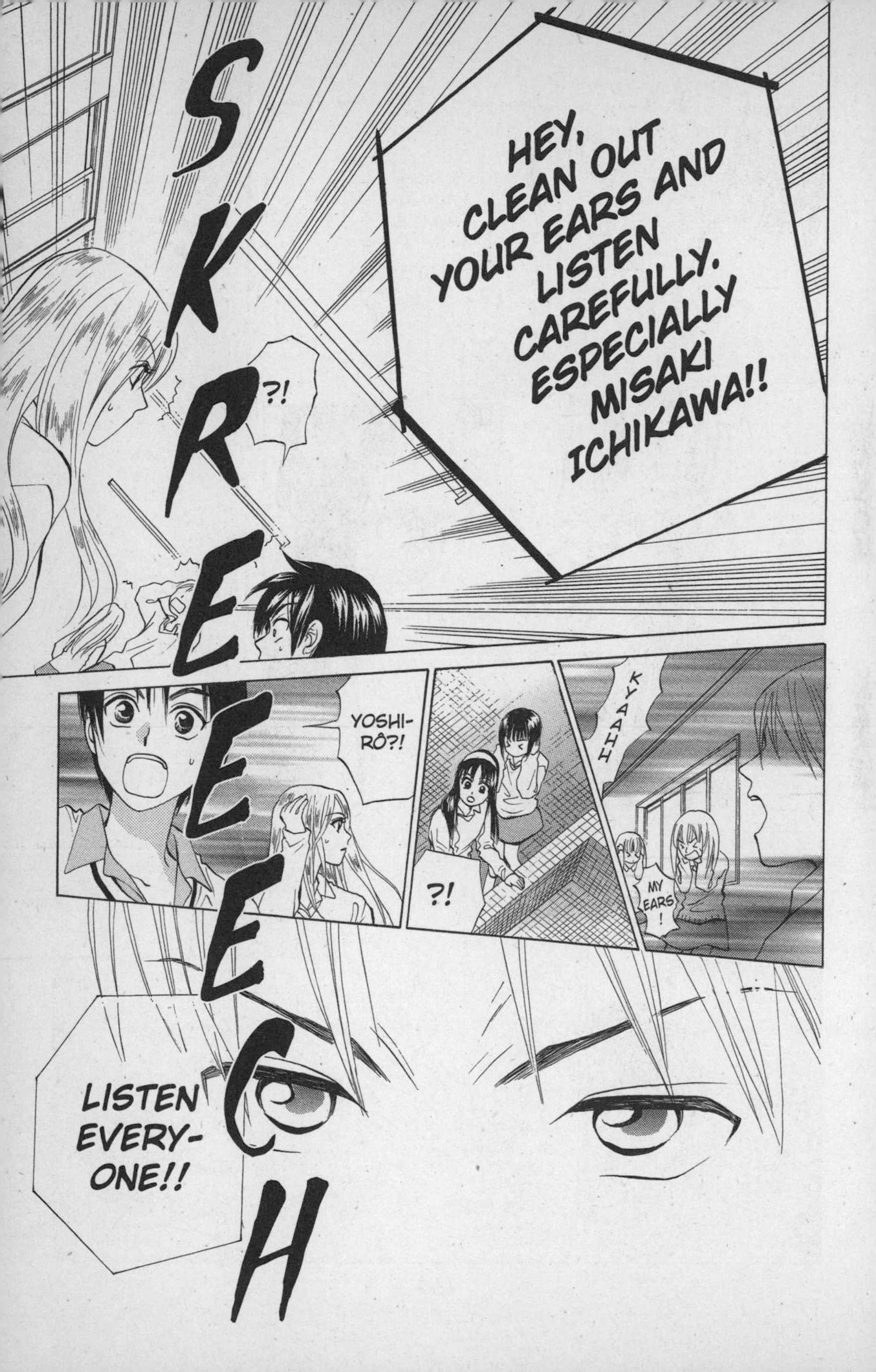
HEY, CLEAN OUT YOUR EARS AND LISTEN CAREFULLY. ESPECIALLY MISAKI ICHIKAWA!!
?!
SKREEECH
KYAAHH
MY EARS!
?!
YOSHI-RÔ?!
LISTEN EVERY-ONE!!

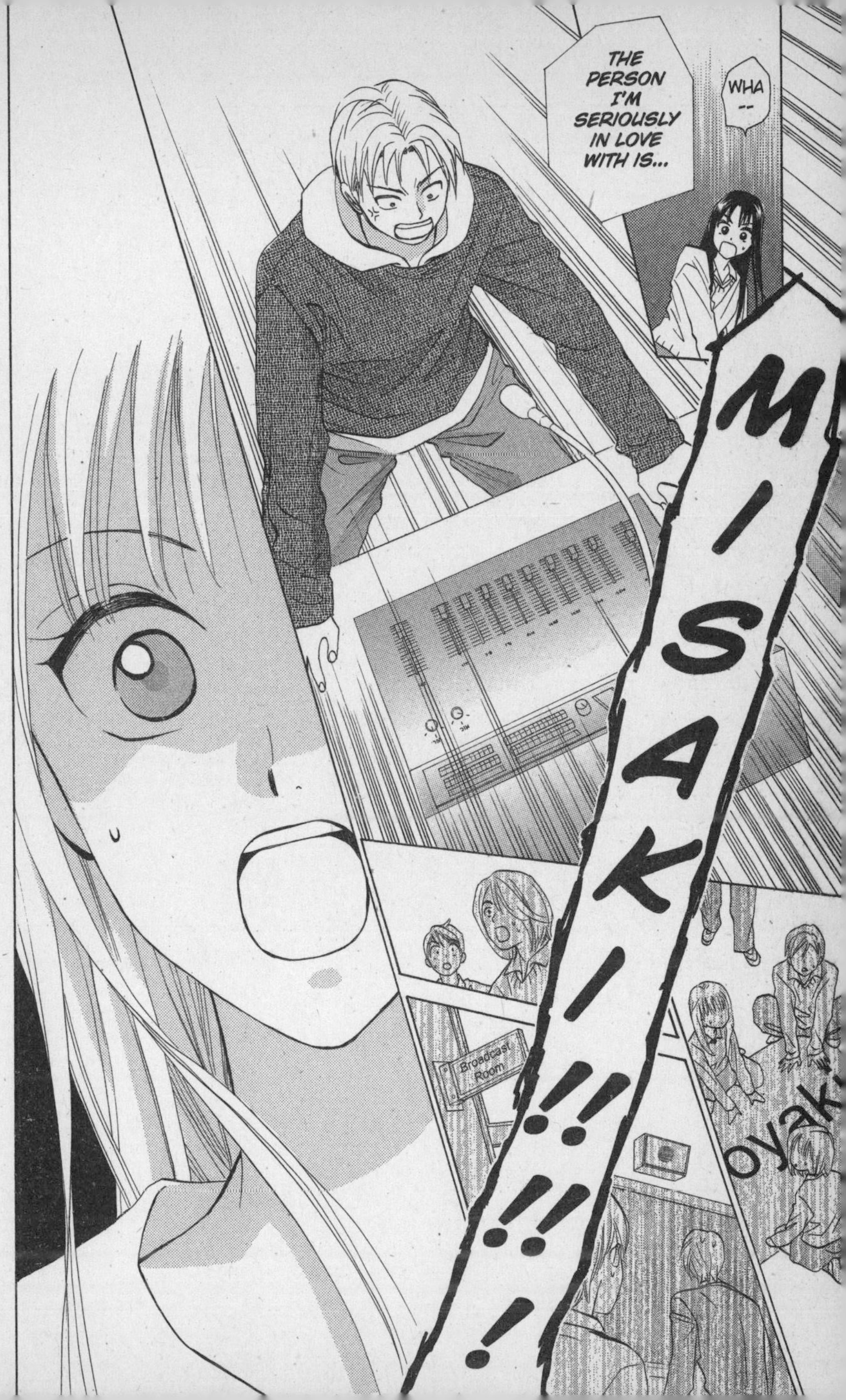
THE PERSON I'M SERIOUSLY IN LOVE WITH IS...
WHA --
MISAKI!!!!!!
Broadcast Room

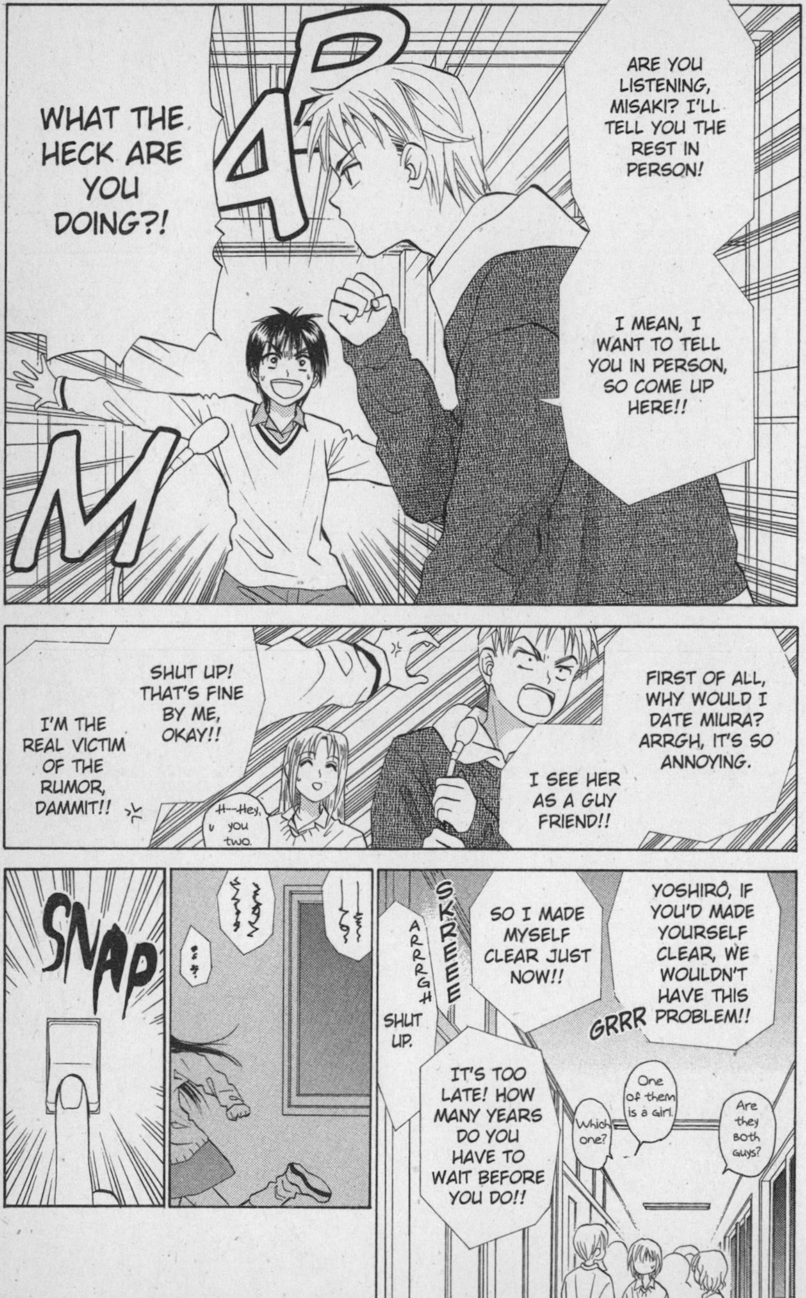
ARE YOU LISTENING, MISAKI? I'LL TELL YOU THE REST IN PERSON!
I MEAN, I WANT TO TELL YOU IN PERSON, SO COME UP HERE!!
WHAT THE HECK ARE YOU DOING?!
FIRST OF ALL, WHY WOULD I DATE MIURA? ARRGH, IT'S SO ANNOYING.
I SEE HER AS A GUY FRIEND!!
SHUT UP! THAT'S FINE BY ME, OKAY!!
H-Hey, you two.
I'M THE REAL VICTIM OF THE RUMOR, DAMMIT!!
YOSHIRÔ, IF YOU'D MADE YOURSELF CLEAR, WE WOULDN'T HAVE THIS PROBLEM!!
GRRR
SO I MADE MYSELF CLEAR JUST NOW!!
SKREEE
ARRRGH
SHUT UP.
IT'S TOO LATE! HOW MANY YEARS DO YOU HAVE TO WAIT BEFORE YOU DO!!
Are they both guys?
One of them is a girl.
Which one?
SNAP

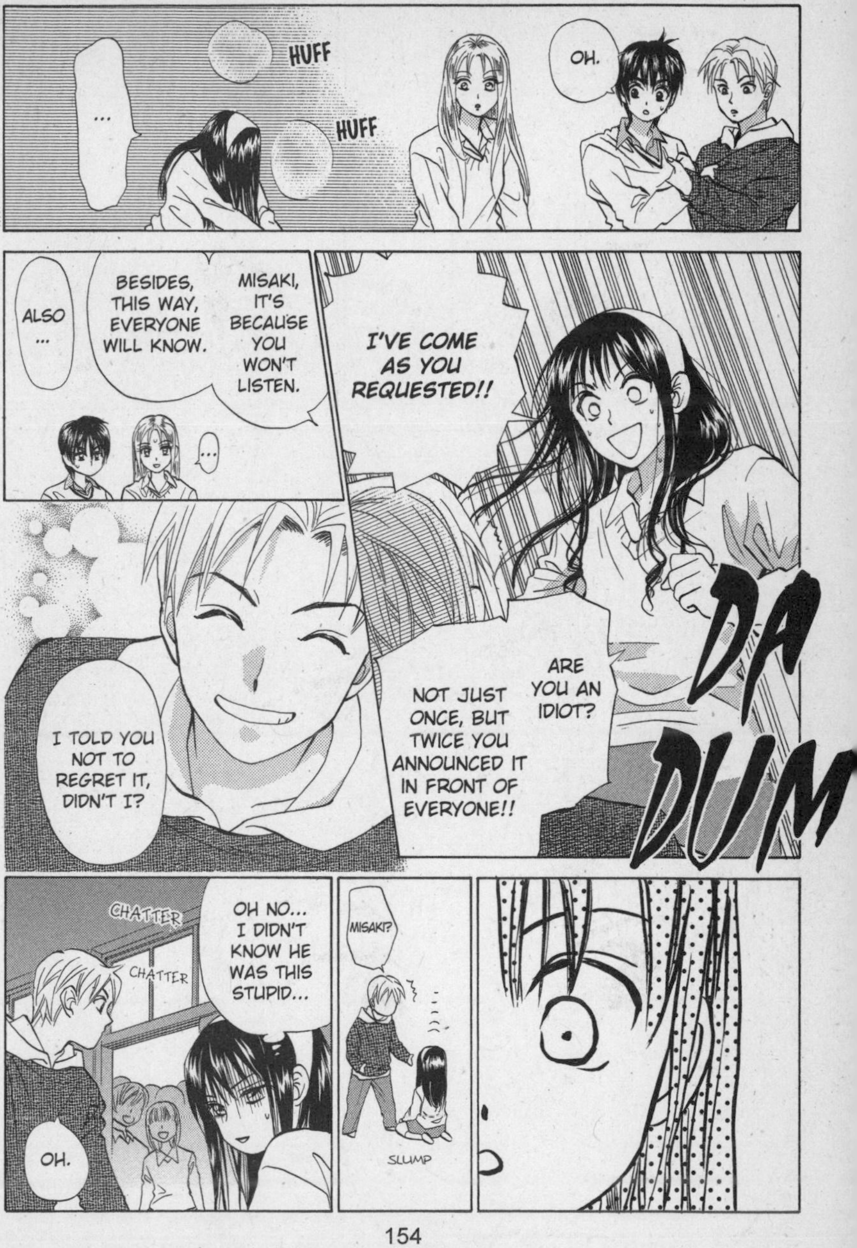
OH.
HUFF
HUFF
...
I'VE COME AS YOU REQUESTED!!
DA DUM
MISAKI, IT'S BECAUSE YOU WON'T LISTEN.
BESIDES, THIS WAY, EVERYONE WILL KNOW.
ALSO ...
...
ARE YOU AN IDIOT?
NOT JUST ONCE, BUT TWICE YOU ANNOUNCED IT IN FRONT OF EVERYONE!!
I TOLD YOU NOT TO REGRET IT, DIDN'T I?
MISAKI?
SLUMP
OH NO... I DIDN'T KNOW HE WAS THIS STUPID...
CHATTER
CHATTER
OH.

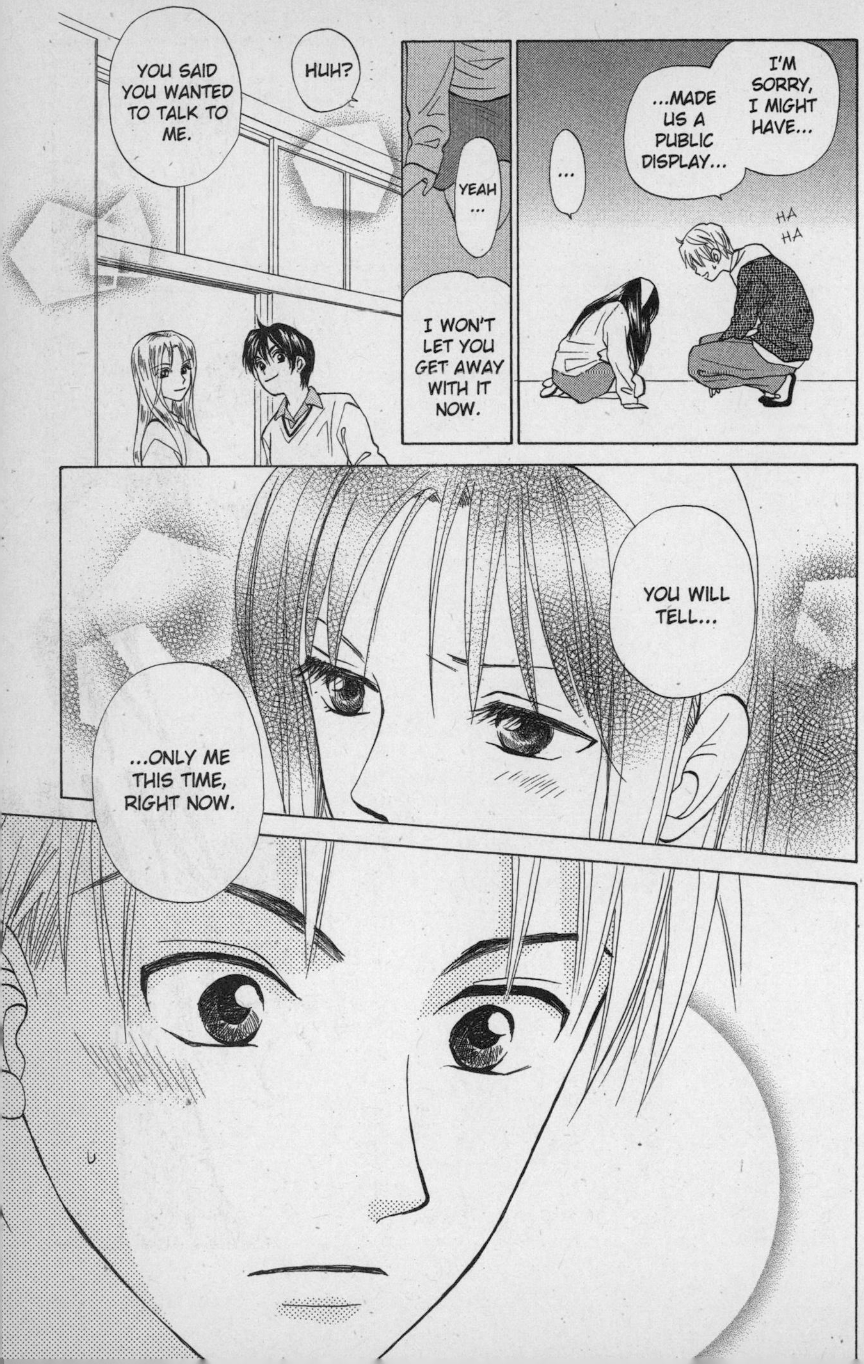
I'M SORRY, I MIGHT HAVE...
...MADE US A PUBLIC DISPLAY...
...
HA HA
YEAH ...
I WON'T LET YOU GET AWAY WITH IT NOW.
HUH?
YOU SAID YOU WANTED TO TALK TO ME.
YOU WILL TELL...
...ONLY ME THIS TIME, RIGHT NOW.

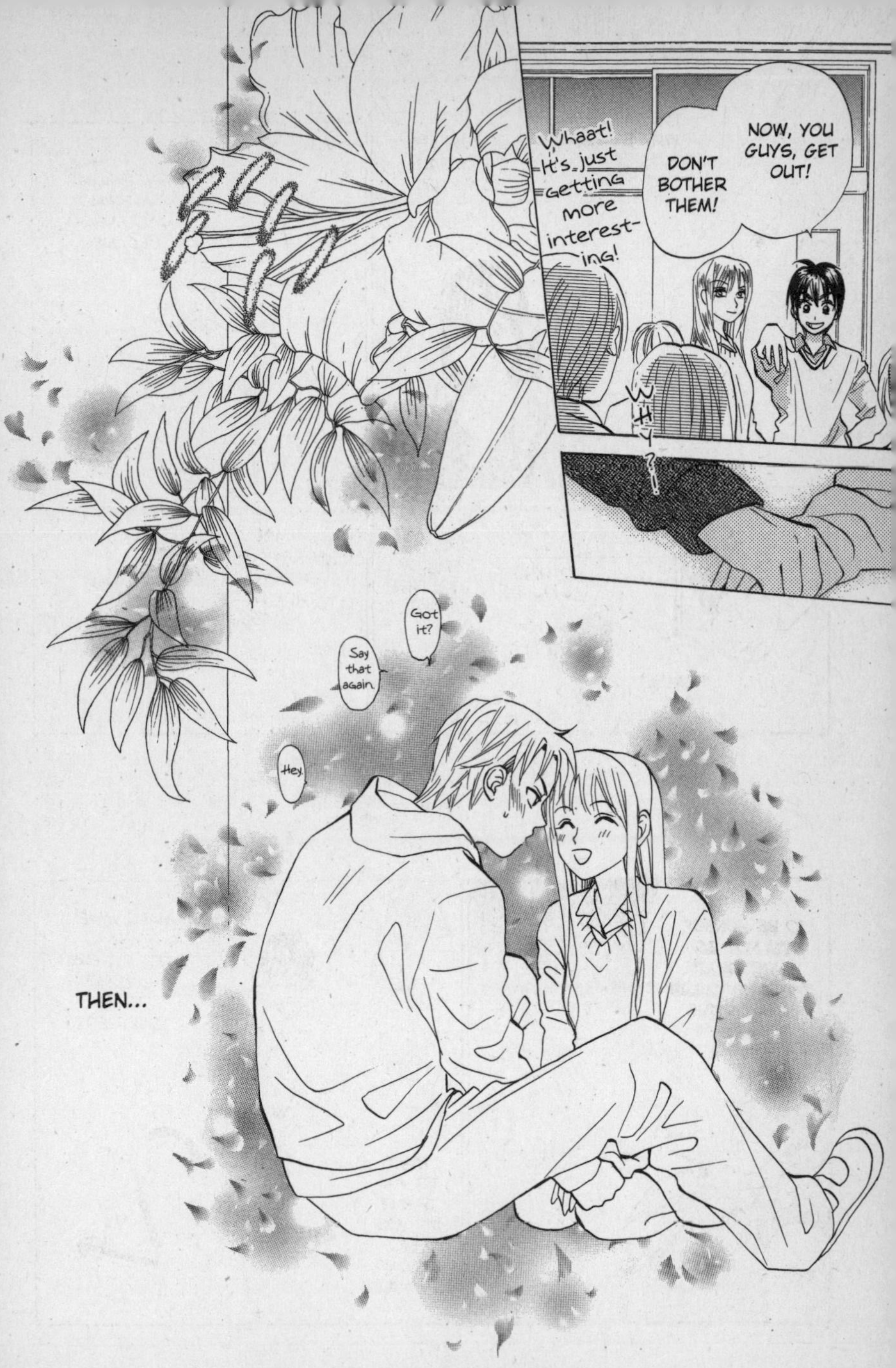
NOW, YOU GUYS, GET OUT!
DON'T BOTHER THEM!
Whaat! It's just getting more interest-ing!
WHY?!
Got it?
Say that again.
Hey.
THEN...

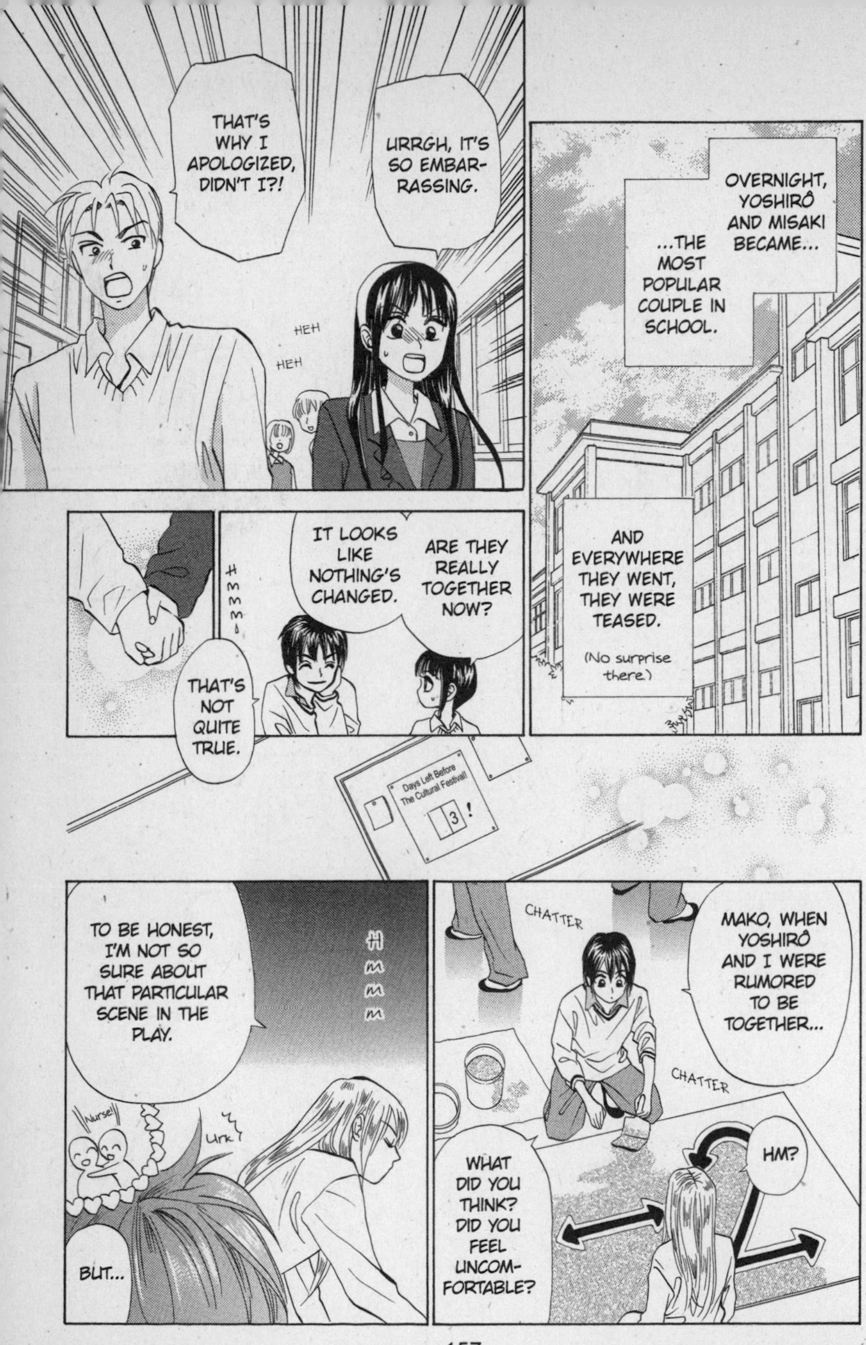

URRGH, IT'S SO EMBARRASSING.
THAT'S WHY I APOLOGIZED, DIDN'T I?!
HEH HEH
OVERNIGHT, YOSHIRÔ AND MISAKI BECAME...
...THE MOST POPULAR COUPLE IN SCHOOL.
AND EVERYWHERE THEY WENT, THEY WERE TEASED.
(No surprise there.)
ARE THEY REALLY TOGETHER NOW?
IT LOOKS LIKE NOTHING'S CHANGED.
HMMM
THAT'S NOT QUITE TRUE.
Days Left Before The Cultural Festival!
3 !
CHATTER
MAKO, WHEN YOSHIRÔ AND I WERE RUMORED TO BE TOGETHER...
CHATTER
HM?
WHAT DID YOU THINK? DID YOU FEEL UNCOMFORTABLE?
HMMM
TO BE HONEST, I'M NOT SO SURE ABOUT THAT PARTICULAR SCENE IN THE PLAY.
Nurse!
Urk
BUT...

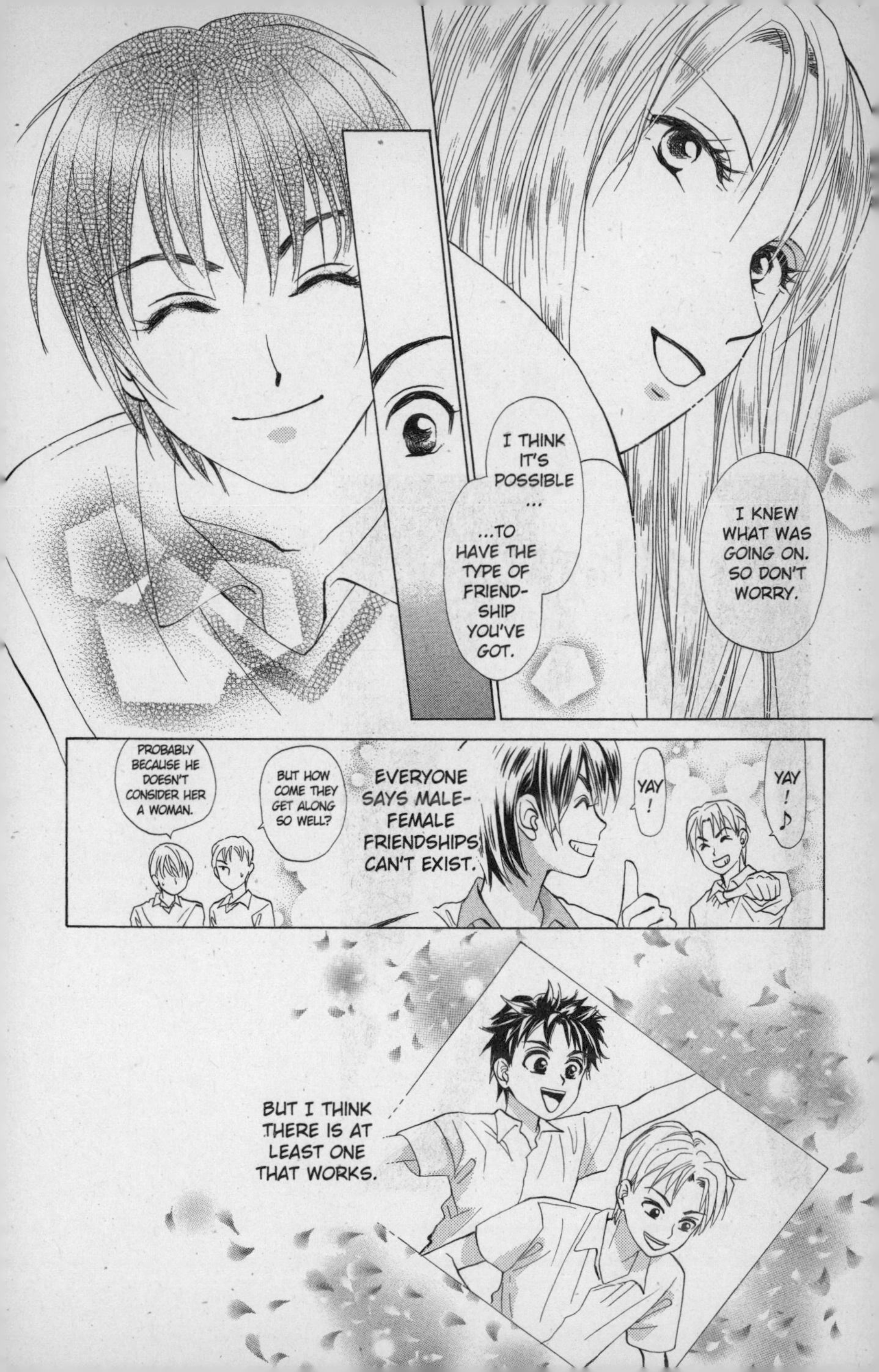
I KNEW WHAT WAS GOING ON. SO DON'T WORRY.
I THINK IT'S POSSIBLE ...
...TO HAVE THE TYPE OF FRIEND-SHIP YOU'VE GOT.
YAY! ♪
YAY!
EVERYONE SAYS MALE-FEMALE FRIENDSHIPS CAN'T EXIST.
BUT HOW COME THEY GET ALONG SO WELL?
PROBABLY BECAUSE HE DOESN'T CONSIDER HER A WOMAN.
BUT I THINK THERE IS AT LEAST ONE THAT WORKS.

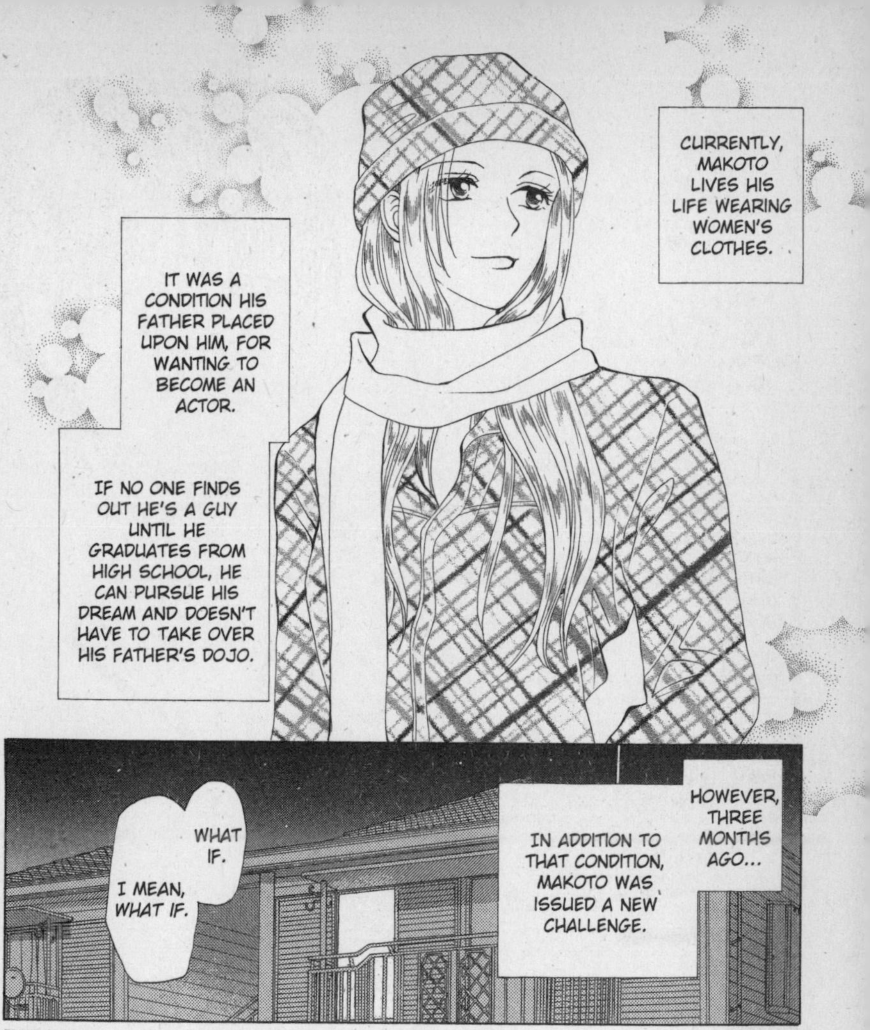
CURRENTLY, MAKOTO LIVES HIS LIFE WEARING WOMEN'S CLOTHES.
IT WAS A CONDITION HIS FATHER PLACED UPON HIM, FOR WANTING TO BECOME AN ACTOR.
IF NO ONE FINDS OUT HE'S A GUY UNTIL HE GRADUATES FROM HIGH SCHOOL, HE CAN PURSUE HIS DREAM AND DOESN'T HAVE TO TAKE OVER HIS FATHER'S DOJO.
HOWEVER, THREE MONTHS AGO...
IN ADDITION TO THAT CONDITION, MAKOTO WAS ISSUED A NEW CHALLENGE.
WHAT IF.
I MEAN, WHAT IF.

—Behind the Scenes Story ⑥—

"What is that ring Ito is wearing...?" The question flew in from everywhere this time. The fact is, it's something Ito received as a gift from Makoto in the HCD story. I included it upon the release of the CD. It was meant as a secret only for those in the know. But it's not really nice to those who read the comics version only! So I'm writing about it now to explain. The CD is available for anyone who orders it. If you're interested, please listen to it. ♪

And don't forget the second CD too!

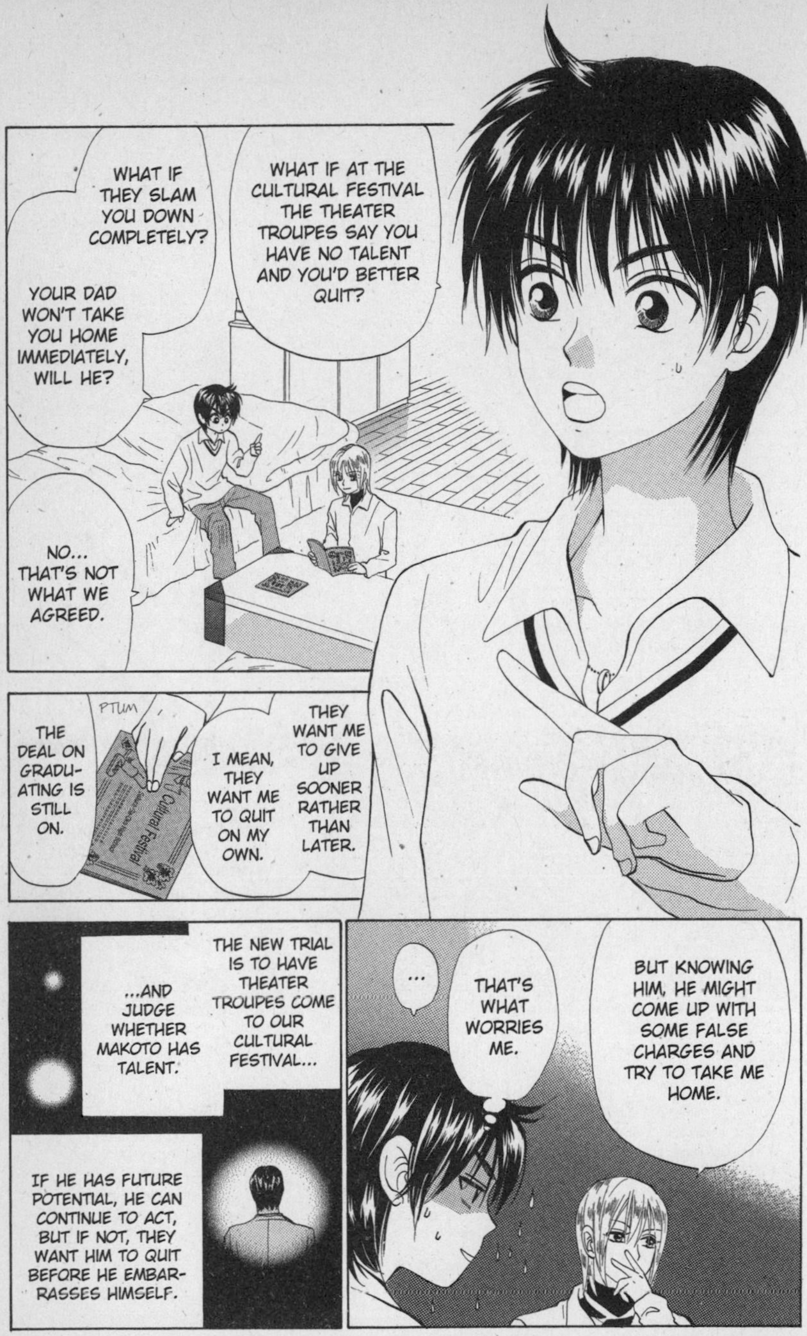
WHAT IF AT THE CULTURAL FESTIVAL THE THEATER TROUPES SAY YOU HAVE NO TALENT AND YOU'D BETTER QUIT?
WHAT IF THEY SLAM YOU DOWN COMPLETELY?
YOUR DAD WON'T TAKE YOU HOME IMMEDIATELY, WILL HE?
NO... THAT'S NOT WHAT WE AGREED.
THEY WANT ME TO GIVE UP SOONER RATHER THAN LATER.
I MEAN, THEY WANT ME TO QUIT ON MY OWN.
PTUM
Cultural Festival
THE DEAL ON GRADU-ATING IS STILL ON.
BUT KNOWING HIM, HE MIGHT COME UP WITH SOME FALSE CHARGES AND TRY TO TAKE ME HOME.
THAT'S WHAT WORRIES ME.
...
THE NEW TRIAL IS TO HAVE THEATER TROUPES COME TO OUR CULTURAL FESTIVAL...
...AND JUDGE WHETHER MAKOTO HAS TALENT.
IF HE HAS FUTURE POTENTIAL, HE CAN CONTINUE TO ACT, BUT IF NOT, THEY WANT HIM TO QUIT BEFORE HE EMBAR-RASSES HIMSELF.

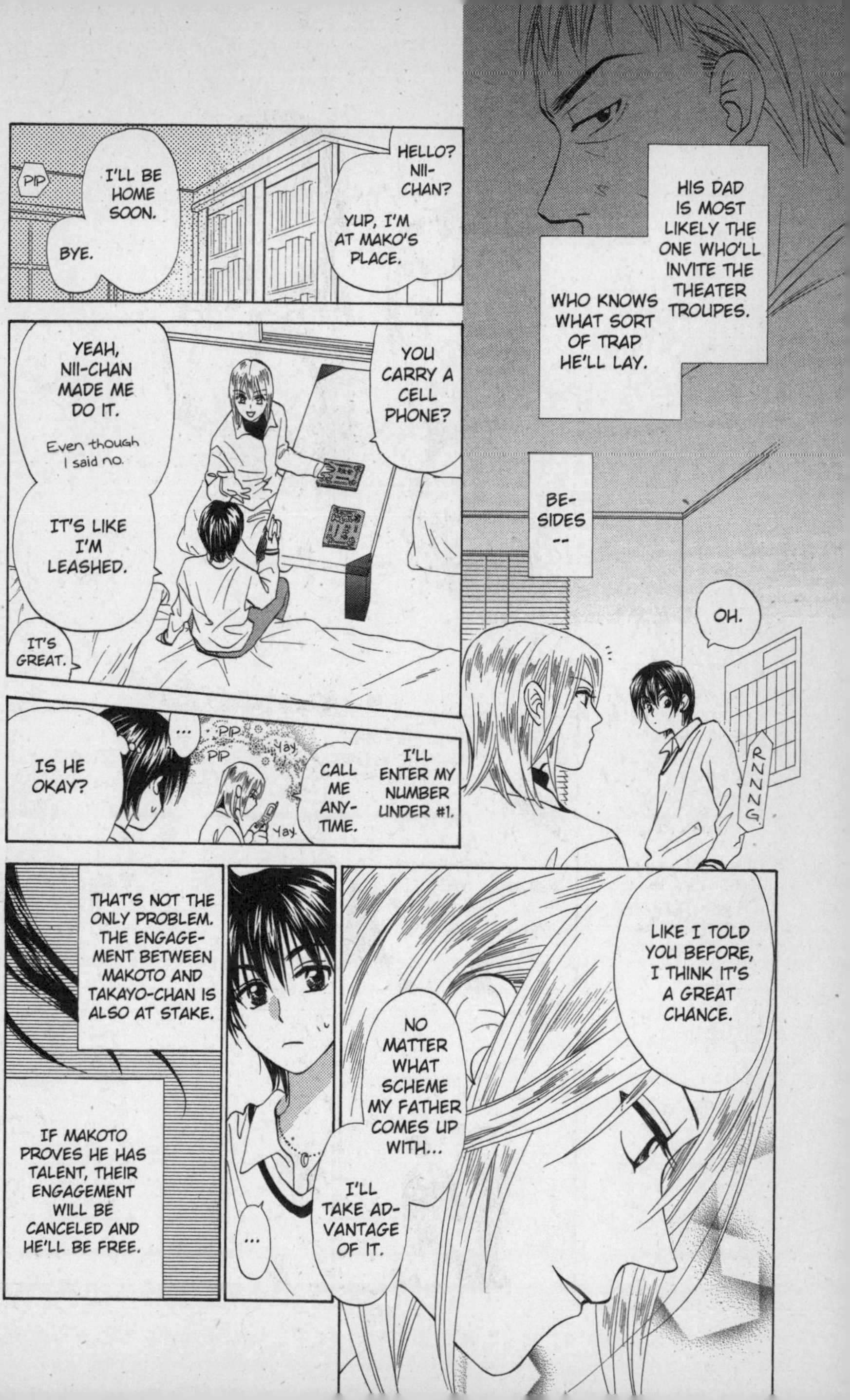
HIS DAD IS MOST LIKELY THE ONE WHO'LL INVITE THE THEATER TROUPES.
WHO KNOWS WHAT SORT OF TRAP HE'LL LAY.
BE-SIDES --
OH.
RNNNG
HELLO? NII-CHAN?
YUP, I'M AT MAKO'S PLACE.
I'LL BE HOME SOON.
BYE.
PIP
YOU CARRY A CELL PHONE?
YEAH, NII-CHAN MADE ME DO IT.
Even though I said no.
IT'S LIKE I'M LEASHED.
IT'S GREAT.
I'LL ENTER MY NUMBER UNDER #1.
CALL ME ANY-TIME.
PIP
PIP
Yay.
Yay.
...
IS HE OKAY?
LIKE I TOLD YOU BEFORE, I THINK IT'S A GREAT CHANCE.
NO MATTER WHAT SCHEME MY FATHER COMES UP WITH...
I'LL TAKE AD-VANTAGE OF IT.
...
THAT'S NOT THE ONLY PROBLEM. THE ENGAGE-MENT BETWEEN MAKOTO AND TAKAYO-CHAN IS ALSO AT STAKE.
IF MAKOTO PROVES HE HAS TALENT, THEIR ENGAGEMENT WILL BE CANCELED AND HE'LL BE FREE.

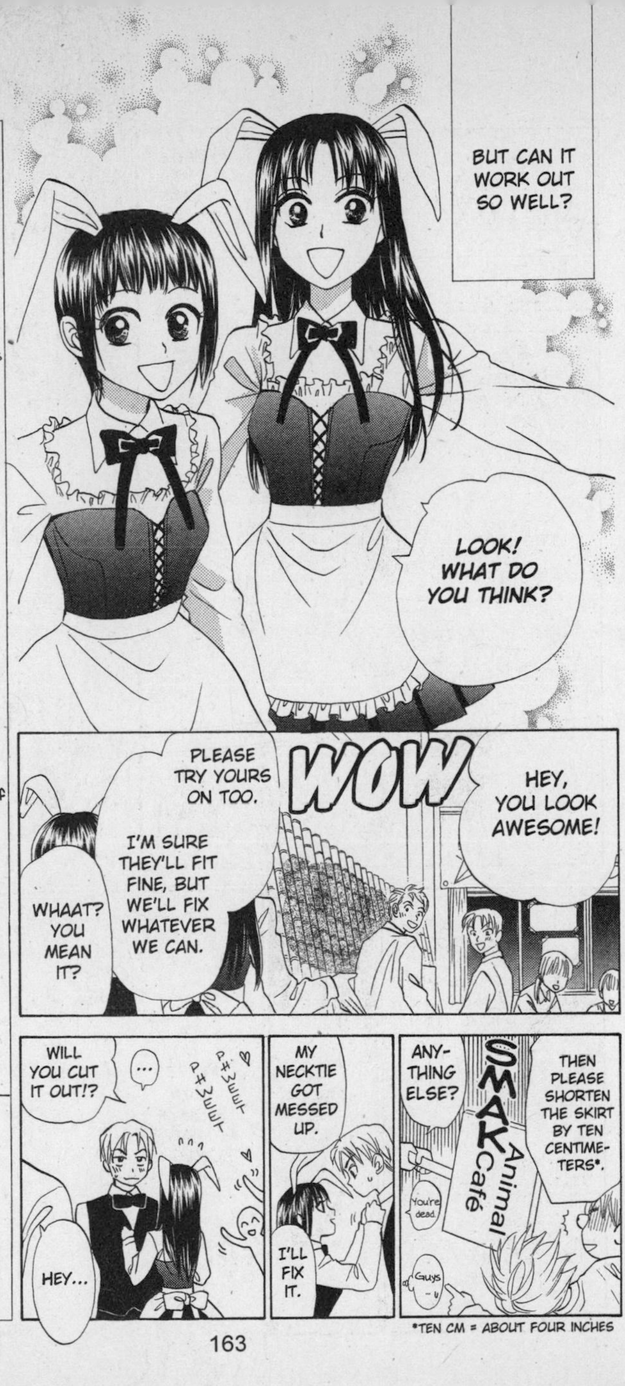
BUT CAN IT WORK OUT SO WELL?
LOOK! WHAT DO YOU THINK?
HEY, YOU LOOK AWESOME!
WOW
PLEASE TRY YOURS ON TOO.
I'M SURE THEY'LL FIT FINE, BUT WE'LL FIX WHATEVER WE CAN.
WHAAT? YOU MEAN IT?
THEN PLEASE SHORTEN THE SKIRT BY TEN CENTIMETERS*.
SMAK
Animal Café
ANYTHING ELSE?
You're dead.
Guys ~
MY NECKTIE GOT MESSED UP.
I'LL FIX IT.
P#WEET
P#WEET
...
WILL YOU CUT IT OUT!?
HEY...

*TEN CM = ABOUT FOUR INCHES

Recently, I've been so busy that I don't have time to go online.

Huh?
Two hours ?!
SKCH

Come on
I'd better work. (Laugh)

My sister bought a PC last year, and I was totally hooked for a while. But since last year (2002), I pretty much stopped looking. Especially after I got injured, I'm always pretty much in an edge-of-a-cliff situation. (Sob)
Er... I guess it's... ...nothing unusual.

I'd love to work with more time. Oh well, I'd better hurry and finish the storyboard.

Anyhow, please continue your support through the next volume. It's the Cultural Festival next at last! There will be an accident.

2002. 7. 14

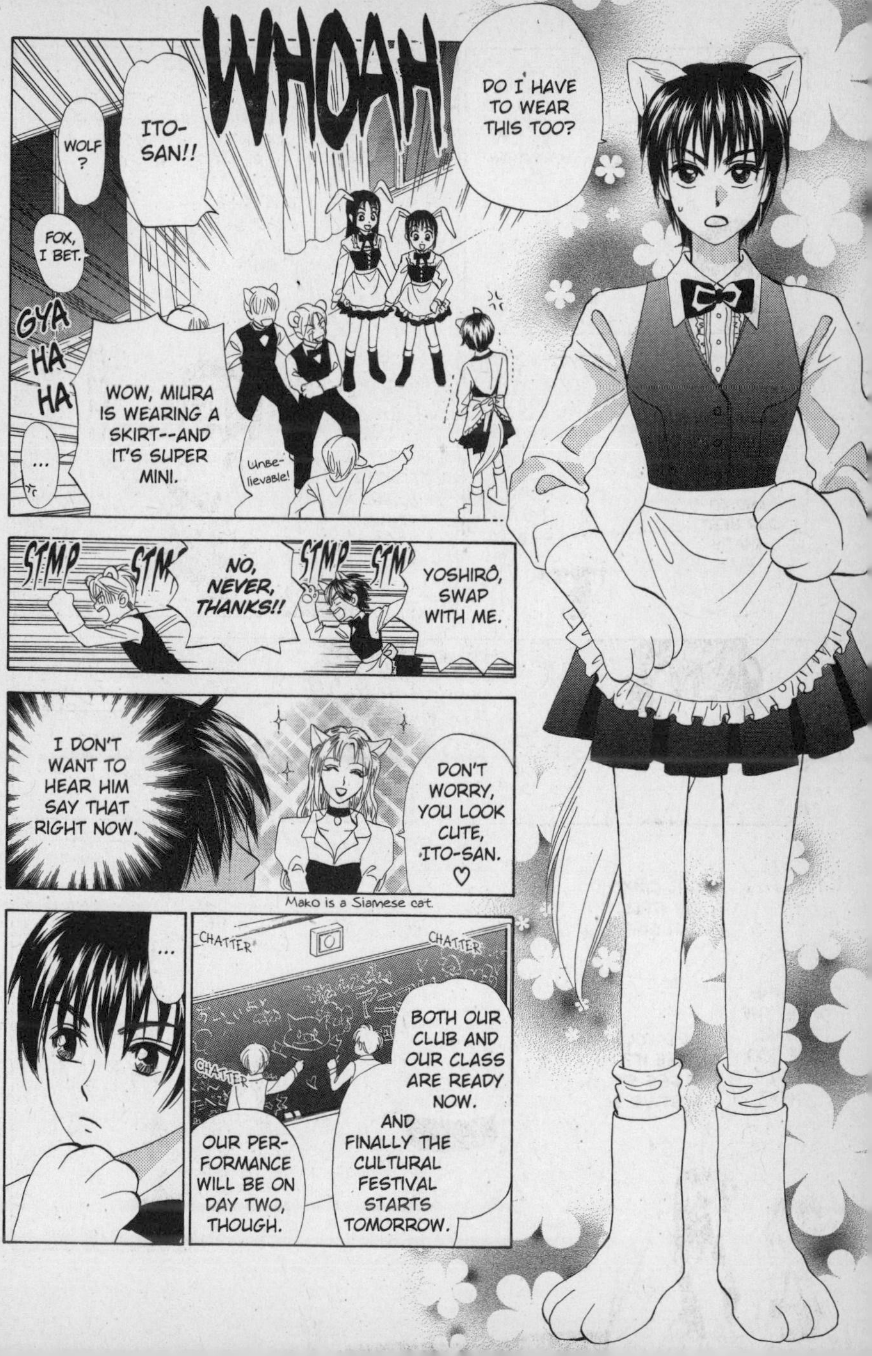
DO I HAVE TO WEAR THIS TOO?
WHOAH
ITO-SAN!!
WOLF?
FOX, I BET.
GYA HA HA
WOW, MIURA IS WEARING A SKIRT--AND IT'S SUPER MINI.
Unbelievable!
...
YOSHIRÔ, SWAP WITH ME.
STMP STM
NO, NEVER, THANKS!!
STMP STM
DON'T WORRY, YOU LOOK CUTE, ITO-SAN. ♡
I DON'T WANT TO HEAR HIM SAY THAT RIGHT NOW.
Mako is a Siamese cat.
CHATTER
CHATTER
CHATTER
BOTH OUR CLUB AND OUR CLASS ARE READY NOW.
AND FINALLY THE CULTURAL FESTIVAL STARTS TOMORROW.
OUR PERFORMANCE WILL BE ON DAY TWO, THOUGH.
...

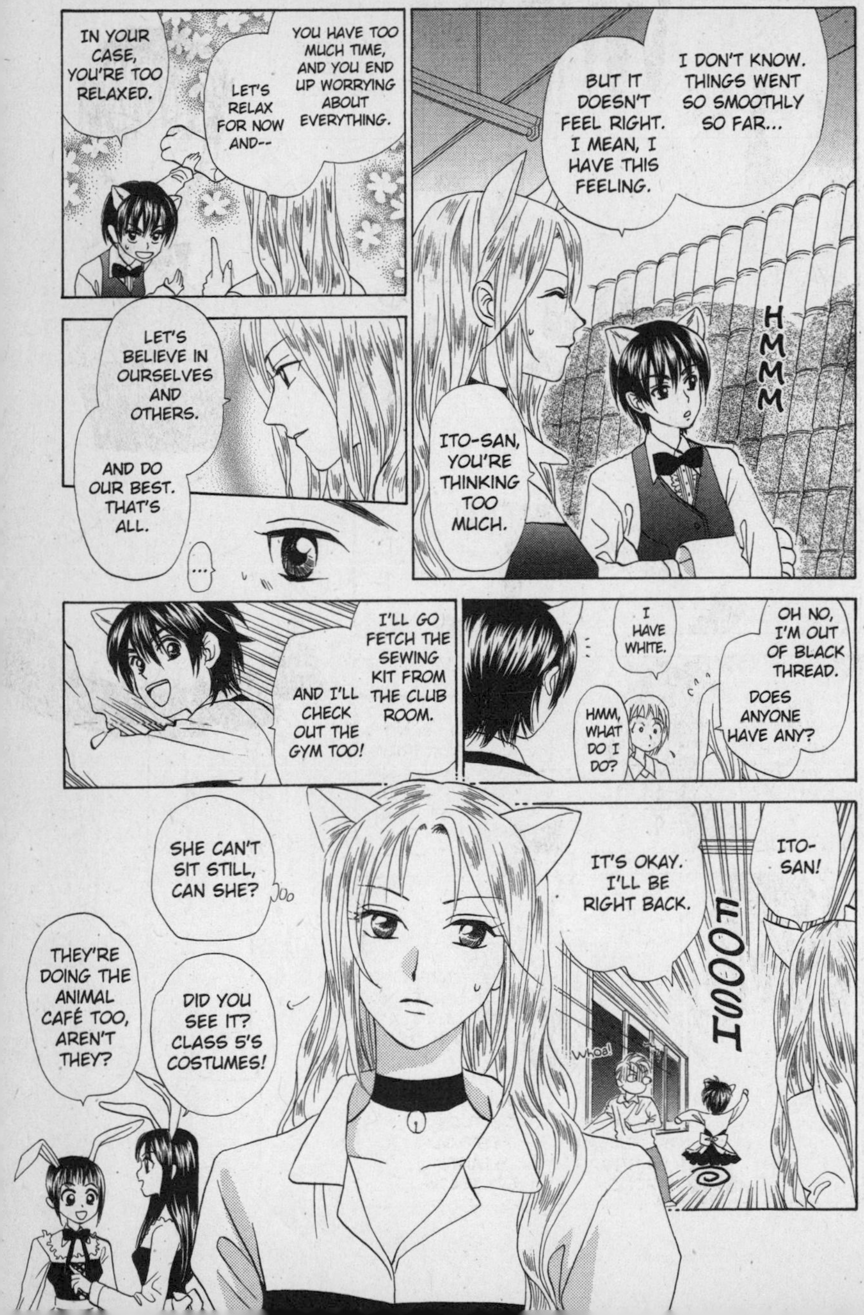
I DON'T KNOW. THINGS WENT SO SMOOTHLY SO FAR...
BUT IT DOESN'T FEEL RIGHT. I MEAN, I HAVE THIS FEELING.
HMMM
ITO-SAN, YOU'RE THINKING TOO MUCH.
YOU HAVE TOO MUCH TIME, AND YOU END UP WORRYING ABOUT EVERYTHING.
LET'S RELAX FOR NOW AND--
IN YOUR CASE, YOU'RE TOO RELAXED.
LET'S BELIEVE IN OURSELVES AND OTHERS.
AND DO OUR BEST. THAT'S ALL.
...
OH NO, I'M OUT OF BLACK THREAD.
DOES ANYONE HAVE ANY?
I HAVE WHITE.
HMM, WHAT DO I DO?
I'LL GO FETCH THE SEWING KIT FROM THE CLUB ROOM.
AND I'LL CHECK OUT THE GYM TOO!
ITO-SAN!
IT'S OKAY. I'LL BE RIGHT BACK.
FOOSH
Whoa!
SHE CAN'T SIT STILL, CAN SHE?
DID YOU SEE IT? CLASS 5'S COSTUMES!
THEY'RE DOING THE ANIMAL CAFÉ TOO, AREN'T THEY?

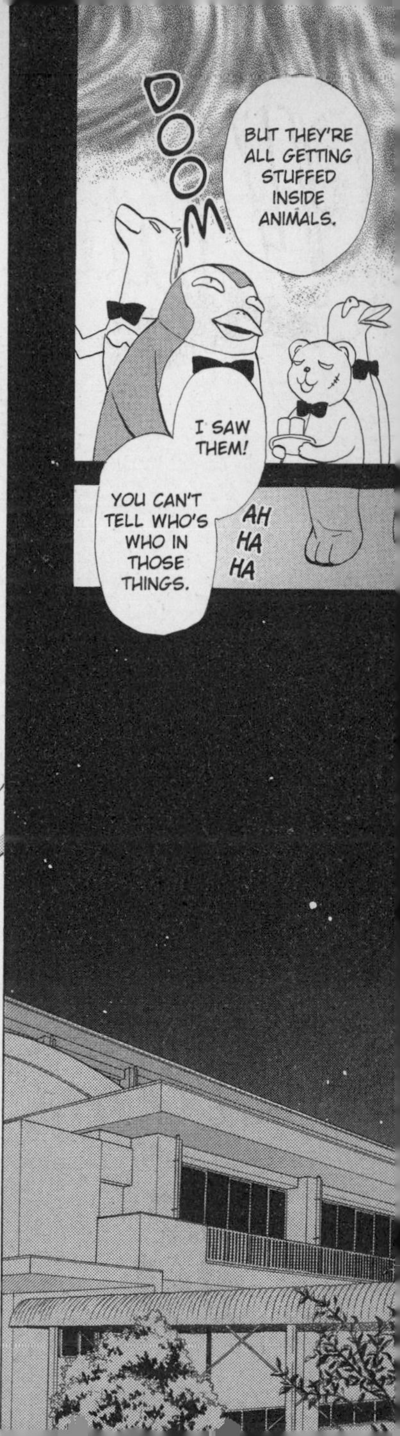
DOOOM
BUT THEY'RE ALL GETTING STUFFED INSIDE ANIMALS.
I SAW THEM!
YOU CAN'T TELL WHO'S WHO IN THOSE THINGS.
AH HA HA

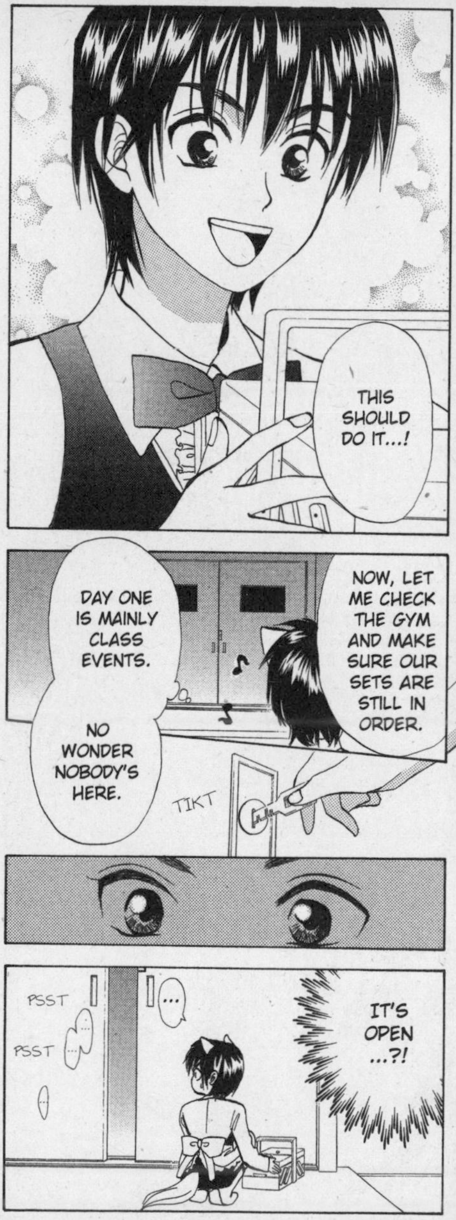
THIS SHOULD DO IT...!
NOW, LET ME CHECK THE GYM AND MAKE SURE OUR SETS ARE STILL IN ORDER.
DAY ONE IS MAINLY CLASS EVENTS.
NO WONDER NOBODY'S HERE.
TIKT
IT'S OPEN ...?!
...
PSST
...
PSST
...
...

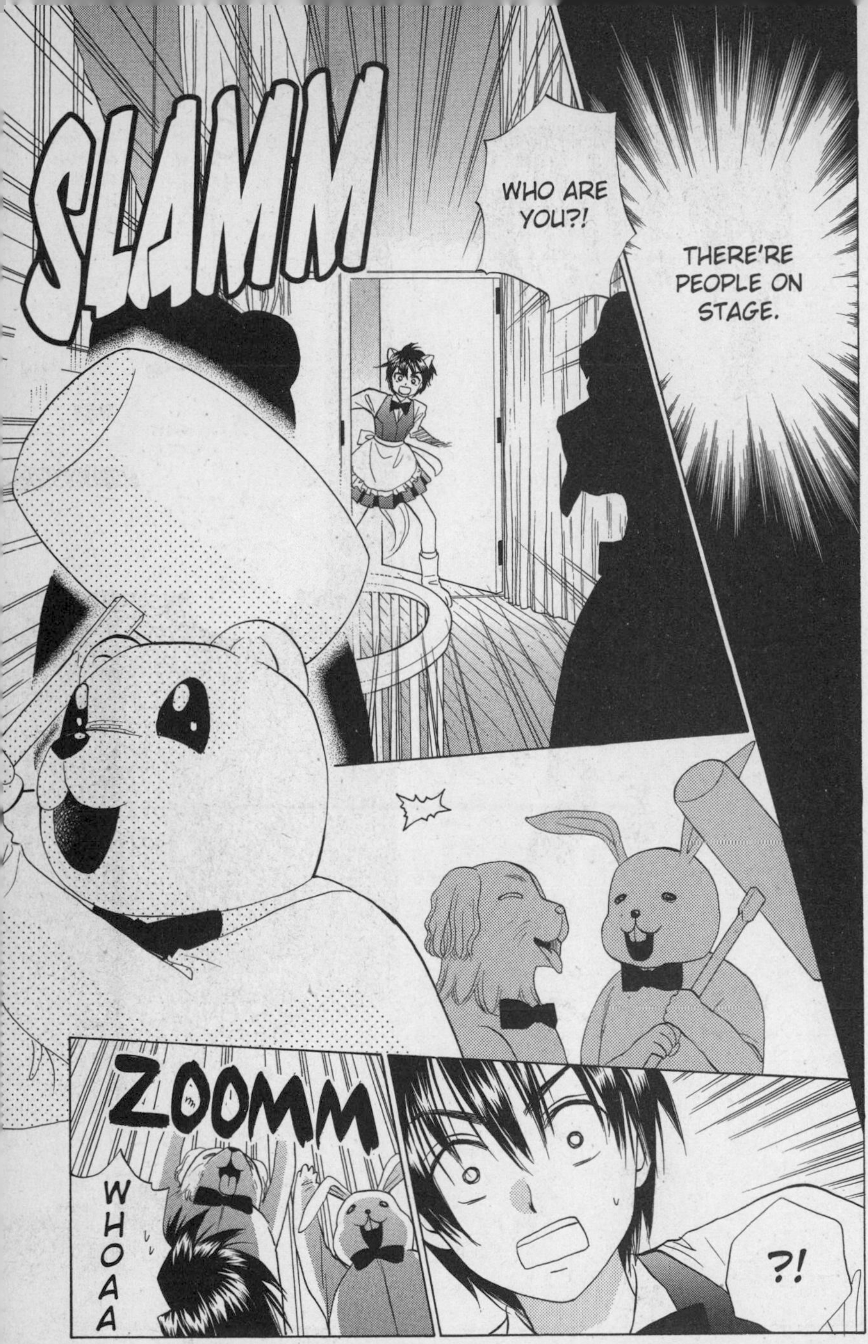
THERE'RE PEOPLE ON STAGE.
WHO ARE YOU?!
SLAMM
?!
ZOOMM
WHOAAA

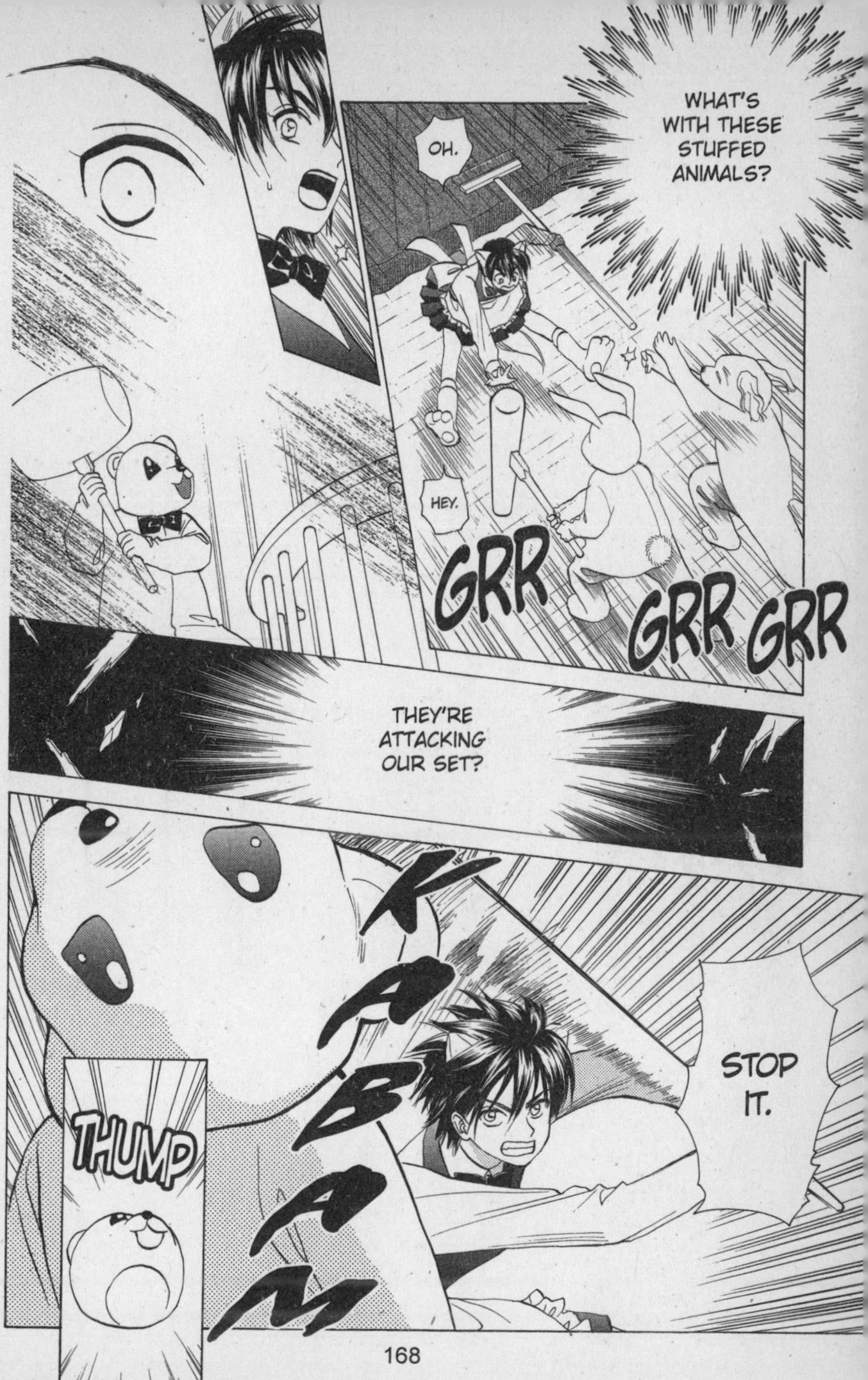
WHAT'S WITH THESE STUFFED ANIMALS?
OH.
HEY.
GRR
GRR GRR
THEY'RE ATTACKING OUR SET?
STOP IT.
KABAMM
THUMP

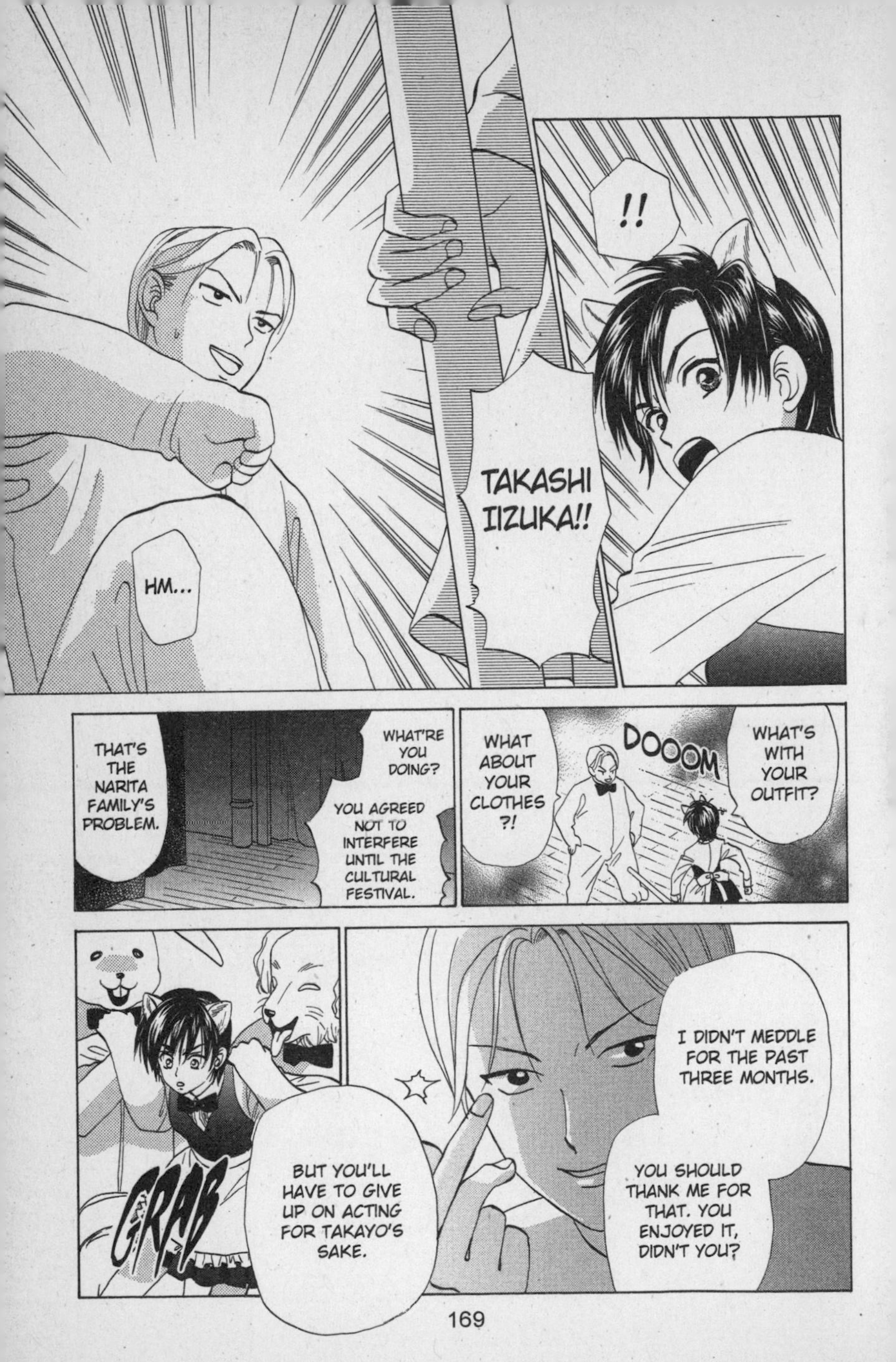
!!
TAKASHI IIZUKA!!
HM...
WHAT'S WITH YOUR OUTFIT?
DOOOM
WHAT ABOUT YOUR CLOTHES?!
WHAT'RE YOU DOING?
YOU AGREED NOT TO INTERFERE UNTIL THE CULTURAL FESTIVAL.
THAT'S THE NARITA FAMILY'S PROBLEM.
I DIDN'T MEDDLE FOR THE PAST THREE MONTHS.
YOU SHOULD THANK ME FOR THAT. YOU ENJOYED IT, DIDN'T YOU?
BUT YOU'LL HAVE TO GIVE UP ON ACTING FOR TAKAYO'S SAKE.
GRAB

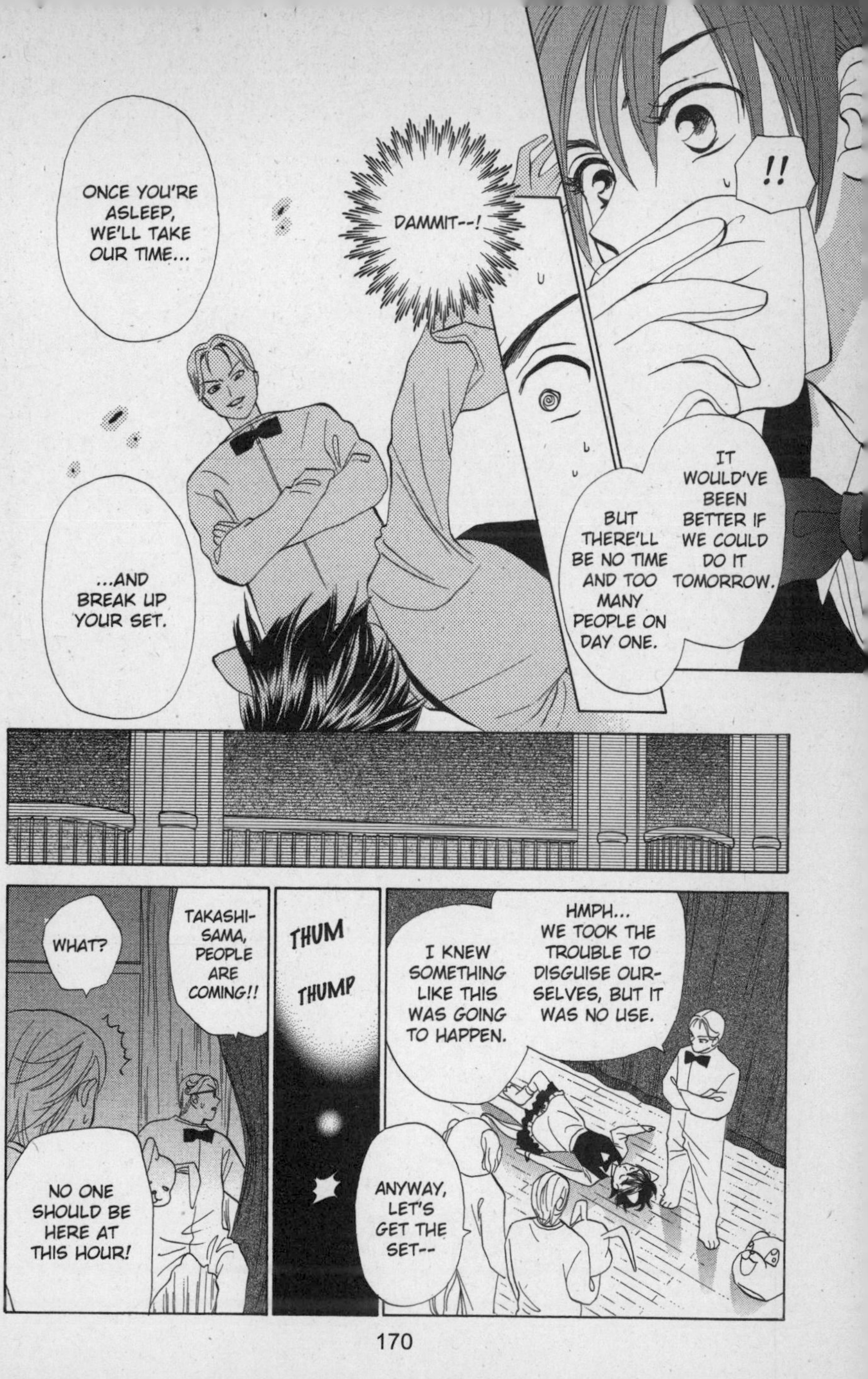
!!
IT WOULD'VE BEEN BETTER IF WE COULD DO IT TOMORROW.
BUT THERE'LL BE NO TIME AND TOO MANY PEOPLE ON DAY ONE.
DAMMIT--!
ONCE YOU'RE ASLEEP, WE'LL TAKE OUR TIME...
...AND BREAK UP YOUR SET.
HMPH... WE TOOK THE TROUBLE TO DISGUISE OUR-SELVES, BUT IT WAS NO USE.
I KNEW SOMETHING LIKE THIS WAS GOING TO HAPPEN.
ANYWAY, LET'S GET THE SET--
THUM
THUMP
TAKASHI-SAMA, PEOPLE ARE COMING!!
WHAT?
NO ONE SHOULD BE HERE AT THIS HOUR!

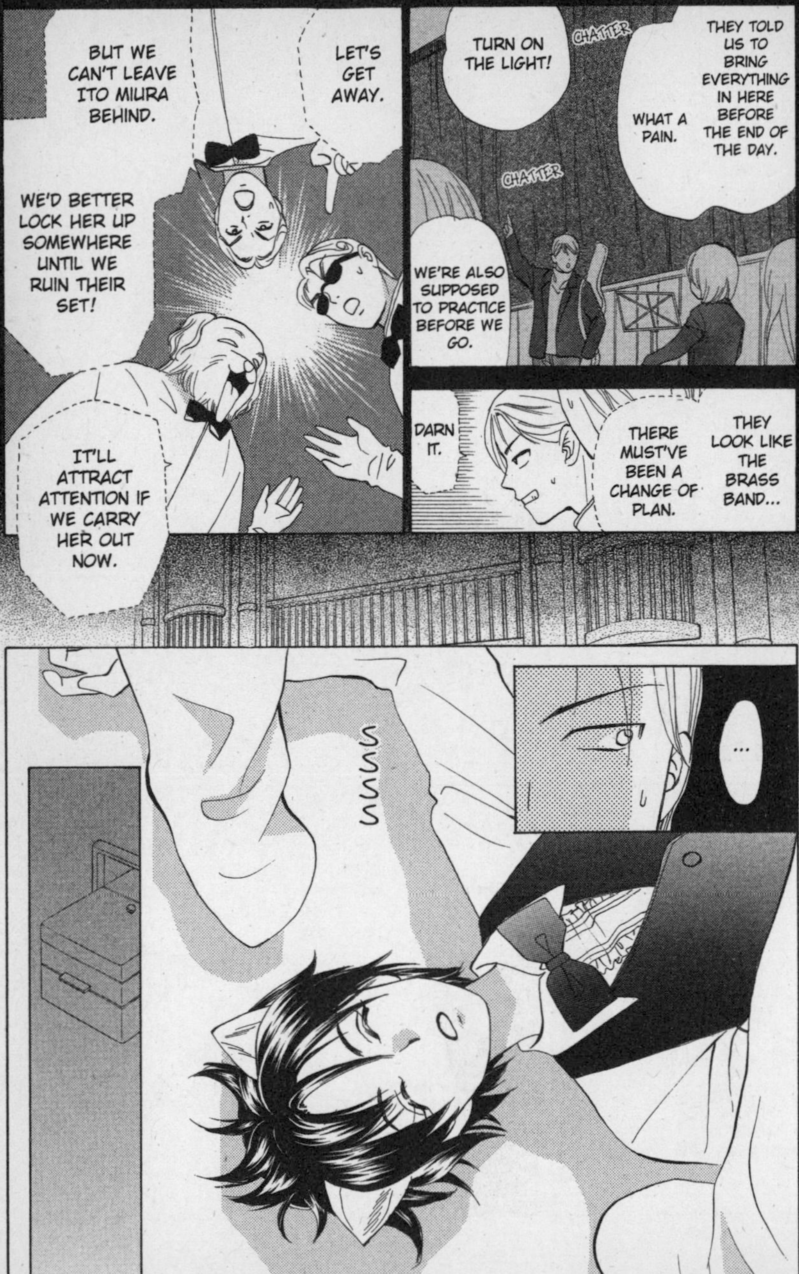
THEY TOLD US TO BRING EVERYTHING IN HERE BEFORE THE END OF THE DAY.
CHATTER
WHAT A PAIN.
TURN ON THE LIGHT!
CHATTER
WE'RE ALSO SUPPOSED TO PRACTICE BEFORE WE GO.
THEY LOOK LIKE THE BRASS BAND...
THERE MUST'VE BEEN A CHANGE OF PLAN.
DARN IT.
LET'S GET AWAY.
BUT WE CAN'T LEAVE ITO MIURA BEHIND.
WE'D BETTER LOCK HER UP SOMEWHERE UNTIL WE RUIN THEIR SET!
IT'LL ATTRACT ATTENTION IF WE CARRY HER OUT NOW.
...
SSSSS

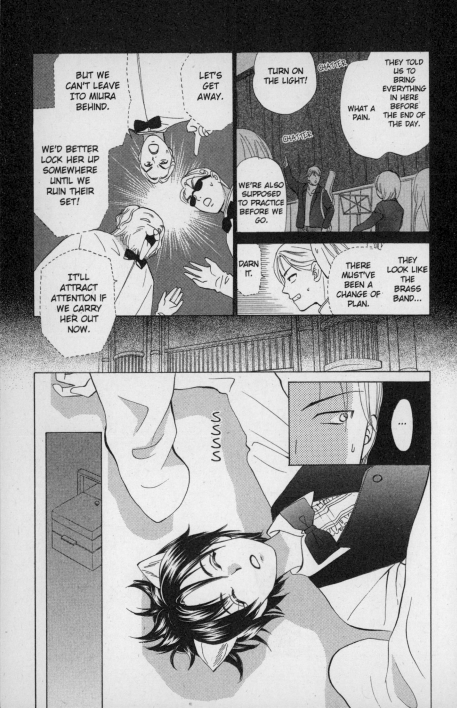

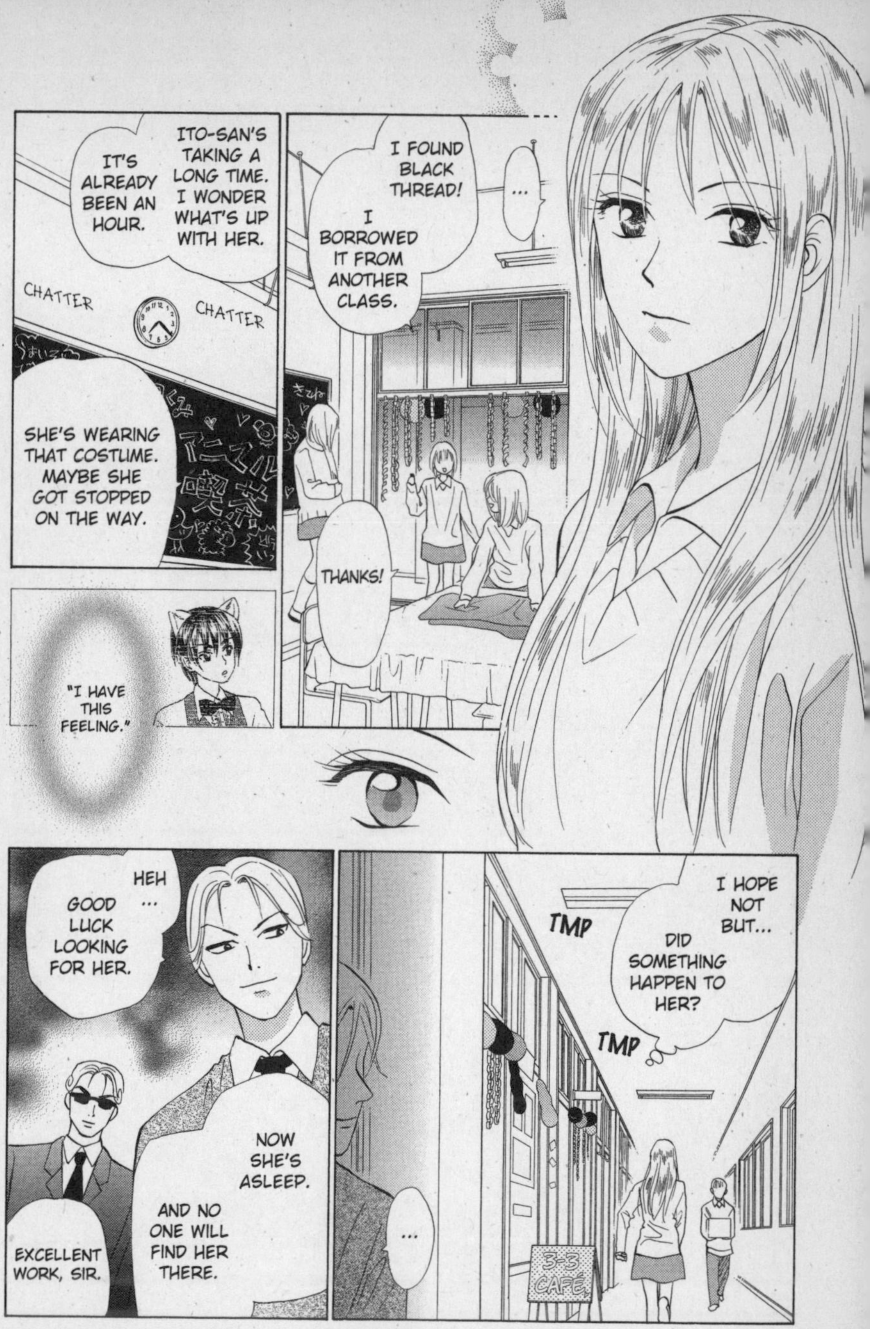
I FOUND BLACK THREAD!
I BORROWED IT FROM ANOTHER CLASS.
...
THANKS!
IT'S ALREADY BEEN AN HOUR. ITO-SAN'S TAKING A LONG TIME. I WONDER WHAT'S UP WITH HER.
CHATTER
CHATTER
SHE'S WEARING THAT COSTUME. MAYBE SHE GOT STOPPED ON THE WAY.
"I HAVE THIS FEELING."
I HOPE NOT BUT...
DID SOMETHING HAPPEN TO HER?
TMP
TMP
3-3 CAFÉ
...
HEH ...
GOOD LUCK LOOKING FOR HER.
NOW SHE'S ASLEEP.
AND NO ONE WILL FIND HER THERE.
EXCELLENT WORK, SIR.

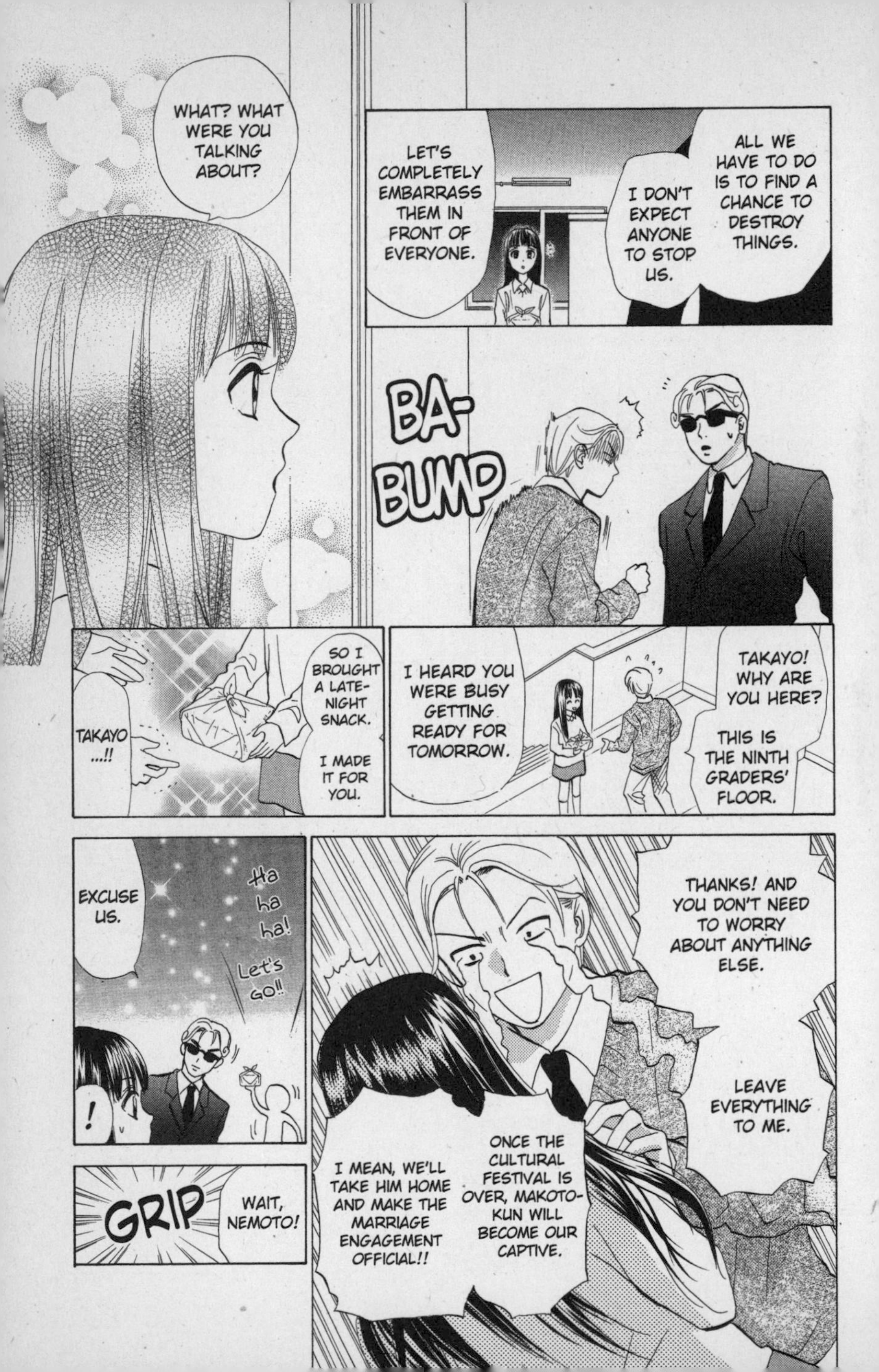
ALL WE HAVE TO DO IS TO FIND A CHANCE TO DESTROY THINGS.
I DON'T EXPECT ANYONE TO STOP US.
LET'S COMPLETELY EMBARRASS THEM IN FRONT OF EVERYONE.
BA-BUMP
WHAT? WHAT WERE YOU TALKING ABOUT?
TAKAYO! WHY ARE YOU HERE?
THIS IS THE NINTH GRADERS' FLOOR.
I HEARD YOU WERE BUSY GETTING READY FOR TOMORROW.
SO I BROUGHT A LATE-NIGHT SNACK.
I MADE IT FOR YOU.
TAKAYO ...!!
THANKS! AND YOU DON'T NEED TO WORRY ABOUT ANYTHING ELSE.
LEAVE EVERYTHING TO ME.
ONCE THE CULTURAL FESTIVAL IS OVER, MAKOTO-KUN WILL BECOME OUR CAPTIVE.
I MEAN, WE'LL TAKE HIM HOME AND MAKE THE MARRIAGE ENGAGEMENT OFFICIAL!!
EXCUSE US.
Ha ha ha!
Let's go!!
!
WAIT, NEMOTO!
GRIP

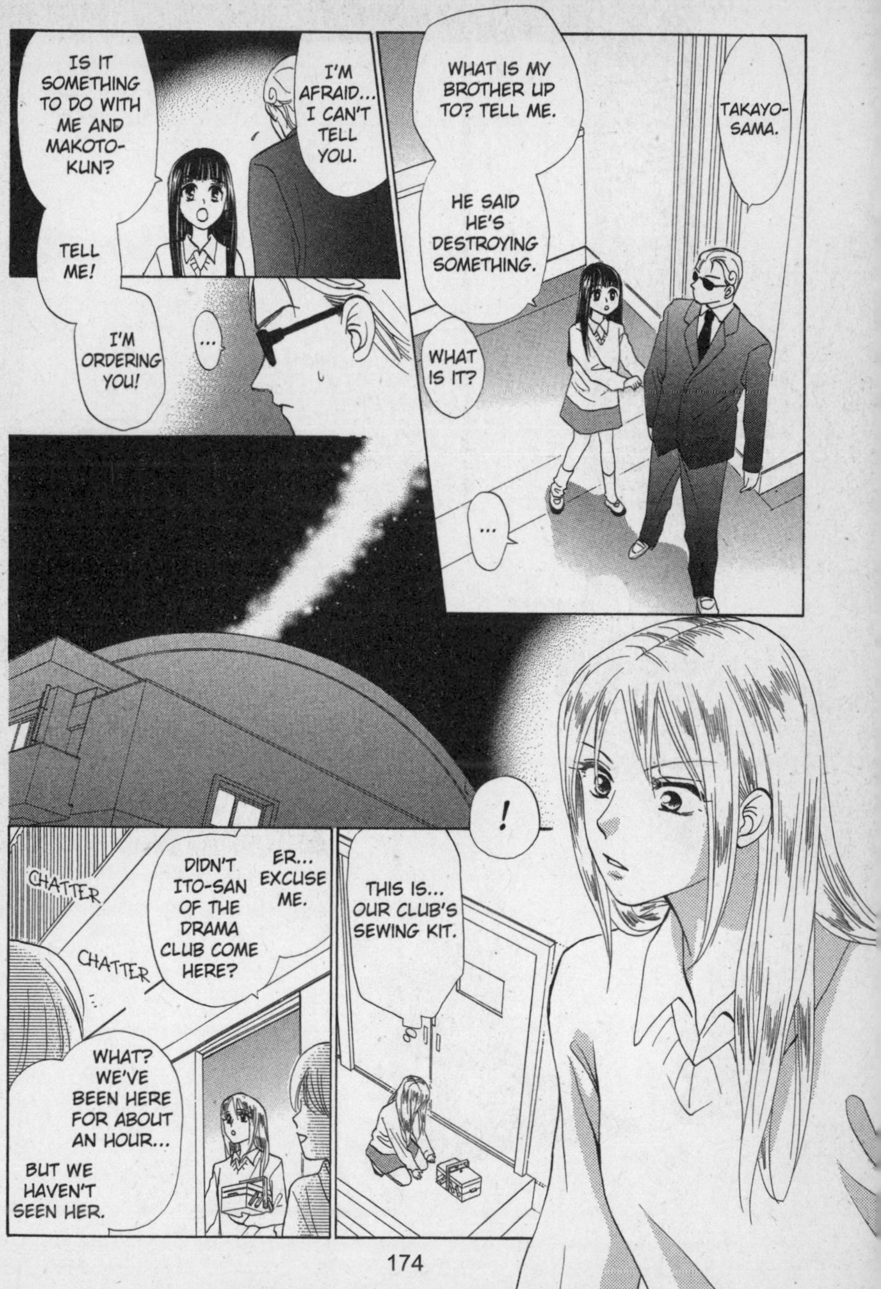
TAKAYO-SAMA.
WHAT IS MY BROTHER UP TO? TELL ME.
HE SAID HE'S DESTROYING SOMETHING.
WHAT IS IT?
...
I'M AFRAID... I CAN'T TELL YOU.
IS IT SOMETHING TO DO WITH ME AND MAKOTO-KUN?
TELL ME!
...
I'M ORDERING YOU!
!
THIS IS... OUR CLUB'S SEWING KIT.
ER... EXCUSE ME.
DIDN'T ITO-SAN OF THE DRAMA CLUB COME HERE?
CHATTER
CHATTER
WHAT? WE'VE BEEN HERE FOR ABOUT AN HOUR...
BUT WE HAVEN'T SEEN HER.

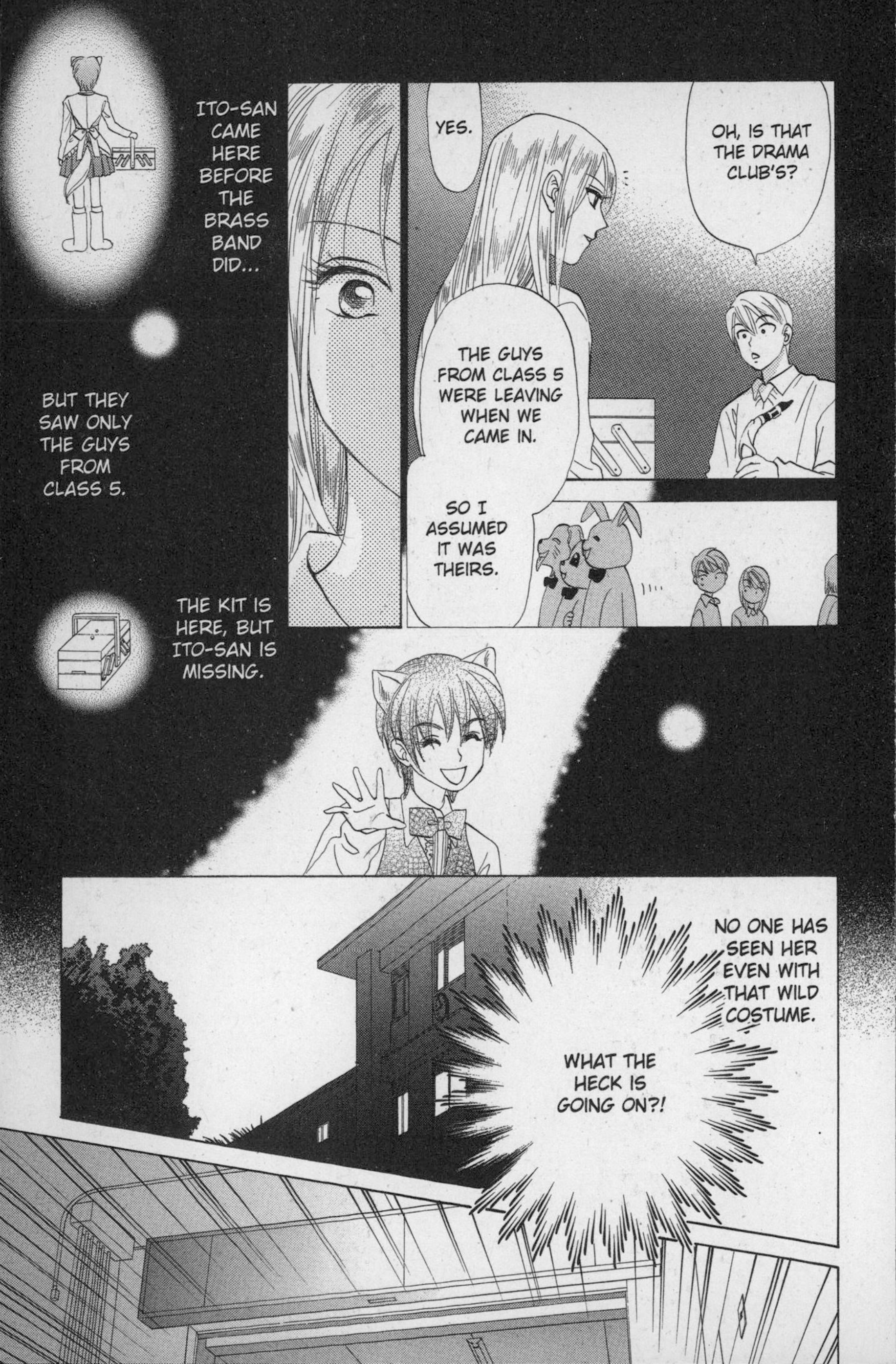
OH, IS THAT THE DRAMA CLUB'S?
YES.
THE GUYS FROM CLASS 5 WERE LEAVING WHEN WE CAME IN.
SO I ASSUMED IT WAS THEIRS.
ITO-SAN CAME HERE BEFORE THE BRASS BAND DID...
BUT THEY SAW ONLY THE GUYS FROM CLASS 5.
THE KIT IS HERE, BUT ITO-SAN IS MISSING.
NO ONE HAS SEEN HER EVEN WITH THAT WILD COSTUME.
WHAT THE HECK IS GOING ON?!

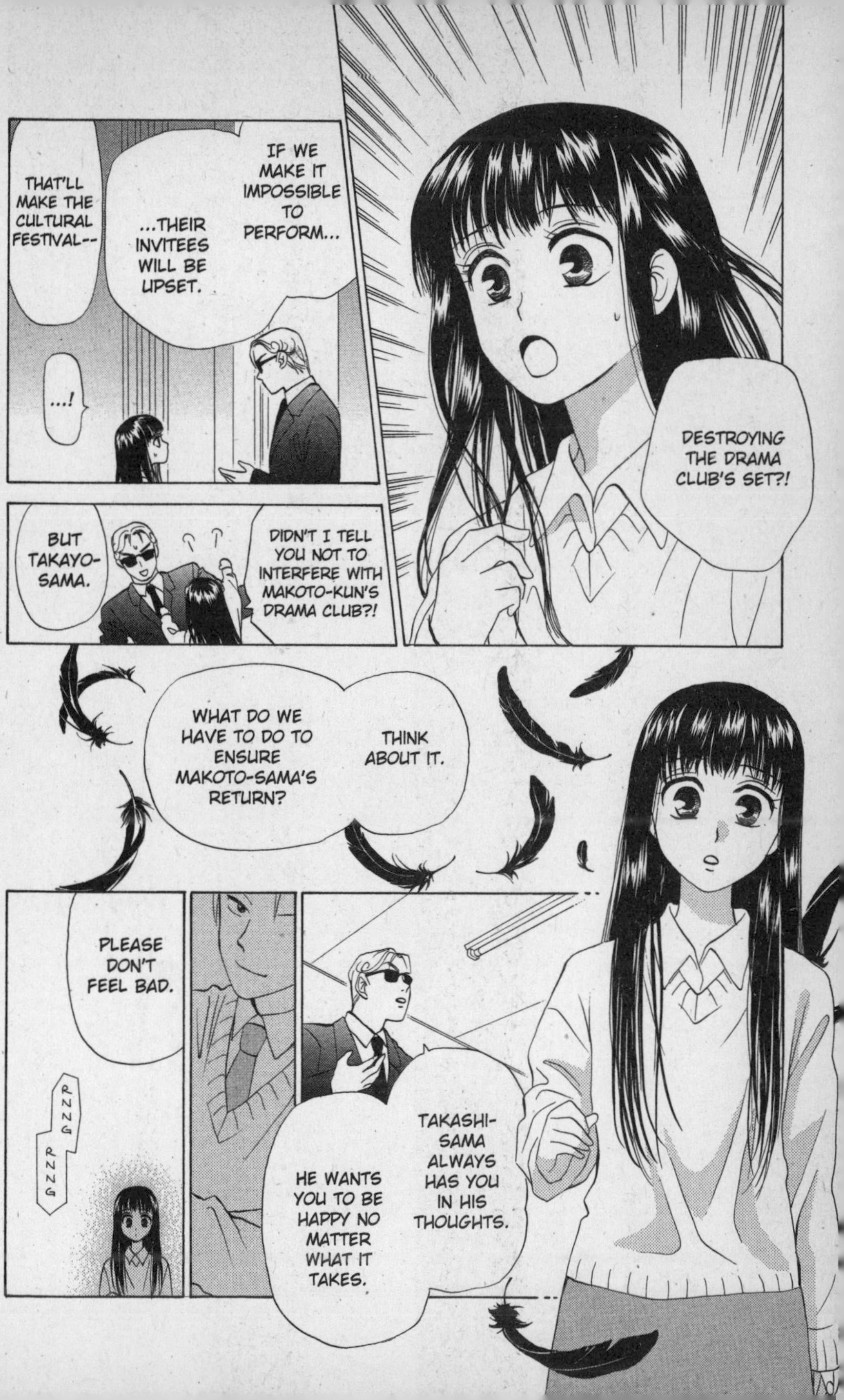
DESTROYING THE DRAMA CLUB'S SET?!
IF WE MAKE IT IMPOSSIBLE TO PERFORM...
...THEIR INVITEES WILL BE UPSET.
THAT'LL MAKE THE CULTURAL FESTIVAL--
...!
DIDN'T I TELL YOU NOT TO INTERFERE WITH MAKOTO-KUN'S DRAMA CLUB?!
BUT TAKAYO-SAMA.
THINK ABOUT IT.
WHAT DO WE HAVE TO DO TO ENSURE MAKOTO-SAMA'S RETURN?
TAKASHI-SAMA ALWAYS HAS YOU IN HIS THOUGHTS.
HE WANTS YOU TO BE HAPPY NO MATTER WHAT IT TAKES.
PLEASE DON'T FEEL BAD.
RNNG
RNNG

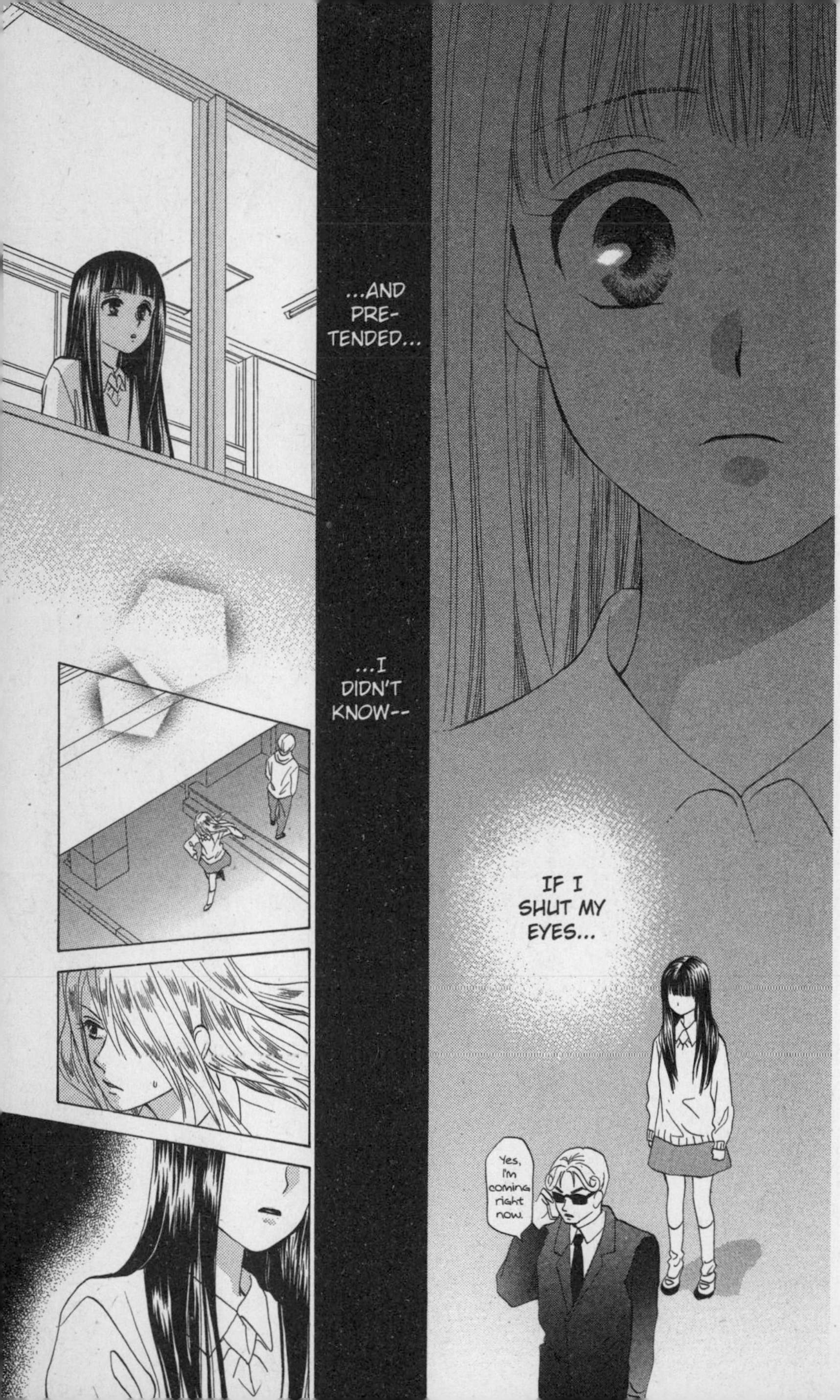
IF I SHUT MY EYES...
Yes, I'm coming right now.
...AND PRE-TENDED...
...I DIDN'T KNOW--

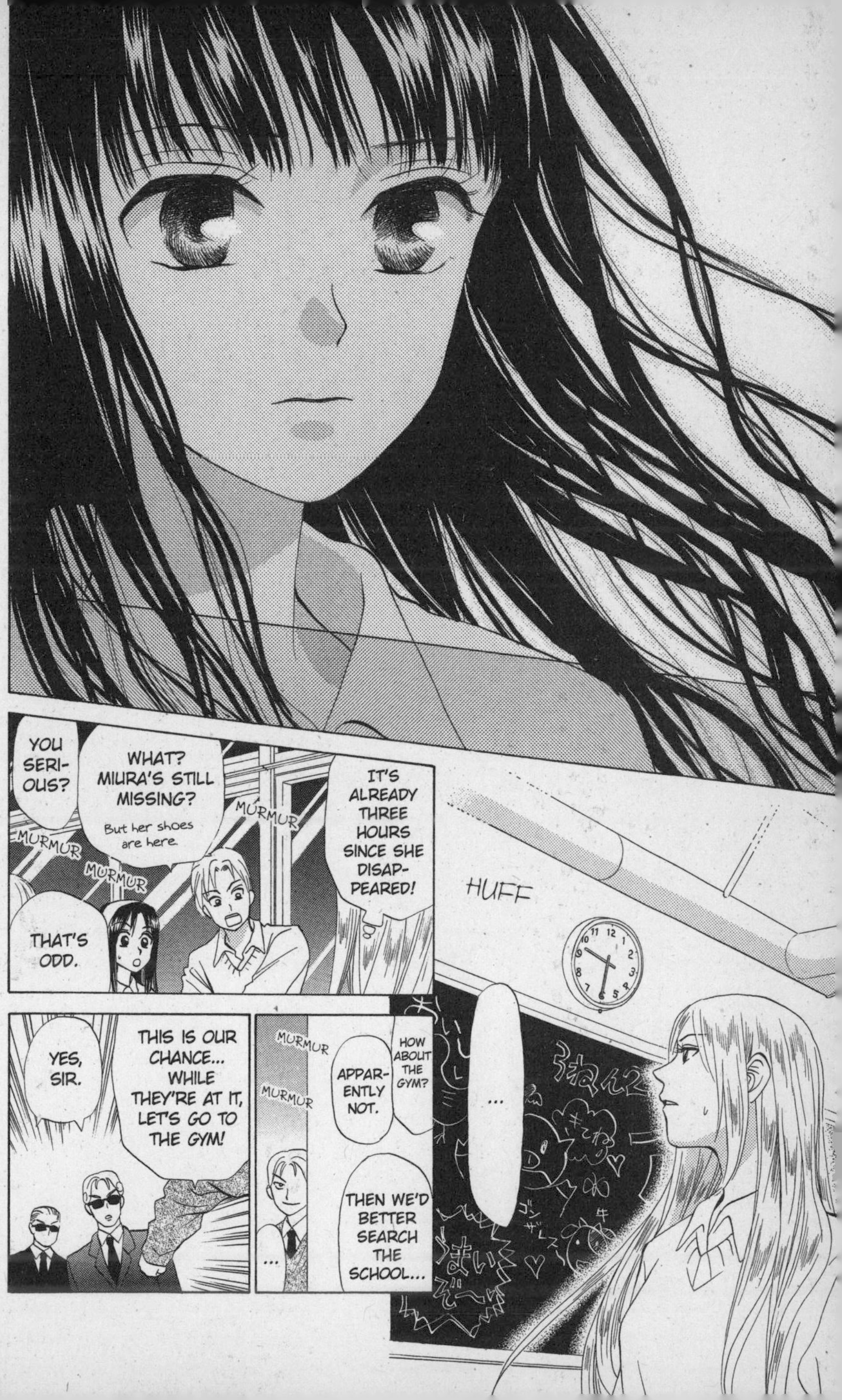
HUFF
...
IT'S ALREADY THREE HOURS SINCE SHE DISAPPEARED!
MURMUR
WHAT? MIURA'S STILL MISSING?
But her shoes are here.
YOU SERIOUS?
MURMUR
MURMUR
THAT'S ODD.
HOW ABOUT THE GYM?
MURMUR
APPARENTLY NOT.
MURMUR
THEN WE'D BETTER SEARCH THE SCHOOL...
...
THIS IS OUR CHANCE... WHILE THEY'RE AT IT, LET'S GO TO THE GYM!
YES, SIR.

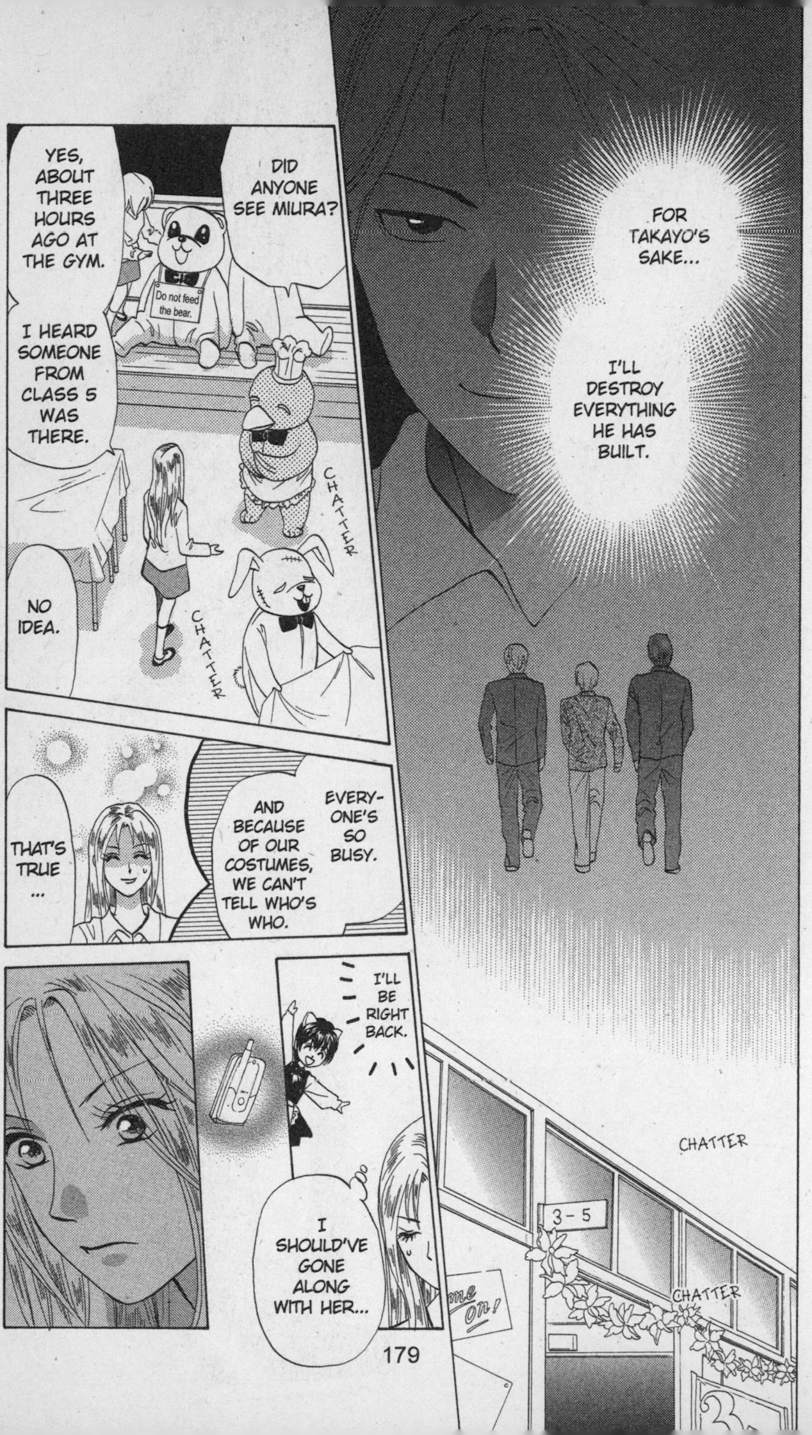
FOR TAKAYO'S SAKE...
I'LL DESTROY EVERYTHING HE HAS BUILT.
CHATTER
3 - 5
CHATTER
DID ANYONE SEE MIURA?
YES, ABOUT THREE HOURS AGO AT THE GYM.
Do not feed the bear.
I HEARD SOMEONE FROM CLASS 5 WAS THERE.
CHATTER
CHATTER
NO IDEA.
EVERY-ONE'S SO BUSY.
AND BECAUSE OF OUR COSTUMES, WE CAN'T TELL WHO'S WHO.
THAT'S TRUE ...
I'LL BE RIGHT BACK.
I SHOULD'VE GONE ALONG WITH HER...

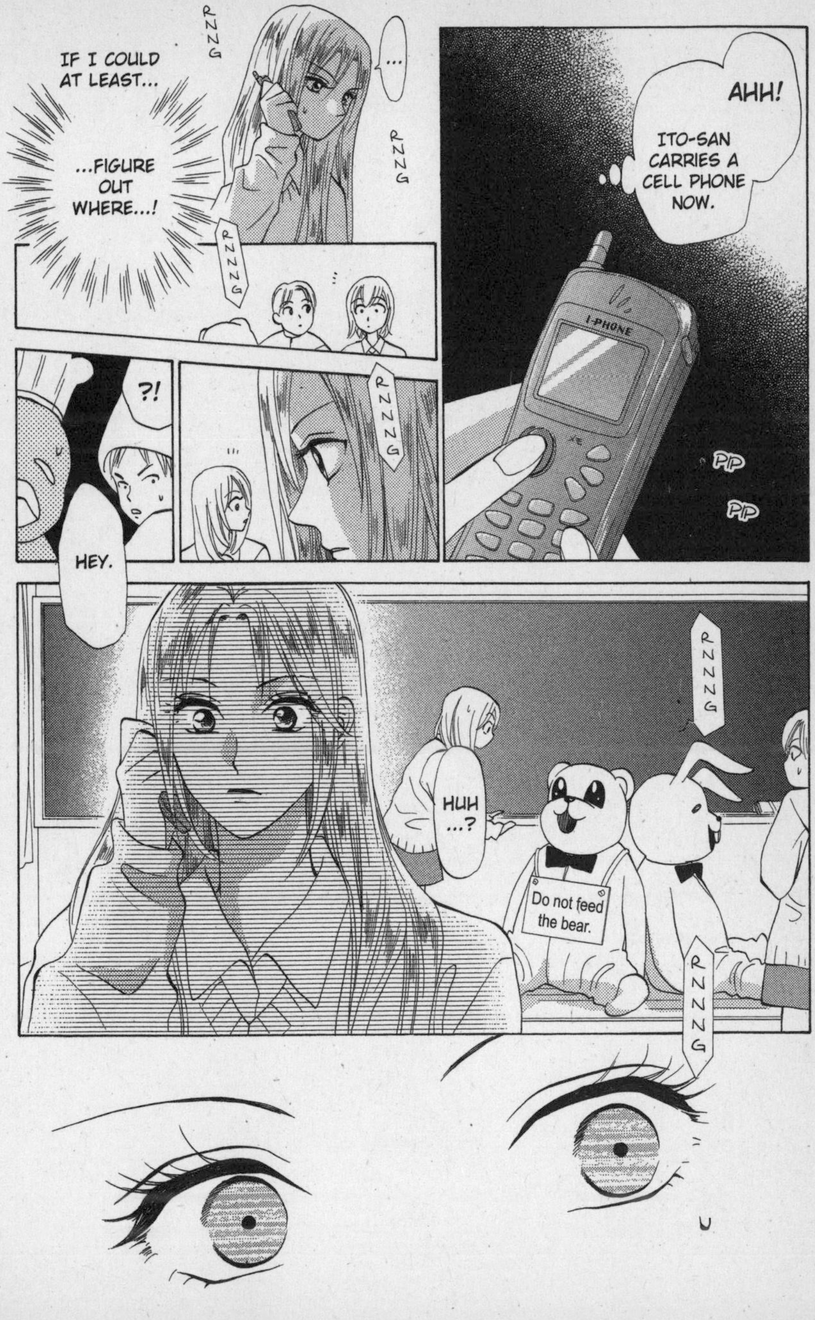
IF I COULD AT LEAST...
RNNG
...
RNNG
...FIGURE OUT WHERE...!
AHH!
ITO-SAN CARRIES A CELL PHONE NOW.
I-PHONE
PP
PP
RNNNG
RNNNG
?!
HEY.
RNNNG
HUH ...?
Do not feed the bear.
RNNNG

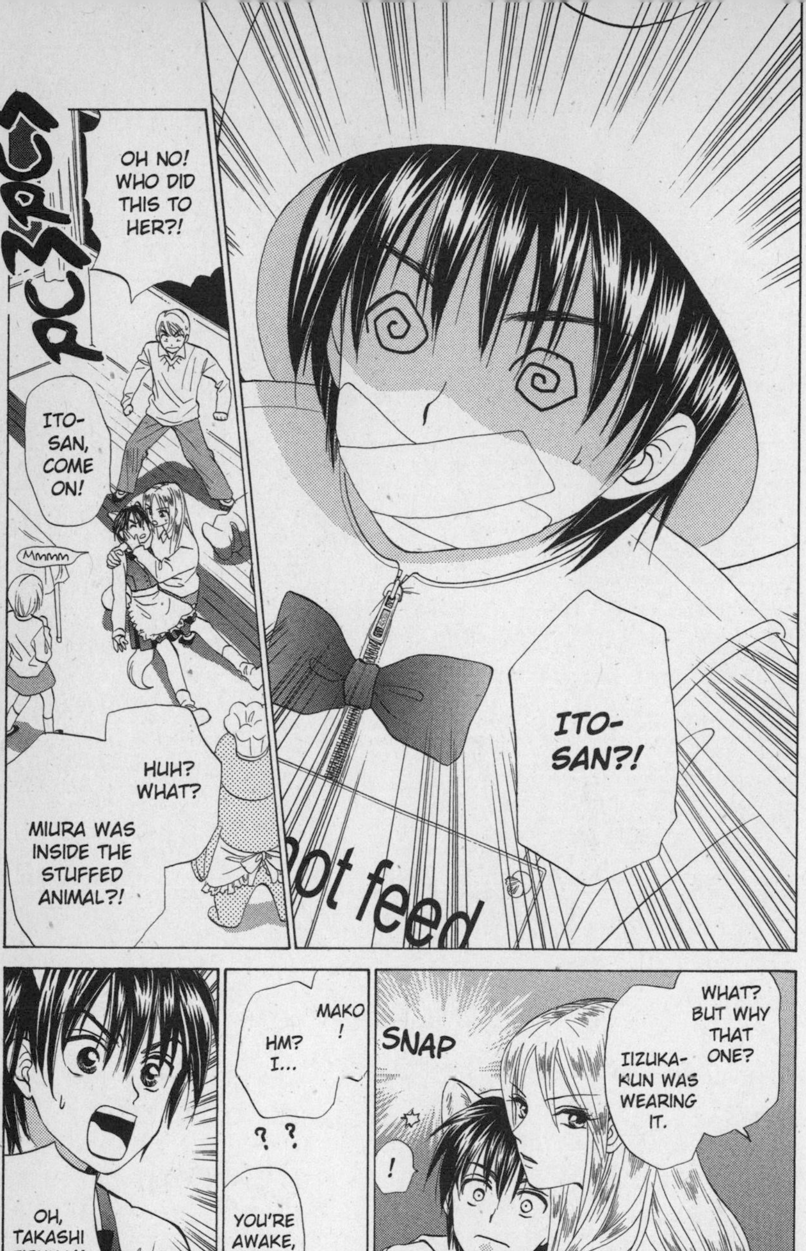
ITO-SAN?!
OH NO! WHO DID THIS TO HER?!
ITO-SAN, COME ON!
Mmmm
HUH? WHAT?
MIURA WAS INSIDE THE STUFFED ANIMAL?!
WHAT? BUT WHY THAT ONE?
IIZUKA-KUN WAS WEARING IT.
SNAP
!
MAKO!
HM? I...
? ?
YOU'RE AWAKE, ITO-SAN!
OH, TAKASHI IIZUKA!!

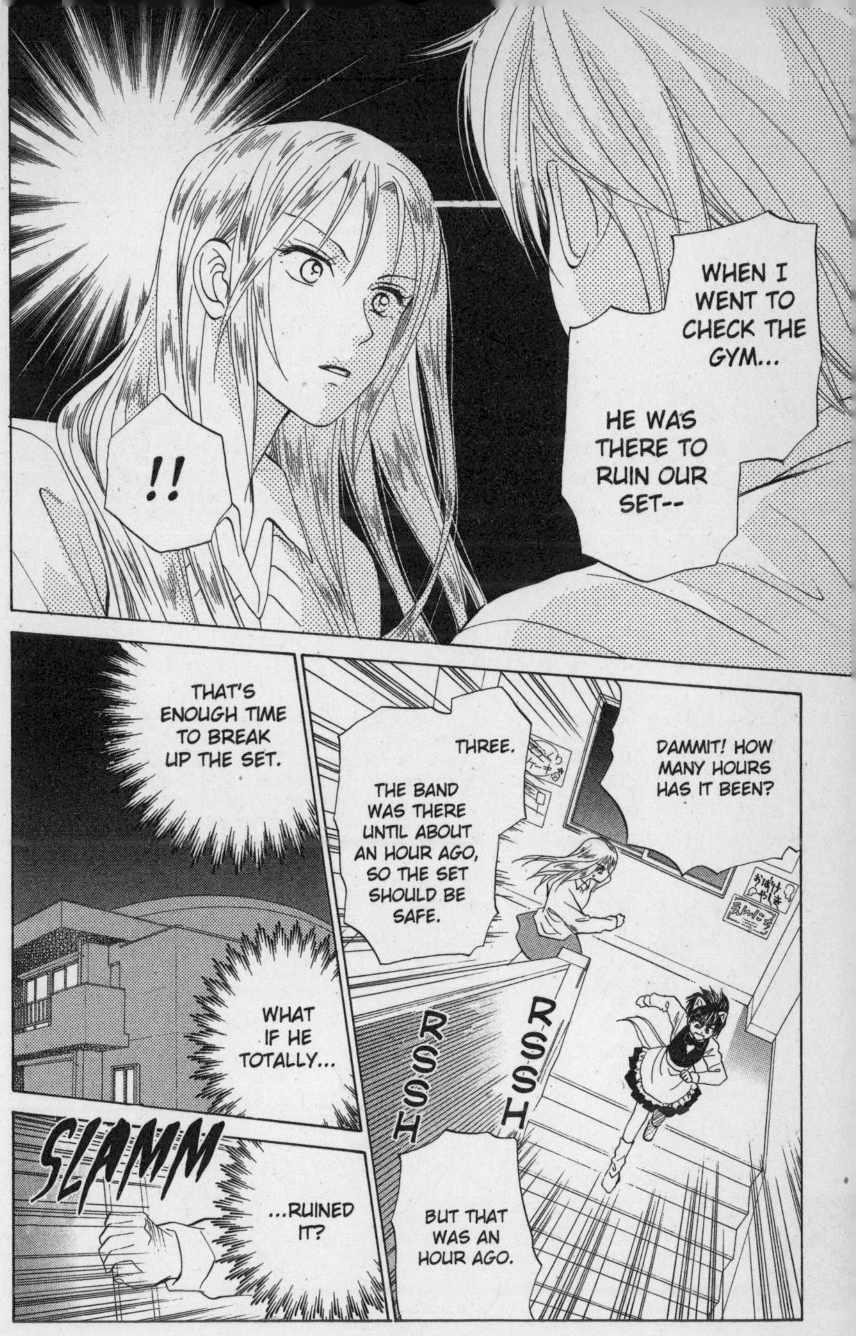
WHEN I WENT TO CHECK THE GYM...
HE WAS THERE TO RUIN OUR SET--
!!
DAMMIT! HOW MANY HOURS HAS IT BEEN?
THREE.
THE BAND WAS THERE UNTIL ABOUT AN HOUR AGO, SO THE SET SHOULD BE SAFE.
RSSH
RSSH
BUT THAT WAS AN HOUR AGO.
THAT'S ENOUGH TIME TO BREAK UP THE SET.
WHAT IF HE TOTALLY...
SLAMM
...RUINED IT?

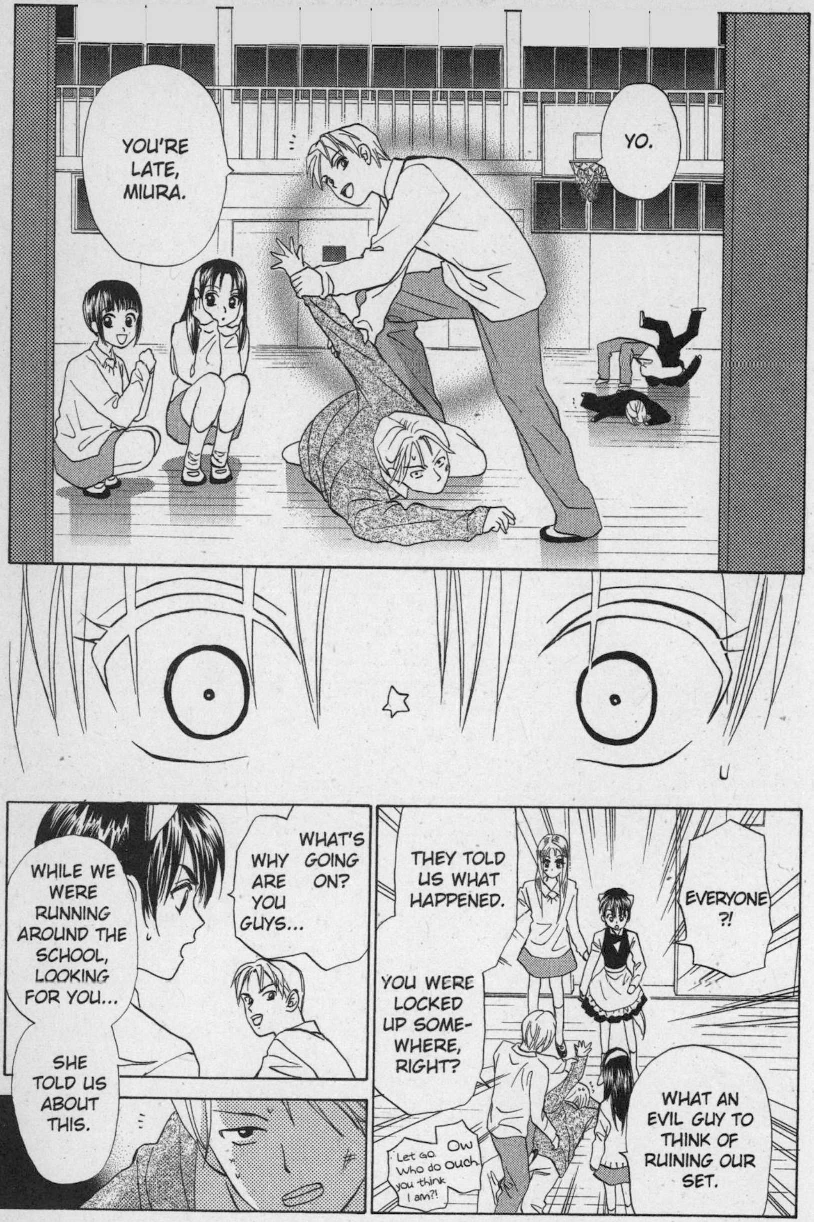
YO.
YOU'RE LATE, MIURA.
EVERYONE ?!
THEY TOLD US WHAT HAPPENED.
YOU WERE LOCKED UP SOME-WHERE, RIGHT?
WHAT AN EVIL GUY TO THINK OF RUINING OUR SET.
Ow Ouch.
Let go. Who do you think I am?!
WHAT'S GOING ON? WHY ARE YOU GUYS...
WHILE WE WERE RUNNING AROUND THE SCHOOL, LOOKING FOR YOU...
SHE TOLD US ABOUT THIS.

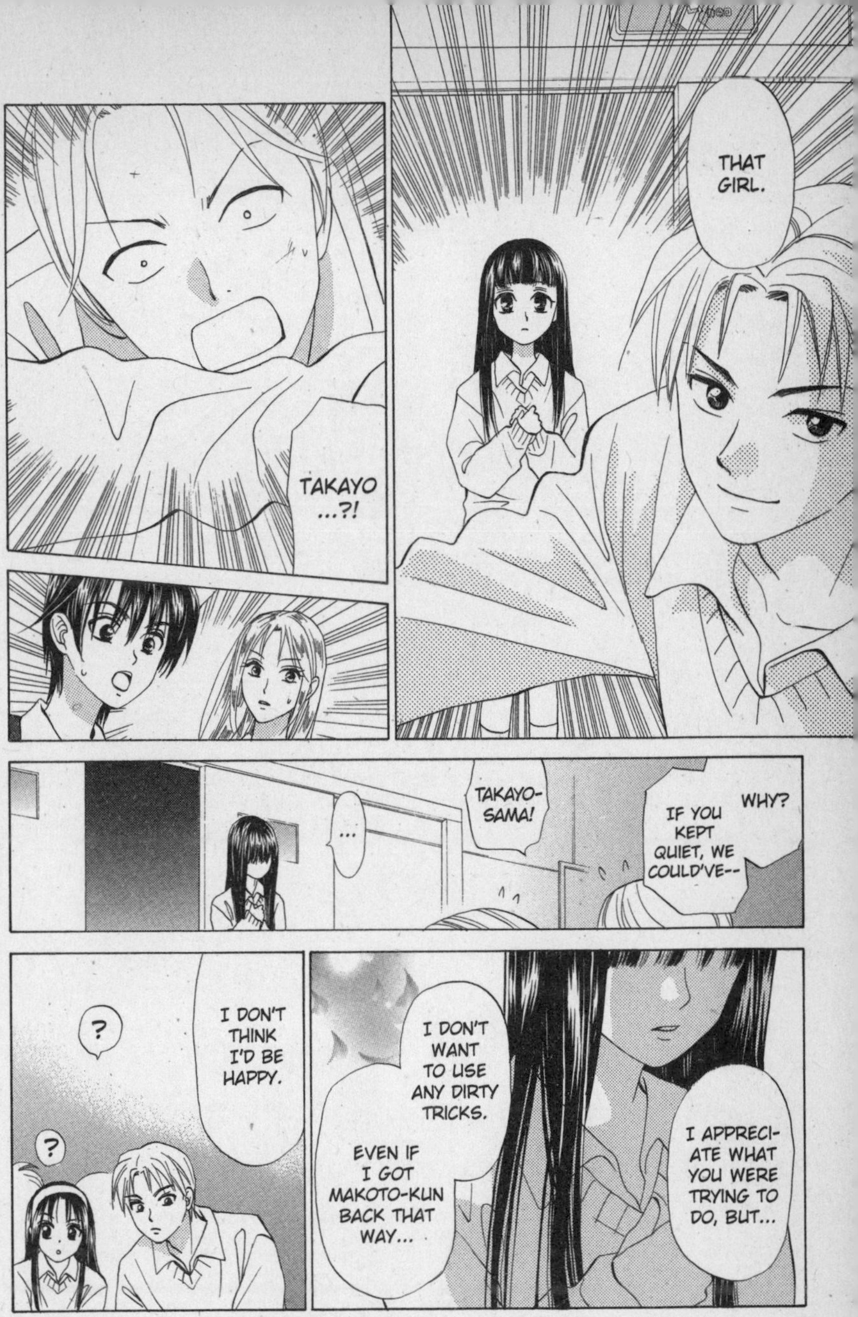
THAT GIRL.
TAKAYO ...?!
WHY?
IF YOU KEPT QUIET, WE COULD'VE--
TAKAYO-SAMA!
...
I APPRECI-ATE WHAT YOU WERE TRYING TO DO, BUT...
I DON'T WANT TO USE ANY DIRTY TRICKS.
EVEN IF I GOT MAKOTO-KUN BACK THAT WAY...
I DON'T THINK I'D BE HAPPY.
?
?

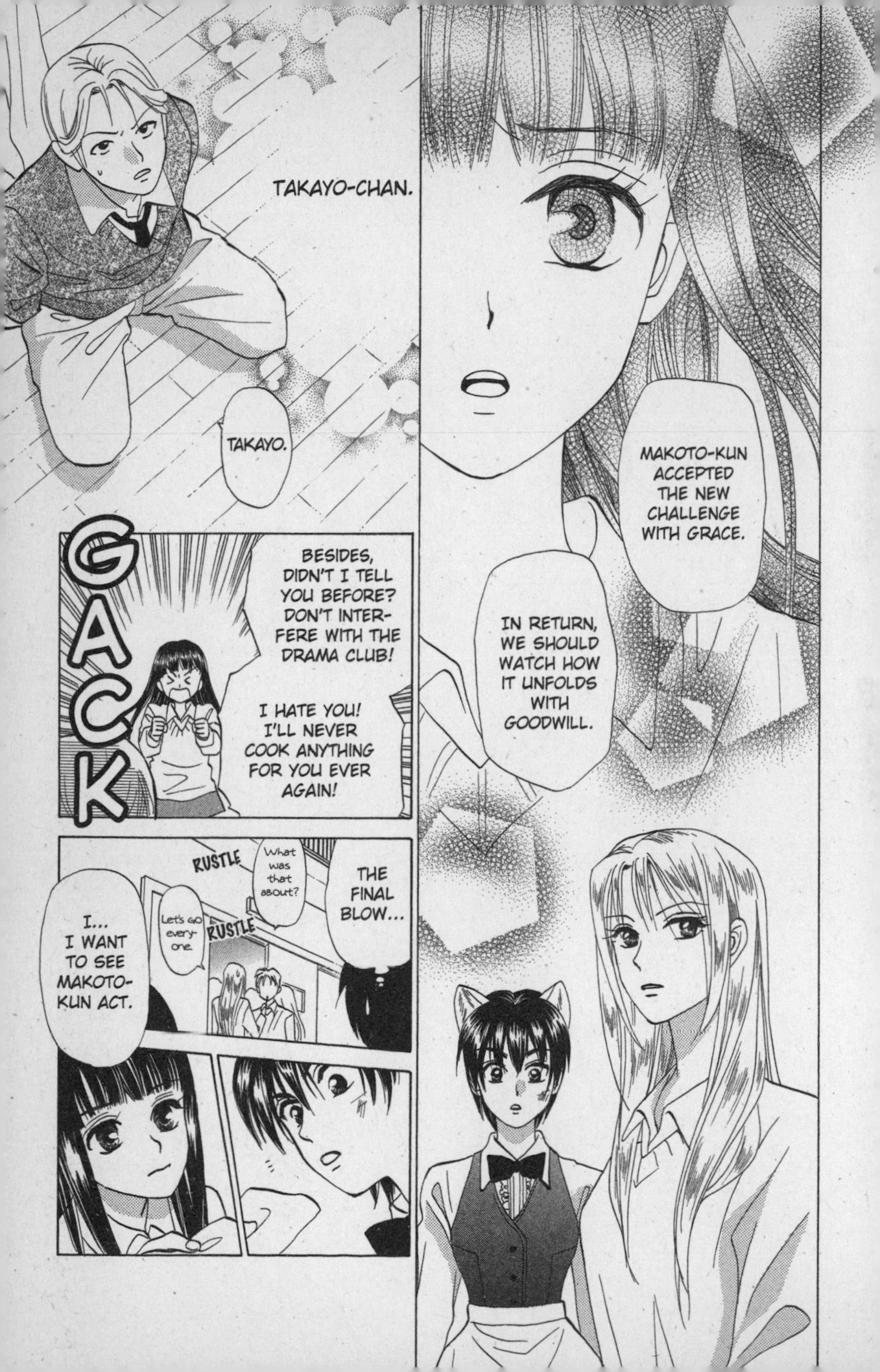
MAKOTO-KUN ACCEPTED THE NEW CHALLENGE WITH GRACE.
IN RETURN, WE SHOULD WATCH HOW IT UNFOLDS WITH GOODWILL.
TAKAYO-CHAN.
TAKAYO.
BESIDES, DIDN'T I TELL YOU BEFORE? DON'T INTER-FERE WITH THE DRAMA CLUB!
I HATE YOU! I'LL NEVER COOK ANYTHING FOR YOU EVER AGAIN!
GACK
THE FINAL BLOW...
What was that about?
RUSTLE
Let's go every-one.
RUSTLE
I... I WANT TO SEE MAKOTO-KUN ACT.

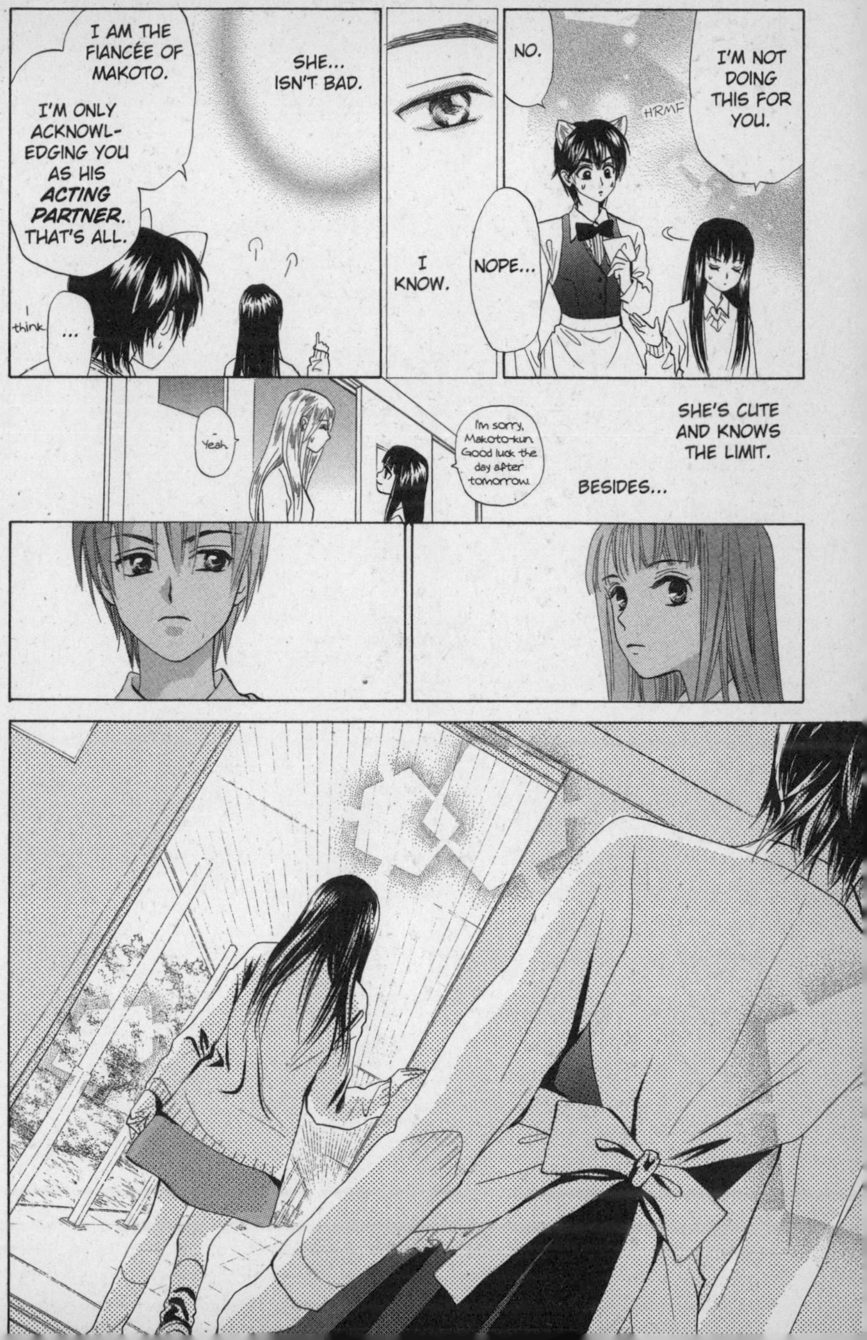
I'M NOT DOING THIS FOR YOU.
NO.
HRMF
NOPE...
I KNOW.
SHE... ISN'T BAD.
I AM THE FIANCÉE OF MAKOTO.
I'M ONLY ACKNOWL-EDGING YOU AS HIS ACTING PARTNER. THAT'S ALL.
I think
...
SHE'S CUTE AND KNOWS THE LIMIT.
BESIDES...
I'm sorry, Makoto-kun. Good luck the day after tomorrow.
Yeah.

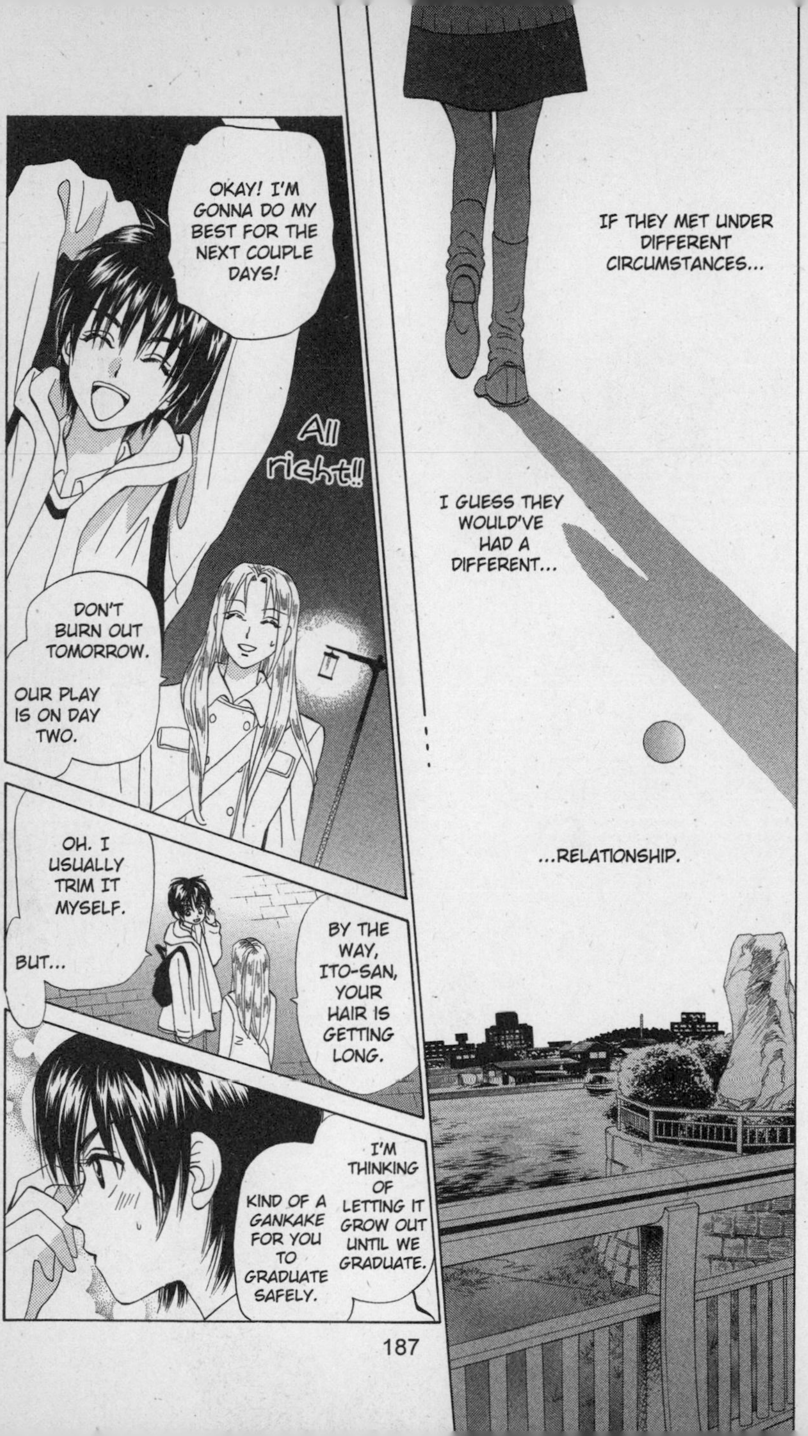
IF THEY MET UNDER DIFFERENT CIRCUMSTANCES...
I GUESS THEY WOULD'VE HAD A DIFFERENT...
...RELATIONSHIP.
OKAY! I'M GONNA DO MY BEST FOR THE NEXT COUPLE DAYS!
All right!!
DON'T BURN OUT TOMORROW.
OUR PLAY IS ON DAY TWO.
BY THE WAY, ITO-SAN, YOUR HAIR IS GETTING LONG.
OH. I USUALLY TRIM IT MYSELF.
BUT...
I'M THINKING OF LETTING IT GROW OUT UNTIL WE GRADUATE.
KIND OF A GANKAKE FOR YOU TO GRADUATE SAFELY.

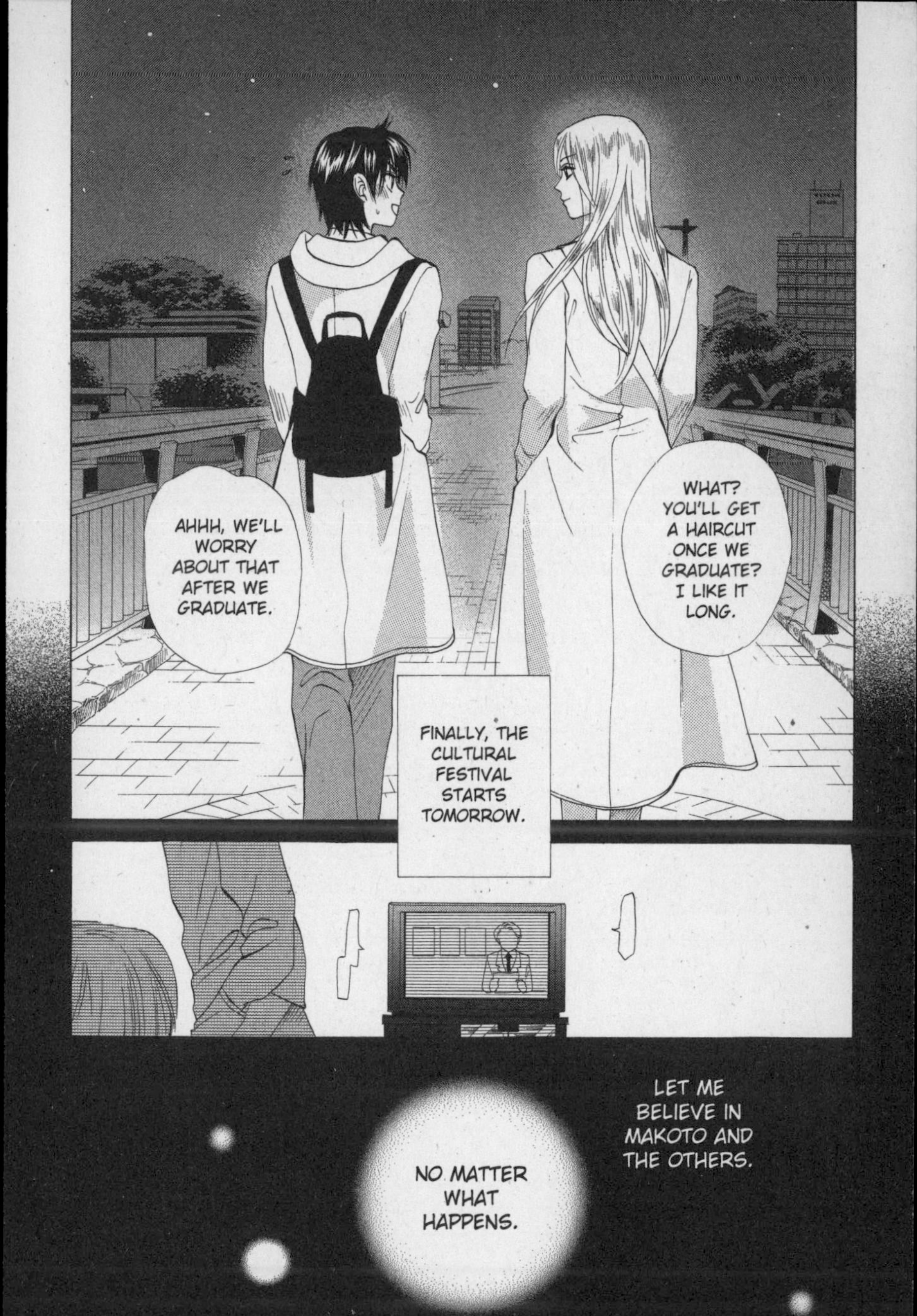
WHAT? YOU'LL GET A HAIRCUT ONCE WE GRADUATE? I LIKE IT LONG.
AHHH, WE'LL WORRY ABOUT THAT AFTER WE GRADUATE.
FINALLY, THE CULTURAL FESTIVAL STARTS TOMORROW.
LET ME BELIEVE IN MAKOTO AND THE OTHERS.
NO MATTER WHAT HAPPENS.

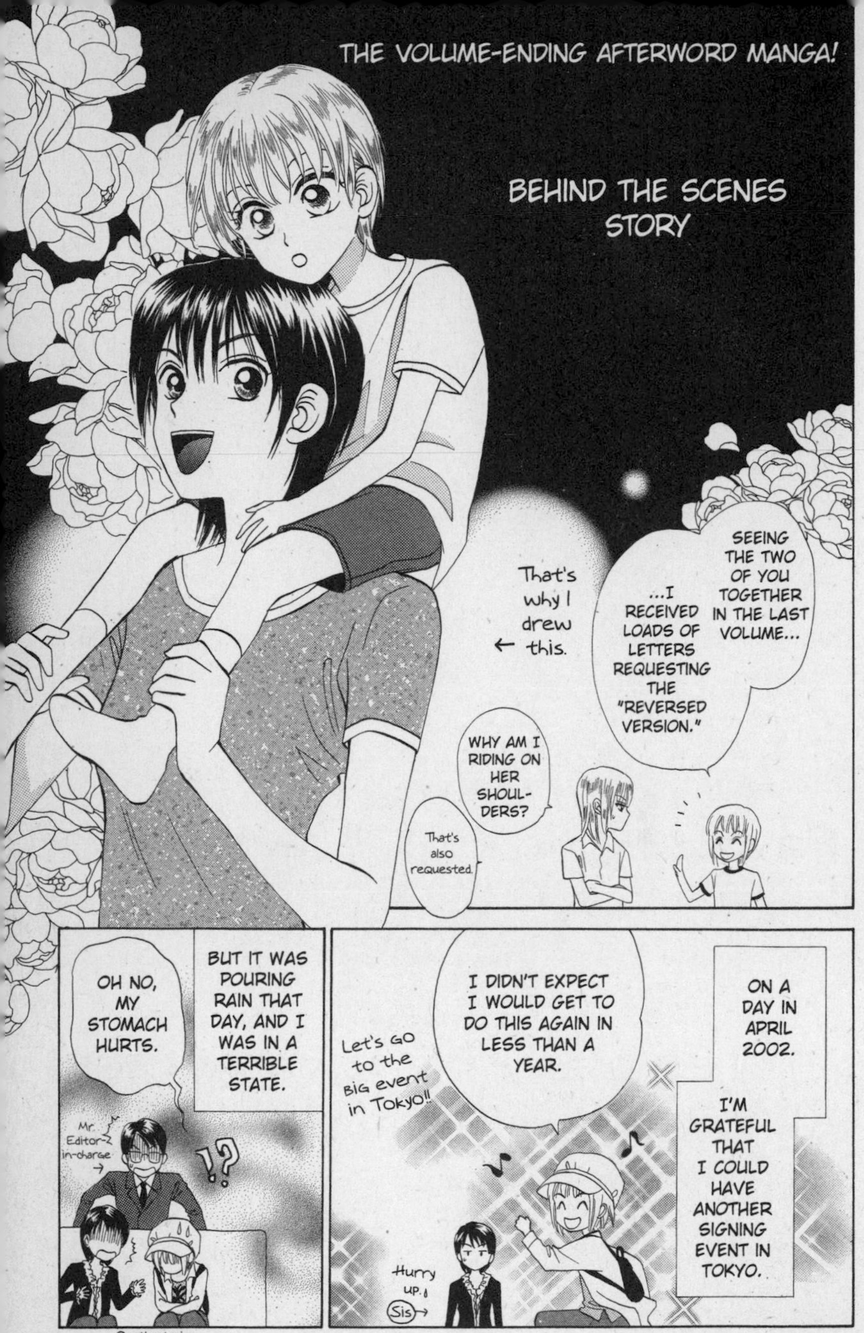
THE VOLUME-ENDING AFTERWORD MANGA!
BEHIND THE SCENES STORY
SEEING THE TWO OF YOU TOGETHER IN THE LAST VOLUME...
...I RECEIVED LOADS OF LETTERS REQUESTING THE "REVERSED VERSION."
That's why I drew ← this.
WHY AM I RIDING ON HER SHOUL-DERS?
That's also requested.
ON A DAY IN APRIL 2002.
I DIDN'T EXPECT I WOULD GET TO DO THIS AGAIN IN LESS THAN A YEAR.
Let's GO to the BIG event in Tokyo!!
I'M GRATEFUL THAT I COULD HAVE ANOTHER SIGNING EVENT IN TOKYO.
Hurry up.
Sis→
BUT IT WAS POURING RAIN THAT DAY, AND I WAS IN A TERRIBLE STATE.
OH NO, MY STOMACH HURTS.
!?
Mr. Editor-in-charge →
On the train.

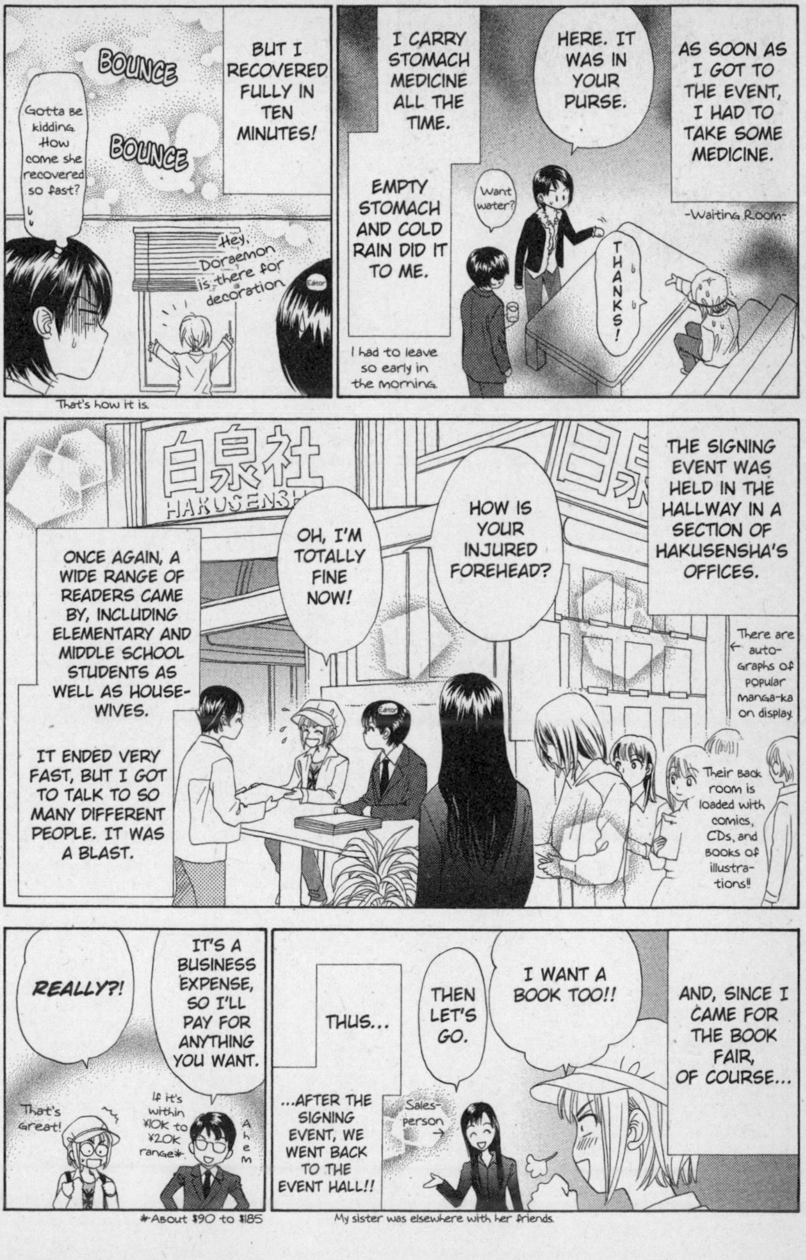
AS SOON AS I GOT TO THE EVENT, I HAD TO TAKE SOME MEDICINE.
-Waiting Room-
HERE. IT WAS IN YOUR PURSE.
Want water?
THANKS!
I CARRY STOMACH MEDICINE ALL THE TIME.
EMPTY STOMACH AND COLD RAIN DID IT TO ME.
I had to leave so early in the morning.
BUT I RECOVERED FULLY IN TEN MINUTES!
BOUNCE
BOUNCE
Gotta be kidding. How come she recovered so fast?
Hey, Doraemon is there for decoration.
Editor
That's how it is.
THE SIGNING EVENT WAS HELD IN THE HALLWAY IN A SECTION OF HAKUSENSHA'S OFFICES.
白泉社
HAKUSENSHA
HOW IS YOUR INJURED FOREHEAD?
OH, I'M TOTALLY FINE NOW!
ONCE AGAIN, A WIDE RANGE OF READERS CAME BY, INCLUDING ELEMENTARY AND MIDDLE SCHOOL STUDENTS AS WELL AS HOUSEWIVES.
IT ENDED VERY FAST, BUT I GOT TO TALK TO SO MANY DIFFERENT PEOPLE. IT WAS A BLAST.
There are autographs of popular manga-ka on display.
Editor
Their back room is loaded with comics, CDs, and books of illustrations!!
AND, SINCE I CAME FOR THE BOOK FAIR, OF COURSE...
I WANT A BOOK TOO!!
THEN LET'S GO.
THUS...
...AFTER THE SIGNING EVENT, WE WENT BACK TO THE EVENT HALL!!
Salesperson
My sister was elsewhere with her friends.
REALLY?!
IT'S A BUSINESS EXPENSE, SO I'LL PAY FOR ANYTHING YOU WANT.
That's Great!
If it's within ¥10K to ¥20K range*.
Ahem
*About $90 to $185

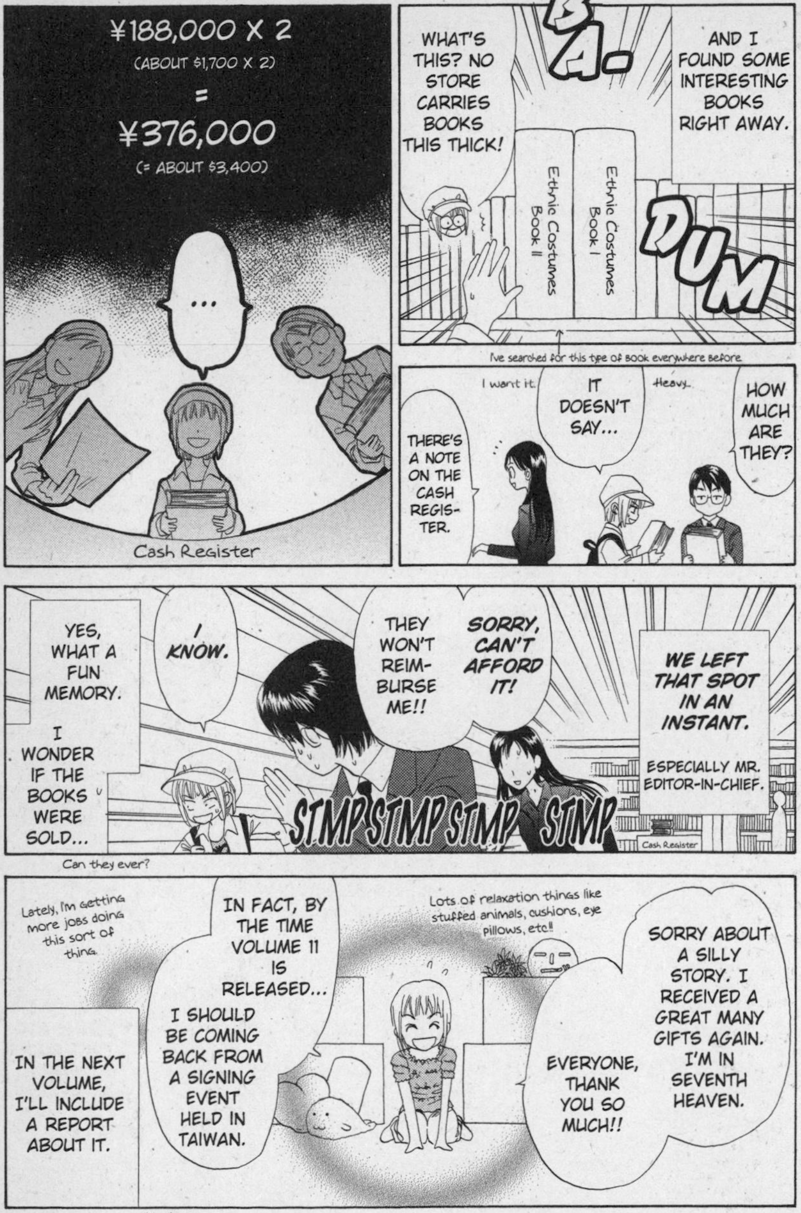
AND I FOUND SOME INTERESTING BOOKS RIGHT AWAY.
BA-
WHAT'S THIS? NO STORE CARRIES BOOKS THIS THICK!
Ethnic Costumes Book I
Ethnic Costumes Book II
DUM
I've searched for this type of book everywhere before.
HOW MUCH ARE THEY?
Heavy...
IT DOESN'T SAY...
I want it.
THERE'S A NOTE ON THE CASH REGISTER.
¥188,000 X 2
(ABOUT $1,700 X 2)
=
¥376,000
(= ABOUT $3,400)
...
Cash Register
WE LEFT THAT SPOT IN AN INSTANT.
ESPECIALLY MR. EDITOR-IN-CHIEF.
SORRY, CAN'T AFFORD IT!
THEY WON'T REIMBURSE ME!!
I KNOW.
YES, WHAT A FUN MEMORY.
I WONDER IF THE BOOKS WERE SOLD...
STMP STMP STMP STMP
Cash Register
Can they ever?
SORRY ABOUT A SILLY STORY. I RECEIVED A GREAT MANY GIFTS AGAIN. I'M IN SEVENTH HEAVEN.
EVERYONE, THANK YOU SO MUCH!!
Lots of relaxation things like stuffed animals, cushions, eye pillows, etc!!
IN FACT, BY THE TIME VOLUME 11 IS RELEASED...
I SHOULD BE COMING BACK FROM A SIGNING EVENT HELD IN TAIWAN.
Lately, I'm getting more jobs doing this sort of thing.
IN THE NEXT VOLUME, I'LL INCLUDE A REPORT ABOUT IT.

2002.7.15 絵夢羅 EMURA

Cultural Notes

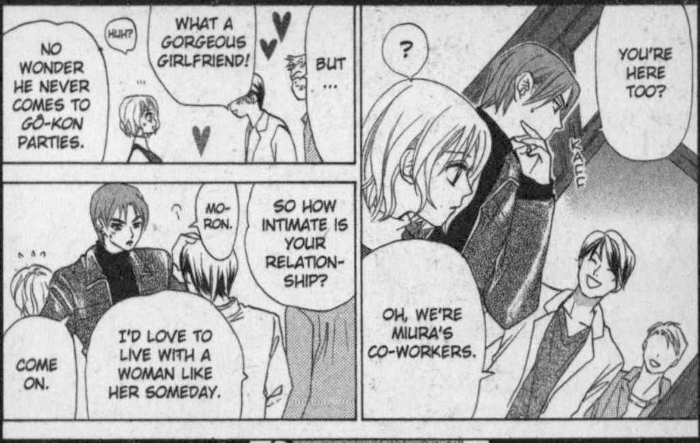
?
YOU'RE HERE TOO?
OH, WE'RE MIURA'S CO-WORKERS.
BUT ...
WHAT A GORGEOUS GIRLFRIEND!
HUH?
NO WONDER HE NEVER COMES TO GÔ-KON PARTIES.
SO HOW INTIMATE IS YOUR RELATIONSHIP?
MO-RON.
I'D LOVE TO LIVE WITH A WOMAN LIKE HER SOMEDAY.
COME ON.

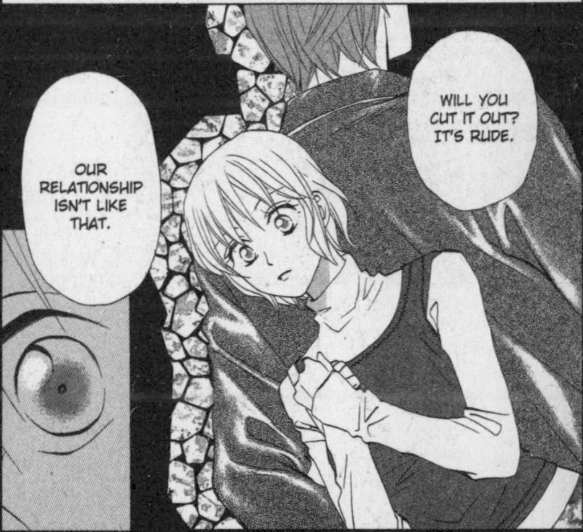
WILL YOU CUT IT OUT? IT'S RUDE.
OUR RELATIONSHIP ISN'T LIKE THAT.

Gô-kon

[reference page 81] The word "gô-kon" comes from "gôdo-compa." "Gôdo" means "joint" or "group," while "compa" is an abbreviation of "companion." A gô-kon is basically a group blind date. The organizers, usually one or two people, invite their friends, and friends of their friends might also be invited. Everyone who comes to a gô-kon knows at least one person in the group. Also, the number of men and women must match. (Some say three men and three women are the optimum number for a gô-kon, while others say five men and five women make it perfect.) Typically, men and women sit opposite each other and hold conversations. Even if a person clicks with someone, participants switch seats throughout the evening, so everyone gets to meet everyone else. The systematical nature of the gô-kon may seem forced, but it is quite useful in overcoming shyness and in finding somebody attractive who might eventually become one's spouse.

Gankake

[reference page 187] Gankake originates from Shinto. A special ritual, gankake is an invocation or a petition to the deities, requesting divine aid in attaining an earnest wish. It usually takes some visible form so it can be seen by others and will also remind oneself of that wish. For instance, Ito chose not to cut her hair until graduation day. Her decision to let her hair grow out is her way of asking the deities to help Makoto graduate without a problem.

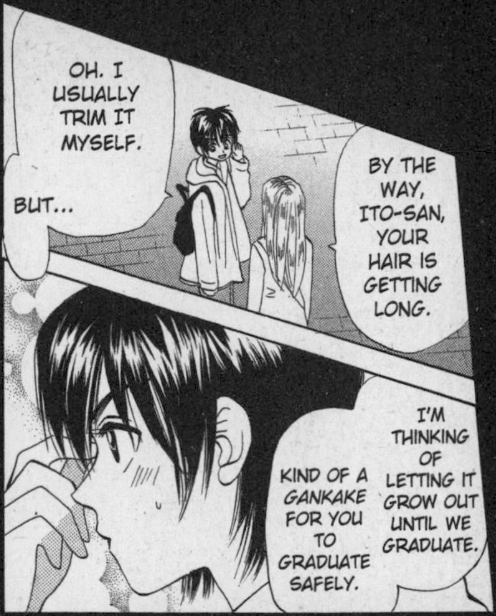
BY THE WAY, ITO-SAN, YOUR HAIR IS GETTING LONG.
OH. I USUALLY TRIM IT MYSELF.
BUT...
I'M THINKING OF LETTING IT GROW OUT UNTIL WE GRADUATE.
KIND OF A GANKAKE FOR YOU TO GRADUATE SAFELY.

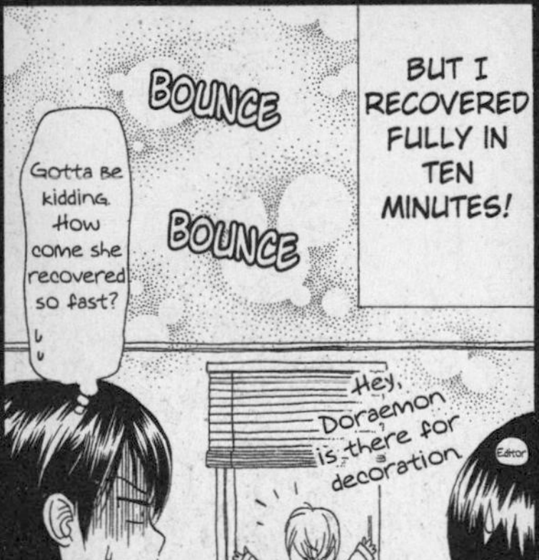
BUT I RECOVERED FULLY IN TEN MINUTES!
BOUNCE
BOUNCE
Gotta be kidding. How come she recovered so fast?
Hey, Doraemon is there for decoration.
Editor

Doraemon

[reference page 190] The *Doraemon* series is an all-time favorite children's manga classic in Japan. It was originally created in 1969-70 by Hiroshi Fujimoto (a.k.a. Fujiko F. Fujio) and Motoo Abiko (a.k.a. Fujiko Fujio). In the late 1970s, the series was first made into anime. Doraemon is a robotic cat from the future who has traveled back in time to aid an incredibly hapless, bespectacled boy named Nobita Nobi.

Since its debut, *Doraemon* stories have been selectively collected into 45 books through 1996--with a circulation of over 80 million. New versions of *Doraemon* are still being produced and telecasted today. It is considered to be a culturally significant work of Japanese pop culture.

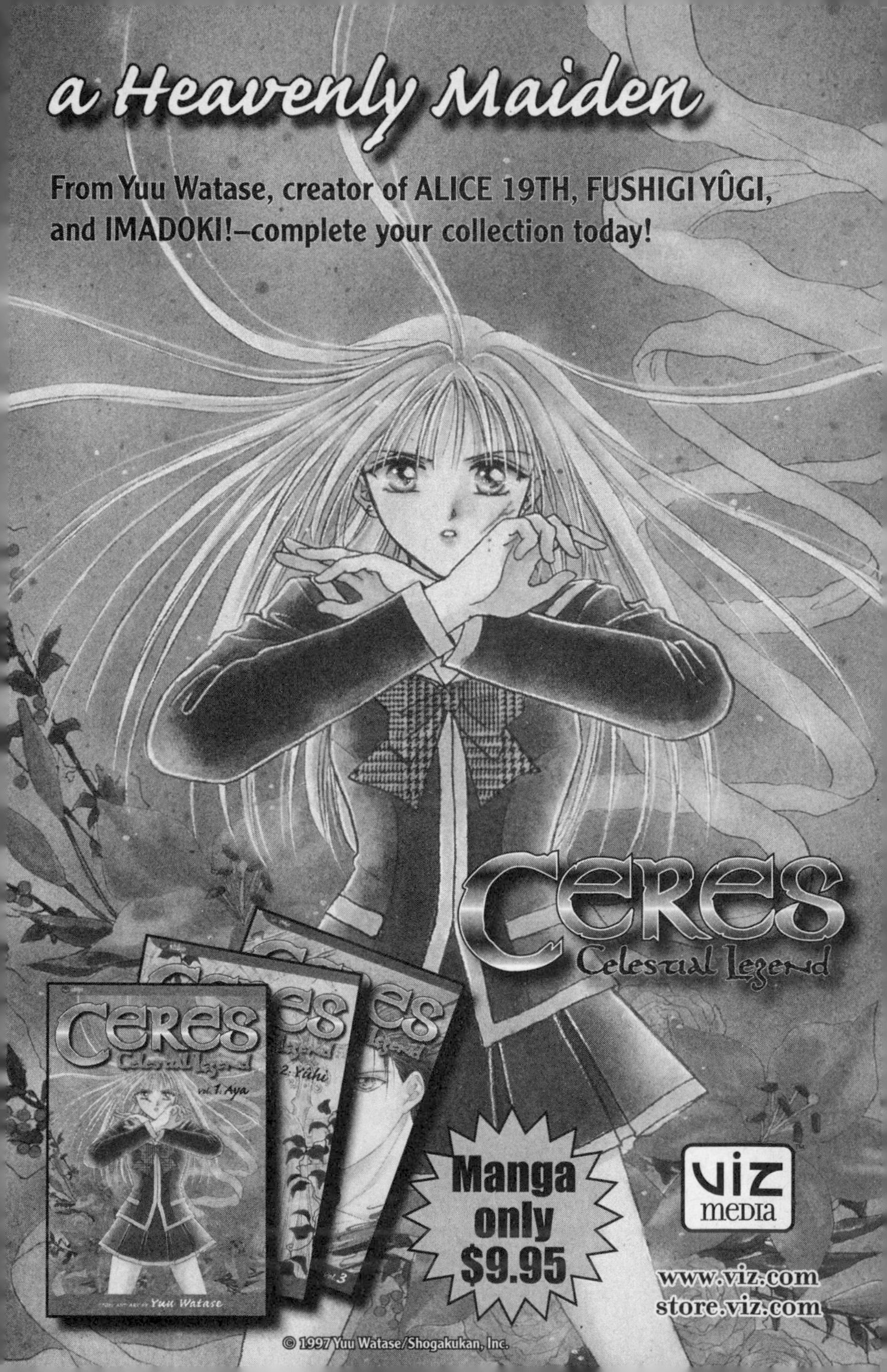
a Heavenly Maiden
From Yuu Watase, creator of ALICE 19TH, FUSHIGI YÛGI, and IMADOKI!–complete your collection today!
Ceres
Celestial Legend
Ceres
Celestial Legend
Manga only $9.95
viz media
www.viz.com
store.viz.com
© 1997 Yuu Watase/Shogakukan, Inc.

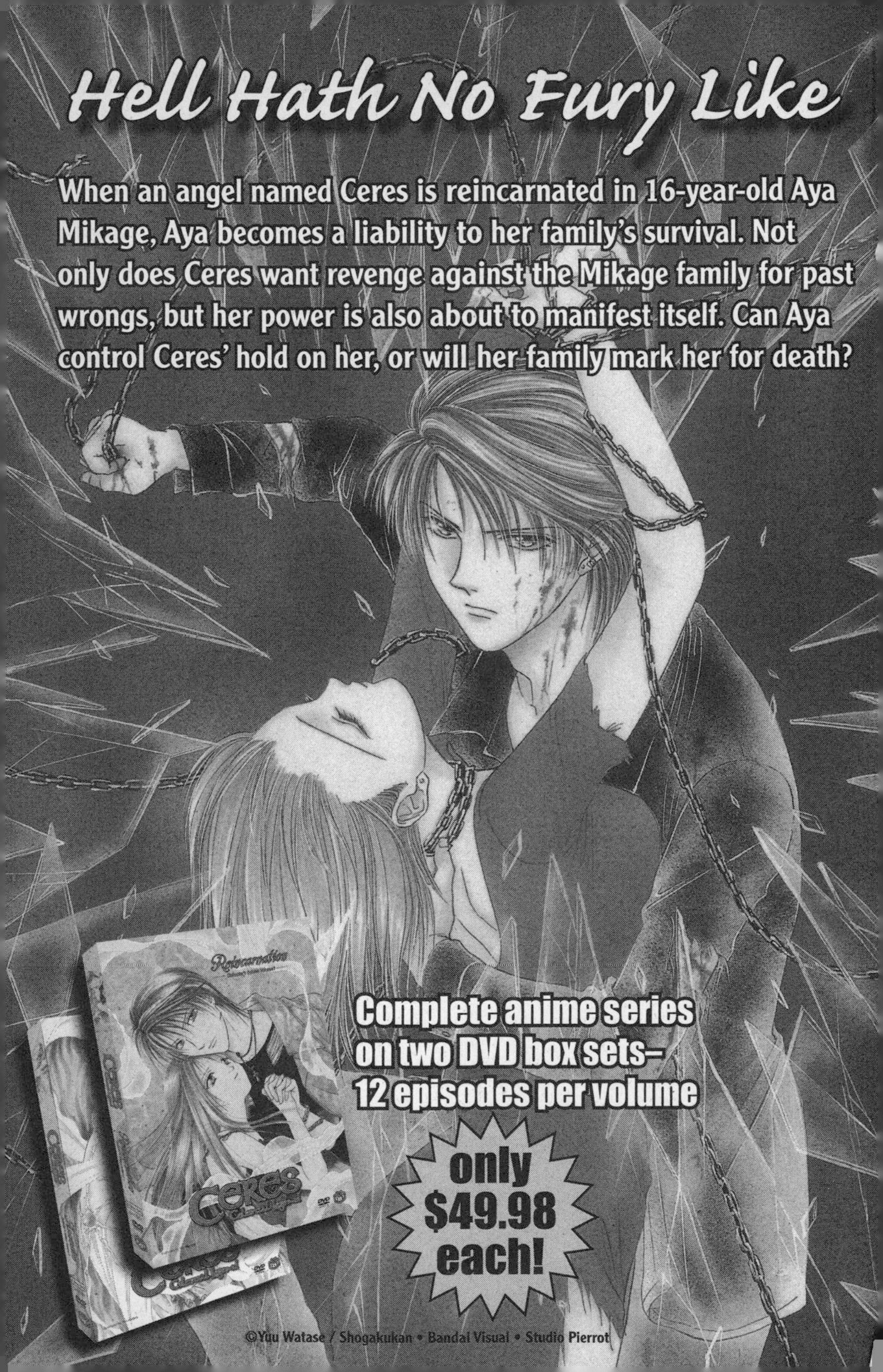
Hell Hath No Fury Like
When an angel named Ceres is reincarnated in 16-year-old Aya Mikage, Aya becomes a liability to her family's survival. Not only does Ceres want revenge against the Mikage family for past wrongs, but her power is also about to manifest itself. Can Aya control Ceres' hold on her, or will her family mark her for death?
Complete anime series on two DVD box sets– 12 episodes per volume
only $49.98 each!
©Yuu Watase / Shogakukan • Bandai Visual • Studio Pierrot

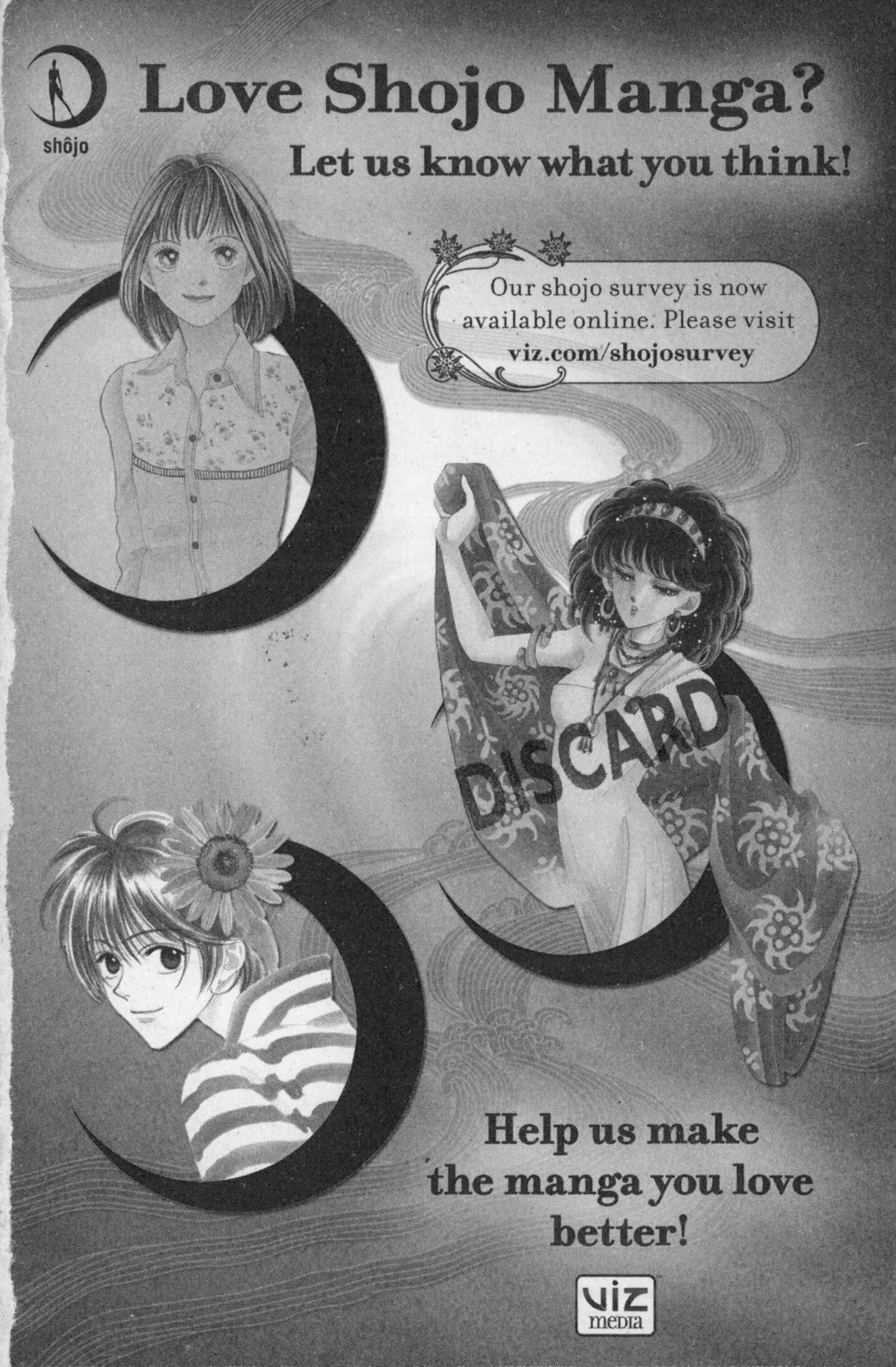

shôjo
Love Shojo Manga?
Let us know what you think!
Our shojo survey is now available online. Please visit viz.com/shojosurvey
DISCARD
Help us make the manga you love better!
VIZ media